Tourism and Animal Ethics

There is a long history of the involvement of animals in circuses, zoos, fairs, ecotourism, and wildlife tourism. The wave of responsibility and sustainability that currently permeates the tourism field is catalysing deeper moral questions about welfare, rights, justice, and values in regard to this use.

Tourism and Animal Ethics represents a required extension of the sustainability imperative and environmental theory by providing a critical account of the role that animals play in tourism. This book explores the rich history of animal ethics research that lies outside the field of tourism for the purpose of providing greater theoretical, empirical, and conceptual guidance inside the field. It examines historical and current practices of the use of animals in the tourism industry from both *in situ* to *ex situ* consumption and production perspectives, identifying a range of ethical issues associated with such use. This detailed examination of current animal ethics theories will be instrumental in determining the rightness or wrongness of these practices, and hence allow tourism practitioners and theorists to think about these issues and practices in a different light, minimizing the impact that the industry has on animals.

This text provides an interdisciplinary overview of the moral issues related to the use of animals in tourism, and contains cutting edge research and boxed international case studies throughout. It will appeal to students, academics and researchers interested in Tourism Ethics, Sustainable Tourism, and Wildlife Tourism.

David A. Fennell teaches and researches in the Department of Tourism and Environment, Brock University, Canada. He has written widely on the topics of ecotourism and tourism ethics, and is the Editor-in-Chief of the *Journal of Ecotourism*.

Contemporary Geographies of Leisure, Tourism and Mobility

Series Editor: C. Michael Hall
Professor at the Department of Management, College of Business & Economics, University of Canterbury, Private Bag 4800, Christchurch, New Zealand

The aim of this series is to explore and communicate the intersections and relationships between leisure, tourism and human mobility within the social sciences.

It will incorporate both traditional and new perspectives on leisure and tourism from contemporary geography, e.g. notions of identity, representation and culture, while also providing for perspectives from cognate areas such as anthropology, cultural studies, gastronomy and food studies, marketing, policy studies and political economy, regional and urban planning, and sociology, within the development of an integrated field of leisure and tourism studies.

Also, increasingly, tourism and leisure are regarded as steps in a continuum of human mobility. Inclusion of mobility in the series offers the prospect to examine the relationship between tourism and migration, the sojourner, educational travel, and second home and retirement travel phenomena.

The series comprises two strands:

Contemporary Geographies of Leisure, Tourism and Mobility aims to address the needs of students and academics, and the titles will be published in hardback and paperback. Titles include:

1. **The Moralisation of Tourism**
   Sun, sand . . . and saving the world?
   Jim Butcher

2. **The Ethics of Tourism Development**
   Mick Smith and Rosaleen Duffy

3. **Tourism in the Caribbean**
   Trends, development, prospects
   Edited by David Timothy Duval

4. **Qualitative Research in Tourism**
   Ontologies, epistemologies and methodologies
   Edited by Jenny Phillimore and Lisa Goodson

5. **The Media and the Tourist Imagination**
   Converging cultures
   Edited by David Crouch, Rhona Jackson and Felix Thompson

6. **Tourism and Global Environmental Change**
Ecological, social, economic and political interrelationships
Edited by Stefan Gössling and C. Michael Hall

7. **Cultural Heritage of Tourism in the Developing World**
Edited by Dallen J. Timothy and Gyan Nyaupane

8. **Understanding and Managing Tourism Impacts**
An integrated approach
Michael Hall and Alan Lew

9. **An Introduction to Visual Research Methods in Tourism**
Edited by Tijana Rakic and Donna Chambers

Forthcoming:
Tourism and Climate Change
Impacts, adaptation and mitigation
C. Michael Hall, Stefan Gössling and Daniel Scott

Routledge Studies in Contemporary Geographies of Leisure, Tourism and Mobility is a forum for innovative new research intended for research students and academics, and the titles will be available in hardback only. Titles include:

1. **Living with Tourism**
Negotiating identities in a Turkish village
Hazel Tucker

2. **Tourism, Diasporas and Space**
Edited by Tim Coles and Dallen J. Timothy

3. **Tourism and Postcolonialism**
Contested discourses, identities and representations
Edited by C. Michael Hall and Hazel Tucker

4. **Tourism, Religion and Spiritual Journeys**
Edited by Dallen J. Timothy and Daniel H. Olsen

5. **China's Outbound Tourism**
Wolfgang Georg Arlt

6. **Tourism, Power and Space**
Edited by Andrew Church and Tim Coles

7. **Tourism, Ethnic Diversity and the City**
Edited by Jan Rath

8. **Ecotourism, NGOs and Development**
A critical analysis
Jim Butcher

9. **Tourism and the Consumption of Wildlife**
Hunting, shooting and sport fishing
Edited by Brent Lovelock

10. **Tourism, Creativity and Development**
Edited by Greg Richards and Julie Wilson

11. **Tourism at the Grassroots**
Villagers and visitors in the Asia-Pacific
Edited by John Connell and Barbara Rugendyke

12. **Tourism and Innovation**
Michael Hall and Allan Williams

13. **World Tourism Cities**
Developing tourism off the beaten track
Edited by Robert Maitland and Peter Newman

14. **Tourism and National Parks**
International perspectives on
development, histories and change
*Edited by Warwick Frost and C.
Michael Hall*

15. **Tourism, Performance and the
Everyday**
Consuming the Orient
*Michael Haldrup and Jonas
Larsen*

16. **Tourism and Change in Polar
Regions**
Climate, environments and
experiences
*Edited by C. Michael Hall and
Jarkko Saarinen*

17. **Fieldwork in Tourism**
Methods, issues and reflections
Edited by C. Michael Hall

18. **Tourism and India**
A critical introduction
*Kevin Hannam and Anya
Diekmann*

19. **Political Economy of Tourism**
A critical perspective
Edited by Jan Mosedale

20. **Volunteer Tourism**
Theoretical frameworks and
practical applications
Edited by Angela Benson

21. **The Study of Tourism**
Past trends and future directions
Richard Sharpley

22. **Children's and Families'
Holiday Experience**
Neil Carr

23. **Tourism and National Identity**
An international perspective
*Edited by Elspeth Frew and
Leanne White*

24. **Tourism and Agriculture**
New geographies of consumption,
production and rural restructuring
*Edited by Rebecca Torres and
Janet Momsen*

25. **Tourism in China**
Policy and development since 1949
David Airey and King Chong

26. **Real Tourism**
Practice, care, and politics in
contemporary travel culture
*Edited by Claudio Minca and Tim
Oaks*

27. **Last Chance Tourism**
Adapting tourism opportunities in
a changing world
*Edited by Raynald Harvey
Lemelin, Jackie Dawson and
Emma Stewart*

28. **Tourism and Animal Ethics**
David A. Fennell

Forthcoming:
Gender and Tourism
Social, cultural and spatial perspectives
Cara Atchinson

Liminal Landscapes
Travel, experience and spaces
in-between
*Edited by Hazel Andrews and Les
Roberts*

Tourism and War
*Edited by Richard Butler and
Wantanee Suntikul*

Tourism in Brazil
Environment, management and
segments
*Edited by Gui Lohmann and Dianne
Dredge*

Sexuality, Women and Tourism
Susan Frohlick

Actor Network Theory and Tourism
Ontologies, methodologies and
performances
*Edited by René van der Duim, Gunnar
Thór Jóhannesson and Carina Ren*

**Backpacker Tourism and Economic
Development in the Less Developed
World**
Mark Hampton

Tourism and Animal Ethics

David A. Fennell

Routledge
Taylor & Francis Group

LONDON AND NEW YORK

First published 2012
by Routledge
2 Park Square, Milton Park, Abingdon, Oxon OX14 4RN

Simultaneously published in the USA and Canada
by Routledge
711 Third Avenue, New York, NY 10017

Routledge is an imprint of the Taylor & Francis Group, an informa business

British Library Cataloguing in Publication Data
A catalogue record for this book is available from the British Library

Library of Congress Cataloging in Publication Data
Fennell, David A., 1963–
Tourism and Animal Ethics/David A. Fennell.
  p. cm.
Includes bibliographical references and index.
1. Tourism—Moral and ethical aspects. 2. Ecotourism. 3. Animal welfare. I. Title.
G155.A1F3726 2011
179'.3—dc23
2011023139

ISBN: 978-0-415-58171-4 (hbk)
ISBN: 978-0-203-15364-2 (ebk)

Typeset in Times New Roman
by RefineCatch Limited, Bungay, Suffolk

Printed and bound in the United States of America by
Edwards Brothers, Inc.

This book is dedicated to the students of tourism studies, both undergraduate and graduate, who stand poised.

'To you from failing hands we throw
The torch; be yours to hold it high.'

—John McCrae

Contents

List of plates   xii
List of figures   xiii
List of tables   xiv
List of boxes   xv
Preface   xvi
Acknowledgements   xvii

1   **Introduction**   1

2   **Animals and humans – an evolving relationship 1: Misothery
    and theriophily in religious, philosophical, and cultural contexts**   13

3   **Animals and humans – an evolving relationship 2: On the use
    of criteria to assign moral value to animals and associated theories**   37

4   **Captives**   70

5   **Animals at work in the service of the tourism industry**   103

6   **Animal combat and competition: Blood, bravado, and betting**   131

7   **Animals pursued for sport and subsistence**   155

8   **Wildlife viewing**   187

9   **The animal threat**   215

10 **Conclusion**   247

References   256
Index   299

Plates

2.1	Hogarth: The *First Stage of Cruelty*	20
2.2	Animal themes that sell: Busch Gardens, Florida	31
2.3	Dog sledding as representative of the character of the 'north': Algonquin Park, Canada	31
3.1	Circus procession, 1888	40
4.1	Bear pit at Bern, Switzerland	77
4.2	Zoo breeding programmes: photo taken by author at Naples Zoo, Florida	80
4.3	Part of the education message regarding conservation, Naples Zoo, Florida	81
4.4	Zoo education, Naples Zoo, Florida	83
5.1	Camel riding at Naples Zoo, Florida	108
5.2	Shanghai monkey working the streets for money	116
6.1	Badger baiting, 1824	136
6.2	Fox tossing, 1719	142
6.3	Mounted bullfighting, Seville, *c.* 1850	143
6.4	Protest against bullfighting	146
6.5	Showing the dogs before a race in Fort Myers, Florida	152
7.1	Hunting dogs with a day off, Griffith Island, Ontario	159
7.2	Market hunting in ivory	160
7.3	Legal hunting and its benefits	171
8.1	Taniwha rock carving, Lake Taupo, New Zealand	198
8.2	Girl swimming with bottlenose dolphin, Hawaii	209
9.1	The female *Anopheles* mosquito	234
9.2	Manatee tours, Florida	245
9.3	Manatee	246

Figures

1.1 Present relationship between tourism, animals, and ethics
in tourism studies   7
1.2 Conceptual framework for tourism, animals, and ethics   10
3.1 Anthropocentrism   39
3.2 The extension of liberty rights under the common law   51
3.3 Anthropocentric 'othering'   65
4.1 Tourist attractions: animals and captivity   71
5.1 Improving equine welfare now and for the long term   111
7.1 Human priorities and actions in recreational interactions with fish   182
8.1 Classification of wildlife appeal   199
8.2 A mindfulness model of wildlife-based tourist experiences   205
9.1 Relationship between various bear–human interactions   219
9.2 A process of species reinvention over time   245

Tables

1.1   Cohen's conceptual framework of human–animal engagement   4
2.1   Types of human attitudes toward animals   17
3.1   Species mentioned in participants' deliberations concerning
where to 'draw the line' between those which can and cannot suffer   52
4.1   The evolution of the circus   92
5.1   Use of draught animals worldwide   107
5.2   Companion animals owned in US population, 2007   121
5.3   The travel veterinary kit   125
6.1   Types of blood sports   133
7.1   Total wildlife-related recreation   158
7.2   Percentage of Swedish groups in support of hunting option   164
8.1   The potential benefits and risks (costs) of bear-to-human
habituation   207
9.1   Terms used in describing bear–human interactions   219
9.2   Some local and systemic symptoms and signs of venomous
snakebite   224
9.3   Human fatalities and marine animal envenomation   227

Boxes

1.1 British Columbia sled dog cull   2
3.1 Did animals sense tsunami was coming?   49
3.2 Swiss say no to animal lawyers   61
4.1 Transporting the Black Rhinoceros   74
4.2 Elephant attacks   94
4.3 *Lolita: Slave to Entertainment*   98
4.4 Animals torn to pieces by lions in front of baying crowds: the spectator sport China DOESN'T want you to see   100
5.1 Iditarod Rules, 2009   115
5.2 The first rescue dogs   118
5.3 German airports use honeybees to sniff out air quality   119
5.4 Your Time Travels   127
5.5 Animal sex tourism   128
6.1 Crackdown appeal after swoops on badger-baiting ring   135
6.2 Turkey: tradition of camel wrestling making a comeback   141
6.3 Bullfighting ban a first for Spain   147
7.1 New South Wales Council of Anglers Code of Conduct   184
8.1 Going anywhere nice this year?   191
8.2 Whale shark tourism: tour guides, boatmen and fishermen   202
9.1 How deadly are stingrays?   229
9.2 Dengue/DHF press release, WHO   233
9.3 Killer bat disease closes Cadomin Cave   240
9.4 Recommendations for best practice in reducing disease transmission to great apes   243
10.1 World Society for the Protection of Animals: animal-friendly tourism   253

Preface

The title of this book could have, and perhaps should have, been 'Tourism, Animals, and Morality'. I follow Loftin's (1984) lead in this regard, who argues that the ethics of hunting is different than the morality of hunting. In the latter case, philosophers talk about whether or not hunting should be allowed in a principled society, whereas the ethics of hunting entails following, for example, regulations and codes of conduct, pertaining to the way we should hunt. My reasoning for keeping the word 'ethics' in the title is for consistency of terminology in the field, despite the fact that most of what the reader will encounter is of a moral rather than ethical nature.

The intended audience for this book – tourism students and scholars, and travel industry practitioners – should be aware at the outset that most of the material sourced for this volume comes from other disciplines. From this perspective, the present work does not deviate far from past projects of mine, which emphasize the importance of theory from outside our field. I view the incorporation of such as vital, especially here, because without this approach a book of this nature *for tourism* could not have been written. Indeed, the shortage of work on animals and ethics in our field is the reason why such a volume has not been written. My hope is that this book induces tourism students and scholars to think broadly about the many uses of animals in the tourism industry, and to undertake critical investigations of these uses to challenge the conventional mindset. It is not as though tourism scholars have left this area completely unattended, but rather for a field relying so much on the importance of animals as attractions, workers, companions, objects of pursuit, and so on, there is much work that needs to be done.

Finally, in venturing outside of my academic 'comfort zone', as I have done here, my hope is that I have represented well the thoughts, ideas, theories, etc., of those who have made animal ethics such an important and exciting area of study. The work of these scholars is deep and textured and in my efforts to synthesize all of this, I sincerely hope that it comes packaged in way that is informative, accessible, and meaningful.

David A. Fennell
May 2011
Fonthill

Acknowledgements

I wish to thank the anonymous reviewers who endorsed this book, and who took time to make valuable suggestions on ways to make it better. I thank Emma Travis at Routledge for her initial support of this book, as well as the editorial staff at Routledge, especially Faye Leerink, for keeping me on track.

My job was made easier because of the work and dedication of two fine undergraduate students: Nicolle Lalonde, initially, and later Olga Yudina. Both students were enormously helpful in tracking down many of the sources used in this book, and both were passionate about the need for a voice that speaks for the interests of the animal 'other' in tourism. Thanks are also extended to Val Sheppard for the time she placed into chapter organisation. I should also acknowledge Brock University for providing me with the support and freedom to engage in this project.

I wish also to thank my wife, Julie, and children, Sam, Jessie, and Lauren, for their ongoing support of this work and the many other large projects of my past, which have often drawn me away from the more important things in life.

1   Introduction

The cull of the wild

The Olympic Games provides the international community with a chance to demonstrate excellence not only in athletics but also in common virtue. We come together as the union of one, developed and less developed nations, to celebrate the accomplishments of humanity as a measure of civilization, progress and, of course, sport. The games also provide the opportunity for one city and its surrounding environs to play host to the world. Along with the prestige of hosting these games, there is the potential for local and regional economies to prosper through substantial gains in international and domestic tourism receipts. The 2010 Winter Olympics in Vancouver is a case in point. The games attracted 2.3 million attendees, with a total contribution to the British Columbia economy of 2.5 billion Canadian dollars in Gross Domestic Product, and the creation of 45,000 jobs (Calgary Herald, 2010).

While the games themselves are the main attraction for visitors, the host region has the opportunity to showcase many of its most important attractions. In British Columbia during the time of the Olympics, one of these attractions was dog sled tours – an activity not confined to British Columbia, but widespread across Canada. The Vancouver Olympics provided the opportunity for international visitors to experience part of the Canadian culture and wilderness through this unique form of adventure tourism. One Canadian dog sled company boasts that tourists are given the opportunity to experience 'beautiful Siberian huskies, awe-inspiring wilderness, and breathtaking adventure'. A testimonial from the same company reads as follows: 'Thank you very much for the experience of a lifetime. We could not be happier with the level of service and the professionalism shown by our guide.' The dog sled tour is thus an archetypal Canadian winter event and carries with it a tremendous amount of pride in heritage. When a Canadian dog sled company – one that offered tours to tourists during the Olympics – was found guilty of culling 100 dogs in January of 2011 because of a slow season less than one year after the games, the Canadian public took this very hard. This event is detailed in Box 1.1.

A reading of a case like the sled dog cull, provides an opportunity to test values – what an individual believes to be important. At first glance we may decide that it is a heinous act and wonder how a tourism organization could ever ask an

Box 1.1 British Columbia sled dog cull

By Darcy Wintonyk, ctvbc.ca
Date: Monday 31 January 2011 8:47pm PT

A prominent animal rights group called for a ban on sled dog tours Monday following the news that 100 healthy sled dogs were killed in a horrific mass slaughter by a Whistler, BC tour company. Police and the BC SPCA launched an investigation after reports an employee dumped the bodies into a mass grave after shooting and stabbing the animals. The unnamed employee has filed a claim with WorkSafe BC, claiming post-traumatic stress. Documents show at least one dog had its eye hanging out of the socket after surviving being shot in the face. The canines panicked as they watched the others being killed, and some tried to attack the worker.

Peter Fricker of the Vancouver Humane Society calls the details 'absolutely shocking.' 'This is what happens when animals are exploited for profit and become surplus to requirements when business is bad,' Fricker said. 'We see this all the time. This is just an extreme example. They just wash their hands of it.'

The Worksafe BC claim states the dogs were killed because of a slow winter season for sled dog tours following the 2010 Olympic Winter Games. Like pet owners, Fricker said sled dog companies should be responsible for the cradle to grave care of an animal. 'It seems like a perfectly normal thing to expect of people but in industries where animals are used for entertainment or profit this just isn't the case,' he said.

The operator of Candle Creek Kennels at Big White, near Kelowna, BC, rejects the idea of a ban on tours. 'These dogs love to do what they do,' Tim Tedford told CTV News. 'That's what they were born and bred for. To take that away from them would be cruel in my opinion.'

The SPCA in BC says it isn't impressed with most sled-dog businesses, but stopped short of calling for a ban. 'In BC we come across far more dogs in horrible conditions in the name of quote-unquote dog-sledding operations,' said Marcie Moriarty, general manager of cruelty investigations. 'It's hard given stories like today for me to say this, but there are good sled-dogging operations out there. I have seen them.'

employee to carry out such a task, and also how an employee could ever succumb to such a request. By contrast we may also decide that it is a justifiable business decision in light of current economic conditions. Moving beyond our own values and beliefs we may seek guidance in regards to what passes as acceptable behaviour within the industry in question – within tourism. There are a couple of ways to do this. The first involves a search for industry-related information, while the second would involve a survey of published research in this area.

In looking at industry, we may find little coordination between tourism operators in regards to the proper guidelines, regulations, policies, or procedures that exist on the appropriate use of dogs for sledding. There may be a disconnect between government policy and industry practice. What this means is that operators may do what they wish in terms of how they handle their animals, within the limits of animal welfare legislation in one's country, without fear of repercussion. It also means that what passes as acceptable care rests on experience of the guide and owners, and this may in fact be exceptional in some cases and limited in others. In the absence of good industry standards, there is no guidance for the operator in the event that he or she would want to know what would be best for his or her animals. We may come to the realization that there are decidedly few voices out there that have established protocols for the health and well-being of sled dogs, but we recognize that many feel that sled dog tourism is an exciting way in which to earn a living and also to spend part of a vacation. Sustained thought on the subject may prompt the agent to widen the circle of investigation beyond this case and begin to consider practices in other areas of tourism that necessitate the use of animals. This is easy to do and might include innumerable species that are used in many different ways in the service of the tourism industry. We might also find, however, that there is a lack of information available on standards for the use of other animals in tourism as well as guidance for tourists interested in the wellbeing of animals (WSPA, 2011).

The second approach is to survey the tourism literature in regards to the issue of the acceptability of sled dog tourism. While there may be academic work on the practice itself, especially activity and marketing components (see for example Mehmetoglu, 2007), there may be little work available that explicitly tackles dog sledding as a tourism practice from an ethical standpoint. Casting the net wider, we find that there is indeed work on the physiological costs to dogs from involvement in dog sled activities, but this has little to do with the tourism industry itself (Burr *et al.*, 1997; Hinchcliff, 1996). What surfaces is a failure to link tourism activities involving animals, the ethical nuances of these activities as tourism enterprises, and work that examines the physiological demands of these activities. As such, we may find that there are certain physiological costs to dogs because of their involvement in dog sledding, but these are not discussed from an ethical standpoint, nor is this discussion nested in a broader discourse on tourism.

Tourism and animal ethics

The pattern of inquiry followed above has yielded certain realities about the use of animals in tourism; foremost is the realization that little knowledge exists both in theory and in practice. This is not a new conclusion, although it is a recent one. Cohen (2009) explains that animal–human interactions as a topic of study in tourism has only recently begun to take shape, with infinite complexities that make it especially exciting for researchers in the social sciences. Cohen also observes that tourism is an ideal domain for the study of animal–human interactions because of the nature of tourism itself (i.e., novelty about the other and the world in general) and that tourism more than most endeavours makes people aware of the animals they interact with from the perspective of observation, play, and consumption – in recreational and culinary contexts. But if Cohen is right, and there is no reason not to think so, what is the state of affairs?

An area of study that tourism scholars have broached is the use of frameworks or typologies to organize how animals are used for tourism purposes. For example, Beardsworth and Bryman (2001) characterize human–animal interaction according to four modes of engagement: (1) encounter, with humans being in the direct physical presence of unrestrained animals in their own habitat; (2) presentation: direct engagement with animals in a captive environment, including zoos and aquaria; (3) representation: figurative images of animals through literary, symbolic or artistic forms (e.g., rock paintings); and (4) quasification, which is a type of representation whereby fakes or jokes allow the perceiver to be entertained by the artifice (e.g., taxidermy presenting animals in fearsome poses). Cohen (2009) adapts these four modes of engagement and packages them into a more elaborate model of human–animal interactions (Table 1.1).

Ballantyne *et al.* (2007) summarize the costs and benefits of different types of wildlife encounters, from first, second and third generation exhibits, through to animal shows and feeding programmes, interactive activities, and finally non-captive wildlife tourism. The benefit of an interactive activity would be that it heightens the emotional connection to an animal, and costs occur through the encouragement of unnatural animal engagement like 'breakfast with a chimpanzee'. Hall *et al.* (2004)

Table 1.1 Cohen's conceptual framework of human–animal engagement

Settings	
Natural	Spaces completely unframed, animal unconstrained
Semi-natural	Managed spaces like parks; animals live unconstrained
Semi-contrived	Zoos, aquaria, theme parks; captured animals with the appearance of wild
Contrived	Animal shows with animals that are tamed, trained or humanized
Mode of engagement	
Non-interactive	Observation or photography
Interactive	Non-symbolic contact between animal and human (fishing)
Relational	Symbolic rapport between human and animal (teasing or taunting animals)
State of the animals	
Wild	Not interfered with by humans
Tamed	Through contact with humans
Trained to work	Work for human masters
Trained to perform	Entertainment value for humans
Mediators	
Unmediated	Direct tourist–animal engagement
Guides	Leading or directing tourists in the engagement
Performers	Presenting animals to tourists

Source: Cohen (2009)

developed a categorization of animal visitor attractions that, although less comprehensive than Cohen's in regards to the mechanisms that facilitate the human–animal interface, provides a good general description of how the tourism industry presents animals to the public. The seven categories are as follows:

1. Wild creatures for discovery: Animals in natural or semi-natural environments with little contact. Feelings of danger, wildness or threat are experiences that tourists are in search of and visitor management must take this into consideration.
2. Tame creatures for interaction: The audience is primarily children, and the animals are deemed safe for handling or viewing, and these animals may be familiar to children because of exposure through the media.
3. Objects for exhibition: This category includes zoos, where animals are arranged in restricted surroundings, and includes the presentation of animals on geographical or ecological bases.
4. Targets for shooting and fishing: Hunting requires a more highly prescribed legal and environmental governance regime, whereas fishing is said to be a more solitary pursuit. Members in these groups have a strong sense of social class identity.
5. A source of education, training or science: This includes visitor education initiatives but with tremendous variance. While zoos claim to incorporate a scientific and educational dimension, the extent to which they satisfy these requirements is open to debate.
6. Mythical or symbolic representation: Includes images in museums, handicrafts or other tourism goods (e.g., the Loch Ness monster).
7. Ancillary roles: Animals may play a minor role at various attractions, and may include visual displays or forms of transportation created in the likeness of an animal.

Bulbeck (1999; see also 2005) defines three different types of animal encounter sites. The first are authentic sites, defined as 'those tourist sites where "wild" animals visit on a regular basis' (p. 132), and include for example the wild dolphins at Monkey Mia in north-western Australia. The second, semi-authentic encounter sites, include those allowing tourists to walk through safari-type events, including various types of sanctuaries where animals can be found in open environments. The final type, 'staged' encounter sites, include experiences where animals are viewed through bars or small enclosures. The basis of Bulbeck's work is that authenticity is a social construct and different socio-economic segments of society might search for different degrees of authenticity, as discussed above – not unlike different degrees of aesthetic appreciation in art. Higher socio-economic groups might have an appreciation of certain forms of art unlike their lower socio-economic counterparts. Bulbeck (2005: 89) has also developed a continuum of five different dolphin–human interactions ranging from the staged to the authentic. These include: (1) captivity (aquaria), (2) regulated tactile settings like Monkey Mia, (3) unregulated settings where lone dolphins choose to socialize with people,

(4) communities of known dolphins living close to human settlements, and (5) chance encounters with unknown dolphins in open waters. The importance of a spectrum of these opportunities is captured by Hall and Brown (2006), who argue that even though wildlife tourism is on the rise, a persistent demand for attractions that display captive animals still exists. The reason for this, they suggest, is the desire for a high-quality close interaction with animals.

Researchers have also started to use a core of philosophical reasoning in the investigation of animal use in tourism. Hughes (2001; see also Garrod, 2007; Franklin, 2008) argues that animals are more often considered objects than subjects in tourism. As objects, they are typically used and manipulated for instrumental purposes. The value of animals lies only in their ability to generate pleasure for tourists (reflected in profits), rather than any inherent value. This instrumental–intrinsic dichotomy is discussed by Hughes (2001) according to environmental ethics, animal welfare, and animal rights theory (more on these theories later). Building on the work of Hughes (2001), Shani and Pizam (2008) argue that tourists and operators who subscribe to the environmental ethics standpoint are accepting of zoos, circuses, safaris, hunting, frequent transportation of animals, and other animal-based tourism attractions because these improve the social-economic conditions. Those who uphold the animal welfare position accept the use of nonhuman animals as part of the tourism trade, and support policies and procedures which maximize animal well-being, but object to situations that are inhumane. By contrast, animal rights proponents reject outright tourism activities that induce pain and suffering in animals, as well as any attempts to remove animals from their natural habitats (Shani and Pizam, 2008).

Holland *et al.* (1998), Fennell (2000), and Holland *et al.* (2000) have debated at length whether the ecotourism label is appropriate for activities like billfishing (marlin and sailfish). Dobson (2009) uses this discussion to infuse more ethical consideration into what is right or wrong with billfishing. He suggests that billfishing as ecotourism might be wrong on utilitarian grounds according to what is in the best interests of the majority. In the absence of billfish re-caught after being tagged by anglers, it is difficult to decide whether the practice is ethically justifiable or not, suggesting that the issue is one that is multifaceted and difficult to evaluate in view of different stakeholder interests.

While ethics has been used in tourism for only a very short period of time (see Fennell, 2000; 2006), ethics turned towards the use of animals in tourism is even more recent. Figure 1.1 is an attempt to illustrate the relationship that exists between tourism, animals, and ethics. The circles in the figure are representative, crude as they may be, of the amount of animal and ethics scholarship taking place in tourism. It shows that the relationship between tourism and animals is not without representation. A good deal of this research comes in the form of ecotourism and wildlife tourism, but also reflects other studies on marketing and imagery, and sustainability and conservation. The number of studies in tourism concentrating on ethics is far less than studies that have animals as a focus in tourism. Studies have advanced over the past 20 years, but the number of these studies in relation to other work surfacing in tourism is still quite small. Perhaps

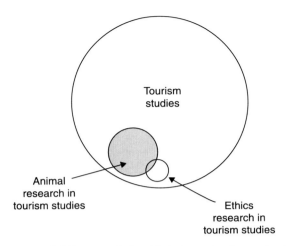

Figure 1.1 Present relationship between tourism, animals, and ethics in tourism studies

most important in Figure 1.1 is the relationship between animal and ethics research. What is shown is that, of the animal research found in the tourism literature, a very small amount of this has to do with ethics, despite the fact that there is a capacious amount of work outside of tourism that would otherwise serve our field extremely well given the reliance of the tourism industry on animals.

It is worth noting that, although work in this area is burgeoning in other fields, especially in the emergence of fields like critical animal studies, there is still the recognition that certain disciplines need to catch up. For example, Mullin (1999) writes that in recent years the relationship between humans and animals has been a topic generating enthusiasm not only in anthropology, but also biology and a number of other fields (see also Bradshaw and Bekoff, 2001). This comes about, Mullin says, because of extensive boundary crossing between humans and animals as well as society and nature and humans and machines, with much of the discourse pointing to the fluid nature of these boundaries between humans and animals. Because they serve as commodities, members of the family, food, and the embodiment of nature itself, Mullin (1999) argues, there is focused attention and a resultant conflict.

The emergence of anthrozoology, a new interdisciplinary field that focuses on animal–human interactions, is testament to this level of commitment. Drawing on ethology, medicine, veterinary medicine, and zoology from the natural sciences standpoint, anthrozoology incorporates social sciences including anthropology, philosophy, geography, literature, art, sociology, and psychology in investigating the positive and negative implications of animal–human interactions. In no way are these interactions static, but rather heavily influenced by culture. Anthrozoology has evolved in part in view of Noske's (2008) contention that anthropologists have amassed huge amounts of knowledge on animal–human relationships in many different cultural contexts, but virtually nothing on animal welfare.

Sociologists have argued that the failure to incorporate animals into scholarship rests in part on the charge of paternalism, i.e., talking for the animals, and the narrowness that comes from viewing the social world as the domain of human beings only, with animals as the ultimate other (Hobson-West, 2007). The last few years, Hobson-West observes, have seen a flurry of activity in sociology which parallels other fields such as geography, history, and science. Traditional social theory has maintained the staunch view that animals used in the service of any industry follow capitalist social relations, where animals are merely valued as resources and commodities to be controlled and consumed. There is also the theme suggestive of the fact that kinship with nonhumans represents womanish sentiment, and that urbanization is yet another tool to further distance animals from humans via pavement, bricks, concrete, policies, zones, and regulations (Wolch and Emel, 1995). Baker (2001) contends that poststructuralists, who occupy territory at the other end of the spectrum from empiricists, have struggled to place their own preferred method over others in attempts to more properly represent animals.

Geography appears to be no different. Philo (1995) writes that geographers have considered animals in their writing in ways that display utility to human beings as a type of 'human chauvinism'. The appearance of animals in the work of geographers comes in the form of beings to be trapped, counted, mapped, and analysed. Geographers have investigated how domesticated animals exist as potent representations of place and livelihood. As rural economies shift and enter into periods of decline, farm tourism emerges as an opportunity for urban inhabitants to reconnect with the land while injecting new life into the rural environment (Weaver and Fennell, 1997). Philo places special emphasis on the urban context by arguing that some animal species are accepted members of the urban context and many are not. For example, cats and dogs are valued members of the urban context, whereas cows, sheep, and pigs were rendered undesirable and expelled to the rural world because of odours, flies, and disease. The products of these animals (e.g., meat) are welcome in the urban world, just not the living animals themselves (see Wolch, 2002 for an overview of recent trends in animal geography).

Aim of the book

The services that animals perform in the name of human progress and enjoyment are many and varied. While Turner (1980: 1) argues that animals have been 'feared, loved, beaten, caressed, starved, stuffed, and ignored', this is really just the tip of the iceberg. The moral dimensions of animal use for human instrumental ends has been partitioned by Vardy and Grosch (1999) into five main categories: (1) animals bred for food; (2) animals bred for their fur and leather (along with other parts); (3) the use of animals in medical experimentation (vivisection); (4) animals used for testing cosmetics; and (5) animals used to facilitate or enable human recreations, like hunting, fishing, racing, and various forms of entertainment. In reference to the five categories above, Hemsworth (2008) states that there are two main principles that we follow in the management of animals for our use. The first includes aims directed toward profit, benefit, or pleasure, while the second includes the duty of care. The purpose of this book is to follow the lead of Hemsworth, in light of the spectrum of various forms of tourism that involve animals, with particular emphasis on the duty of care, broadly conceived. This spectrum of use includes animals kept as captives, animals at work in the service of the tourism industry, animals forced into combat and competition, animals pursued for sport and subsistence, animals viewed *in situ*, and animals that act as pests and vectors of disease (Figure 1.2). In light of these uses, the following two questions are central to this work:

How are animals involved in the service of the tourism industry?

What are the ethical issues tied to this use?

It is the intersection of tourism and animals that is most important here, along with the moral issues that stem from this intersection. These questions are deemed important because (1) animal use has not really been foremost in the minds of tourism theorists in any sustained fashion based on a survey of the tourism literature, nor is it foremost in the mind of most tourists, and (2) there is little regard for the interests of the animal other.

This book ties into the emerging interest of ethics in tourism, but also into the vast changes that have been taking place in society over the last three decades in regards to the ethical treatment of animals (Hemsworth, 2008). There has been a major shift in the way humans regard animals over time, and the transition of thought appears to be getting stronger. Animals are no longer viewed as just property to be used and abused without regard for welfare, and this shift represents one of the greatest changes in Western morality (Bowman, as cited in MacQueen, 2009). These changing sentiments have catalysed a foundation of literature that is said to be 'bounteous, diverse, and sophisticated' (Burgess-Jackson, 1998: 159). If one aspect of this research stands out, it is how much information currently exists on animals and animal ethics outside our field, and how little exists within it. The tourism industry can ill afford to remain external to these changing values and attitudes. It is worth noting that Patrick O'Donnell's extended bibliography on animals, ethics, rights, and law (on the web) contains almost 500 entries. None of these sources are explicitly about tourism and animals.

When animals are the object of our gaze, at zoos or aquaria, or when we birdwatch, visit farms, hunt, fish, or travel with our companion animals, we often consider 'them' with the aid of a mirror pointed not at the animal object but rather at ourselves (Berger, 1980). Because they have the inability to reveal their thoughts to us, and we have the inability to fully understand animal behaviour in detail, we impose our own interpretations of their world – our emotions, experiences, language, and so forth. As Haraway observes, 'We polish an animal mirror to look for ourselves' (Haraway, 1991: 21). The problem with being classified as 'other' is that it makes it easy to argue for the exclusion of these others in the moral

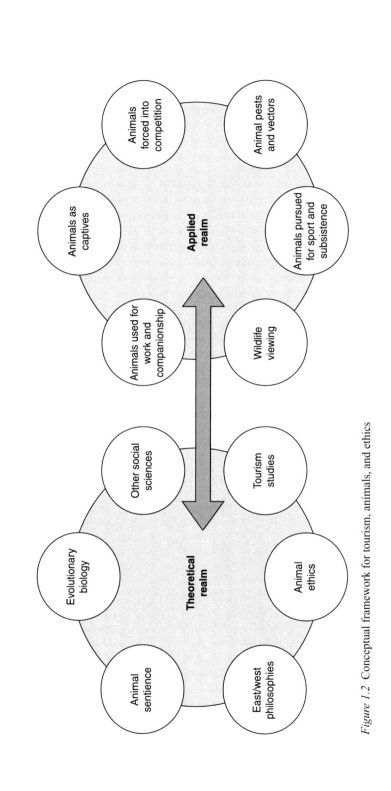

Figure 1.2 Conceptual framework for tourism, animals, and ethics

universe. Yates (2004) places this into perspective according to the boundaries of inclusion and exclusion:

> Boundaries effectively produce 'moral distance' with regard to constructed 'others'; thus boundaries keep 'them' at bay, serving to emphasise distance *and* difference, perhaps holding 'them' up to ridicule or 'humorous' debasement. Often jokes and joking relations can construct and reflect the distancing of 'others': often jokes and joking can amplify the putative stupidity of 'the other', serving to dehumanise and depersonalise those placed in 'them' categories, while the moral status of 'us' is simultaneously elevated. A sufficiency of distance (social and moral) can apparently result in untold cruelty and utter disregard for the rights of those successfully classified as 'other'.

The result is that animals, despite their intelligence or other unique qualities, are not accorded equal consideration. But it is naive to suggest that the category 'nonhuman animal' is one general category. Animals are not all treated on an equal footing. Companion animals are more highly regarded over livestock, and livestock are more highly valued over pests like rats. It all boils down to what the animal means to, and does for, us. We protest the seal hunt because the pups are cute with big sad eyes and they pose no threat to our safety, yet we ignore the killing of rats or sharks, which threaten our health or well-being, because 'one less pest or predator is a good thing'. One category of animal is a foe (predators), another is viewed as a tool (food-producing animals), while a third category is given the status of friend (companion animals) (Arluke and Sanders, 1996). This book examines all of these different categories and, as above, the acceptability of using animals as such.

Theorists have also pointed out that people's feelings about the use of animals are highly ambivalent and often not reliable as a rational guide; the beliefs that people hold towards the use of animals are highly resistant to change; and these issues lead in turn to polarized positions on the topic of animal welfare, making the topic emotionally charged and especially challenging to applied ethicists (Huntingford *et al.*, 2006): 'Personal experience shapes moral beliefs' (Wemmer and Christen, 2008: 4). But as Ehrlich (2000) has suggested in reference to the naturalistic fallacy, i.e., the ethical 'ought' versus the biological 'is', the 'way we do behave or have behaved gives us no guidance about the way we ought to behave' (Ehrlich, 2000: 309). Old habits and traditions often die hard, culturally derived or naturally derived (or indeed both), but it does not mean that we need to be firmly seated in entrenched, instrumental reason.

Animal ethics as a new, vibrant interdisciplinary field of enquiry offers guidance for a way forward in tourism studies. It is defined as the branch of study that 'considers the acceptability of the use of animals in different contexts' (Collins *et al.*, 2008: 752). It deals with the issue of moral responsibility that humans have toward animals and the quality and quantity of care that should be extended (Håstein *et al.*, 2005), and is a derivative of other branches of applied ethics that have been evolving since the mid-1960s to tackle the gamut of moral issues within society (Gunn, 1983).

But what is often good in theory is not so good in practice. In this there is a cautionary note to consider as we venture forward. Saul (2001) argues that ethics is the most demanding of our human qualities and this can be discernable on two basic fronts. First, our capacity to be moral is contingent upon the will to resist the vast spectrum of human needs, wants, and desires that we must have at any cost the recognition that we cannot have whatever we want at any price (Preece, 2005). Second, because morality can be taken to culturally derived extremes, it must be rooted in everyday life. In order for ethics to have utility, it needs to be exercised regularly – not unlike the muscles of the body that, if not exercised, will atrophy and be of less use. How can we claim to be inclusive of thought in tourism if we are only now beginning to ask questions that have moral significance? And how is it that we can take pleasure in our touristic pursuits if they come at a cost to others? The pleasure principle continues to prevail in this field in practice, with little resistance from the philosophical domain. This statement, bold as it may seem, continues to hold weight.

Finally, it is important to situate the subject of the discussion as a matter of process. The word 'animal' is from the late fourteenth century from Latin *animale* 'living being, being which breathes,' neuter of *animalis* 'living, of air,' from *anima* 'breath, soul'. As an adjective, it is attested from the 1540s; *animal rights* is attested from 1879; *animal liberation* from 1973 (Online Etymology Dictionary, 2011). In Latin, animals are referred to as (*animans*) 'animate beings', because they are 'animated (*animare*) by life and moved by spirit' (Isidore, 2007: 247). In common usage, an animal is any member of the kingdom *Animalia* other than a human, such as another species of mammal, or a bird, fish, insect, or reptile (Canada Revenue Agency, 2011). More specifically, an animal is 'a living organism which feeds on organic matter, typically having specialized sense organs and a nervous system and able to respond rapidly to stimuli' (Oxford Dictionary, 2011). The literature often refers to animals as 'nonhuman animals', to make a distinction from human animals. In this work the word 'animal' will be used almost exclusively over 'nonhuman animal'.

2 Animals and humans – an evolving relationship 1

Misothery and theriophily in religious, philosophical, and cultural contexts

Introduction

This chapter concentrates on the dichotomous positions that humans have held, and continue to hold, towards animals. On one hand, cultures have shown atrocious disregard for the welfare of animals, as evident through fear and hatred for types of animals as an evolutionary adaptation. On the other hand we have shown a strong tendency for admirable sympathy. We venerate animals through totems, religion, philosophical thought, and even through the enactment of laws that have animal interests in mind. This veneration surfaces because of an inherent or innate love of nature expressed through the concept of biophilia, which also has evolutionary origins. The section concludes with a discussion on contemporary expressions of animals in art, books and media. There is the recognition that the treatment of animals differs between cultures, and this is reflected in different systems of beliefs, values, and customs, and associated moral significance of different animals or animals in general (FAO, 2009).

Misothery

The term *misothery*, coined by Mason (2005), refers to humans' strong negative feelings about animals; feelings that include contempt, prejudice, and hatred. Mason argues that speciesism, or the discrimination against animals (more on this in Chapter 3), is far too mild because it fails to capture more deep-seated negative feelings toward animals that humans have maintained over millennia. Examples of this contempt include intense fear of certain species, dislike on the basis of competition for resources, and hatred induced through various cultural practices. The evolutionary connection mentioned briefly above is as relevant in this discussion as the cultural context, and both will be used as lenses to more fully appreciate the nature of misothery.

Attitudes of fear and disgust

Evidence points to the fact that early hominids were threatened by predatory species. Kruuk (2002) argues that our ancestors were about the size range of prey species for a number of predatory animals during the Pliocene and Pleistocene eras. Just as lions seek out and kill cheetahs and other predatory animals in Africa, early man would have been a direct competitor to these other predatory animals. Tsukahara (1993) reports that chimpanzee remains (hair and bones) were discovered in the faeces of lions in Mahale Mountains National Park, Tanzania. This is the first such evidence of lion–chimpanzee predation, and suggests that this predator–prey relationship may have taken place over millennia.

This position is corroborated by Brantingham (1998), who found that consistent overlap in food-attaining strategies of hominids and other large carnivores contributed to coevolution in the predatory guild. Coevolution is defined as 'reciprocal selective pressures that operate to make the evolution of one taxon partially dependent on the evolution of another' (p. 327). This suggests that the arrival of hominids would have created a number of new selective pressures (e.g., competition) that would have affected the evolution of hominid and carnivore species: the type of food sought and how they transported food to avoid scavenging in the face of constant attention from other species. Adaptations that improve hunting skills in predators have matched selective forces that make prey more efficient in eluding predators. This loop, played out over time, has meant that both predator and prey have been able to cope with adaptive changes in defining a relatively dynamic relationship.

Öhman (1986; see also Öhman *et al.*, 2007) contends that our human nature – in particular our emotions – has been shaped by encounters with animals that posed a threat to our survival and those that did not. Thus, it is no accident that the embodiment of evil in humans is intricately tied to beastly origins. When we flee a snake or spider in fear, we do so on the basis of the activation of time-honed behaviours that are a result of biological evolution. The function of this fear is to 'protect the organism from harmful or noxious circumstances, whether actual or anticipated' (p. 124).

Animal fear responses typically include escape and avoidance, keeping a safe distance between animals and the potential victim, but more specifically fear can be explained on the basis of causal factors operating at three different time frames, which cannot be examined in isolation (Öhman, 2009). The first level is the short-term adaptive process. This level deals with the moment-to-moment adjustments that the organism makes of the immediate situation. Using the example of the snake in the garden, the individual may, upon seeing the snake, be scared and leave the vicinity of the garden altogether. The second level concerns the attitudes of an individual over his or her lifespan and the socialization and types of exposure that he or she has had towards snakes. Learning is important and provides the opportunity to gain an appreciation of the importance of snakes in the environment as well as to address any conceptions or misconceptions in regards to the threat of snakes to human well-being. The third level pertains to our deep evolutionary heritage that is represented in processes controlled by the gene pool – what Öhman refers to as evolutionarily anchored behavioural systems. In understanding our fear of snakes, all three levels need to be examined (see also Jacobs, 2009).

Of animals that we are most fearful of, it is the reptiles that occupy a privileged position on the scale of prototypical predators (Öhman, 2000; see also Prokop *et al.*, 2009). Snakes are a perfect example of the fascination and fear that humans have with animals. There is a deep-seated evolutionary explanation for this, Wilson (1998) argues, with genetics and the environment working in tandem. Snakes represent polar emotional states in humans, including good vs evil, male vs female, and medicine vs poison, and also conjure up tales and narratives that laid the foundation for a moral code among the ancient societies of Japan (Koopmans-de Bruijn, 2005).

Isbell (2006) posits that snakes were the chief factor responsible in better vision of primates. Snakes, first constrictor snakes and later venomous snakes, have a long and shared evolutionary existence with placental mammals and were quite likely their first predators (see also Öhman, 2007). The fear of snakes, particularly venomous snakes because of their smaller size and ability to hide in foliage, led to a greatly improved visual system in primates with more cortex than non-primate animals. This more refined visual system led to a more refined integration with the amygdala and associated defence mechanisms. Isbell observes that raptors that specialize in eating snakes have larger eyes than more generalized raptors, adding weight to this hypothesis.

A key question for theorists is whether snakes and spiders are natural triggers for humans at birth. The preparedness theory (Seligman, 1971) is cited by Jacobs as an alternative to the natural trigger body of literature. This theory is based on the belief that we are hard-wired with the capacity to learn once we are exposed to a threat like a spider or snake, which in turn results in a predisposition to react emotionally to the threat. That is, we are born with a preparedness to acquire fear towards fear-relevant animals like spiders and snakes (see New *et al.*, 2007). Jacobs feels that because of the heightened interest in activities like wildlife viewing, emotions research may prove to be a fruitful avenue of investigation in increasing our understanding of the benefits that people derive from this type of activity.

Arrindell *et al.* (1991) summarize a number of studies on the factor loadings of fear inventories amongst adults, and find that most factors can be organized into four categories: (1) social fears (e.g., interpersonal interactions); (2) fear of death, injury, blood, surgery, etc.; (3) fear of animals; and (4) agoraphobic fears, including being in crowds or going out of the house alone. (See also Taylor (1998), who developed a hierarchic model of fears based on genetic and environmental factors.) In relation to the third category, above, Arrindell (2000) reports that there are four reliable and independent dimensions in relation to the structure of animal fears. These include fear-relevant animals (e.g., rat, bat, snake, lizard), dry or non-slimy invertebrates (e.g., wasp, maggot, beetle), slimy or wet-looking animals (e.g., slug, eel, fish), and farm animals (e.g., goat, cow, goose). The fear of animals, or at least the fear of some animals over others, occurs for several reasons according to Arrindell (2000): appearance and predictability, environmental aspects such as exposure to the animal, cultural factors such as attitudes toward certain species, biases in information on species, the perception of dangerousness, and correctness of information on routes of transmission of disease in livestock animals.

A study by Davey (1994) of self-reported fears of indigenous animals offered an empirical contribution to the understanding of animal fears. Of 261 students representing all major geographic regions of the UK, female subjects reported being more fearful of prevalently feared animals than males, but there were no consistent patterns of fear with age. Two factors, invertebrates (e.g., slug, worm) and fear-relevant animals (e.g., snake, rat), accounted for one-third of the variance in the fear of indigenous animals. The snake topped the list of percentages of adults reporting at least some anxiety towards an animal (53.3 per cent), followed by wasp (39.5 per cent), rat (36.7 per cent), cockroach (36.4 per cent), and spider (27.6 per cent).

In addition to fear there are various layers of disgust that humans feel towards animals. For example, urban dwellers often despise animals that exploit changes that we have made to the natural world, like seagulls, raccoons, and rats (Herda-Rapp and Goedeke, 2005). In this capacity, Rozin, Haidt, and McCauley (2000) have shown that disgust can arise form nine different domains in North Americans: food, body products, animals, sexual behaviours, contact with death or corpses, violations of the exterior envelope of the body (gore and deformity), poor hygiene, interpersonal contamination (contact with unsavoury humans), and various moral offences. Core disgust is an emotion that is linked to three components, including (1) oral incorporation (food or eating), (2) a sense of offensiveness, and (3) contamination. In regards to the ingestion of animals, the authors contend that most cultures eat a small subset of available animals as food and, in North America, of those that are eaten, not all of the animal is consumed. The head is left off the dinner plate as well as the viscera. Animals are avoided as a food source because they resemble body products such as mucus (slugs) or because their niche requirements involve close contact with garbage or rotting flesh. Those carnivorous animals that eat dead or decaying animals and produce putrid faeces are said to be disgusting at both ends of the animal. Other animals are avoided as a food source because they have similar phenotypic characteristics to humans (primates) or because they are socially acceptable as pets. Finally, there are those animals that motivate disgust, e.g., snakes and spiders, which are not favoured by humans (Davey, 1993 for example suggests that we avoid snakes and spiders more out of disgust than of fear.) Rozin and Fallon (1987) find that most of the objects that humans find disgusting have an animal origin. That is, the things that we encounter that remind us that we are animals elicit disgust. For example, if a person behaves outside of our cultural norms in regards to the consumption of certain animals, hygiene, or sexual practices, s/he is condemned as disgusting and animal-like (Rozin, Haidt, and McCauley, 2000).

Certain animals may become stigmatized as a function of cohabitation with humans. Using content analysis of *New York Times* articles from 1851 to 2006, Jerolmack (2008) writes that the pigeon or 'rat with wings' has been labelled a problem animal because of its disruption of the boundaries that exist between human and nature. There is a general trend suggesting that Westerners have become less tolerant of wildlife in urban environments, and while some species are revered because of certain characteristics such as usefulness, rarity, or beauty, others are castigated, like the pigeon, because they are deemed useless and because they are scavengers – eating the waste of society in the same manner as rats. As such, the pigeon appears to be the antithesis of the orderly, sanitized urban centre, its main offence being that it pollutes spaces dedicated for human use.

Stephen Kellert's (1980, 1993) work on attitudes, knowledge, and behaviour of Americans toward animals provides one of the most comprehensive statements on the topic. His typology of basic attitudes towards the natural environment, and animals more specifically, has been useful in describing the underlying values that people attach to the nonhuman world. The typology includes nine general attitudes and is accompanied by a definition of each (Table 2.1). Kellert captures the spirit of the discussion above, linking well to Mason's concept of misothery, with his negativistic dimension in which avoidance of animals is based on indifference, dislike, or fear.

Kellert developed a number of separate scales and studies to measure these attitude types. Kellert and Berry (1987) investigated the attitudes, knowledge, and behaviour toward wildlife of US male and female adults, with findings that substantiate much of the data on gender differences in regard to wildlife. Females were found to be much more humanistic in terms of their attitudes towards animals, especially domestic pets. Females also demonstrated stronger anthropomorphic feelings towards animals, and scored higher on the moralistic scale, with emphasis on animal cruelty issues and far less support for the exploitation and dominance of animals, including opposition to laboratory experimentation, trapping, hunting, and rodeos. Finally, females had higher scores on the negativistic scale, and were found to be more indifferent and fearful of animals than their male counterparts. Males, on the other hand, demonstrated higher scores relative to women on questions pertaining to the utilitarian and dominionistic use of animals.

Table 2.1 Types of human attitudes toward animals

Attitude	Definition
Naturalistic	Primary interest and affection for wildlife and the outdoors.
Ecologistic	Primary concern for the environment as a system, for interrelationships between wildlife species and natural habitats.
Humanistic	Primary interest and strong affection for individual animals, principally pets. Regarding wildlife, focus on large attractive animals with strong anthropomorphic associations.
Moralistic	Primary concern for the right and wrong treatment of animals, with strong opposition to exploitation or cruelty toward animals.
Scientistic	Primary interest in the physical attributes and biological functioning of animals.
Aesthetic	Primary interest in the artistic and symbolic characteristics of animals.
Utilitarian	Primary concern for the practical and material value of animals or the animal's habitat.
Dominionistic	Primary interest in the mastery and control of animals, typically in sporting situations.
Negativistic	Primary orientation an avoidance of animals due to indifference, dislike, or fear.

Source: Kellert and Berry, 1987: 364

Men more than women would sanction the exploitation of animals for material human gains and derive personal satisfaction from the mastery/control of animals. (See Kellert, 1993 for a cross-cultural study on the attitudes of Germans, Americans, and Japanese toward animals. In general, the Japanese are not as concerned about overexploitation and cruelty toward animals as Americans or Germans.)

The wolf – an animal much maligned over centuries – is a good example of the impact that utilitarian and dominionistic attitudes can have on a species. Emel (1995) writes that history points to the fact that as a top predator the wolf competed with hunters as well as with landholders in the US, especially ranchers. Sport hunters killed wolves because wolves killed their game, and ranchers killed wolves because wolves, in an era of declining populations of bison (anthropogenic causes), sometimes killed cattle and other livestock.

> Like the Native American, the wolf was killed to secure land and investment. No less important, it was killed to sustain big game animals so that human hunters could kill them. It was killed for pelts, for data, for science, and for trophies. It was tortured, set on fire, and annihilated … Wild animals, and particularly predators such as the wolf, have represented longings, needs, and urges that were suppressed in the particular construction of masculinity that dominated during the late nineteenth and early twentieth century. They have been targets of hatred, the same hatred that launched armies and lynch mobs against human 'others'.
>
> (Emel, 1995: 720)

The principal stance adopted by Emel is reflected in the latter part of the quote above. Her aim is to show that during this time society placed value in representations of virility that could be demonstrated through acts of hunting and killing fierce animals. The frontier mentality provoked a frontier masculinity, and the construction of the wolf as a merciless killer in lore and legend elevated the status of the wolf on the list of animals most hated. Those who were able to kill the animal were simply playing out a culturally accepted practice in elevating their own fitness and status within the community; one that symbolized masculinity and mastery over nature.

But this is not a relatively recent set of values held by people toward the wolf. This animal has been persecuted for centuries. Commenting on a journalistic book she read on wolves, Midgley (2002) says that the book described how wolves when caught in Medieval Europe were often flayed (whipped) alive. The author quipped that this might be considered cruel, but then again the wolf itself is a very cruel beast. The author further complained that wolves were treacherous in the way they crept up on unsuspecting victims before they could defend themselves. It never crossed the author's mind, Midgley writes, that the cruelty might only be found in *Homo sapiens*; those that would whip an animal until it died and who would blame an animal for being a carnivore when in fact those responsible for blaming were likely carnivores themselves. The killing of wolves as such was thought to be a punishment for their ferocity and wickedness, justifying this form of treatment.

The preceding example involves just one species. To be sure, the literature is replete with examples of how animals have been tortured and abused as a matter of public enjoyment. The hanging of cats in bags for targets in archery is a case in point. These killings, and the killing of other animals as public spectacle, were practised as rituals or ceremonies with therapeutic value for local people as these displays were meant to rid the community of guilt (Cohen, 1994).

In 1751, William Hogarth, the famous English artist, satirist, and columnist became troubled with British society's culture of disrespect in regards to the treatment of animals. The streets, he said, were filled with examples of inhumane regard for the well-being of dogs, cats, and the various animals that people used for food and transportation. This compelled him to publish four engravings known as *The Four Stages of Cruelty*, with each engraving representing four different stages of the life of the fictional character Tom Nero. In the *First Stage of Cruelty*, Nero as a young boy is seen torturing a dog, while other children in the engraving are burning out the eyes of a bird with a hot needle, throwing at a cock, tying a bone to a dog's tail and abusing cats (Plate 2.1). The engraving contains the following text:

> While various Scenes of sportive Woe
> The Infant Race employ,
> And tortur'd Victims bleeding shew
> The Tyrant in the boy.
>
> Behold a Youth of gentler Heart
> To spare the Creature's pain
> O take, he cries – take all my Tart.
> But Tears and Tart are vain.
>
> Learn from this fair Example – You
> Whom savage Sports delight
> How Cruelty disgusts the view
> While Pity charms the sight.

Equally cruel are the acts depicted in the *Second Stage of Cruelty*, where Nero as a man has turned his cruelty towards his horse, which has collapsed from years of overwork with a broken leg, overturning the carriage it was pulling. Infuriated with the beast, Nero is seen beating the horse so badly that he has taken out an eye, a lamb is beaten to death by a drover, and an ass is driven forward by its handler despite being overloaded with goods. In the third plate, *Cruelty in Perfection*, Nero has moved from being cruel to animals to robbery, seduction, and murder, and finally in the fourth scene, *The Reward of Cruelty*, Nero is hanged for his misdeeds and his body is dissected by surgeons in a surgical theatre without

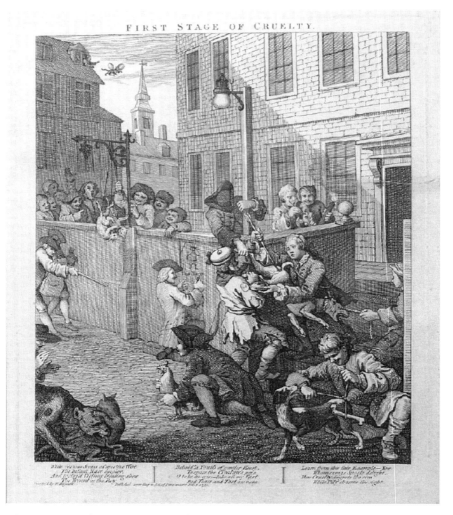

Plate 2.1 Hogarth: *The First Stage of Cruelty*

proper burial as a deterrent for others thinking that they may choose the same path as Tom Nero.

Misothery has also been documented in a curious form of animal treatment during the Middle Ages known as animal trials. In 1906, E.P. Evans published a book entitled *The Criminal Prosecution and Capital Punishment of Animals*, which detailed dozens of accounts not of humans committing crimes against animals, but rather of animals committing crimes against humans – and the prosecution and punishment of these transgressors (Evans, 1906/1987). The book was the first of its kind by many accounts, and it unlocked a chapter in the history of legal process that lay dormant for almost two hundred years (see also Coulton,

1967, describing this phenomenon in detail including animals copulating, causing injury to humans, and involved in theft and vandalism, all offences requiring trials). Boehrer (2007) writes that of some 200 documented cases of animal prosecution and punishment, 75 per cent occurred between 1400 and 1700.

The ontological platform sanctioning animal trials in medieval Europe, according to Beirnes (1994), was based on the chain of being: male God, followed by his earthly representatives, multi-tiered social strata based on feudalism, all of which sat atop the nonhuman animal kingdom and the various strata inherent in this from primates down to plant life (discussed in detail in Chapter 3). This belief was upheld in the ecclesiastical court in Berne in 1666, stating that 'an ox is created for man's sake, and can therefore be killed for his sake; and in doing this there is no question of right or wrong as regards the ox' (Beirnes, 1994: 30). Oxen that gored people were not executed on the basis of whether this was right or wrong – but because oxen were lower beings that threatened or challenged the divinely ordained hierarchy as established by God himself.

Animal trials and executions were of two types: ecclesiastical and secular. In the former case, untamed animals such as moles, mice, snakes, birds, insects, or eels that caused a public nuisance were tried for their crimes. Swarms of insects, for example, were tried *in absentia* for the destruction of crops. The history of these trials dates back to 824, where there is reliable documentation of the excommunication of moles in the Valley of Aosta, Italy. Unsubstantiated cases include the burning of storks in 666 by St Agricola, in Avignon, France, and the expulsion of venomous snakes from the island of Reichenau, Germany by St Perminius in 728 (Evans, 1906/1987; see also Girgen, 2003). Ecclesiastical trials were first held in France, Germany, Italy, and Switzerland, and because of the internationalization of ecclesiastical jurisdiction, such trials spread widely to other places including Ethiopia, Scandinavia, Spain, Canada, Brazil, and Turkey (Girgen, 2003).

Secular trials involved domesticated animals like pigs, bulls, horses, and goats held accountable for causing physical harm or death to a human (Girgen, 2003). These were not mock or show trials, according to Humphrey (2002), but trials in every sense of the word. Every effort was expended to guarantee that the defendant, offered lawyers free as a form of legal aid, had a fair trial with all the principles of natural justice. Perhaps the most oft-quoted example of one of these trials (the one that graces the front of Evans' book) involves an infanticidal pig in the city of Falaise in 1386. The proceedings were recorded thus:

> Having been duly tried in a court of law, presided over by a judge with counsel attending, the sow was dressed in human clothes, mutilated in the head and hind legs, and executed in the public square by an official hangman (*'maître des hautes oeuvres'*) on whom had been bestowed a pair of new gloves befitting the solemnity of the occasion.
>
> (Evans, 1987: 140; cited also in Beirnes, 1994: 31)

The use of clothing was deemed important as a means by which to mock the animal, but more likely to make the pig more humanlike for the purpose of imparting a moral lesson to those in attendance (Girgen, 2003; see also Hyde, 1916). Although the prosecution and punishment of animals in the manner above has not taken place for centuries, humans continue to punish animals in other ways according to Girgen (see the example of the wolf, above). We do so for the purpose of restoring order in our communities as well as to achieve revenge, with the belief that there should be renewed emphasis on due process for animals who are threatened with punishment and possible extermination for their crimes (see also Finkelstein, 1981).

Theriophily

George Boas' concept of *theriophily*, which is a combination of two Greek words – *therion* (beast, an animal of a wild or feral nature) with *philos* (love of, or loving) – is appropriate in framing the section that follows. Theriophily is the view that animals are models of good behaviour, demonstrating industriousness, prudence, and fidelity, and possessing qualities less prone to vice and passion, which might otherwise be copied by humans (Newmyer, 2005; Gill, 1969). By the beginning of the twentieth century there were over 170 English-speaking clergy, laypersons and authors who had supported the belief in the immortality of animals, i.e., that they possessed souls (Preece, 2007). In this, the history of animal–human relations is not defined by the orthodoxy of ideas that positions humans against animals, i.e., animals, apart from a few commentators, have always been subordinate to humans in thought and action. Preece's main point is to demonstrate that much of the most recent writing on the topic of the status of animals is simply misleading because it fails to give credit to these older sources. What surface as novel, cutting edge propositions on the importance of animal well-being in the present age, are often replications of similar views that have been expressed throughout human history (see also Midgley, 2002).

Religious theriophily

Before organized religions emerged, reverence towards animals often took the form of religious-like or spiritually based veneration. Paleolithic humans expressed reverence for animals on cave walls, shelters were built 125,000 years ago that were guarded by the skulls of wolves, and bear bones were placed in ceremonial positions in underground chambers to signify any number of characteristics or traits of the deceased (Kalof, 2007a). During the Late Palaeolithic period in numerous places around the world, most notably France, South Africa, and Australia, the human illustrations of animals are said to express admiration for animals and this was linked to ritual and ceremony (Kalof, 2007b). The animals most often depicted in these caves are the horse (30 per cent of paintings), bison and aurochs (30 per cent), deer, ibex, and mammoth (30 per cent), and bears, cats, and rhinos (10 per cent) (see Bahn and Vertut, 1997).

In his discussion on the objects of religion among the primitive atheists, Durant (1963) talks of the importance of the sun, stars, the earth, sex, totemism, and animals. In the latter it is observed that most animals in nature, from the Hindu elephant to the Egyptian scarab, have been worshipped as a god. In select places around the world, including North America, Australia, and Africa, *totem* was used to signify a sacred animal, and in turn to distinguish one group of primitive people from another. The use of animals as religious symbols was thought to have emerged out of fear and the need to appease these powerful beings, and perhaps out of reverence. As hunting thinned the forests of these animals and hunting and gathering gave way to a primarily agricultural existence, human gods replaced animal gods, but not completely. In Egypt, the most popular gods were animals, Durant tells us, including the bull, crocodile, hawk, cow, goose, goat, ram, baboon, cat, dog, chicken, swallow, jackal, and serpent. When the gods later became human they often did so with animal representations as symbols, for example Osiris as a bull or ram. Primates are revered by different societies because of myth or other historical conceptions. The monkey god Hanuman is an important figure in India because he represents faithfulness, obedience, and devotion (Hill, 2002). Cretans in ancient Greece worshipped goats and doves, but especially bulls and snakes because of their reproductive vitality. There is not the same reverence towards animals in Greek religion as compared to Egypt and India, the former of which is comparatively more anthropomorphic in design (Durant, 1966). Some traditional societies felt that by consuming a certain type of animal, the human consumer would take on characteristics of that animal (see Frazer's classic, *The Golden Bough* 1890/1959).

In reference to veneration in organized religion there is much ground to cover on this topic and, in view of this, only Buddhism and Islamic law are discussed briefly here. It is fundamental to note that the world's religions have not faced an ecological crisis in the past of the magnitude we are facing now. There is no precedent for this in the past, which is why religion in general has not fashioned a more specific environmental ethic. In this context, a rhetoric based on reverence, which can be supplied by the world's religions, is said by Gross (1997) not to be enough. Most pressing are issues related to excessive consumption and repro-duction, and any religion-based environmental ethic needs to be able to address these in its teachings. What is troubling are changes like the 1994 revised Catholic Church Catechism declaring that: 'Animals, like plants and inanimate things, are by nature destined for the common good of past, present and future humanity' (Waldau, 2006: 69). The domination of nature, at least in the Christian doctrine, was established in Genesis where God commands both man and woman to have sovereignty over the animals (Derrida, 2002). Waldau suggests that in practice the record of many religious institutions demonstrates hopeless failure at the hands of arrogance and ignorance. The proof of this lies in the fact that since the inception of the animal protection movement during the 1960s and early 1970s there has been little reliance on religion for leadership in this area, even though some Christian animal liberationists insist that animals have rights given by God, although they cannot themselves claim such rights (see Linzey, 1994, 2000), while others view our stewardship priorities not on the basis of rights but rather mercy (Scully, 2002; see also White Jr., 1967).

Buddhism

During the sixth century BCE, The Buddha, drawing heavily on existing Indian philosophy, developed a religion premised on a non-teleological lack of permanency – no final end – but rather a life of continuous birth and death for sentient beings (Harris, 2009). Rebirth takes place in one of six destinies or *gati*, including the realm of the gods, demigods, humans, animals, ghosts, and hell, none of which are permanent. The motivation for practising a life of virtue, i.e., to practise a form of ethics based on compassion and love and to do the least harm to other beings, is to be reborn in a higher or more favourable future state. Virtuous souls may thus be reborn in a higher state in their next life, whilst those less virtuous, those accumulating negative karma, find themselves reborn as a lower being (Waldau, 2006).

Traditional forms of Buddhist ethics have as their foundation the Eightfold Path, which includes non-injury (*ahimsa*) of others including animals, and abstinence in regards to stealing, lying, sexual misconduct, and intoxicants. The focus on non-injury to other beings has elevated Buddhism in the eyes of some commentators as an ecologically conscious religion – non-violence has led to a more caring relationship with nonhuman entities. Buddhists must abstain from taking the lives of other humans and animals, even injuring these others, including insects and unicellular organisms. Of 16 practices that Buddhist scripture (the *Mahayana Mahaparinirvana Sutra*) says are to be shunned unendingly, 13 of these are centred on the abuse of animals (Page, 1999: 143):

1. Keeping, feeding, and fattening sheep for profit and sale.
2. Buying and killing sheep for profit.
3. Raising, fattening, and killing pigs for profit.
4. Buying and killing pigs for profit.
5. Raising, fattening, and selling calves for profit.
6. Buying and killing calves for profit.
7. Raising hens for profit and selling them when fully grown.
8. Buying hens for profit and killing them.
9. Fishing.
10. Hunting.
11. Selling fish.
12. Catching birds by net.
13. Charming snakes.

Living with the purpose of securing the rights of animals or helping to liberate condemned animals serves three purposes for the Buddhist: the suffering of the sentient being is lessened, the Buddhist experiences spiritual growth, and this, in turn, produces positive karma. In the end, however, Phelps contends that animal activism is not about Buddhists or about the abusers of animals, but rather about the animals themselves. In this regard, Phelps explains that 'Only individual sentient beings are able to suffer, and therefore, a compassion-based ethical system must always place the individual above the collective' (Phelps, 2004: 89). This means that arguments for the acceptance of practices that injure or stress animals, the perspective adopted by conservation biologists, in the name of some ecological types of tourism, like ecotourism, cannot be condoned on this basis alone. The removal of a hierarchy of beings opens the door for a protracted ethics based not only on the compassion for all sentient beings, their use for pleasure and profit, but also the protection, preservation, and sustainable use of the environment (Phelps, 2004; see also McDermott, 1989).

Islamic law

Cross-cultural work by Wescoat (1995) shows how Islamic law has made important provisions for the well-being of animals, which are on a par with provisions made for humans. Laws securing *haq-i shurb*, or 'right of thirst', are designed to provide animals with access to water, and these provisions are clearly outlined in Islam. The structure of Islamic law follows a unified approach to thought and behaviour that is referred to as *shari'a*, translated as 'the way', and provides a foundation for all of the various branches of Islamic jurisprudence (Wescoat, 1995). Within this structure there are four roots of the law, the most important being the Qur'an (the word of Allah as revealed by Muhammad). While the Qur'an makes it clear that animals have a lower status than humans and that animals are created to serve humans, it also makes clear that animals possess souls, have a spiritual function, and that animals are no different than people in terms of their resource requirements, i.e., their need for water. So, it is not human beings that control the resources that sustain life, but more importantly Allah. Wescoat (1995) also points out that shari'a law has stimulated a more enhanced commitment to the rights of animals in Pakistan, through support of various organizations charged with the responsibility of preventing abuse. In other places like the USA, there does not exist a constitutional basis for the provision of drinking rights for animals, which makes these cross-cultural studies important – other models and parameters that would be useful in broadening our moral landscape when it comes to the well-being of animals.

Secular theriophily

In the literature pertaining to veneration in philosophical thought, Preece's (2002, 2005) work is noteworthy, outlining the ideas of many philosophers who possessed the view that animals were not soulless machines but rather thinking, feeling entities. The reader is urged to source Preece for detailed accounts of this position. For purposes of consistency, one philosopher is included here, Michel de Montaigne (1533–92), because of the influence of his stance during a time of great resistance.

Montaigne's *An Apology for Raymond Sebond* made a clear statement about the capacity for emotion and communication in animals that stood in contrast to the sentiment of the day, said by Derrida (2002) to be one of the finest anti-Cartesian texts on animals. The book pokes fun at man's propensity to reject the cognitive and emotion faculties of animals. Animals have an inherent power of reason, which makes them able to learn, communicate, and respond. This communication is said to be as acute within a species as it is between species, when Montaigne argues that 'we manifestly perceive that there is a full and perfect communication amongst them, and that not only those of one same kinde understand one another, but even such as are of different kindes ... By one kinde of barking of a dogge, the horse knoweth he is angrie; by another voice of his, he is nothing dismaid' (as cited in Kalof and Fitzgerald, 2007: 58).

Shklar (1982) points out that Montaigne was immersed in cruelty in European society, and he felt that, because it was everywhere, this moral disease was foremost among the vices. Two dominant forces in European society at the time provided the impetus for his philosophy. Montaigne felt that Christianity had done little to suppress cruelty, and in fact reinforced the notion that cruel acts could be sanctioned in the name of Christianity. He cites the Spanish conquest of other worlds as particularly representative of their supposed superiority over others, and the approval of this in an effort to reorder reality. The other main force according to Shklar, which influenced the Spaniards and other conquering tribes, was Machiavellianism. Governance through cruelty was said to be more efficient than leniency, and success in politics, i.e., in efforts to become a good prince, was founded on this rationale. For a way out of this social milieu, Montaigne sought guidance from nature. Animals, Montaigne argued, are morally superior in almost every capacity because of their unimpaired grasp of reality. While humans seek renown, reason, and material goods, animals seek only that which is able to provide security, health, and peace (Shklar, 1982). As such, nature is the most exemplary guide to proper behaviour.

Up until the early modern period, there was a sustained emphasis on reason and virtue as signposts of what it meant to be a good person. This has been referred to as the Inward Government Theory (IGT) (Hallie, 1977). To be good, one used reason to exercise self-control over the passions, because it is the latter, seen through the desire of the body, which levelled humans down to the rank of the beasts. Fudge (2005) argues that one of the principal aspects of the IGT was that because animals lacked reason, awareness, and control they were unable to govern their urges. The possession of reason meant that humans by contrast could control themselves – they could exercise heroic virtue – in being good (Henry, 2000). Animals were thus viewed as the absolute other (Fudge, 2005).

In the early modern period, however, Montaigne dispatched this approach to ethics. He understood that ethics was not about egocentric concern for the moral agent, but rather how these moral agents act in the interests of others. This was a radical departure from the conventional mindset, although not unprecedented in practice, and it opened up a new ethics that was based on trust, pliant goodness, and a feeling for the other – the capacity to feel over the capacity to reason (Quint, 1998; Fudge, 2005). For Montaigne, a feeling for the other meant not only humans, but also animals, and he often pitched this ethics through his beliefs on cruelty. In his final thoughts in the essay *On Cruelty*, first published in 1580, Montaigne argues that

There is nevertheless a certain respect, a general duty of humanity, not only to beasts that have life and sense, but even to trees, and plants. We owe justice to men, and graciousness and benignity to other creatures that are capable of it ...

(Montaigne, n.d.)

By the onset of the Age of Enlightenment there was a gradual move away from the Cartesian way of looking at the world to one that opens the door to animal sentiment (Senior, 2007). Turner (1980) has suggested the revolutionary changes taking place at this time converged in the creation of a new sensitivity towards animals. These were (1) the recognition that humans were descended from beasts, (2) a rising esteem for science, (3) a sensitivity to pain and the suffering of others, and (4) industrialization and urbanization that placed humans and nature on a new foundation. All of these, Turner argues, culminated in a new question: 'How ought people to treat the animals around them'? (1980: xii). So, at the dawn of the 1800s, kindness and sympathy toward others was sporadic and tenuous. By 1900 sympathy was of a second nature. And for the Victorians, 'learning kindness to animals was part of the process of learning to live with their own animality. Partly they redefined the animal, but they also redefined themselves' (Turner, 1980: 139).

Keeping pace with societal shifts was legislation enacted for the protection of animals in European society. One of the first animal-friendly articles of legislation in Europe was an Irish law (1635) prohibiting the use of a horse's tail for ploughing or draught, as well as the pulling of wool from living sheep. In this latter case, clipping or shearing was to be the preferred method (Kalof, 2007b). The English Protectorate ordinance of 1654, facilitated by Puritans, was enacted in response to practices like cock throwing and cockfighting, which were fuelled by drunkenness and idleness (Kete, 2002). But at a broader level, Kete tells us that the ordinance was based on two assumptions: first, traditional actions toward animals were socially unsettling; and second, humans had a duty not to cause unnecessary pain. Kete writes that the ordinance was overturned during the time of the Restoration, but middle-class opinion had already started to sway in favour of the abolishment of blood sport practices. By the end of the eighteenth century, municipalities were enacting laws against many blood sports (Allen, 2004). Middle-class reform had generated so much support against lower-class popular violence that new Acts were swiftly being passed. Martin's Act of 1822 preventing the cruel treatment of cattle is a case in point. The Irishman Richard Martin, MP for Galway, submitted a bill in 1822 that sailed with ease through both houses, becoming an Act on 22 July of that year, recognizing the rights of animals – but not all animals. The Act protected 'horses, mares, geldings, mules, asses, cows, heifers, steers, oxen, sheep, and other cattle', but not cats and dogs. In addition, bulls were apparently classified as a different form of cattle, leaving them off the list of protection and allowing for the continuation of bull baiting (Turner, 1980). This was later changed via the British Cruelty to Animals Act passed in 1835, outlawing the use of any animal for purposes of baiting, running, and fighting. The

Grammont Law, passed by the French National Assembly in 1850, prohibited civic cruelty towards animals.

Independent societies also started to take shape in the nineteenth century. The Society for the Prevention of Cruelty to Animals (SPCA) emerged by the initiative of Arthur Broome, an Anglican clergyman, who organized a meeting on 16 June 1824 at a coffeehouse by the name of Old Slaughter's in London (Turner, 1980). Queen Victoria gave royal approval in 1840 after a period of remarkable growth and financial stability. This was followed by German and Swiss societies in the 1830s and 1840s respectively, in France in 1845, the American SPCA in 1866, and in Sweden in 1875. What emerged according to Kete (2002) was a new bourgeois morality based on the valorization of compassion to animals, which was being viewed as a mark of civilization in Europe, and henceforth carried over into the masses to become a global norm in the twentieth century. Countries that carried on ritual practices of cruelty towards animals, like Spain in reference to bullfighting, were looked down upon by other European nations at the forefront of change.

In contemporary times, animal welfare laws have further broadened to protect the interests of animals. The 1986 British Animals Act was amended in 1993 to expand protection to all mammals, birds, reptiles, fish, and amphibians (see Allen, 2004). Laws in the United States and Canada have experienced similar amendments. In Canada, for example, Bill C-15B moved the cruelty to animal provisions away from crimes against property to Part V: Sexual Offences, Public Morals and Disorderly Conduct. This means that animals are no longer treated as property, but rather beings that feel pain.

Biophilia

The term biophilia, made popular by E.O. Wilson, is defined as an 'innately emotional affiliation of human beings to other living organisms' (Wilson, 1993: 31). It explains why we go to such lengths to speak on behalf of those who cannot speak for themselves, as illustrated in the previous section. Wilson asserts that this affiliation with nature can be explained in evolutionary terms. The extensive history and intricate involvement of our species with the natural environment as hunters and gatherers meant that we had to learn and adapt to a range of natural stimuli, which must be reinforced through continual contact with nature (Heerwagen, 2009). There is thus a subconscious love or affective bond that we have for other living beings and systems, and this biophilia is a product of biological evolution. As modern life pulls away from this relationship, there is a yearning on the part of humans to reconnect.

An alternative hypothesis is offered by Tooby and Cosmides (1992), who feel that biophilia is a function of the hard-wiring of the brain over the course of human evolution as a result of the navigation of persistent problems encountered regularly in the environment. As explained by Heerwagen, these problems included the avoidance of predators, the ingestion of toxic vs non-toxic foods, and understanding cloud formations in predicting the weather. Different reasoning processes would be used for different problems because each situation is different. This reasoning is also supported by Herzog (2002), who suggests that our ancestors had to tackle different sets of rather specific problems and conditions, including predation, securing food, attracting mates, and so on. As such, the mind is not a general-purpose problem solver, but rather contains separate components that have evolved to get to the bottom of many different adaptive problems, which Herzog refers to as domain specificity. In our deep evolutionary past, hominids in Africa would have encountered helper animals (canids that warned of impending danger), foes (venomous snakes), and prey. Herzog finds it improbable that biophilia, as a general overriding hypothesis directing us to respect nature, could provide us with adaptive advantages to cope with all of these separate domains. On one hand our interactions with animals may be of a biophilic nature (the regard we have for canids as helper organisms), and on the other hand we have an inherent biophobic side to our natures, with adverse reactions to animals like spiders, as discussed earlier in this chapter.

The strength of the amount of empathy toward others is a function of rather nested relationships between kin, neighbours, other members of the community, our nation, and humanity in general. Midgley (1998) argues that since animals and humans evolved in often co-dependent ways (and of course competitive ways) there was the extension of compassion to these others, but not to the same extent as this cooperation and compassion was extended to the human members within the community. This, she explains, is why there is a higher degree of moral regard for people than for animals. Following this strand of thought it would appear that wild animals fall on the margins of this human–human and human–animal nested set of relationships, because the former are not part of the immediate extended family of the human community. It follows therefore that these wild animals would be extended less moral regard than, say, domesticated animals that fall more closely within the community or family unit. Yet in some cases the bond between animal and person/community can be extended and strengthened on cultural (ritual and totemism) grounds (see also Roszak's (1992) concept of ecopsychology).

Contemporary culture

There has been a broad shift in contemporary society with regards to the treatment of animals according to Benton and Redfearn (1996), which has occurred because of three main drivers. The first is ethology, which has allowed television and film to safely delve into the 'social, psychological and emotional richness and complexity of the lives of other animal species' (Benton and Redfearn, 1996: 48). Animals are portrayed in these works as possessing cognitive and emotional properties and capacities that viewers can relate to. At the same time, the practice of pet-keeping has reinforced these sensitivities in children as well as adults. Finally, the emergence of changing values in regards to the fragility of the earth – new green sensitivities – in response to the human-induced impacts that have so negatively affected the earth and its innumerable inhabitants, beyond humans, has converged well with the animal agenda. Riding on the wave of these changes is the media, which has been successful at exposing the underbelly of enterprises that sacrifice the well-being of animals for human productivity and efficiency via animal experimentation, agriculture, hunting, and so on. This heightened sensitivity is demonstrated in opinion polls. In 2009, Canadians were polled on 21 moral issues ranging from abortion to animal testing. The study found that there is a higher level of reverence for animals than for some facets of human life. Whereas 31 per cent of Canadians have misgivings about wearing animal fur and 41 per cent are opposed to medical tests on animals, only 34 per cent are in opposition to capital punishment (MacQueen, 2009).

Animal representation

Central to the discourse here is the representation of the animal through human eyes. Malamud (2007) writes that it is a challenge in this day and age to be an animal amidst the demands of human existence. Foremost, animals are viewed as a resource for consumption on two different levels. We not only eat, skin, harvest, or physically devour the animal, but we also consume these beings culturally, according to Malamud: 'watching, framing, representing, characterizing, and reproducing the subject in a certain way – that may comparatively devour animals' (2007: 1). A myriad set of postmodern dislocations, Malamud suggests, has rendered animals' habitat as almost irrelevant. Animals go anywhere we want them to go, and we demand they do anything we want them to do. This is tantamount to the worst form of alienation, by removing them from their domains and shaping their behaviours (silly, violent, or otherwise) in the service of our own selfish enterprises. As Baker (2001) contends, how we attempt to represent the animal through art, media, science, and so on, can never truly represent the real animal. Photographers such as Britta Jaschinski have argued that photographs don't tell the real story of the photographer actually knowing the animal. The camera sees the animal image, but one doesn't really know the subject (Baker, 2001).

The inability or unwillingness to learn and appreciate the animal beyond its cultural or financial value is a form of arrogance and ignorance, which sometimes gets us into trouble. Pictures of park visitors happily feeding bears demonstrate this animal–human disconnect. Timothy Treadwell, 'The Grizzly Man', demonstrated a type of arrogance that proved fatal in presuming to truly predict animal behaviour and nature on the basis of *his* own personal experience. The Australian icon Steve Irwin, who had accomplished so much in the name of conservation and awareness of the needs of animals, surely stepped over the line in presuming to fully understand the nature and behaviour of stingrays.

In plain view of this arrogance and ignorance, theorists have suggested that we need to explore a different ontology in reference to the relationship between humans and animals. In *A Thousand Plateaus*, Deleuze and Guattari (1987) explore this new terrain. Their concept of the becoming-animal is about undoing identity – about the sweeping away of both animal and human identities as they come closer to each other's realities (Baker, 2002). Deleuze and Guattari suggest,

Plate 2.2 Animal themes that sell: Busch Gardens, Florida

Plate 2.3 Dog sledding as representative of the character of the 'north': Algonquin Park, Canada

for example, that we need to move away from the naturalist's preoccupation with ordering and relationships on the basis of series and structures. Looking at the world through the reductionist lens is limiting and fails to understand the dynamism that is not locked in 'degradations of the mythic order'. What the authors are after is an escape from order, series, and structure towards a new construction of the human–animal interface towards this becoming-animal, where there is permeability between what is human and animal. This means that we cannot simply level an animal down to its cultural representation – how we have chosen to represent an animal through media, commerce, and so on – but rather we need to understand the whole animal including its life course and its life force. This entails learning about each other from the ground up, our own animal nature as well as the natures of other nonhuman forms.

> A becoming is not a correspondence between relations. But neither is it a resemblance, an imitation, or, at the limit, an identification …To become is not to progress or regress along a series … Above all, becoming does not occur in the imagination, even when the imagination reaches the highest cosmic or dynamic level, as in Jung or Bachelard. Becomings-animal are neither dreams nor phantasies. They are perfectly real.
>
> (Deleuze and Guattari, 1987: 262)

Becoming-animal means, in the case of tourists and television stars, knowing when not to pursue the animal, how much personal space to afford the animal, and the dimensions of threat in the face of personal and commercial prizes.

A recent application of this theoretical position can be found in the work of Wolch (2003), who explores the human–animal divide via the process of urbanization. City builders and dwellers have developed a moral compass that is based on instrumental reason – profit, reason, progress – the calculative mindset as postulated by Heidegger. Proof of this may be found in the elimination of wild animals that pose a threat to development and the virtual elimination of animals from contemporary urban theory. Humans therefore interact with animals through their diet, by keeping captives of exotic species, through their pets, going to *ex situ* establishments like Marineland, or by watching shows on television where the true representation of the animal is questionable. The outcome of this disassociation with real animals is the slip with apparent ease into misinterpretations of what is real and not real, because of the redefinition of what is and is not authentic. Wolch argues that a new theory of urban design premised on allowing the animals back in ought to be established – a reconceptualized cityscape or zoöpolis. This amounts to a transspecies urban practice based on an emerging science of urban animal ecology. This demands conservation, collaboration, and critique in an effort to forge coexistence 'for a future in which animals and nature would no longer be incarcerated beyond the reach of our everyday lives' (Wolch, 2003: 268). This perspective is not too far removed from the Spanish philosopher Jose Ferrater-Mora (1912–91). Ferrater-Mora argued for a type of integrationism which was characterized by the need to establish a continuous ontology based on levels of reality: physical, biological, neural-mental, biological-social, and social-cultural, with each stemming from the previous one (Honderich, 1995). He wrote frequently on issues of animal justice as a more practical outgrowth of this ontology, whereby differences between nonhuman and human animals were thought to be differences not of kind, but rather of degree (see also Midgley, 2002).

Art, books and the screen

Poststructuralist, postmodern art has attempted to re-imagine the human–animal interface over the past couple of decades. Baker (2002) cites for example the work of Joseph Beuys, *Coyote* (1974), in which both the artist and coyote lived for a week in a confined space in New York City during 1974. While Beuys viewed the event as ecology, others felt that the relationship was akin to slave or ringmaster in some sort of grand performance. The British artists, Olly and Suzi, have also explored this fertile ground where there is an attempt to come closer to the reality of the animal other by painting dangerous predators in the animals' spaces. Works include sharks off the coast of South Africa, tarantulas, wolves in close proximity, and the green anaconda. In the case of the anaconda, the artists got the animal in its own habitat to move across a canvas in creating its own distinctive mark, rendering the imprint, according to the artists, as 'a genuine artefact of the event' (Baker, 2002: 88). The intent of such a procedure, Baker adds, is to allow Western audiences to capture the truth and immediacy of the event and, in so doing, gain an appreciation for the animal's reality.

The Ukrainian Nathalia Edenmont has generated a great deal of controversy in the world of art through the use of dead animals as the subject of her work, challenging Western morality in the process. Her exhibition entitled 'Still Life' presents sections of freshly killed rabbits, mice, and cats, which she kills herself just prior to the exhibition in order to preserve the freshness of life (Meleshkevich, 2005). Turkish-born Pinar Yolacan makes clothes out of fresh meat, and explains the process as follows:

> I make the clothes the morning of the shoot, so the meat doesn't rot. In Bahia, I froze it beforehand, so it wouldn't get smelly, because it's really hot. It's quite domestic, really – I have to buy meat, clean up, sew. For this series, I got the fabrics in local markets, and the meat, too. I try to accentuate each woman's skin tone and expression with the clothes; I take Polaroids of them when I first meet them, then I work from those.
>
> (MacDonnell, 2007)

Baker (2005) queries whether or not contemporary art can adequately address the killing of animals, especially through work that is both ethically and aesthetically disturbing. He uses the example of Cindy Sherman's *Untitled No. 140*, which shows the artist in an outdoor scene at night, wearing a pig snout in profile, eating something, with blood or dirt covering the face. Critics argue that the work fails in its ability to be art because viewers see it primarily as an example of instrumental use of an animal, and further that it represents a pig's death more than anything else. This is a theme taken forward in Baker's (2000) *The Postmodern Animal*, which describes these works of art more as 'botched taxidermy' than art. Animals in these works take on often shocking forms, which say more about the artists' views on identity and creativity in humans than any accurate depiction of natural history.

Perhaps most noteworthy of these artists is Damien Hirst, who has raised controversy over themes of death and decay in his art. His most famous piece, a full tiger shark suspended in a glass box of formaldehyde called *The Physical Impossibility of Death in the Mind of Someone Living*, has been at the centre of this controversy. The shark used in the art was caught off the coast of Queensland, but was later replaced in the piece of art because of poor methods of preservation. In his artwork, *Some Comfort Gained from the Acceptance of the Inherent Lies in Everything* (1995), Hirst sliced up cows and preserved these sections in glass, steel, and formaldehyde, like the shark, so that viewers could walk between each section/slice. Hirst claims that these works prompt us to develop more compassionate feelings for the species and for animals more generally. So despite the fact that an animal may be used and presented as a piece of art, one of the outcomes of this is the 'acute shame, humiliation and guilt for the instrumental and systematic abuse of those that deserve our care' (Cashell, 2009: 175). But to others this simply represents an 'international carnival of anthrozoological weirdness' (Malamud, 2008: 75).

Proponents of this 'shock art' argue such art lies in the belief that if the artist hasn't harmed the animals in the production of the work (the animals are in fact dead before their use) then the works are defensible on ethical grounds (Cashell, 2009). Artists are able to claim ethical immunity, at least on utilitarian grounds, because no pain was inflicted on the organism. From the perspective of rights, however, the argument may take another turn. Beings have interests and therefore ethical rights, which are designed to protect these interests. The issue of the use of animals in an instrumental way, as means to our own ends, in this case to make lots of money, is one that bears weight. There is a violation of the animal's dignity in the face of instrumental gain or exploitation of one form or another. Whether this argument bears fruit in the face of so much animal exploitation by humans for food, entertainment, work, and so on, is worthy of further debate. (See the work of Sue Coe and Britta Jaschinski, who have crafted their art in defence of animals that have been exploited or injured through anthropogenic causes.)

In reference to books, the portrayal of animals in the popular 'Christian fantasy series' Harry Potter (Rowling), Narnia (Lewis), and Middle Earth (Tolkien) are compared and contrasted by Morris (2009) from an animal liberationist perspective. Morris observes that Harry Potter is the least sensitive to issues of animal cruelty (beasts used in a variety of capacities are offered little intrinsic value) and the use of animals as food. The food consumed by students at Hogwarts is rich in saturated fats, sugar, and animal products, and the only student offering protests, Fleur Delacour, is criticized for doing so. The direction of the Harry Potter series follows from an era when animals garnered far less respect. Morris finds Lewis's 'Narnia' series and other popular works to be far more enlightened in comparison to Rowling. Although vegetarianism is criticized in the author's work, vivisection is frowned upon and a much more respectful attitude is demonstrated consistently throughout the books. Finally, Morris argues that in Middle Earth, Tolkien takes an even stronger animal liberationist stance than Lewis by demonstrating kindness to animals as a virtue and cruelty as a deficiency of disposition (see also Donovan, 2009, for an explanation of how Tolstoy discards speciesist ideology in favour of an approach that respects the subjectivity of animals).

Although the popularity of the preceding books is without question, increasingly it is the screen that has become the dominant forum by which contemporary society fixes meaning to nature. Disney films like *Finding Nemo* and *The Lion King* are cases in point, where human values and characteristics are projected on to the nature of animals. How animals and the environment are depicted has vast implications in an era of habitat destruction, extinctions, climate change, and hunting and fishing (Rothfels, 2002a).

The success of these films, however, points to the fact that there is a connection between humans and animals on many levels. Despite the rampant anthropomorphism, Disney has realized that there is a real deep-rooted fascination with the image of animals – how they look and behave, how they are different or similar to ourselves, and perhaps where we all fit into the broader scheme of things. Disney is right to have channelled its efforts into the children's market, but the packaging of these films with adult humour makes these productions accessible to a much wider audience.

But as Malamud (2007) has argued, the animals we spend so much time viewing – the animals we make famous in modern culture – are not empowered. We don't truly know these animals, but only configure them in our minds according to how they are presented to us, which in turn is influenced by our current place in culture. They are subjects of 'fetishistic voyeurism' (p. 25). Large-budget films like *Babe* and *Chicken Run* became powerful representations and cultural evaluations of the often unbalanced relationships that exist between animals and humans (Wolch, 2002). The same can be said of cartoons like Bugs Bunny, Mickey Mouse, and 'real-life' television shows like *Rin-Tin-Tin*, *Lassie*, and *Flipper*. These animals lived and died in the service of an industry. We loved them, but we depersonalized them for commercial reasons; because we knew that we might exploit a niche that wasn't otherwise exploited and because there was something novel about how these animals could behave as almost human. But far from being autonomous beings in control of their own destiny, their perverse lives, according to Malamud (2007), were fashioned according to the expectations and desires of those who were really in control: industry and, even more powerful, those who chose to watch.

Conclusion

In this chapter the spectrum between fear and veneration has been discussed for the purpose of establishing belief, value, and attitude dimensions of the animal–human relationship. Mullin (2002) reminds us that culture is often the great divider in this relationship. Culture has been problematic because it has constructed systems of hierarchical dualisms such as culture/nature, human/animal, mind/body, and male/female (Mullin, 2002). But evolution has played a part in all of this too. On one hand we have a very real deep-seated fear and contempt for certain animals, and on the other a fascination and love for nature that is also very real. What is encouraging according to Wolch and Emel (1995) is that the rights- and utilitarian-based philosophies that started to emerge over the course of the last two hundred years have begun to penetrate the consciousness of popular culture in laying the foundation of a new moral landscape. The acceptance of the animal-other is important because it shapes who we are in self, society, politics, and environment, and this acceptance carries with it the manner by which we might assign moral value to animals. This is the topic of the next chapter.

3 Animals and humans – an evolving relationship 2

On the use of criteria to assign moral value to animals and associated theories

They eat without pleasure, cry without pain, grow without knowing it; they desire nothing, fear nothing, know nothing
(Nicolas Malebranche (1638–1715), cited in Harrison, 1992)

Introduction

This chapter is assembled into two main sections. Following from Aaltola (2005), the first section discusses the criteria (e.g. consciousness, reason) that we use to assign value to animals. The issue is that if animals are found to have these qualities, we might extend greater moral consideration to them. Many scholars contend that the most important of these criteria for the extension of moral consideration in including animals, or certain species of animals, is consciousness – experiencing the world as something. As such, consciousness is given greater consideration in the discussion below. The second part of the chapter examines the justification of the moral value of animals on the basis of many different important ethical theories, including rights theory, utilitarianism, and virtue ethics, among others. These theories are important to the latter chapters of the book, as these will be used to reflect more deeply upon the tourism industry's use of animals.

The great chain of being

There has long been a continuity between humans and animals and this has been referenced through the idea of the great chain of being, otherwise known as *scala naturae* (scale of nature) in classical Greece and used more intensively from the early Middle Ages up until the latter part of the nineteenth century (Preece, 2005). The chain is arranged such that all beings in nature are positioned from highest to lowest according to worthiness and superiority in comparison to others. The highest position is occupied by God, followed by angels, humans, other mammals, right on down to insects, plants, and rocks. The chain has been a convenient tool by which to define the essence of what it is to be human on the basis of what other species lack, including speech, consciousness, sentience, religion, and so on. The absence of these human qualities obliges us to use these lower beings as instruments to satisfy our own goals and interests, giving rise to the 'lower' and 'higher' animals according to their position on the ladder.

Both Plato and Aristotle felt that there was a hierarchy of animals, with predatory animals towards the bottom and the more gentle and social animals towards the top (Preece, 2005). Aristotle discussed an upward scale of existence in plants and animals, with nature proceeding 'little by little from things lifeless to animal life in such a way that it is impossible to determine the exact line of demarcation, not on which side thereof an intermediate form should lie' (*The History of Animals*, Book VIII, 1). His work was a precursor to this *scala naturae* and dominated the discourse on human and nonhuman animals for centuries after. St Thomas Aquinas is another who believed that animals were below humans in the great chain of being. In fact it was wrong for humans not to consume animals, because these beings had been provided to us by God. Even the Darwinists have been unable to break free of the *scala naturae*. Although evolution by natural selection replaced the great chain of being in theory, i.e., as a biological explanation for the relationships that exist between humans and animals, the chain lives on as a moral model for these relationships (Preece, 2005).

The great chain of being is not a defunct idea, but rather one that continues to exist in scholarly work. For example, Machan (2002) has argued that there is a hierarchy of complexity in nature with humans at the top – this status affording us the opportunity to use animals for a number of purposes including sport and experimentation. We can do this because of our advanced cognitive capacities that allow for moral reasoning giving us higher value than other animals, which therefore gives us usufructuary rights over less complex beings in allowing us to succeed in life or flourish.

Speciesism, anthropocentrism, and anthropomorphsim

Two concepts that are direct descendents of the great chain of being are speciesism and anthropocentrism, and both have particular relevance to animal ethics in contemporary times. The term 'speciesism' was first used by Richard Ryder (1971), and was meant to correspond to discrimination against animals in the same way that humans discriminate against each other, e.g., sexism and racism. Instead of intra-group discrimination it refers to inter-group discrimination according to biological categories, or species (see Ryder, 1970; see also Noske, 2008). To Singer the speciesist gives 'greater weight to the interests of members of their own species when there is a clash between their interests and the interests of those of other species' (Singer, 1993: 58; see also Shanks, 2009). It is the assumption of human superiority and we can justify the poor treatment of nonhuman animals based on this supremacy. Speciesism thus makes it patently convenient to formulate difficult decisions about the order of species in a hierarchy. Humans are higher than gorillas, for example, which in turn are higher than chimpanzees, monkeys, dogs, cats, birds, and fish, and so on down the ladder (Bekoff, 1998). In this capacity:

Whenever you see a bird in a cage, fish in a tank, or nonhuman mammal on a chain, you're seeing speciesism. If you believe a bee or frog has less right to life and liberty than a chimpanzee or human, or you consider humans superior to other animals, you subscribe to speciesism. If you visit aquaprisons and zoos, attend circuses that include 'animal acts', wear nonhuman skin or hair, or eat flesh, eggs, or cow-milk products, you practice speciesism.

(Dunayer, 2004: 1)

Rachels (1990), like Dunayer above, argues that speciesism is not a uniform concept, but may be conceptualized on the basis of mild and radical forms. Mild speciesism occurs when interests might be comparable but priority is still given to humans. A radical form of speciesism occurs when even the most minor or insignificant interests of humans take priority over the essential interests of animals (see also Fjellström, 2002; Graft, 1997; Holland, 1984; Gray, 1991).

Anthropocentrism or human supremacy relates to the predisposition that humans have in regarding themselves as the centre of the universe. All other entities are secondary to the needs of humans, and these other entities are used as resources to fulfil human desire. Because of the idea of supremacy, there is a lost connection to other beings that might otherwise be considered as part (perhaps equal parts) of the web of life. Figure 3.1 demonstrates that while humans are assigned intrinsic value there is a moral boundary that excludes animals and the rest of nature, which are otherwise assigned only instrumental value, i.e., resources to be used for human ends.

Anthropocentrism is closely related to speciesism, according to Noske (2008), with the latter relating more to practice and the former more to attitude.

Anthropomorphism is the term we use when we treat animals as if they were people, where 'humanity is and should be the measure of all things' (Noske, 2008: 78). This includes attributing human characteristics to the behaviour, emotions, and appearance of animals (see Plate 3.1). We do this, Midgley (2002) suggests, because we have a failure to understand the special unique sentience of animals – feelings that are a complete mystery to us – which equates to a lack of an interspecies sympathy. In using anthropomorphic thought we lessen the distance between animals and humans, because the offering of virtue to animals is a signpost for humans to be virtuous too (Fudge, 2005). When we idolize animals

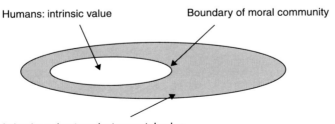

Figure 3.1 Anthropocentrism

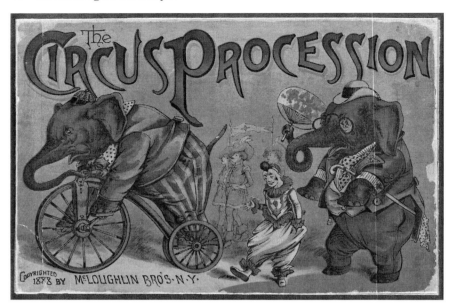

Plate 3.1 Circus procession, 1888

this simply represents another form of anthropomorphism beyond the more frequent examples of animal denigration. When groups idolize animals and revere them because of the virtues they are said to possess, and to which humans aspire, they are simply making a comparison on the basis of what is wicked and repulsive within their own societies without really understanding the nature of the animals that they revere. Suggesting that animals don't lie, cheat, murder, rape, steal, or kill has been refuted by current research (Masson and McCarthy, 1995). The fear of treating animals as if they were people, or attributing human qualities to other beings or objects, is called *anthropomorphophobia*.

The moral value of animals

The terrain on the moral value of animals is complex. The area incorporates the use of a number of basic concepts, the knowledge of which is thought to be essential in grasping this complexity. In this section interests, moral agency, and moral consideration are discussed for the purpose of establishing a base of familiarity with the criteria used to assign moral value.

We ought to be concerned over the question of whether only some animals have interests, such as chimpanzees, over others that may or may not have interests, such as slugs and snails. The key component in addressing this issue is whether these animals have the capacity to experience pain or if they are capable of consciousness. If they are, then, as stated above, we can conclude that these others have interests, and as humans we should take these interests into consideration.

For philosophers like Peter Singer, similar interests need to be counted equally, and this would hinge on the nature of the animal in question, including its nervous system and other associated aspects of physiology. Those animals with a higher capacity to suffer should be treated differently than those with a lower capacity for suffering. To other philosophers like Tom Regan it is not so much a question of the assessment of interests but rather the fact that we should all count equally based on inherent value.

Animals have an interest in their own survival. Not unlike humans, animals possess an innate drive to increase their own well-being or fitness for purposes of longevity, survival, reproduction, and so on. Intra-group competition exists to secure reproductive rights, so it makes sense that there is a drive that compels the animal to advantage itself to fulfil these basic needs or interests. Furthermore, seeking optimal conditions in which to secure these factors would mean fulfilling certain niche and habitat requirements. Midgley (1983) argues that animals may have different levels of interests – trivial and urgent. The former includes those aspects that may be in the best interests of the animal, but do not relate more specifically to the animal's physiological well-being or the avoidance of pain. By contrast, urgent interests include those that have a direct bearing on the need to avoid pain and suffering (see for example Dobson, 2009 in the context of ethics and marine wildlife tourism). Gruen (2010) also makes a distinction between different types of interests in a hierarchical formation: crucial interests are more significant than important interests, which in turn are more significant than replaceable interests, which are further weightier than trivial interests. According to Gruen (2010):

> So if an animal has an interest in not suffering, which is arguably a crucial interest, or at least an important one, and a person has an interest in eating that animal when there are other things to eat, meaning that interest is replaceable, then the animal has the stronger interest and it would be wrong to violate that interest by killing the animal for food if there is another source of food available.
>
> (p. 10)

If we do care about the animals, i.e., we are sensitive to their interests, we extend to them moral consideration, in similar ways to how we extend it to ourselves. Moral consideration relates to what some theorists argue as acceptance into the moral community. Both the willingness to extend moral consideration and the degree of this consideration are questions essential to the equation. How far, for example, should we extend moral consideration beyond our own species?

It has been a matter of much debate that only human beings can make claims of moral consideration, but it is increasingly recognized that membership within a species is a 'morally irrelevant characteristic', according to Gruen. We simply cannot say that just because humans are members of *Homo sapiens*, they deserve moral consideration over all other species. Theorists have gotten around the membership argument by stressing that humans possess certain capacities that make them different than other species. Because we can reason (reflect), this gives us the ability to be successful in navigating the subtleties of our moral terrain – a capacity that is not shared in the nonhuman animal realm (Korsgaard, 1996). This means that animals do not have reasons to act and reasons not to act, which further means that they fail to have an identity 'from which they reflect and for which they act' (Gruen, 2010: 4). The problem with this reasoning, according to Gruen and many other philosophers, amounts to the problem of 'marginal humans'. Using Korsgaard's rationale, it is the case that many human beings do not possess the capacity for rational thought, yet we extend to these individuals moral consideration. They have the right to life regardless of their debilitating condition, and we work to protect these rights (see Hadley, 2004).

The foregoing is suggestive of the fact that the decision to ascribe moral consideration to an animal rests on the issue of moral agency. Moral agents are beings that are capable of understanding the rightness or wrongness of their behaviours, and who may be responsible or accountable for their behaviours. These behaviours can be subject to evaluation according to the norms of society. By contrast, a moral patient 'is a being whose treatment may be subject to moral evaluation' (Cavalieri, 2001: 29). While moral patients are not held accountable for their actions, moral agents are because they are in the possession of moral principles that direct their actions. Moral agency also comes packaged with obligations, and there is general agreement in the literature suggesting that the obligations we have toward others are limited to one's level of understanding. Consistent with the foregoing discussion, a three-year-old would have a lower level of responsibility or obligation than an adult based on this level of understanding.

According to Shapiro (2006), some animals are thought to act as moral agents even in the absence of the ability to master moral principles. Shapiro's position comes in response to Machan's (2002) argument that it is ethically justifiable for humans to use animals for experimentation and sport because humans are capable of undertaking moral tasks by virtue of their ability to reason, whereas animals presumably cannot. This capability makes humans more important than nonhuman animals, suggesting that this lack of moral agency is a reason to limit the moral status of animals. Shapiro proposes two ways to deal with this issue. The first is to suggest that the criterion of moral agency is not as important as other characteristics, like pain, in according moral status. The second argument is that some nonhuman animals are in fact moral agents because of their behaviour toward other members of their species and other species. While some theorists argue for an ability to understand and act upon moral principles as the benchmark for moral agency (see Pluhar 1995; Machan, 2002), Shapiro contends that the standard for moral agency should be the capability to engage in virtuous behaviour along a continuum with the capacity to act according to principles at one end and the rudiments of virtuous behaviour at the other end. This would place many animals somewhere in the middle of the continuum, based on current scientific evidence. Displays of reciprocal altruism include whales placing themselves between harpooned whales and whaling ships, dolphins keeping other injured dolphins afloat, animals dying of grief over the death of a mate, the cooperative relationship between wolves, and blood sharing between vampire bats (Wilkinson, 1986).

Accordingly, ethologists, those who study animal behaviour, have been successful at proving that all of these capacities are in one form or another attributes that are worthy of elevating the moral status of animals in the eyes of critics. But if this way of looking at animals seems intuitive or only natural, the reality is that only recently have scientists bothered to look beyond behaviour to the emotional domain in animal science, despite a promising start by Darwin in his *The Expression of the Emotions in Man and Animals*, published in 1872. In this volume, Darwin made several observations on a range of emotions in humans and animals with a characteristic leaning towards a shared ancestry between animals and humans based on evolution by natural selection. For example, Darwin argued that 'pain is expressed by dogs in nearly the same way as by many other animals, namely, by howling, writhing, and contortions of the whole body' (Darwin, 1872).

Research on the emotions of animals has received scant attention until recently for two main reasons. On one hand, even though Darwin had built the foundation for continuity between humans and animals, the fact that there was no evidence pointing to the existence of an animal mind served to further derail attempts at building a case for animal sentience. If animals were not experiencing subjects, there was little reason to treat them as anything more than a means to an end. The use of animals in laboratories to serve behaviourism emphasizes this point. Behaviourism was a product of logical positivism, where experimentation and quantitative methods were seen as the hallmark of good science. In fact, any terms not definable on the basis of the relationship between stimulus and response were excluded (Cavalieri, 2001).

Based on Morgan's Canon, 'in no case may we interpret an action as the outcome of the exercise of a higher psychical faculty, if it can be interpreted as the outcome of the exercise of one which stands lower in the psychological scale' (Morgan, 1894, cited in Allen and Bekoff, 2007b: 306–7). It is also the case that exploring the emotional domain of animal minds had much to do with professional and financial interests, according to Masson and McCarthy (1995). Scientists would have had to come to grips with the notion that their subjects did in fact suffer from pain, as they showed compassion and altruism, and experienced terror, loneliness, and anguish. But what we can infer from all of this is that not understanding or not being willing to understand the capacity for animals to feel is perhaps a limitation in the sensory capacity of humans. Even in humans the extension of moral status has relatively little to do with reason, and much more to do with emotion (Rollin, 2005; see also Burghardt, 2009).

Evolving in the early twentieth century from the works of Oskar Heinroth, Julian Huxley, Konrad Lorenz, and Niko Tinbergen on the behaviour of animals in the wild, the field of ethology changed further through the efforts of Jane Goodall, who helped to influence a new vision for the scientific community. Through rigorous academic methods and objectivity, Goodall advanced the idea that there is certainly a lot more going on in the mind of a chimpanzee beyond basic instincts.

Donald Griffin is perhaps foremost in the emergence of a cognitive ethology that is suggestive of the fact that scientists ought to keep an open mind to the possibility of animal consciousness. Cognitive ethology is defined as 'the comparative, evolutionary, and ecological study of nonhuman animal minds, including thought processes, beliefs, rationality, information processing, intentionality, and consciousness' (Allen and Bekoff, 2007b: 304). Good ethologists, according to Bekoff (1998), strive to uncover what it is like to be the animal under study, including investigations of the senses that they use to be successful in their worlds. Bekoff argues for a deep, reflective ethology in the same line of thinking as deep ecology, where both scientists and laypersons have deep moral responsibilities and obligations towards animals. Restrictions ought to be imposed on how animals are used for research, amusement, and food, but this might only take place if a more biocentric and holistic reorientation takes place (see Taylor, 1986).

The animal mind

Consciousness remains a difficult area of study both in humans and nonhuman animals. This topic surfaces in our discussion of animal ethics because moral consideration extended to animals is often premised on the capacity for consciousness. Consciousness means that an animal is aware of its environment, and responds to it, learns from it, and feels the effect of it. Animals are said to be conscious because they are able to be unconscious, as when they have been knocked out or anaesthetized (Scruton, 2002). Furthermore, since animals have similar nerves and organs of sensation to human beings, as well as similar cries and groans, they may experience pain in the same way as humans but perhaps not to the same extent (Turner, 1980; Lynch, 1994). Part of the issue surrounds the belief on the part of some theorists that animals simply respond reflexively when exposed to painful stimuli and without conscious understanding of the nature of the episode and how it is built into experience (see DeGrazia, 1996).

While it is beyond the scope of this work to examine consciousness in great detail, a basic understanding of the concept is required, and an excellent summary is provided by Rowlands (2009b) in the form of different types of consciousness in ascending order of complexity. There is the recognition that in higher order organisms, these different forms of consciousness once in place would have been subject to adaptive processes leading to refined and higher levels of consciousness (see Baars, 1993). The six types of consciousness outlined by Rowlands include (2009b: 166):

1. Waking state: A creature is conscious when it is awake as opposed to asleep or otherwise unconscious.
2. Sensitivity: A creature is able to detect salient features of its environment.
3. Access consciousness: A creature's mental representations (neural states that carry information about the environment) are poised for use in the control of action (including, but not restricted to, verbal action).

4. Phenomenal consciousness: A creature has experiences, and there is something that it is like to have these experiences. Suppose you stub your toe. This feels a certain way – it hurts. This way that it feels to stub your toe is one example of what philosophers have in mind when they talk of phenomenal consciousness as raw experience.

5. Self-consciousness: This mode of consciousness can take two forms: (a) awareness of oneself as an entity that is distinct from other entities and which persists through time, and (b) awareness of one's own mental states.

6. Mentality: In discussions of nonhuman animals the term consciousness is often used as a catch-all for mental states or abilities; judging whether an animal is conscious or not is often seen as tantamount to working out whether it can believe, think, remember, reason, and so on.

Rowlands suggests that the ability to arrive at a unified definition of consciousness is difficult and unlikely because these different conditions or states lack unifying phenomena that might be used to tie them together. Categories 4 through 6 appear to be the groups most highly debated in the study of animal consciousness, and suitable for further discussion here.

Category 4: Phenomenal consciousness

Sentience implies foremost the capacity to feel pleasure and pain, and there is a long history of its relevance to animal–human studies. Those animals that are more distant down the great chain of being than humans, and thus in possession of fewer characteristics similar to humans, suffer because we choose not to believe that these animals are capable of experiencing conscious pain (Allen, 2004; see also Perrett, 1997). There is an analogical argument developed by Peter Singer (1993) in reference to whether or not animals feel pain. It is structured according to a correlation between how humans and animals experience pain. Given that humans share many of the fundamental structures and systems of physiology with other vertebrates, including birds and mammals, it follows that they have the capacity to feel in the same way we do.

   Although sentience pertains to pleasure and pain, it is the latter that has garnered more interest because of its implications for the use of animals. The utilitarian philosopher Jeremy Bentham opened the door to debate on pain in his oft-quoted line, 'The question is not, can they *reason*? Nor, can they *talk*? But, can they *suffer*?' (*An Introduction to the Principles of Morals and Legislation*, XVII, 5n; see also Harrison, 1997: 41). If we base moral status on sentiency, not rationality, and animals are sentient beings, then how is it that we should treat animals as morally inferior? For Derrida (2002), Bentham's viewpoint changed everything, as it asked the type of moral question that carries with it a lack of certainty that has possibilities in every direction. (See Boddice, 2008, who writes that nobody has bothered to emphasize the fact that Bentham, in the same stanza, also made reference to humans' entitlement to kill and consume animals, and that animals are 'never the worse for being dead' (p. 127).)

The emphasis that we place on suffering should also be placed on the understanding of pain and fear, the former of which is 'a sensation, and sensations are non-cognitive states, characterized by their intensity, duration and locality' (Scruton, 2002: 551), while the latter is characterized by 'cognitive states, which are not felt in any particular part of the body and which involve a mental assessment that may have no precise duration' (Scruton, 2002: 551; see also Casimir, 2009). Assembling this together, Scruton argues that the level of emotion that an animal can experience is a function of the thoughts that it can think, which means that animal fear is probably not the same as the fear experienced by a human. While we have a concept of death from a metaphysical standpoint, it is not at all clear the level of awareness that certain animals have of this. Furthermore, the value of pain is that it has survival value, meaning that we learn through adaptive and selective processes from those elements of the environment that bring pain and pleasure (see Lynch, 1994).

Category 5: Self-consciousness

This category of consciousness includes awareness of oneself as an entity that is distinct from other entities and which persists through time, and awareness of one's own mental states. The question of animal selves has been addressed by the sociologist Irvine (2007), who argues there is ample evidence pointing to the fact that animals have the ability to see themselves as objects – a characteristic of selfhood. While sceptics argue that language is a chief criterion of consciousness, Irvine argues that there are many other factors that need to be considered, including behavioural flexibility (the monitoring and adjustment of behaviour depending on situation). This indicates consciousness because it demands the capacity to monitor and adapt. Some animals such as dogs have the ability to share the focus of attention. This entails a directing of the dog's own gaze in the direction of the gaze of a human. Dogs are also adept at following human signals for food or other items. The failure of sociologists and other scientists to use such evidence in the creation of a broader definition of self is said to be a result of entrenched anthropocentric ideals.

The mirror test for self-recognition, pioneered by Gallup (1970), has been a useful tool to measure self-consciousness in animals. After a period of time which allowed chimpanzees to see themselves in a mirror, Gallup anesthetized chimps and placed two red marks on each chimp: one over an eye and the other on the opposite ear. Once presented with the mirrors again, the chimps repeatedly touched the marks and at times smelled their fingers to see if there was an accompanying scent.

The only other species found to self-recognize are orang-utans and bonobos, suggesting that it is only the great apes that have this capacity. Gallup, Anderson and Shillito (2002) argue that self-recognition is a metric of self-awareness, which indicates the aptitude to become the object of one's own attention (see also de Veer *et al.*, 2002). In all other cases besides the great apes, organisms respond to the image in the mirror as if it was another organism, indicating no pre-existing sense of self.

The mirror test has been criticized as simplistic by Rowlands (2009b), who argues that mirror-recognition may not be the only condition for self-awareness. In this vein, Allen and Bekoff (2007b) suggest that the study only included species that match motor and visual information, excluding countless others that rely on, for example, chemical clues. Animals like chimps and gorillas regularly involve themselves in self-inspection and so may be more sensitive to positioning of spots or other markers on portions of their body. For those animals who do not engage in this behaviour, the test would not be as relevant.

Category 6: Mentality

Consciousness is often used as a catch-all phrase for mental states or abilities – judging whether an animal can believe, think, remember, reason, and so on. From this, theorists attribute cognitive and affective abilities (beliefs and desires) to animals largely on the basis of common sense, not empirical evidence, in consideration of how they behave under various conditions (Rowlands, 2009b). In attempts to move beyond this common sense approach, a number of measures have been developed to more accurately assess advanced consciousness. One example is Varner's (2008) work – the Autonoetic Consciousness Paradigm (ACP). Autonoetic refers to self-knowledge and autonoetic consciousness pertains to consciousness of one's own past, present, and future, which, among the animals, gives way to a heightened form of respectful treatment over other animals that do not posses this capacity. Varner says that this should translate into rights, and there are moral strings tied to this status; we should not treat poorly animals that display autonoetic consciousness. Also, there should be a hierarchy of animals according to self-knowledge. He explains this hierarchy as follows:

> At the bottom are *merely sentient* organisms – organisms that can consciously experience pain, but have no robust sense of their own future and past – they 'live entirely in the present'. At the top of the ACP hierarchy are full-blown *persons*, with a biographical sense of their lives as wholes. Probably only human beings are persons in this strong sense, but among sentient nonpersons a further distinction can be drawn between merely sentient animals and those that qualify as *near-persons* because they have a robust, conscious sense of their own past and future, but fall short of having the normal human sense of their lives as complete biographies. Persons are claimed to deserve a special kind of respect over both near-persons and the merely sentient, and near-persons deserve some kind of special respect over the merely sentient.
>
> (Varner, 2008: 43)

Three approaches have been used to look at the three temporal states of this autonoetic consciousness: (1) episodic memory (past); (2) mirror self-recognition (present) as above; and (3) a theory of mind (future) (Varner, 2008). As regards elephants, the focus of his article, Varner says that no studies have been completed on (1), only three have been undertaken on (2), and just one on (3). This issue relates strongly to tourism; we often use near-persons as the focus of our touristic endeavours (elephants, cetaceans, primates) yet extend as little regard to their interests as we would to animals that are merely sentient or not sentient at all. The problem is that we throw them all into one category – animals – without any knowledge of their inherent value.

Measures of intelligence include long-term memory in those species with large brains and especially the neocortex part of the brain responsible for learning and memory. Elephants are especially adept at retaining a great deal of knowledge of place, as well as aspects of ecology and social interactions with people and other elephants. Machiavellian Intelligence tests make use of competitive tactics in socially oriented interactions with others. Socially relevant information is said to have selection advantages, such that it enables the individual to navigate through a labyrinth of social situations that demand acuity for survival. This includes the ability to form long-term relationships, the use of a third party for interventions, the use of allies, grooming, reconciliation for mending relationships, tactical deception, and sensitivity to social hierarchies based on dominance or other characteristics. Elephants were found to score highly on all of these measures (Poole and Moss, 2008; see also Sumumar, 2008). These animals demonstrate an understanding of the concept of death and display a number of behaviours to those elephants and even humans that are dying or dead, including touching, lifting and carrying of bones, as well as guarding and covering. Scientists argue that elephants and other higher-order mammals demonstrate theory of mind, or 'the ability to understand and predict another [animal's] behavior by attributing mental states' (Wise, 2002: 5). Poole and Moss (2008) write that a good example of this is when the elephant Chandrasekhan would not insert a wood pillar into a hole until a sleeping dog had been chased away, indicative of the use of knowledge to predict behaviour. (Also see Dunayer, 2004, who challenges the conventional mindset by presenting evidence suggesting that honeybees can in fact reason through their choices of new hives. If a bee 'sister' finds a better site, a scout will stop dancing the directions to the one that she found and start advocating for the better site.)

In the end, some, including Dawkins (2000), argue that there is too much focus on intellectual and cognitive research, i.e., the forming of abstract concepts and the use of language that may prove damaging to our understanding of animal consciousness. She argues for the extension of research to include animal emotions in rounding out our understanding of consciousness in animals. For example, investigating the conditions under which animals suffer or experience strong or persistent negative emotions would be helpful in structuring a more balanced approach to the animal mind (see above). It is all well and good that animal behaviourists are teaching animals how to communicate in sign language, but the questions are all wrong according to Malamud (2008). Instead of teaching them how to buy an ice cream, with rewards for correct change, we should be asking them more meaningful questions on how to survive tsunamis and how best to preserve our forests. Box 3.1 relates to the 'sixth sense' that animals have demonstrated in avoiding harm during events like tsunamis that claimed the lives of so many humans but virtually no animals.

Box 3.1 Did animals sense tsunami was coming?

By Maryann Mott
for National Geographic News
Date: 4 January 2005

Before giant waves slammed into Sri Lanka and India coastlines ten days ago, wild and domestic animals seemed to know what was about to happen and fled to safety. According to eyewitness accounts, the following events happened:

- Elephants screamed and ran for higher ground.
- Dogs refused to go outdoors.
- Flamingos abandoned breeding areas.
- Zoo animals rushed into shelters and could not be enticed to come back out.

The belief that wild and domestic animals possess a sixth sense – and know in advance when the earth is going to shake – has been around for centuries. Wildlife experts believe animals' more acute hearing and other senses might enable them to hear or feel the Earth's vibration, tipping them off to approaching disaster long before humans realize what's going on.

The massive tsunami was triggered by a magnitude 9 tremor off the coast of northern Sumatra island on December 26. The giant waves rolled through the Indian Ocean, killing more than 150,000 people in a dozen countries. Relatively few animals have been reported dead, however, reviving speculation that animals somehow sense impending disaster.

Ravi Corea, president of the Sri Lanka Wildlife Conservation Society, which is based in Nutley, New Jersey, was in Sri Lanka when the massive waves struck. Afterward, he traveled to the Patangangala beach inside Yala National Park, where some 60 visitors were washed away. The beach was one of the worst hit areas of the 500-square-mile (1,300-square-kilometer) wildlife reserve, which is home to a variety of animals, including elephants, leopards, and 130 species of birds. Corea did not see any animal carcasses nor did the park personnel know of any, other than two water buffalos that had died, he said.

Corea, a Sri Lankan who emigrated to the United States 20 years ago, said two of his friends noticed unusual animal behavior before the tsunami. One friend, in the southern Sri Lankan town of Dickwella, recalls bats frantically flying away just before the tsunami struck. Another friend, who lives on the coast near Galle, said his two dogs would not go for their daily run on the beach. 'They are usually excited to go on this outing,' Corea said. But on this day they refused to go and most probably saved his life.

<http://news.nationalgeographic.com/news/2005/01/0104_050104_tsunami_animals.html>, accessed 15 April 2011

A chink in the chain

In 1993 scientists and philosophers came together for the purpose of addressing the moral gap between humans and the great apes. Their meetings culminated in the *Great Ape Project (GAP): Equality beyond Humanity* (Cavalieri and Singer, 1993), an international movement, and book, with the objective of extending rights to nonhuman primates by accepting great apes into the sphere of moral equality with humans. These rights, outlined in the book's 'Declaration on Great Apes', include: (a) the right to life, as part of the community of equals; (b) the protection of individual liberty; and (c) the prohibition of torture.

For Bekoff (1998), while the value of GAP is obvious, added value comes in the form of recognition that there is importance placed on the individual. Our relationship with animals should not be based on how we manage a population, but rather on the fact that individuals are important in these populations, just as they are with our own species. Furthermore, while gains have been made in regards to primates, the net needs to be cast much further. Bekoff argues that the basic principles afforded to primates – which he refers to as primatocentrism – should be extended to all animals. We cannot just think that primates are smart or intelligent, because these terms are loaded and misused. Monkeys are smart in their own way, just as dogs and cats do what they need to do in order to be dogs and cats, which contributes to their success as species.

This species-specific intelligence has been discussed at length by the philosopher Thomas Nagel (1974). Nagel seems to have hit the mark in suggesting that consciousness and subjective experience are a function of the ability to understand what it is like to be an organism. He calls this the subjective character of the experience. Using the example of bats – close to us as mammals on the phylogenetic tree – Nagel argues that it is impossible for us to understand what it is like for a bat to be a bat because of the limits of our nature. Bats function according to bat physiology, not human physiology, and if we try to imagine this we simply cannot. Our own experience, Nagel adds, is the basis of our imagination, the range of which is restricted to the resources of our minds.

In one fell swoop, philosophers argue that Nagel was able to refute two cornerstones of behaviourism. First is the notion that science and/or philosophy should eliminate the subjective factor from the analysis of the mind. Second is the idea that the complexity of appreciating the experiences of other mentalities invalidates the declaration that they have experiences (Cavalieri, 2001). And for Searle (1998), the issue is more matter-of-fact when he suggests that 'it doesn't matter really how I know whether my dog is conscious, or even whether or not I do "know" that he is conscious. The fact is, he is conscious and epistemology in this area has to start with this fact' (p. 50).

Where to draw the line?

The discussion on moral value, emotion, consciousness, and subjectivity has much to do with the discussion on the great chain of being. The moral community is based on a hierarchy of beings, but the question is which species to admit to the community of morals and which to leave out (Sumner, 1981).

Wise (2002) offers an excellent discussion of where to draw the line in the context of certain basic rights, which apply to animals under common law. He argues that autonomy is a key factor in the extension of rights to a species; that there are less complex autonomies that are in existence; and further that 'a being can be autonomous if she has preferences and the ability to act to satisfy them' (p. 32). Wise calls this 'practical autonomy' and this being should be extended these basic legal rights if she: (1) can desire; (2) can intentionally try to fulfil her desires; and (3) possesses a sense of self-sufficiency to allow her to understand, even dimly, that it is she who wants something and that it is she who is trying to get it (p. 32).

Wise employs the use of Griffin's (2001) work on the mental capabilities of different species of animal in making an attempt to draw the line. Griffin argued that the more an animal acts intentionally (thinking, feeling, wanting, and demonstrating a sense of self), the closer the probability is to 1.0 (humans would be assigned the value of 1.0). If there is no chance that an animal performs in any of these capacities the probability is 0.0. For those animals, Wise argues, where there is the possibility in the absence of good knowledge, the probability would be 0.50. Figure 3.2 represents Wise's (2002) approximations of who should get basic liberty rights under common law according to four categories.

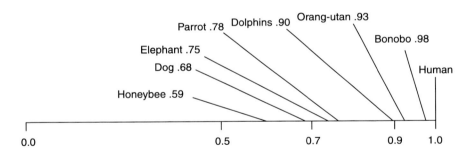

Category 1: Nonhuman animal who clearly possesses sufficient autonomy for basic liberty rights. An autonomy value of .90 is the cut-off from basic legal rights using a narrow reading of the precautionary principle (PP).

Category 2: Nonhuman animals who, according to increasing evidence, possess sufficient autonomy for basic liberty rights. An autonomy value of .70 is the cut-off for basic liberty rights using a moderate reading of PP.

Category 3: Nonhuman animals about whom we do not know enough to reasonably determine whether they possess sufficient autonomy for basic liberty rights. This category probably includes most species.

Category 4: Nonhuman animals who, according to increasing evidence, lack sufficient autonomy for basic liberty rights.

Figure 3.2 The extension of liberty rights under the common law

The difficulty in assigning these values is validated in surveys of different cohorts within society. For example, in a study investigating attitudes of scientists, laypersons, and animal welfare advocates towards the possibility of an animal mind, Knight *et al.* (2009; see also Knight *et al.*, 2003) found consistent differences between all three groups. On a scale of 1 (no capacity) to 5 (humanlike capacity), the pro-science group had a lower mean score (mean = 2.81) for the possibility that animals have cognition compared to 3.62 for the pro-animal group. Furthermore, the mean score for the possibility of animals being sentient was 3.50 for the pro-science group compared to 4.34 for the pro-animal group. Layperson scores on these measures fell between the two other groups.

In related work, Paul (1995) found that scientists and animal rights campaigners have different attitudes towards animal experimentation. Paul (1995) wrote that both groups had a negative view of the other. When it came to drawing the line as a cut-off point in reference to those species that do have the capacity to suffer and those that don't, both groups found this to be a difficult task. Half of the scientists and animal rights advocates could not draw such a line, while half of both groups attempted to do this. Higher order animals such as mammals in general were shown greater concern than lower order animals (e.g., invertebrates), demonstrating a hierarchy along phylogenetic lines. Both groups accepted the reality of a phylogenetic hierarchy of animals in regards to the capacity to suffer, but they placed emphasis in different areas. While researchers tended to draw the line at humans, other primates, other mammals, vertebrates, or invertebrates (most drew the line at other mammals), animal rights campaigners had a broader range of where to draw the line, with most drawing it at invertebrates (Table 3.1).

Theories of animal ethics

The spectrum of theoretical approaches used in animal ethics has been categorized within a number of relatively discrete categories or schools (see for example Aaltola, 2009; Wade, 1990; and Taylor, 2003). In this section Garner's (2005)

Table 3.1 Species mentioned in participants' deliberations concerning where to 'draw the line' between those which can and cannot suffer

Species	Species mentioned by animal researchers	Species mentioned by animal rights campaigners
Humans	2	0
Other primates	5	1
Other mammals	14	7
Other vertebrates	11	5
Invertebrates	11	20
Microscopic organisms	1	5
Bacteria and viruses	0	2
Plants and fungi	0	5
Computer	0	1

Adapted from Paul (1995)

scheme is used, which is organized according to three main schools: (1) theoretical approaches that argue for the lack of moral status in animals on the basis of sentiency; (2) moral orthodoxy or animal welfare; and (3) moral heterodoxy, which includes most of the new theoretical positions on animal ethics. These will be examined in more detail below.

Completely lacking moral status, with only indirect duties owed to animals

Animals lack sentiency

Representative of this position is René Descartes, who maintained that animals are machines without souls – natural automata – regulated, mechanistic, and involuntary like the workings of a clock. Animals act without consciousness, and this action is not of their own volition but rather from external forces like nature. In Descartes' day the only primates that were known to Western humans were North African macaques. Morris and Morris (1966) suggest that these animals were viewed as inferior imitators of the human condition, and served to further elevate the esteem of humans in light of these other beasts.

The neo-Cartesian Peter Carruthers (1989) has argued that the experiences of animals are all *nonconscious*. Nonconscious experiences are those that feel like nothing, because the animal is not conscious of it – the experience is not available to conscious thought. Consequently, although pain is an experience, it is of the nonconscious variety and so it should not be the object of our sympathy or our moral concern. Carruthers' argument follows accordingly:

- A being counts, morally speaking, only if it is conscious;
- Consciousness is a product of the ability to think (reason);
- Animals cannot think;
- Since they cannot think their pain, in whatever form it manifests itself, is unconscious;
- Questions regarding animal pain are therefore a moot point, since animals don't really feel pain;
- Therefore, animals exist outside the realm of moral concern.

Duran (1994) feels Carruthers' work is a serious abuse of terminology surrounding 'conscious' and 'nonconscious' – equivocation in her opinion – that does nothing to advance the debate on animal minds (see also Wilson, 2001). In response, Carruthers (2000) has advanced a theory of consciousness based on higher-order thought processes (HOT). This means that an animal would be conscious if it could actually think about or conceptualize its thoughts, which means that the animal has a theory of mind. Based on his review of relevant literature, there is no solid evidence to support the argument that animals (apart from perhaps chimps) have a theory of mind. Since animals cannot feel what it is like to be an entity at all because of their nonconscious state, it really is a moot point. Carruthers makes the analogy of consciousness as the turning on of a light. Because animals lack conscious thought, they apparently live in a world of darkness.

Joining Carruthers in this stance is Harrison (1989, 1991, 1992), who argues that all human experiences of pain are functions of distinctive human consciousness and cannot be mutually shared by animals. Harrison advances the following formal argument in support of this position: (1) Continuity of experience is the crucial aspect of the human awareness of pain; (2) animals lack that continuity of experience, and therefore, animals do not experience pain as we do. By continuity of experience, Harrison means that animals don't learn from painful experiences because there is simply no memory to allow this to take place. Instead, animals have a more reflexive type of pain where there is no conscious knowledge of a painful event. Animals cannot experience pain because they have no sense of self, and therefore there is no sense of 'I' to own any experience like pain. They are like chronic amnesiacs, who lose their individuality at every passing moment. In the absence of the continuity of experience, pain is felt momentarily and there may be a reaction, but this is not internalized in the same way that humans experience pain. (See also Tye (2000), who argues that simple creatures like bees and fish do not suffer because they are incapable of feeling pain. Suffering, Tye argues, 'requires the cognitive awareness of pain' (p. 182).)

Animals are sentient but lack morally significant interests

The leading advocate for this position is Kant, who argued that rationality is the key element in deciding whether to extend moral consideration to a being, because reason alone provides the means by which to make and abide by moral judgements (Bull, 2005). Beings that are rational have inherent value, and those that do not merely possess relative value and cannot be ends in themselves – as things they have exchange value while humans have dignity. This perception prompted Kant to observe that 'Our duties to animals are merely indirect duties to mankind' (Bull, 2005: 46). As such, because animals are not ends in and of themselves we do not have any responsibilities towards them. We can treat them as means to our own selfish ends because they simply do not have the same value as humans.

Kant's work is important because it provides the foundation for human rights, though it lacks a connection between human dignity and moral worth. There is no basis from which to conclude that only rational beings have intrinsic worth. The moral issue of contention for animals is whether or not this ability to reason may be used as a manner to distinguish one species from another, but also the degree of the ability to reason, or even in what capacity this rationality comes packaged within a species. As Hoff illustrates, 'Human dignity is here being deployed axiomatically to deny moral status to animals' (1983: 66). Hoff (1983: 70) cites Schopenhauer (1998) in illustrating his point:

> Now just as those two definitions offend against logic, so is genuine morality outraged by the proposition that beings devoid of reason (hence animals) are

things and therefore would be treated merely as means that are not at the same time an *end ... I regard such propositions as revolting and abominable.*

Kant's indirect duties argument is problematic because it includes assessments of actions that are independent of the fact that these may directly harm an animal (Wilson, 2002). We do not torture animals in the park, according to Wilson, because doing so would affect or hurt human beings; we do not kill zoo animals because this would cut into the zoo owner's ability to make a living; we do not take someone else's pet and use it as a dartboard because this would make the pet's owner sad. This perspective has direct relevance to the contractarianist perspective outlined below.

Another major theorist to argue in favour of the dimension of interest in ascribing moral worth to animals is Frey (1980, 1983). To have moral rights, according to Frey, a being needs to have interests, but in having interests they must first have higher-order intelligence, including the ability to believe or desire. There is a causal link in Frey's work moving from the inability to talk, to the inability to desire, to the intermediate position of having no interests, and finally to the conclusion that they should not, therefore, have rights (as discussed in Namkoong and Regan, 1988).

Moral orthodoxy (animal welfare/humane treatment/pragmatic); some moral status but inferior to humans

Animals have an interest in not suffering but this is overridden to promote the greatest good of humans who are autonomous agents

At its simplest, animal welfare 'deals with the humane treatment of animals' (Håstein *et al.*, 2005: 529; see Wearing and Jobberns, 2011, for a discussion of animal welfare and ethics in zoos), and deciding what is humane or even whether humans ought to extend care to other beings necessitates examining the values behind the relationship between animals and humans. Animal welfare means how an animal is coping with the conditions in which it lives. An animal is in a good state of welfare if (as indicated by scientific evidence) it is healthy, comfortable, well nourished, safe, able to express innate behaviour, and if it is not suffering from unpleasant states such as pain, fear, and distress. Good animal welfare requires disease prevention and veterinary treatment, appropriate shelter, management, nutrition, humane handling, and humane slaughter/killing (see Dawkins 1998, 1990; Stevens and McAlister, 2003).

Animal welfare has been a discourse triggered by emotion rather than reason according to Korte *et al.* (2007) and its failure to incorporate science has stunted its growth and effectiveness. Even though law recognizes animals as being sentient and having intrinsic value, significant gains in themselves, there still remains anthropocentric thinking about how animals ought to be handled in the absence of new developments in science that would better inform the debate. To illuminate the inadequacies of more ethical than science-based measures of animal welfare,

Korte *et al.* examine the UK Farm Animal Welfare council's 'Five Freedoms' of animal welfare (Farm Animal Welfare Council, 2009). These 'Five Freedoms' are:

1. Freedom from Hunger and Thirst: Ready access to fresh water and a diet to maintain full health and vigour.
2. Freedom from Discomfort: Providing an appropriate environment including shelter and a comfortable resting area.
3. Freedom from Pain, Injury or Disease: Prevention or rapid diagnosis and treatment.
4. Freedom to Express Normal Behaviour: Providing sufficient space, proper facilities and company of the animal's own kind.
5. Freedom from Fear and Distress: Ensuring conditions and treatment, which avoid mental suffering.

The authors feel that these five freedoms are no longer helpful because they fail to consider the conditions and complexities of the natural environment that individuals face on a daily basis. Freedom from fear is a case in point. Fear has fitness value in how it enables the organism to negotiate its environment, survive, and pass this 'knowledge' on to successive generations. As such, an event can benefit reproductive success, yet be a negative experience for the individual, leading to poor animal welfare. The authors further argue that freedom from pain, injury, and disease is decidedly utopian. For example, the experience of pain allows animals to build resilience against further threats with eventual fitness implications. In addition, freedom from hunger and thirst is also problematic because hunger is one of a number of different challenges confronted on a daily, weekly, or monthly basis. The upshot of this is that good animal welfare is premised on the notion that animals should not be exposed to environmental challenges that might take them outside of a controlled or balanced set point.

An animal that is fit possesses a wide regulatory range of allostatic (stability through change) mechanisms, according to Korte *et al.*, but the activation of mechanisms outside of this range can have dramatic effects on the organism, leading to a chronic deviation of the normal system. As such, when allostatic loads are higher these can contribute to hyperstimulation and certain pathologies, and in contrast hypostimulation leads to depression and other disease types. Poor animal welfare, therefore, is reflected in these extreme allostatic states, while good animal welfare may be realized by maintaining optimal states. This means that welfare is not just a function of constancy or freedoms, but rather the capacity to change; 'by a broad predictive physiological and behavioural capacity to anticipate environmental challenges … .' Or 'when the regulatory range of allostatic mechanisms matches the environmental demands' (Korte *et al.*, 2007: 426).

The welfarist platform is said to be old-speciesist because it condones actions and systems that violate the moral rights of animals (Dunayer, 2004). There is concern over the conditions of captivity, for example through veterinarian care and fresh food, but it does not attempt to address what many animal rights people see as the root of the problem: enslavement, slaughter, and other abuses. Better conditions, yes; emancipation, no.

Francione (1996) follows this line of thinking in discussing the new animal welfare platform. He argues that almost everyone agrees that animals ought to be treated humanely. But although more animals are being used every year in horrifying ways, welfarist reforms lead to more exploitation of animals, not abolition. The new animal welfarism, according to Francione, is based on the premise 'that animal welfare leads to animal rights' (1996: 87). That animals might possess rights is simply a long-term goal of this altered movement. So, whereas animal welfare advocates 'seek the *regulation* of animal exploitation; the rightists seek its *abolition*' (Francione, 1996: 1). The modern animal rights movement has therefore adopted the mentality of the welfare regime. Animals are still the property of humans, and still exploited, and reform is supported but human benefit remains foremost.

Organizations such as PETA, the Humane Society of the United States, and the American Society for the Prevention of Cruelty to Animals are rejecting the animal rights platform because there is the sense that animal rights' position of all or nothing is unrealistic to attain (Francione, 1996). Participants are referred to not as animal rights advocates but rather as 'animal advocates' or the 'humane movement'. The message is that there is little that can be distinguished between welfare and rights approaches, with no one theory any better than another, and attempts to dichotomize these are divisive of the importance of unity in the animal movement.

Ecocentrism, where holism is advocated over individual rights or interests

The ecocentric approach is characterized by the placement of moral value at the level of the natural environment on the whole. Individual members that comprise this whole are extended only secondary moral consideration (Wade, 1990; see Belshaw, 2001 for an explanation of how ecocentrism fits into environmental philosophy). Aldo Leopold's land ethic is a good example of this holistic approach. Actions are judged as good or right based not on the effects on individuals, but rather on the whole. Hunting is morally sanctionable, therefore, if it secures benefits for the entire population (Varner, 1998). Hunting needs to be done with respect to limiting the pain and discomfort as much as possible in the process (Callicott, 1985; see Wade 1990, who suggests that it may be in the best interests of the biosphere to sport hunt humans). If we were to hunt the last few members of a species, this would be morally indefensible because the absence of this species might have a bearing on the proper ecological functioning of the whole. By contrast, taking a few fish out of the system is justifiable because the absence of these has little to no bearing on the health of the species and system in question. Callicott (1985) observes that Leopold's main precept of 'a thing is right when it tends to preserve the integrity, stability, and beauty of the biotic community. It is wrong when it tends otherwise' (Leopold, 1966: 262) acts as an ecological categorical imperative. The ultimate measure of the good therefore is action that preserves this whole.

For animal rights scholars like Regan (1983) ecocentrism can never be accepted because of the fact that these interests or basic rights become sacrificed in the name of 'integrity', 'stability', and 'beauty' of the whole. Respect accorded to the subject-of-a-life, which is so important to rights theorists, is not a concern in the ecocentric view. In Regan's rather extreme example – but perhaps not unfair given the limits of ecocentric philosophy – if

> the situation we faced was either to kill a rare wildflower or a (plentiful) human being, and if the wildflower, as a 'team member' would contribute more to the 'integrity, stability, and beauty of the biotic community' than the human, then presumably we would not be doing wrong if we killed the human and saved the wildflower.
>
> (Regan, 1983: 362)

The argument for the ethical treatment of animals on the basis of individuals of a species as compared to the population or species in general is addressed by Loftin (1985). In the case of the medical treatment of wild animals, Loftin finds that although there are many how-to books on caring for birds injured in the wild, this energy would be far better spent at a broader level. By contrast, those who are interested in preserving wildlife ought to do so at the level of the population along with habitat, rather then channelling energy into individuals, the latter possessing no real value. His major criticism lies in the belief that wild animal hospitals compete for scarce resources, and that this money might be better spent on other conservation measures. In this Loftin argues that taking care of injured wild animals is not wrong, but neither is it right. As such, in not taking care of a cardinal after it flies into his or her front window, an agent does not fail in his or her moral duty as humans have no moral obligations to that animal, except in ending its suffering. In the end, time and money are better spent trying to save habitat in benefiting animals, than on a focus on individual animals.

Another example of the application of ecocentric thinking is the International Convention for the Regulation of Whaling, where whales are conserved not because they have intrinsic value but because they have economic value. We need whales only in as much as they serve our instrumental needs. Garner (2004) uses the CAMPFIRE (Communal Areas Management Programme for Indigenous Resources) programme in Zimbabwe to exemplify this. He argues that although the culling of elephants is said to be a good example of sustainable use because benefits go to local people in the form of meat, ivory, hides, and the selling of permits to hunters, the real problem is the re-opening of the ivory trade. Southern African countries have been successful at transferring elephants from the endangered species list (Appendix 1 of CITES) to Appendix 2 (threatened species), thus allowing for the selling of ivory to Japan as the sole trading partner (see also Stokey and Zeckhauser, 1978; Norton, 1982).

Challenges to moral orthodoxy (moral heterodoxy)

Animals have rights

BASED ON INHERENT VALUE (REGAN)

The primary academic figure arguing in favour of animal rights is Tom Regan. Regan's subject-of-a-life theory argues that animals should have equal inherent value, irrespective of the fact that they are rational or non-rational, and even though animals may possess minimum inherent value, this is still reason to argue for their reason to exist (Bull, 2005). The animal rights attitude is absolutist. Human action that fails to take into consideration an animal's moral claims is deemed troubling.

> Any being that is subject of a life has inherent worth and the rights that protect such worth, and all subjects of a life have these rights equally. Thus any practice that fails to respect the rights of those animals who have them, e.g., eating animals, hunting animals, experimenting on animals, using animals for entertainment, is wrong, irrespective of human need, context, or culture.
>
> (Bull, 2005: 8)

Animal rights advocates don't restrict their views on animals to just their pets or charismatic others, Regan (2004) suggests. They feel the same way towards pigs and elephants (the examples he uses) as they do about animals that are close to them. He does not propose that we make pets out of these others, but rather that 'we just want people to stop doing terrible things to them' (p. 3).

Regan's theory is deontological. It means that if an animal has a right, such a right cannot be violated if the consequences of violating such a right are found to be more pleasing than the defence of that right (Francione, 1996). So the individual is not necessarily intrinsically valuable, but rather possesses some other quality like pleasure or knowledge as this applies to others, like humans. This means that those in support of animal rights reject utilitarianism based on the belief that it licenses what might be considered to be evil acts in increasing pleasure and satisfaction.

A recent practical application of the rights-based perspective is the Balearic islands, which extended legal rights to apes in 2007 in following through on leadership provided by the Great Ape Project, with Spain's parliament following suit in June of 2008 (see Sorenson, 2009). Hill (2002), however, finds that there is not universal acceptance over the idea that primates deserve rights. This is an emerging belief in the western world, but not necessarily in traditional societies where these animals are viewed as a source of food, as an agricultural pest, and as a physical threat to human beings.

Benton and Redfearn (1996) suggest that the rights platform may be criticized on three fronts. First, it is very difficult to extend rights over the species boundary, which is not the case with utilitarianism, where the focus on sentience is difficult to refute. Second, it demands equality between humans and animals, which would entail massive transformations within society from veganism to discontinuing the use of animals in the manufacture of clothing and other personal items that make our lifestyle more comfortable or enjoyable. Finally, Benton and Redfearn argue that the rights approach is more sympathetic to animals that share human characteristics, and less sympathetic to animals that fail to qualify according to the subject of a life criterion (see also Frank, 2002; Watson, 1979; Povilitis, 1980; Willard, 1982).

For Cohen (1997), the rights perspective is a moot point because animals cannot be the bearers of rights. The concept of rights is uniquely human and has applicability only to humans. Nonhuman animals, he argues, are completely amoral and there is nothing close to a concept of morality. They are never wrong because there is no sense of the meaning of wrong and by extension there are no rights to differentiate what is 'right' or 'wrong'.

> But a rat can no more be said to have rights than a table can be said to have ambition. To say of a rat that it has rights is to confuse categories, to apply to its world a moral category that has content only in the human moral world.
>
> (Cohen, 1997: 95)

The practical application of Cohen's work is to imagine a world where experimentation on animals was never allowed (the call by Regan and other animal rights activists), and the subsequent implications. In 1952, there were just fewer than 60,000 cases of polio in the United States, with approximately 3,000 deaths. Three years later a vaccine was created, resulting in a reduction to only 12 cases, on average, per year and total eradication of the disease in the Western hemisphere not long after. His point is that after initial tests on children proved disastrous, the only way to eradicate the disease was to use animals. So although we have obligations toward animals, i.e., to treat them with respect and dignity, they cannot claim the right to be treated with respect and dignity. His example of his dog serves to illustrate this point: 'My dog has no right to daily exercise and veterinary care, but I do have the obligation to provide these things for her' (p. 94). In the end, Cohen asks us to consider whether animals would still have rights if humans suddenly disappeared off the face of the earth.

BASED ON SENTIENCY

Sentiency is used as a position to argue for the rights of animals, and this perspective can be found in the work of Richard Ryder (1993) and Bernard Rollin (2005), who are key contributors to this idea. To these we might add Franklin (2005), who develops a comprehensive account of the duties that humans have toward not only other humans (in the tradition of Rawls and Kant) but also animals. He suggests that we emend Kant's categorical imperative as well as

Box 3.2 Swiss say no to animal lawyers

By Frank Jordans, Associated Press
Monday, 8 March 2010

Swiss voters have soundly rejected a plan to appoint special lawyers for animals that are abused by humans. Results in yesterday's referendum showed that 70.5 per cent of voters cast their ballot against the proposal. Switzerland already has among the world's strictest rules when it comes to caring for pets and farm animals.

Opponents of the proposal, including key farmers' groups and the government, had argued that existing laws are sufficient and appointing special lawyers to act on behalf of animals would be unnecessarily expensive for taxpayers. 'The Swiss people have clearly said our animal protection laws are so good we don't need animal lawyers,' Jakob Buechler, a lawmaker for the centrist Christian People's Party, told Swiss television SF1.

According to the country's only animal lawyer, Antoine F. Goetschel, public prosecutors are often unsure about animal rights and shy away from pursuing cases even if there is clear evidence of abuse. He said the cost of Sunday's measure would have been less than 1 Swiss franc ($1) per person a year.

The country's 160-page animal protection law stipulates that pigs, budgies, goldfish and other social animals cannot be kept alone. Horses and cows must have regular exercise outside their stalls and dog owners have to take a training course to learn how to properly look after their pets.

Like in other countries, the law also forbids killing animals in a cruel fashion or for fun.

Swiss daily *Tribune de Genève* reported earlier this year that a woman who decapitated four chickens and left their heads on the doorstep of her love rival received a 90-day suspended sentence.

Goetschel said he represents about 150–200 animals annually in Zurich, while in other cantons (states), only a handful of cases go to court each year.

Most of his clients are dogs, cows and cats, Goetschel told The Associated Press in a recent interview. Many cases involve the serious abuse of animals, such as deliberate wounding, rape and neglect.

But in one high-profile case last month, Goetschel represented a dead pike after an animal protection group accused the angler who caught it of cruelty for taking 10 minutes to haul the fish in.

The angler was found not guilty.

<http://www.independent.co.uk/news/world/europe/swiss-say-no-to-animal-lawyers-1917809. html>, accessed 19 April 2011

Locke's views on the law of nature as bound by a speciesist hierarchy to life. It follows that

> ... no sentient being shall ever be treated solely as a means but also at the same time as an end. The obligations of moral agents to respect life are not now restricted to other moral agents; they would also extend to animals as moral patients.
>
> (Franklin, 2005: 73)

This theory puts forward the rule that humans cannot use sentient nonhuman animals instrumentally and this should sit as the 'ultimate foundation of a theory of justice' (p. 75). Acting otherwise, Franklin observes, is to deny the value of justice as a virtue and instead use power as a representative of what we hold as the ultimate good.

Utilitarianism

The main proponent of the utilitarian position is Peter Singer, whose influence on the world of animal ethics has been enormous. His article in *The New York Review* in April of 1973 ushered in a new term, 'animal liberation', as well as a new era. Previous to this the treatment of animals was simply not a topic that held serious merit (Singer, 1975, 1987, 2003). He argued that because animals share the same capacity to suffer as we do, they have interests, and we cannot ignore these interests. In revisiting his initial ideas 30 years later, Singer argues that although humans have a superior ability to reason and other cognitive capacities that animals do not, this is not enough to justify a line of demarcation between those that matter in regards to rights (humans) and those that do not (animals). His principal argument in favour of the interests of animals follows the concept of speciesism, or 'the idea that it is justifiable to give preference to beings simply on the grounds that they are members of the species *Homo sapiens*' (Singer, 2003: 2). Philosophers, he adds, have continually failed to develop a plausible theory advocating the moral importance or significance of one species over others.

The essence of Singer's argument is the recognition of animals as moral subjects, and more specifically the suffering these subjects bear against the benefits that humans gain from their use. The focus is not whose interests are at stake, but rather the potency and nature of the interests at hand. In this capacity, Gruen (2010) illustrates that the utilitarianist position stipulates that it is sometimes a better option to impose harm or suffering in animals if this is the lesser of two evils. Given a choice of imposing significant amounts of suffering that ultimately lead to death versus moderate amounts of suffering with the eventual painless death of the agent, the utilitarianist would choose the second as morally preferable to the first. Similarly, if an animal has lived a healthy, happy existence and is killed painlessly later in its life course by hunters who are hunting to feed a hungry family, this can be morally justified by the ends-based philosophy. Equality does not imply equal or identical treatment, but rather equal consideration, and animals that suffer more than others must be entitled to more benefits. Furthermore, utilitarianists eliminate the need to focus on rationality as the primary driver of moral consideration, and replace this with an ends-based rationale: pleasure and the satisfaction of various interests. If other beings have the capacity to suffer, there is no way that we can avoid assigning these others moral consideration. This is not a hedonistic utilitarianist perspective (measures of pleasure and pain), but rather preference utilitarianism based on attempts to satisfy various preferences.

According to Wade (1990), the above theory gives no preference to the interests of humans. Equal interests count equally no matter what species is under consideration. Because utilitarians base their argument on that which maximizes the good and minimizes the bad without necessarily any regard for the groups and circumstances around which these decisions are made, the theory opens itself up to scrutiny. For example, Wade argues that there is little guidance to help us navigate around the issue of the moral correctness in regards to the satisfaction that a majority race would receive in hunting for sport a minority race even if the kills made are clean ones (i.e., to limit suffering). Stripping utilitarianism down to the letter of the law, there may be little that a utilitarianist might find wrong with this practice.

The answer to why we do not hunt a minority community for sport, even if we are decidedly racist, is because every human being has a right to a life, which includes not being killed by another. Where utilitarianism fails, according to the above example, is where rights approaches excel. And what applies to humans must also apply to animals from the animal liberation standpoint. The burden of proof for the reasoning behind why we should not kill humans, because of this right to a life, but feel comfortable killing animals lies in the demonstration that humans are empirically different than animals, i.e., through sentience, intelligence, or other capacities. If no such difference can be found, then hunting animals is just as wrong as hunting human beings. If animals are seen to possess interests there is the belief that they have moral rights (see also Sapontzis, 1987).

Contractarianism

Building from Kantian deontological ethics, contractarianists argue that animals are not afforded direct rights, only indirect rights, because they are said not to be rational agents. Contracts can only be agreed upon either implicitly or explicitly by rational agents. So, the killing of another's ox is in fact a sin. But the sin is not in the killing, but rather in the destruction of someone else's property. The ox is not a subject but rather an object such as a cart or a shovel (Fudge, 2005; see also Boonin-Vail, 1994).

The extension of indirect rights to animals takes place under two conditions (from Rowlands, 2009a). In the first case, even though an animal does not have a right not to be harmed (this is a direct right), the owner of the dog has a right to insist that his or her dog not be harmed. Harming the animal is an infringement, therefore, not of the dog's rights but rather of the owner's direct rights. The animal in this case has indirect rights but only insofar as these are tied to the direct rights of the owner. The second form of indirect rights follows from Kantian ethics. If we treat an animal with cruelty this is wrong not because of the damage it does to the animal, but rather because of the harm it does to the perpetrator (Skidmore, 2001). By extension, this behaviour is injurious to the reputation of the perpetrator, because he who is tough in his dealings with animals is likely to be tough in his dealings with human beings, which is an infringement of these others' direct rights.

Narveson (2001) has adopted the same position by arguing that only those who are rational can enter the moral community. Animals fall outside the circle of morality because they simply are not rational. Taylor (1996b), however, objects to Narveson's reasoning on the basis of the fact that animals enter into contracts in their own special ways. The sheepdog who works for food, and the cat that provides companionship, each do so with an understanding that is forged between animal and human. This is especially true within and between species in the way animals mark their territories, for example, as markers of the rules of their daily lives. We understand the nature of a verbal or written contract as these apply to us, but animals may be just as effective in specifying the nature of their own interactions through capacities of their own (see also Carruthers, 1992 for controversial uses of contractarianism in animal ethics based on a Rawlsian notion of an imaginary contract between rational agents, who have agreed upon rules for their ensuing conduct; see also Wenz, 1993; Tucker and MacDonald, 2004).

Postmodern, including feminist ethics

Feminist theory takes its lead from the work of Gilligan (1982), who argues that studies on morality take a decidedly masculine focus that is not representative of the way women see the world. While men are said to have a stronger orientation towards justice, fairness, rights, and rules, women are more strongly oriented towards responsibility, and ethics of care and connection rather than separation. The strength of the feminist approach rests on three main arguments: (1) opposition to animals as the most oppressed beings on the planet; (2) feminist scholars are adept at uncovering myths and rationalizations that serve the purpose of legitimizing oppressive practices, or hiding practices that support oppression; and (3) feminist scholars look at the world differently than those who use more traditional approaches to ethics, and thus are able to provide depth to the debate on animal ethics issues (DeGrazia, 1999; Kheel, 1985; Curtin, 1991). The strong ethic of care that women extend towards animal others is backed by research, where women more than men are drawn to humane societies, and disapprove of inhumane treatment of animals (including culling animals and farming animals for human consumption), animal experimentation, hunting, keeping animals in captivity, meat-eating, and killing animal pests around the house (Bulbeck, 1999; see also work on this topic from Jamison and Lunch, 1992; Garner, 2005; Paul, 1995).

For Donovan (1990) there exists a cultural feminism that has occurred in waves over time, starting perhaps with the denial of the Cartesian manner of nature in the

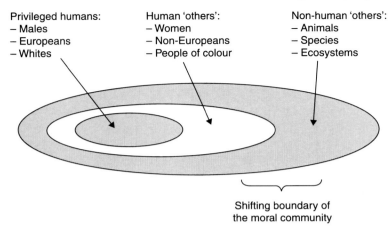

Privileged humans:
– Males
– Europeans
– Whites

Human 'others':
– Women
– Non-Europeans
– People of colour

Non-human 'others':
– Animals
– Species
– Ecosystems

Shifting boundary of
the moral community

Figure 3.3 Anthropocentric 'othering'

1600s, but this has been suppressed by the dominant male discourse in parallel with the exploitation of nature. There is a natural kinship between women and animals because 'Both were erased (at best) or manipulated (at worst) to behave in accordance with paradigms imposed by the rationalist lords – whether vivisectors or sexologists' (Donovan, 1990: 366; see also Dixon, 1996). In much of this Western discourse women have been assigned a status somewhere in between men and animals (Garner, 2005). The term 'human' is not neutral at all, as it refers more to the human male than female (*man* in English is *l'homme* in French). According to Noske (1997), women are not quite as human as men, with men more strongly equated with culture and women with nature, and with animals assigned an object status, as passive and inferior (Noske, 1997). Lynn's (1998) illustration of anthropocentric 'othering' (Figure 3.3) demonstrates that privileged humans like white males garner more respect, power, and influence over human 'others' including women and minorities. The figure also shows that nonhuman animal 'others' are one step removed from women and two steps removed from privileged males.

Perhaps the most powerful application of the foregoing discussion comes to us from Carol Adams in her seminal *The Sexual Politics of Meat* (Adams, 1990; 2008), whereby animals used for meat are referred to as absent referents. In this sense, behind every meal of meat that we enjoy there is an absence, which corresponds to the reality of a dead animal whose place has been taken by the meal itself. Looking deeper, it is the culture that separates the animal from the food itself that is most troubling to Adams:

> This is the function of the absent referent: to keep our 'meat' separated from any idea that she or he was once a nonhuman animal, to keep the moo away from the meat, to keep *something* from being seen as having been *someone*.
>
> (Adams, 2008: 48)

The relevance of the ethic of care position has been discussed by Luke (1996), who contrasts it with other theoretical positions based on justice (rights and utilitarianism). Justice-based approaches fail, he argues, because they tend to frame the issue as one of a comparison between how animals are treated and how humans are treated. He is appalled by the abuses themselves, independent of the thought that humans have been spared these usages, and this 'moral condemnation' stems from his sympathy for the animals, not out of fairness. Luke references Herzog and McGee's (1983) study on the psychological aspects of slaughter, in which university students were asked to record their thoughts on witnessing first-hand the killing and butchering of cattle and hogs. One 19-year-old woman in this study recorded:

> The first time I went into the slaughter room I had just haltered and pulled a steer into the waiting line. I could tell that the steer sensed what was going to happen to him. He was doing anything to get away. Then when I walked to the slaughter room I was amazed at the amount of blood. It was an awful feeling to look at that steer with its eyes open and his feet pointing up, so I had to look at the ceiling. Mr. ------ told me to cut off the head with a saw. I couldn't do it so I left.

> (Luke, 1996: 82)

What Luke demonstrates is that the students' observations were not comparative judgements based on justice, i.e., 'I can't saw off the head because this is something that I could never do to a human', but were instead based on elements of care and sympathy for the animal struggling for its life. More generally, Luke feels that this care and sympathy for animals is a normal state of human nature, crossing cultures, demonstrated through the keeping of animal companions, the use of animals in human therapy, our willingness to rescue animals like whales and dolphins at great personal cost, and expiation, or the mediating of guilt in those who harm or kill animals.

Virtue ethics

The emphasis on the ethic of care and personal relationships that is important in feminist ethics shares a kinship with Aristotelian virtue ethics. The focus is not on following rules or adhering to obligations, but rather on the traits or aspects of one's character that should be demonstrated in an effort to live the good life. Virtues are positive traits of character that include, for example, courage, honesty, loyalty, compassion, altruism, and so on. Cruelty and dishonesty are vices. The focus is thus not on the predetermined rule regarding what I should do, but on what sort of person I should be.

Virtuous conduct is not merely a conditioned reflex in an 'unthinking' manner, but rather a function of reason through pre-established attitudes and will. Aristotle would argue that sex is not a demonstration of the human's extraordinary capacity to reason but rather satisfaction of a physical need shared with other animals.

Aristotle suggests that there is a more profound form of happiness that we should have as our life's target, one that we do not share with other animals, and which might only be reached via our capacity to reason. This is us as humans choosing rather than nature choosing for us. Reason then gives us the ability to think through options and to determine the quality of happiness we seek, which might only be refined through training and habituation. Furthermore, virtuous decisions come about through the selection of the middle path or the 'golden mean', as explained by Aristotle. For example, the mean between underdevelopment of a natural resource and a scorched-earth policy is the virtue of sustainable development. And where simple forms of happiness can be relative and subjective according to the particular tastes of individuals and cultures, the target of eudaimonia is a universal and objective good (Fennell and Malloy, 2007; Tribe, 2002).

The problem with the use of virtue ethics in animal studies or indeed other disciplines has been summarized by Rowlands (2009a), who contends that there are three main issues that will remain challenging. These are (1) subjectivity, which means that while one person may view courage as a vice someone else may see it as a virtue; (2) vagueness, which suggests that there is too much flexibility in the treatment of the virtue rendering it open for debate; and (3) conflicts that occur between virtues and vices. The way to circumvent these issues is to employ a pluralistic approach including virtue ethics in addition to other theoretical positions such as utilitarianism and justice (Sapontzis, 1987).

Respect

Paul Taylor's (1986) work on biocentrism is an example of how respect can be used as a theoretical position, where moral worth is extended to living parts of nature, including plants and animals, but does not extend this to non-living matter. Taylor feels that all living things deserve equal respect. Each individual has intrinsic or inherent worth because each is a teleological centre of life with the purpose of maintaining its own existence. This is a departure from the rights perspective because this latter position is said by Taylor to be too misleading, as animals do not have the traits that characterize moral agents. He, like Mary Midgley, prefers the use of the word 'duty', as in our duties toward other sentient or non-sentient beings.

Among the various elements that make up Taylor's biocentric outlook, foremost is the complete rejection of human superiority over other living things. The author contends the idea of human superiority by contrasting our unique abilities of free will, self-awareness, and reason, with other abilities held by nonhuman organisms, which we lack. The posed question is which of these abilities are to be taken as the signs of superiority – e.g., the dolphins' advanced speech, the eagles' eyesight, the wolves' sense of smell. Clearly, only the human/anthropocentric standpoint can view human abilities as desirable and useful, unless human superiority claims are interpreted from a nonhuman standpoint and based on the judgement of comparative merits as opposed to human inherent worth.

A further take on the value of respect in animal ethics comes from Nussbaum

(2006), who suggests that justice is a theoretical position that has been underrepresented in examining the moral status of animals. When we prevent animal from realizing their capabilities, this is a justice issue that infringes upon their dignity. Animals possess innumerable needs, functions, abilities, and so on, and not allowing them the opportunity to exercise these is to deny respect and dignity. Bridging over from Aristotle, who discussed the various characteristics of animals, Nussbaum argues that different species have different capabilities and it is up to us to appreciate and not deny these capabilities in the extension of full benefits to the species. It is therefore not up to us to determine which capacities are good and which are bad, as in doing so we violate the moral agency of the species.

Taylor's theory has been widely embraced, but also, and not surprisingly, criticized for being too individualistic, employing principles that are thought to be at odds with the theory, and for not dealing with domesticated animals (see Sterba, 1995). In the case of individualism, Sterba writes that individuals and species populations can be both benefited and harmed as well as have a good of their own. This qualifies them as moral subjects. Species as an entity do not have a good of their own because they are a class name and classes in this capacity cannot have a good of their own.

Other theorists embracing respect of other living beings include Goodpaster (1978; see also Schmidtz, 1998; Warren, 1992), who argues for a hierarchical basis for respect, with some organisms afforded a higher level of respect than others.

> ... the clearest and most decisive refutation of the principle of respect for life is that one cannot live according to it, nor is there any indication in nature that we were intended to. We must eat, experiment to gain knowledge, protect ourselves from predation (macroscopic and microscopic), and in general deal with the overwhelming complexities of the moral life while remaining psychologically intact.
>
> (Goodpaster, 1978: 324)

Conclusion

Perhaps the most controversial element of the scientific and moral deliberations on animals and their capabilities falls within the realm of the animal mind. It is vitally important because to prove that animals plan or feel pain, or even remember, is to change the way we use animals completely for food, science, work, or a range of other endeavours, including tourism. The problem is the use of standards to measure cognitive abilities. These may be different amongst scientists, not to mention that scientists and philosophers are often on opposite pages of the debate to begin with (Allen and Bekoff, 2007b). For the agenda to move forward, it is essential for both to have a working, up-to-date base of knowledge on each other's work.

What further complicates the terrain is the argument on the part of some theorists that hinging animal ethics on just a couple of contemporary ethical systems, i.e., rights and utilitarianism, is problematic because these are based on impartiality and abstractness. Better for these critics would be an emphasis on an ethic of care, which places value on the long history of successful animal husbandry (Anthony, 2003). Critics of the ethics of care perspective would counter by suggesting that moral judgements must be grounded in reason, not emotion. When we see animals in photographs that have in some way been abused, these often induce the most profound emotional reactions in viewers. Others contend that while normative theory, again rights and utilitarianism for example, have served the animal ethics community well, they have had little value in solving real-world problems (see Preece, 2005). Singer's solution for stopping factory farming, according to Rollin (2005), is simply to become a vegetarian. It is difficult to mix the applied with the theoretical, but this is what is needed in attempts to move forward.

The task in the following chapters is to examine those questions posed at the beginning of the book in regards to tourism, animals, and ethics: how animals are involved in the service of the tourism industry, and with ethical issues tied to this use. In addressing these we might also be able to assess the broader questions posed by Cavell (1995), i.e., who we are (in tourism) and what we conceive knowledge to be in our field.

4 Captives

The wild, cruel animal is not behind the bars of a cage. He is in front of it.

(Munthe, 2011)

Introduction

The focus of this chapter is on the animals that we capture and present, in a variety of different forums, for a public that has as its central motivation the pleasure and entertainment value derived from the gaze. The spectrum of different types of attractions based on the animals that we keep in captivity is presented by Shackley (1996). These forms range from those that offer no freedom to complete freedom, in association with those that have a conservation and education mandate contrasted with those that are purely for entertainment (Figure 4.1). The moral significance of these forms is tied to the fact that, although studies show that animals are considered necessary for consumption or other human endeavours, respondents demonstrate the least amount of support for purposes of entertainment – which is deemed simply unnecessary (Knight *et al.*, 2003). Even so, the number of people visiting zoos and other captive environments in some countries exceeds the spectators of all major professional sports, attesting to the popularity of these captive animal leisure attractions.

In this chapter, the history of the zoo concept is examined through a discussion of the evolution of the menagerie into the modern-day zoo. Zoos are also contrasted with circuses, the latter differing from the former on the basis of their mission and non-sedentary nature. The chapter also includes a discussion of aquaria and the relationship between aquaria and other captive environments as 'circuses of the sea'. This chapter is the first to introduce an 'ethics in action' section, which is the application of ethical theory to a practical situation raised in the chapter – a routine that will continue up to and including Chapter 9.

The menagerie

The capture and keeping of animals is a concept that is not new. Stevens and McAlister (2003) illustrate that zoological collections were kept by Chinese and Aztec emperors as early as the fifteenth century BC as a sign of wealth and fame,

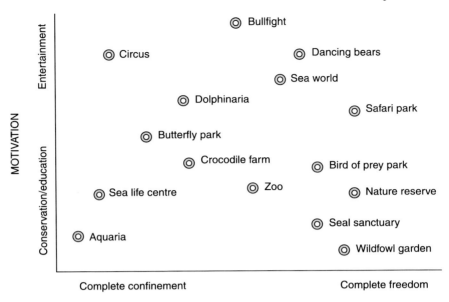

Figure 4.1 Tourist attractions: animals and captivity

and Charlemagne collected wild animals as a sign of his power (Miller, 2005). Queen Hatshepsut of Egypt in 1490 BC made a garden for animals that her soldiers brought back from other countries, animals that were not known in Egypt. Five hundred years later the first emperor of the Zhou dynasty, Wen, established a 'Garden of Intelligence' where animals from different parts of the empire were exhibited for purposes of education (Ehrlich and Ehrlich, 1981). Alexander the Great sent animals back to Greece from his military expeditions, and the public was charged admission to view them – the earliest recorded fees to see captive animals (Hoage, Roskell, and Mansour, 1996). Exotic and endemic animals were often kept in paradise parks adjacent to estates during Antiquity in the Assyrian, Babylonian, and Egyptian empires, which made it convenient to both observe and hunt (Kalof, 2007a; see also Shelton, 2004).

There began a fascination with animals through exploration and conquest during the earliest parts of the fifteenth century, which continued via the movement of species between cultures at unprecedented speeds. The arrival of exotic animals to Western Europe from places like the Far East and Africa brought profound changes to the material culture of the time. Those that could manage to own these animals were afforded higher status. The menageries (*serragli*) of Renaissance princes grew significantly in number and in the types of exotic species held from the 1400s onward (Boehrer, 2007). By the early sixteenth century, the papal menagerie was being constructed largely from gifts offered by Catholic princes from their travels or from their own stock, including elephants, rhinoceros, leopards, panthers, apes, parrots, and so on. Animals even provided the means for diplomatic cooperation between nations, as visiting dignitaries brought with them animals as representations of the fauna of their homeland.

Veltre (1996) writes that the word menagerie was thought to have come from French for farmyard, but instead stems from the word *ménage* (to manage), as well as *rie* which indicates a place: to manage a place, or a place for the management of animals, in the literal sense. It is not only containment that symbolizes the menagerie, Veltre argues, but also domination, control, and the novelty of keeping and showing animals that are so different than those indigenous to the area. He also posits that the viewing of animals did not become popular until the development of cities, whereby a yearning for animals was satisfied through the menagerie as a new form of art connecting people to the wilds. The menagerie became an art form that was supported by artisans and labourers, who constructed elaborate means in which to manage the animals (Kalof, 2007b; see also Anderson, 1997).

During the late seventeenth century, those who could afford to do so assembled private collections of caged animals as status symbols. Anderson (1995) uses the example of the Versailles menagerie, which opened in 1665, as a case in point. The Versailles collection was thought to be the first site to organize animals according to a single vantage point, with a separation of animals on the basis of phylogenetics (Senior, 2007); another example of royal privilege of the day. This menagerie was a representation of absolute monarchy, with political and social factors at work in latter eighteenth-century French society controlling just about every aspect of society and nature. In August of 1792, at the height of the French Revolution, the Jacobins were successful in dismantling the menagerie on the foundation of principle of citizenship that extended beyond concern for human community, 'in the name of the People and Nature [that the King] return to liberty creatures that leave the hands of the Creator free and have been unjustifiably detained by the vanity and pomp of tyrants' (Senior, 2007: 19). According to Loisel (1912):

> The Revolution was three years old, France had been declared a republic, and the menagerie, which had been founded by Louis XIV, was now the republic's property. Met by the menagerie's director, the group's leader addressed him in stirring words. They had come in the name of the people and of Nature, to demand the liberty of beings intended by their Creator for freedom but detained by the pride and pomp of tyrants.
>
> (cited in Bostock, 1993: 1)

The story has it that the director gave the keys to the mob and walked away, and with nowhere to take the animals the Jacobins left them in place until other arrangements could be made. These other arrangements were the Jardin des Plantes – the main botanical gardens in France. In 1804 the animals of Versailles were moved there and it became open to members of the public (Anderson, 1995).

Gathering and holding exotic animal collections by royal and noble families was a tradition that continued through the eighteenth century (Hancocks, 2001) and well into the twentieth century. Yugoslavian leader Marshal Tito maintained a private zoo on the island of Veli Brijun (part of the Brioni islands of Croatia, near Pula on the mainland). Indira Ghandi, for example, presented a bull elephant named Sony to the communist leader in 1970, when the elephant was just two years old. The elephant died in early April 2010.

Life for the beasts living in these facilities was not easy (Boehrer, 2007). Given the lack of expertise of those charged with the responsibility of maintaining the animals, many died because of the poor conditions of captivity. Hanno the elephant, given as a gift to the Vatican, died after two years, and a rhinoceros on route to the Vatican died before it arrived. In the Tower zoo, Boehrer writes, all the lions were dead within a few months of captivity. Animals from warmer climates had to endure colder conditions, food inconsistent with their dietary needs and, not unlike in zoos of the present day, these animals developed all manner of psychological and physiological deformities that seriously compromised their health (Baratay and Hardouin-Fugier, 2002).

Capture

Rothfels (2002b) writes that the capture and presentation of animals for zoos by the end of the nineteenth century often involved questionable ethical practices. The most cost-effective method was to simply shoot the adults of a given species, often in large numbers, and later round up the young. This way, the young remained better mannered, easier to capture and transport (Donald, 2005). For obvious reasons, this part of the industry was not made readily available to the public, as summarized by William Hornaday, the director of the Bronx Zoo in 1902 (the same director who in 1906 put a Pygmy male in the monkey exhibit for display):

> We must keep very still about forty large Indian rhinoceroses being killed in capturing the four young ones. If that should get into the newspapers, right here or in London, there would be things published in condemnation of the whole business of capturing wild animals for exhibition.
>
> (Rothfels, 2002b: 67)

The French zoologist Jean-Yves Domalain (1978) writes of his personal experiences as an international animal dealer. He goes to great lengths to illustrate the depth of animal suffering and the substandard level of treatment afforded to animals captured and bound for zoos. He estimates that one out of ten animals survived the ordeal from wild state to captivity in a zoo. The others perished because of the nature of capture as well as the appalling conditions of transport. This is confirmed by Moriarty (1998), who found that many of the animals trapped in far-off lands and destined for zoos never actually made it.

Those in defence of the capture and use of animals in zoos acknowledge that capture is justifiable if welfare conditions are secured such that the animal is not made to suffer. Bostock feels that if an animal is caught and transported with as little stress as possible and kept under the best conditions, zoo keepers will 'have gone a long way towards respecting its right to freedom' (1993: 187). The argument follows that preference be given to breeding animals in captivity so the need to capture is eliminated. The justification for the continuation of the zoo concept would be easier (Bostock, 1993).

The questionable practices of wild animal capture have led to more recent standards designed according to the welfare needs of these animals. Specialized loading and unloading equipment must be used in addition to human resources trained in the use of this equipment. Animals should be introduced to the cage some two weeks before transport (e.g., feeding in the cage), to ensure that the cage is viewed as a safe and secure refuge. Practitioners in this area have found that animals often make positive associations with cages. Linhart *et al.* (2008) observe that a breeding male cheetah would instantly board the cage because of the positive association with the opportunity to breed. The World Association of Zoos and Aquariums' virtual zoo (select an animal, then select 'in the zoo') provides information on the procedures for transport crates for specific species, as shown in Box 4.1.

The World Association of Zoos and Aquariums (WAZA) is the professional organization that oversees the practices of zoos internationally, and is administered by individuals who represent zoos and aquariums. WAZA must meet regulations established by the Convention on International Trade in Endangered Species of Wild Fauna and Flora (CITES). This member-based organization has as its mission the long-term viability of species of animals and plants that might otherwise be negatively jeopardized by trade. But as Marino *et al.* establish, this voluntary

---

Box 4.1 Transporting the Black Rhinoceros

How this animal should be transported

Rhinos should be allowed to get used to the transport crate, which may take from 1–6 weeks depending on the individual rhino's temperament. Transport crates should allow the rhino to stand comfortably, provide drainage for urine, be adequately reinforced, have adequate ventilation holes or spacing, permit access for food and water for longer transports, and allow handlers to adequately monitor the rhino's condition. Temperature in the crate should range from 12–20°C. Handlers familiar with the individual rhino should travel with the animal to the receiving institution. They should regularly monitor the condition of the animal during transport. For air transport, Container Requirement 71 of the IATA Live Animals Regulations should be followed.

Road transport (according to the South African Standard SANS 10331): Transport in special rhino crates under tranquillization. Professional assistance from competent nature conservation staff or an experienced capture team is necessary for loading and transportation since special facilities are required.

<http://www.waza.org/en/zoo/diceros-bicornis>, accessed 16 September 2010

membership essentially amounts to a 'gentleman's agreement' among parties to use their own domestic laws in controlling the flow of plants and animals between nations – laws that are not at all consistent across the board (Marino *et al.*, 2009). WAZA also provides guidance on the long-distance travel of animals, reported in Linhart *et al.* (2008), who write that the first step involves communication with CITES, including any documentation on the status of the species involved. Planning is facilitated by the Live Animal Regulations of the International Air Transport Association (IATA), which maintains guidelines for the safe transport of live animals (IATA, 2011).

Zoos

Altick (1978) writes that during the Age of Enlightenment the conditions of European society (the mix of Descartes' and Newton's work along with the French Revolution and ideas by Rousseau) opened the door for a more educational component to the use of animals for entertainment. Knowledgeable persons often accompanied animal shows on natural history to inform the audience on specific aspects of the biology and geography of the species under examination. This is corroborated by Anderson (1995), who observes that Cartesian legacies, i.e., the irrational nature of animals in relation to the rational capacity of man, along with new scientific realities opened the door for the public's acceptance of zoos as new institutions. Linnaeus's classification of plants and animals and the emergence of animal physiology and comparative anatomy for research purposes – and also display – supported the practice of animal confinement.

By the early nineteenth century the menagerie had metamorphosed from the exotic collections of Renaissance princes into the zoo as a formal institution (Boehrer, 2007; see also Ehrlich and Ehrlich, 1981). As European powers spread about the globe, they collected animals as a hobby and in fulfilment of a heightened interest in presenting these animals for public viewing as the spoils of imperialism – mastering the globe and all its inhabitants.

> We still capture them, 'acclimatize' them, and make them visual targets of our whims. By definition, confinement subordinates its captives and gives the viewer complete power over them. Ideally, the experience of interacting with other animals should enhance our understanding of the interconnected, mutually shared web of life, but the institution of the zoo forestalls any such insights. We are out there; they are in here.
>
> (Marino *et al.*, 2009: 25)

There is a strong base of literature on the topic of zoos and most of this, not surprisingly, comes to us from outside the field of tourism. As Mason (2000) suggests in reference to the little, comparatively, work available on zoos in tourism research, there is much more that needs to be accomplished in areas like ethics and welfare, education, conservation, and a range of other issues. More specifically, the following four questions posed by Mason are worth more investigation:

- Should animals be kept in captivity to entertain visitors?
- Are zoos appropriate attractions given concern for animal welfare?
- Is it not better to view animals in their natural setting than in captivity?
- Do zoos encourage visitors to anthropomorphize natural heritage and wildlife? (e.g., cuddly pandas; see also Mullan and Marvin, 1987; Shackley, 1996).

Of interest to the nature-based theorists, and particularly the ecotourism group, is the belief that viewing animals in captivity is a form of ecotourism (see Ryan and Saward, 2004; see also Tremblay, 2008). Wearing and Jobberns (2011) argue that such a link is tenuous since zoos fail to contribute to genuine sustainable tourism because of the mistreatment of animals, and because captivity in general is the antithesis of what ecotourism ought to represent. The topic of animal captives in tourism, however, has started to generate enthusiasm. Readers should source the special edition of *Tourism Review International* of 2007 (vol. 11, no. 3), which highlights the importance of the zoo as a major tourism attraction, as well as a recent book by Frost (2011).

By definition, zoos 'are public parks which display animals, primarily for the purposes of recreation or education' (Jamieson, 2006: 132), and broadly conceived they include game preserves and animal or safari parks, petting zoos, city zoos, rural and roadside zoos, aquaria and animal theme parks like Busch Gardens, and hundreds of specialized collections of reptiles, mammals, birds, insects, or fish. But as Tribe (2004) argues, not all zoos are created – or managed – the same. The simple fact is that there are good zoos and not so good zoos, with many in the developing countries substandard in how they manage living conditions for their inhabitants. Only about one-third of the 1,000 zoos in the European Union were found to be reputable enough to be included in the *International Zoo Yearbook*. Many other zoos are poor and still others are not subject to regulations in their jurisdictions. Spain, Portugal, Italy, and Greece, for example, have no laws governing zoos (Garner, 2004). The 'zoo as menagerie' is simply the trend towards keeping animals in cramped quarters for the amusement of spectators, with virtually no emphasis on the science or natural history of these animals (Turley, 1999a). On the other hand, zoos have evolved significantly along the lines of immersion exhibits that create more space for animals and immerse them (and humans) in more natural habitats.

The World Association of Zoos and Aquariums (WAZA) says that 600 million visitors, upwards of 10 per cent of the world's population (Stevens and McAlister, 2003), visit the over 1,300 member zoos worldwide. Two hundred and fifty of these are strictly members of WAZA and another 1,100 are members through regional or national associations (WAZA, 2011). Miller (2005) writes that two of the world's foremost economic superpowers, Japan and the United States, also have the highest number of zoos. Over one-third of the Japanese population visits an aquarium or zoo each year, while in the United States more people visit zoos annually than all of the visitors to the major professional sports combined. In the UK alone there are 50 wildlife parks, zoos, and animal attractions listed in the *Britain's Finest* directory (Britain's Finest, 2011). At least 6,000 species are kept in zoos worldwide (Flesness *et al.*, 1995).

By way of history, the modern zoo has its foundation in the Versailles menagerie in France, although even before this a zoo had been established at the Schönbrunn Palace of the Habsburg monarchy in Vienna, opened to the public in 1765, and another in Madrid in 1775. The London Zoo opened in 1828 as the first zoo of its kind incorporating a scientific component as part of its mission. One of the most popular attractions at zoos during the nineteenth century, at least in London and Bern, was the bear pit. In London the bear pit was immortalized in George Scharf's (1835) painting, depicting a bear that has ascended a fixed pole for the purpose of obtaining a bun from the tip of an extended pole for the delight of the crowd. The Bern bear pit is immortalized in the painting by an unknown artist of around 1880 reproduced as Plate 4.1.

To say that the zoo was a setting only for members of high society is patently incorrect according to Ito (2006). In London, for example, many tiers of society frequented the zoo during the nineteenth century and along with the eclectic nature of spectators, there was also a diverse response to the fundamental nature of the zoo itself, including idealization and excitement on one hand and disappointment and critical reflection on the other (see also Turley, 1999a, 1999b in reference to the zoos' congenial atmosphere tied to recreational and social uses). Essential in a discussion of the historical roots and acceptance of the zoo culture is the recognition that in the mind's eye of the public the zoo experience played out and extended the efforts put forth in building the empire (Ritvo, 1987). For Miller, 'Human order reigns within the walls of the zoo as the primacy of human culture over animal nature is reasserted at every turn, and this order is presented as both benevolent and rational' (2005: 275).

Plate 4.1 Bear pit at Bern, Switzerland

In this capacity, Anderson (1995) argues that even though zoos have gone through a transition from the menagerie during the late nineteenth century to the fairground between the mid-1930s and early 1960s, into the era of naturalistic enclosures to the present day, the zoo remains a cultural institution. Elements of nature are messaged into iconic representations of human-produced order and control in the creation of human–animal boundaries and animal–animal boundaries that domesticate, mythologize, and aestheticize the animal universe for human consumption. The following quote from Anderson summarizes well the conditions that exist even in the new naturalistic enclosures where the conditions of life are said to be far superior to previous conditions:

> At the same time, visitors are spared the knowledge that the objects of their gaze are subject to complete dependence on a caretaker; an artificial diet; immunity from disease they would encounter outside the zoo; strictly controlled mate selection; regulated reproductive practices, including (in some cases) artificial insemination; reduced life expectancy; drugs; social company not of their choosing; severely restricted ranges; and so-called 'behavioural enrichment' programmes devised by zoo staff. Moreover, the animal behaviour that the public witnesses is heavily controlled. There is no animal mating or fighting on display; no eating of each other or hunting, for example; On the other hand, captive bears and jaguars often pace, zoo baboons and monkeys are known to display increased aggression and many animals exhibit stereotypic behaviour. Some captive animals even mutilate themselves and eat their young.
>
> (Anderson, 1995: 291)

The concept of the zoological gaze is also helpful in better understanding the nature of human–animal interactions in the zoo setting – the socially, culturally, and historically organized ways in which visitors to zoos relate to animals (Franklin, 1999). The zoological gaze has been discussed by Berger (1980), who feels that this environment is the epitome of animal marginalization, with humans able to gaze upon animals but animals unable to 'see' or regard humans – the one-way gaze. There is simply a passiveness and dependence based on small cages, isolation, and programmed feeding times that render the animal as more like a distorted cultural version or image of what the animal would be like in its natural form (see Malamud, 1998). This has prompted Mullan and Marvin (1987) to argue that part of the draw of the zoo experience is the fascination built into analyses that focus on 'like us' or 'not like us', with culture weighing heavily into the ways in which animals are regarded. To be more specific, Haraway (1989) illustrates that natural history museums carry on the tradition of using large, impressive males of a charismatic species to look directly back at the onlooker as if still alive and perhaps to signify what might be construed as a form of dominance if the scene was in fact a real-life scene in a real-life setting.

Continued evolution

Zoos have the difficult task of proving their viability through the provision of services geared towards enjoyment, while at the same time acting as a conduit for education, research, and conservation (see Turley, 1999a). As an *ex situ* conservation strategy, the zoo shares some of the same basic challenges as *in situ* parks and protected areas which must balance conservation with visitor use. They have evolved as such in recognition of the fact that the keeping of animals in captivity strictly for entertainment purposes was not going to work in the eye of the general public.

From the standpoint of conservation, Miller *et al.* (2004) argue that with an increasing human population invading and destroying natural areas, one-half and two-thirds of all species will be lost in the next four generations. They suggest that collection-based institutions like botanical gardens and zoos, because of their educational roles, may play a part in shifting this trend. Many zoos have taken up this challenge by becoming internationally oriented conservation centres containing vast amounts of genetic information as *ex situ* gene banks. This genetic information is important for large vertebrates threatened with extinction, as well as small population biology through the use of simulation modelling to help predict scenarios in similar sized groups in the wild (see Rabb, 1994). The key to this conservation mandate is to convince visitors and the public at large that the institution should remain viable as a source of pleasure and entertainment because of the legitimate work being done in the area of conservation and research. Communication and an emotional connection have become essential.

Conservation can take place through a number of different initiatives, including captive breeding, education, research, animal welfare, environmental enrichment, reintroduction, and further support for *in situ* conservation of species and their habitats (Catibog-Sinha, 2008). Koontz (1995) identifies three scenarios in which it might be ethically justified for zoos to acquire wild animals. These are: (1) when stock is needed to set up a long-term captive breeding programme for conservation; (2) when genetic or demographic immigrants are required to enhance an established captive programme; and (3) when more animals are needed for purposes of companionship or other conservation goals. If zoos are committed to conservation, and the quality of animal care increases, Hutchins and Keele (2006) contend, populations such as elephants, which are in demographic peril in zoos, may be aided by the capture of new animals to help sustain populations over the long term. Protocols have been established by the Association of Zoos and Aquariums (AZA) for targeted animals, which include first, captive animals in private hands (e.g., logging camps), second, animals in professionally managed foreign zoos, and third, wild animals. Furthermore, preference should be given to animals that may be culled in parks or reserves, or animals that are living in substandard conditions. For Stevens and McAlister (2003), zoos have a right to hold animals in captivity if these animals are part of a management programme with the intent of releasing these animals back into the wild. While in the possession of the zoo, these animals must also be part of a structured education programme, so that they are not displayed for enjoyment purposes only.

Through such conservation efforts, zoos have been able to achieve some victories and successful outcomes. For example, Jamieson (2006) reports that zoos have saved from extinction the Père David deer, Mongolian wild horse, and the California condor. Still, the conservation potential of zoos is highly controversial. As Garner suggests, captive breeding programmes as a conservation strategy have many challenges, not least of which is diminishing habitat for reintroduction – there is simply no more room for these animals. Furthermore, it is questionable whether zoos ought to be the venues responsible for these breeding programmes. The interests of a species might be better met by species-specific breeding centres that have higher levels of knowledge about these species and are not open to the public. The research component of zoos is called into question by restricting outside influences in gaining traction in the zoo environment. Princée (2001) argues that zoos can broaden their societal utility by allowing ethologists and other zoologists to study the species of interest in the zoo environment. In this vein, Maple (2007) puts forward a strong argument for the need for doctoral-level animal behaviouralists in developing appropriate management standards and best practices for the unique needs of the many different species that inhabit the zoo.

But social scientists have discovered that the educational component that zoo proponents say is so integral to the zoo experience appears to be unfounded. A move towards conservation mindedness does not appear to be a sustained outcome

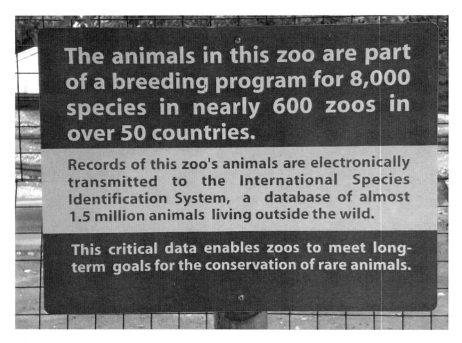

Plate 4.2 Zoo breeding programmes: photo taken by author at Naples Zoo, Florida

Plate 4.3 Part of the education message regarding conservation, Naples Zoo, Florida

of the zoo experience, and this is backed up by an increasing body of work (see Smith *et al.*, 2008), including a landmark study by Kellert (1979), who reports that the typical zoo visitor is a lot less environmentally aware than those such as hunters, anglers, and backpackers who actually spend time in the natural world. Perhaps most damning is that the zoo visitor is only marginally more knowledgeable than people who have little to no interest in animals at all, according to Kellert (see also Smith *et al.*, 2008; Bulbeck, 2005). Despite monumental efforts, visitors still perceive the zoo as a place of recreation and entertainment rather than a place for conservation and education (Ballantyne *et al.*, 2007; Reade and Waran, 1996; Shackley, 1996; Ryan and Saward, 2004; Dunlap and Kellert, 1989).

In a study of 1,340 adult visitors to a number of zoos in the UK, Balmford *et al.* (2007) found that not only were the conservation knowledge scores among visitors low (measured on the basis of knowledge about threatened species internationally and in the UK), but, more troubling, there were no differences between arriving and departing visitors in regards to knowledge scores. The same result has been documented in previous studies, according to the authors; and even in studies that demonstrate increased knowledge, follow-ups with respondents confirm that effects diminish over time. More specifically, the authors conclude: 'We found very little evidence, in the zoos we sampled, of any measurable effect of a single informal visit on adults' conservation knowledge, concern, or ability to do something useful' (Balmford *et al.*, 2007: 133). While zoos might claim that education and conservation are cornerstones of their principles and practices, evidence points more to recreation and enjoyment benefits for visitors.

In 1994 The World Society for the Protection of Animals (WSPA), in association with the Born Free Foundation (BFF), published a report entitled *The Zoo Inquiry*. This report specified welfare recommendations including enforceable minimum animal welfare standards and a passport system for animals in transfer, exchange, sale, and disposal. Perhaps most damning to the zoo industry was the conclusion

> that the captive breeding of wild animals for true conservation objectives, while a worthy aim, can only, at best, play a marginal role in species conservation; that most zoos do little to educate people about how the public can help to conserve wild species and that many zoos cause considerable physical and psychological animal suffering.
>
> (WSPA, 1994)

The public, it seems, is largely indifferent to the efforts of zoo professionals and their exhibits, much to their chagrin; animals are viewed rapidly, and there is a tendency to focus more on 'babies and beggars' (Ludwig, 1981). For example, Markwell and Cushing (2009) found that visitors to the Australian Reptile Park (ARP) spent very little time in front of smaller reptile exhibits, only stopping long enough to take a photograph. To the authors this meant that the gaze was mediated by photography – interacting or relating to the animals through the viewfinders of their cameras. By contrast, animals that were most charismatic, like reticulated pythons, generated the most interest amongst visitors, who spent more time at these exhibits and read interpretive displays in more detail. The managers of the ARP drew upon the cultural anxieties of visitors in structuring exhibits and programmes that allowed for awe and fascination in a risk-free setting. The approach garnered a zoological gaze that was said to be consciously anthropocentric, highlighting the danger to humans that venomous and non-venomous snakes represent.

Still others argue that educational efforts do in fact have positive outcomes for visitors as well as zoos. For example, Weiler and Smith (2009) discovered that the more layers of interpretation that a visitor experiences, the higher the visitor rates this interpretation according to ten cognitive, affective, and behavioural measures (e.g., the desire to stay longer and the desire to visit again in the future). In a study of 206 zoo visitors, Clayton *et al.* (2009) found that there is a strong correlation between zoo exhibits and the connection that people feel towards individual animal and a species. Therefore, the more effective exhibits are in generating pro-animal feelings, the more likely it is for these individuals to support conservation initiatives.

In the process, these changes, however positive, come packaged with what has been termed a process of Disneyization (Beardsworth and Bryman, 2001). This is characterized as 'the impact of Disney theme park principles on a range of organizations and institutional settings' (p. 90). This diffusion of principles includes: (1) theming, for example Africa in Busch Gardens, Florida; (2) dedifferentiation of consumption, which refers to the interlocking of different institutions such as theme parks and shopping malls; (3) merchandizing; and (4) emotional labour, which refers to the expression of socially desirable attitudes and emotions towards the public. The upshot of this is a shift in the tourist's gaze from the animals themselves, according to Beardsworth and Bryman, to the settings in which the animals are situated.

Some of these efforts can be found in the new immersion exhibits, such as the gorilla exhibit at the Bronx Zoo, which is designed to immerse both the animal and spectator in a natural world (see also Smith and Broad, 2007, in reference to the elephant immersion exhibit at the Melbourne Zoo). Rothfels (2005) explains that the idea behind the immersion exhibit can be traced back to the German Carl Hagenbeck, who opened a zoo in 1907 in the Stellingen region of Hamburg based on natural animal enclosures that contained characteristics of the animals' natural habitats in larger areas or pits that maintained the animals without bars. This was designed to provide the illusion of total freedom, and to mask the fact that the animals were captive. A narrative that emerged out of the construction of Hagenbeck's zoo was the vision that people ought to learn to love animals and further to strive for their protection. Yet despite the changes in the form and function of animals at Hagenbeck's 'revolution', it was still difficult to convince all people that the zoo, in whatever form, was not based on the capture, trade, and display of animals for commerce, and that the animals might not be better off in the zoo than in the wild.

Plate 4.4 Zoo education, Naples Zoo, Florida

In order for zoos to be viable in the future, they must do a better job at marketing for the core markets (children and seniors), embrace visitors and their needs from the recreational standpoint, address the issue of animal welfare head-on through communication of new developments in design, and finally public relations personnel need to do a better job at enhancing the credibility of the zoo in the face of mounting criticism from lobby groups. This seems to be the case in New Zealand, where 35 per cent of visitors to the Wellington Zoo were unaware that the zoo had a conservation role to play at all (Mason, 2007). The importance of the family market is corroborated by several studies. A US-based study on demand for zoos and aquaria, for example, found that the market cohort showing the highest demand for the zoo experience is the family with young children (Cain and Meritt, 2007; see also Mullan and Marvin, 1987; Davallon and Davallon, 1987).

Welfare evaluations in zoos

The focus on conservation and education discussed above is said to permeate every aspect of the zoo environment, from the gift shop to how doctors and trainers are described, with the belief that captivity is an essential part of saving wildlife. What is glossed over in this arrangement is the fact that confinement is brutal and cruel. Human-created spaces for these animals in no way meet the ecological needs of animals, and this leads to a wide range of psychological stressors that contribute to poor health:

> Hard concrete, limited movement, noise, near-constant exposure to visitors, lack of family groups, and threat or actual violence by keepers all undermine the animals' well-being. For these reasons, many animals display behaviors and emotional states indicative of psychological trauma and distress: self-injuries, eating disorders, infanticide, hyper-aggression, depression and many others.
>
> (Marino *et al.*, 2009: 27)

The first studies on the effects of visitors on zoo captives were undertaken in the 1970s and progressed with intensity into the 1980s. These early studies, and subsequent ones, according to Davey (2007b) pointed to the fact that there was indeed a 'visitor effect'. That is, the presence of zoo visitors did have an effect on the apes, and many other species including cats and birds. More specifically, such effects were found for the most part to be negative, including mainly higher levels of stress and aggression. By contrast, some studies indicated that the visitor effect was positive, with the presence of humans enriching the lives of animals and acting as a source of variety in animal lives. Davey argues that attributing behavioural responses of animals to visitors is problematic because it is difficult to prove that visitors in fact contribute to stress and aggression. Furthermore, more detailed studies of stress need to be devised, including the incorporation of physiological measures beyond behavioural changes.

The welfare discourse is complicated by the knowledge that, while some animals like polar bears and elephants are unable to behave naturally while in captivity, they suffer from repetitive stereotypic behaviours, they have trouble breeding and suffer poor general health, others like the snow leopard and lemur thrive (Clubb and Mason, 2003). In an analysis of pacing behaviour of 35 caged carnivores, these authors found that it was the widest-ranging species that showed a higher tendency toward stress and/or psychological impairment in the zoo environment. The authors conclude by suggesting that these wide-ranging species are unable to cope with range restrictions and so should not be kept in zoos at all.

Pacing in zoos by lions, tigers, and many other species are stereotypic behaviours that are an indication of a compromised well-being (see Broom, 1991a, 1991b). In a study of two Sumatran tigers and three African lions, Bashaw *et al.* (2007) found that although changes to the animals' environments reduced pacing, the addition of a visual barrier between a tiger and a holding area failed to reduce pacing. For some captive animals, the spatial characteristics of the zoo environment are a poor substitute for their natural habitat. For example, fieldwork data on elephants in the wild has found that these animals travel up to 40 miles in a day, with home ranges covering hundreds of square miles. Maple (2007) contends that the space offered to elephants in zoos is only a fraction of this space. Similarly, the land area of all zoos in the world does not even match the range requirement of a single jaguar in the wild (Preece and Chamberlain, 1993). This perspective gains further traction in the understanding that animals rely on the ability to hide themselves from predators, and humans have been the ultimate predators for just about every animal on the planet for millennia (Knight, 2009). The zoo environment is said to be doubly unnatural for animals because 'they are subject not only to forcible *enclosure*, but to forcible *exposure* too' (Knight, 2009: 173). There is no place to hide.

Not surprisingly, compromised well-being can affect the life expectancy of captive animals. Garner reports that while Asian elephants can live up to the age of 65 in the wild, their average life expectancy in captivity is 15. Zoo elephants have higher infant mortality rates, shorter adult lifespans and lower reproductive capacity (fecundity) than their wild counterparts (Clubb *et al.*, 2008, 2009). While *in situ* elephants breed well into their forties, their captive counterparts begin to breed minimally in their thirties. These problems are attributed to stress and obesity, with the latter a function of the former, i.e., higher levels of stress induce increased consumption of food. It is important to realize that even though animals in captivity may experience the same stressors, they may act differently because of their life experiences. In the case of elephants, the wild live longer than the captive, and in captivity elephants contained in intensively managed sites have a higher mortality rate than elephants living in extensively managed sites (Brown *et al.*, 2008). Between the years 2006 and 2009, four elephants died unexpectedly, with the international zoo watchdog organization In Defense of Animals (IDA) calling for the closure of the elephant exhibit based on scientific evidence that zoos have devastating effects on this species (Weese, 2009). Bradshaw and Lindner (2009) suggest that zoos often use excessive force, pain, and deprivation in efforts to control elephants. The deprivation of food, in particular, they say, has deep implications. The ability to eat when, where, and what one wants is instrumental in how one self-governs oneself. If this is taken away from elephants, they develop eating disorders that compromise health.

Furthermore, there is new evidence to suggest that, just like humans, animals such as elephants are subject to Post-Traumatic Stress Disorder (PTSD). It has been shown that human children who have witnessed atrocities involving their parents have lasting psychophysiological effects on their behaviour. Bradshaw *et al.* (2005) illustrate that normal parent–child interactions help to develop normal self-regulatory structures in the corticolimbic region of the right hemisphere. However, trauma can offset this normal development, leading to a higher predisposition to PTSD and violence as an adult. Bradshaw and her colleagues suggest that the same holds true for adolescent elephants who have witnessed their parents culled or poached in large numbers. These elephants display the same symptoms as human adolescents and young adults, including abnormal startle responses, depression, unpredictable asocial behaviour, and hyperaggression. This is a concern for the tourism industry in as much as *in situ* and *ex situ* conservation programmes like wildlife parks and zoos have to contend with the potential violence of elephants that have been subjected to these conditions. The authors suggest that zoos and parks need to implement strategies that promote the normal ecological and familial relationships that exist in elephant herds in curtailing such behaviour.

These incidents have made the elephant the centre of attention of animal rights and welfare organizations bent on removing elephants completely from zoos. In stemming the tide, AZA leaders have crafted a political strategy that includes alliances with protectionists and politicians and a resolve to educate the public on the expanded mission of zoos, including education and conservation (Donahue and Trump (2006).

Masson and McCarthy (1995) summon the old German term *funktionslust* to refer to those behaviours in animals that they do best and which give them the most pleasure: flying high in the sky, climbing trees, running at full speed, hanging out in groups, and so on. The problem with zoos is that if animals enjoy these behaviours in their natural environment, it is just as likely that they will miss these activities if not allowed to participate in them whilst in captivity. In this vein:

> It would be comforting to believe that they [animals in zoos] are happy there, delighted to receive medical care and grateful to be sure of their next meal. Unfortunately, in the main, there is no evidence to suppose that they are. Most take every possible opportunity to escape. Most will not breed. Probably they want to go home. Some captive animals die of grief when taken from the wild … Wild animals may refuse to eat, killing themselves in the only way open to them.
>
> (Masson and McCarthy, 1995: 99)

Issues raised in the foregoing quote have increasingly been the subject of media scrutiny, which has only increased in sensitivity. The Calgary Zoo in Canada is a case in point, proving that there is great difficulty balancing conservation with profit. In 2009, the Calgary Zoo experienced the death of a number of animals due to human error. The preoccupation by senior members of the organization with raising money and cutting costs had led to job cuts, which in turn contributed to overworking existing staff, insufficient training, and low morale. The maintenance of old facilities suffered as new facilities and projects, containing new charismatic species, were being built to attract more visitors. Animal deaths included 41 cownose stingrays, a spider monkey killed from frostbite when it was left out in the cold, and a capybara crushed by heavy machinery because of a staff member not following proper protocol. Other animals that have recently died include a young elephant, a hippo, a wild goat, and four gorillas. As if this was not enough, a tourist snapped a photo of a gorilla holding a knife, which had been carelessly left in the enclosure by a staff member (Cuthbertson, 2010).

Sadly, Calgary is not the only example of such happenings. The National Zoo in Washington DC came under attack due to animal neglect and the misdiagnosis of animal illnesses that led to the death of 23 animals over a six-year period. Two older giraffes received treatment for lameness, but failed to receive a diagnosis of a digestive ailment that later killed them. A lion and a giraffe died after anaesthesia procedures, and red pandas died after consuming rat poison left in their yard. To make matters worse, veterinarians altered records or failed to file records at all in regards to many of these unfortunate deaths. Keepers and curators blame vets for not heeding their advice, and vets in turn blame keepers and curators for not being more attentive to the animals' needs (Barker and Grimaldi, 2003). At the San Diego Zoo, the finest in the US, Griner (1983) found that over a fourteen-year period, necropsies of animals showed that a number of animals suffered from malnutrition as well as injury and high mortality from transport, infanticide, cannibalism, and intra-group hostility.

Studies of zoos in South East Asia yielded other disturbing welfare conditions. A methodology developed by Agoramoorthy and Harrison (2002) and employed by Agoramoorthy (2004) was used to examine some of the ethical issues tied to three zoos in the region. Part of the study was designed to see how representatives of the zoos themselves evaluated welfare issues at their own zoo (in addition to other regional representatives). Questions and standards (94 in total) were organized according to the following seven categories: (1) freedom from hunger and thirst, (2) freedom from thermal and physical discomfort, (3) freedom from pain, disease, and injury, (4) freedom to express normal behaviour, (5) freedom from fear and distress, (6) general management, and (7) conservation programmes, finance, and responsibility. Of a range of problems, the following welfare issues were discovered: elephants were underfed, Asiatic black bears were not given adequate shelter, not enough ropes were offered to gibbons, a chimpanzee was kept in an enclosure measuring 3m × 3m × 2m, a male pigtail macaque had a hernia and was weak and motionless, two sun bears had mouth tumours, some exhibits had conditions that were unhygienic, and an orang-utan exhibit had no water and lacked enrichment devices. A similar methodology was employed in the welfare evaluations of three zoos in the Philippines (Almazan, Rubio, and

Agoramoorthy, 2005), with similar findings. In general, local evaluators judging the state of their own zoos gave higher scores, because of their inability to fully understand the extent of welfare problems of the animals in their care.

Using primates as forms of entertainment has also been cited as a problem in zoos in South East Asia. Agoramoorthy and Hsu (2005) evaluated 13 different zoos, four recreational parks, and three resorts in the region and discovered that orang-utans were the most commonly used primates for entertainment purposes, followed by gibbons and macaques. Acts the animals were made to perform include brachiation, underwater diving, plucking coconuts from trees, magic tricks, dancing, roller-skating, boxing, playing golf, and riding a bicycle. Orang-utans in particular were used frequently for photography sessions with visitors as well as to attend breakfasts and teas. A further problem with their use as such was that these animals were typically kept away from their conspecifics, in small cages for ease of handling. Negative reinforcement was used frequently, including punishment and intimidation tactics with signs of distress and fear. Agoramoorthy and Hsu found the animals to be heavily imprinted on human trainers, with a tendency to interact more with humans than their conspecifics.

Wickins-Drazilová (2006) illustrates that the usual metrics of acceptable animal welfare in zoos are physical health, long life, and reproductive success. These are limiting according to Wickins-Drazilová because they fail to incorporate other more difficult or qualitative measures of welfare such as natural behaviour, freedom of choice, and dignity. While it is the aim of many zoos to provide naturalistic environments, in the end they cannot replicate or simulate climate, migration, or predator–prey relationships. Zoos also cannot avoid the fact that many unnatural stressors (exposure to humans and close proximity to other stress-inducing species) lead to maladaptive behaviours, such as bar licking, head swaying, and marching for hours in predictable patterns. Lack of freedom comes from the inability to move normally and the impossibility of making decisions for oneself regarding food, reproduction, shelter, and climate. Finally, although it is difficult to appreciate the capacity for dignity in nonhuman animals, animals possess many of the same abilities as us in self-awareness, communication, intrinsic autonomy of the being, and the ability to suffer. By keeping animals in captivity, in a manner similar to our insane asylums of the eighteenth and nineteenth centuries, we diminish the dignity not only of animals but of ourselves, according to Wickins-Drazilová. Future welfare assessments in zoos should be based on the effective tracking, reporting, and communicating of trends in the behaviour and health at the level of the population, and these must be derived from both formal and informal reports. Improvements in technology and database management software will greatly improve this process (Barber, 2009).

Related to the concept of zoos, yet distinct in its essence, is that of sanctuaries. Sanctuaries have been created for the purpose of taking on excess numbers of animals that, for whatever reason, cannot be used at a zoo or transported home (primarily for reasons of logistics and cost). Marino *et al.* (2009) suggest that sanctuaries and zoos/aquaria are vastly different in philosophy and mission because the culture of viewing and entertainment is not at odds with animal welfare.

The Elephant Sanctuary in Tennessee is a representative example of the sanctuary model discussed above. In recognition of the neurobiological similarities between elephants and humans in regards to PTSD, as previously discussed, this organization's main goal is to implement the following treatment goals, recognizing that there is no cure for PTSD (Bradshaw and Lindner, 2009):

- agency, or the ability to exercise one's own free will, along with self-efficacy, mastery, and perceived control
- self-esteem, hope and optimism
- relaxation, competence, and assertiveness
- telling your story
- elephant social bonding
- human social bonding
- health and well-being
- avoidance of isolation or marginalization
- no threats or domination
- healthy, safe living environment
- personal change in mood, diet, behaviour, and social alliances.

The value of animal sanctuaries, however, has been called into question by Michael Hutchins, who has spent 15 years as Director/William Conway Chair at the Department of Conservation and Science of the Association of Zoos and Aquariums (AZA), and has compared zoos and sanctuaries according to space, breeding, accreditation, and other factors in reference to the holding of elephants (Hutchins, 2004). He argues that media reports and animal activists suggest that elephants would be better off living at sanctuaries rather than AZA accredited zoos. While sanctuaries offer significantly more space than zoos – hundreds of acres in the former case and perhaps four acres in the latter – Hutchins argues that bigger is not necessarily better, with many other factors weighing in on the success of elephant management. These include enclosure complexity, environmental enrichment, group size/composition, training, safety, veterinary care, and nutrition. In reference to breeding, sanctuaries do not breed or transfer animals – their focus is only on animal welfare – but zoos are involved in both. Animals may be used in Species Survival programmes, and moved from one facility to another either permanently or temporarily. One of Hutchins' chief concerns about sanctuaries is their level of accreditation. Although they are not accredited by the AZA, they do apparently have their own accrediting body but there is some question about its effectiveness in the following areas:

- staffing in the event that more elephants are added
- the level of training of the keepers
- number and quality of veterinary staff
- facilities for proper veterinary care
- science-based care programmes for the elephants
- procedures for care in the event of emergencies

- the procedures in place to allow elephants to perform key social behaviours
- long-term financial stability of the facility.

In regards to this last concern, Hutchins takes issue with the claim by animal activists that zoos are primarily profit-oriented. He argues that while zoos offer programmes for a diverse audience, sanctuaries often offer more exclusive opportunities in generating funds. To say that one organization is exploitative and the other altruistic is misleading and inaccurate.

To keep or not to keep

Supporters of the zoo, like Bostock, argue that if properly run, the zoo is 'an acceptable community of animals and humans' (1993: 182). Bostock feels that an animal's right to freedom is not compromised if it is kept under conditions that allow for the expression of most of its natural behaviour. Animals such as elephants and camels are able to give rides and thus meet the public, in leading active lives. Feeding, although now outlawed, is also seen by Bostock to be a positive element for animals and humans alike because in offering the animals a present, like food, humans indulge them, establishing a relationship and possibly producing some interesting behaviour to observe. In this capacity, Fraser *et al.* (2007) use the biophilia hypothesis to argue that the zoo is an important conduit allowing urban folks to connect with wild animals, leading to the development of environmental awareness. Another argument in support of zoos follows, that since many animals added to zoo collections are captive-bred and have never known freedom to begin with, there is no ethical dilemma. Jamieson (2006) argues that this is like suggesting that a caged bird has no other interests to engage (like flying), or that a human born into slavery has no interest in freedom. The tragedy here, he says, is that these animals have in fact never known liberty.

Theorists have discussed a number of ethical issues tied to the zoo as an institution. Tribe (2004), for example, observes that there are basically two ethical concerns with zoos. The first is that people feel the zoo is unacceptable because of the belief that animals ought to be living their lives free in an authentic state of wilderness. The second concerns the welfare of animals, who must endure cramped conditions simply for the pleasure of the visitor. These relate to observations made by Zamir (2007), who argues that the keeping of animals in zoos can be challenged on moral grounds according to limited movement and paternalism. Limitations on movement, or making it impossible for an animal to exercise its right to move where and when it wants to – in short exercising normal behaviour – is what Zamir refers to as an extreme form of deprivation. Dysfunctions like the inability to reproduce as discussed above and many behaviour problems underscore this. In regards to paternalism, Zamir says that although some farm and companion animals might enjoy a give-and-take relationship with humans, wild animals all live outside of human companionship and do so successfully – their existence does not depend on human paternalism, unlike a companion animal. The placing in captivity of animals that could otherwise live successfully in the wild is not morally acceptable, and captivity is tolerable only as a temporary stage in the preparation for the animal to live a normal life in the wild.

These moral complications are further discussed by Acampora (2005), who argues that captivity is consistent with what Foucault (1979) called the 'carceral archipelago'. Zoos are like prisons, where artificial space is created to impose occupancy, and, in the case of zoos, demonstration. Both of these conditions, i.e., occupancy and demonstration, violate animals' status as free living creatures, denying them the ability to express natural behaviours that would otherwise define their very being. Acampora (2005) also suggests that the zoo is like a form of pornography, whereby animals are made to disappear because of the way they are overexposed. Animals are representations of their species, along with their supposed role within nature, just like sex shows, which are really not pure presentations of women or men but rather 'graphically and textually sedimented portrayals of reified stereotypes' (Acampora, 2005: 72), for example nymph or seductress. In other work Acampora (1998) suggests that the zoo essentially erases the true wild nature of animals. They have had taken away their capacity to freely elude or engage with others, and further there is a structural inauthenticity based on the impossibility of full otherness: 'their presence is still essentially assigned *to or for us*' (Acampora, 1998: 2). To Garner (2004, 2005), quite simply no matter how dressed up zoos become through new exhibits of larger size, they will always be morally objectionable because they keep animals as captives (see Hancocks, 2001, who discusses the difficulty of ever abolishing zoos because of strong cultural ties, and his proposal for the *uninvention* of the zoo concept of holism and a respect for all animals.)

The circus

The word circus is derived from the Latin word meaning circle (Kreger, 2008). In Rome, the circus referred to chariot racing because of the circuitous route followed by the participants (Cameron, 1976). The modern circus was invented by Philip Astley, who built his first amphitheatre in Lambeth in London in 1768, followed by other amphitheatres in Paris, London, and Dublin in the 1770s (Mosier, 1999). The Royal Circus opened its doors in 1782.

In Victorian times, the circus was said to defy the limits of man and nature (Assael, 2005). It evolved at a time when there seemed to be an insatiable need for exposure to the exotic – things that had never been seen. Its spontaneity, release, freedom, enjoyment, and curiosity satisfied the desire to experience the unexperienced. According to Assael, the circus helped define a new leisure world during a time when the working week was reduced from six to five-and-a-half days, and there was a range of new leisure services available for a yearning public. Attractions included equestrians who possessed excellent trick riding skills honed during the Seven Years War (1756–63), and who found profit by demonstrating these skills at fairs and pleasure gardens across Britain at the end of the war (Kwint, 2002). Circus performances also often involved pigs and horses among other beasts, trained to count, communicate, or perform physical feats (e.g., tightrope walking) in one way or another for the amusement of the audience.

Assael writes that the circus, beyond the enjoyment and spontaneity described above, also contributed to a sense of order in the world. The audience was able to process, define, order, and classify different species of animal against each other, but also against humans. This was important, as in the case of zoos, in that the acquisition of exotic animals from abroad served to reinforce in the minds of Britons and other European nations their ascendant status. This status often took the form of the direct comparison between animals and humans, and the disparagement of the former through a variety of speciesist jokes (Leach, 1964).

The circus also adopted characteristics that defined the carnival, including the pursuit of desire, premised on the need to escape repressive social and religious conditions in favour of periods of misrule, and the suspension of taboos and hierarchies. Kwint (2002) says that women dominated men, animals were dressed up as humans, and night became festive day. Much of this symbolism could be found in the circus through the antics of clowns and other performers, but in a restricted commercial space that was utilized not by the masses, as in the carnival, but by the performers themselves.

The history and evolution of the circus is summarized in Table 4.1. Four rather discrete time periods are developed which correspond to the scale and base of attractions and performances that accompanied these periods of time (Assael,

Table 4.1 The evolution of the circus

Circus phase	Attractions
1768–1820	1768, Astley's first amphitheatre in Lambeth: the birth of the modern circus.
	Competition coming towards the end of the eighteenth century, with many smaller family acts emerging.
	Combination of discrete scenes that focus on comedy and elite horsemanship.
	Development of burlettas (plays based on song).
	Development of military scenes on horseback depicting and glorifying events of war.
1820–1860	Astley's circus differs significantly in scale from the rest of the circus establishments.
	Elaborate equestrian dramas dominate the performance. Up to 30 horses involved in performances like *The Battle of Waterloo*.
	Smaller acts of clowning, juggling, acrobatics follow.
1860–1880	In this phase, variety acts begin to overshadow the grand equestrian acts, which have almost disappeared altogether, as a result of the closure of many important fairs.
1880–1900	Increases in capital and size continue.
	Larger outfits purchase exotic animals like lions and tigers from around the globe, in the absence of protective legislation.
	Barnum and Bailey's three-ring circus and menagerie provide a new benchmark for the circus's use of animals.

2005). The period between 1880 and 1990 was characterized by important changes in the use of large animals to correspond to changes in scale. In the case of the US, the elephant is said by Mosier (1999) to have been a key reason for the development and success of the circus on US soil. It was a combination of the animal's size, unusual appearance, and intelligence that it made it so popular. Its arrival in the US came at a time when the US was defining its independence, and the elephant was used heavily as a patriotic symbol, according to Mosier.

While similarities exist between zoos and the circus, largely on the basis of the use of animals for human entertainment, there are characteristics of the circus that make it different from a zoo. The first is that the circus is mobile. The circus brings the event to the audience, whereas the audience needs to travel to attend the zoo (Beardsworth and Bryman, 2001). Furthermore, zoos are often promoted as advancing science and education, whereas the circus is viewed more as a collection of curiosities with strictly entertainment value (Hall and Brown, 2006). In providing the service of entertainment, the animals must work hard to be properly trained and endure a lifestyle that is marked by frequent transportation, unnatural food sources, meagre living conditions, and the stress of being away from their own kind in the wild. Despite these differences, or perhaps because of them, the two institutions are historically interconnected. Zoos and circuses often supported each other morally as well as practically via the exchange of animals (Kreger, 2008). Circuses loaned animals to zoos in the off-season, and in return the circus animals were given veterinary care, winter care, and feeding.

During the latter half of the nineteenth century, Romanticism, secular humanitarianism and religious sensitivities paved the way for a changing attitude towards the use of animals for human amusement in circuses – the legacy of various acts and organizations (RSPCA 1824, Martin's Act 1822, Cruelty to Animals Act 1849) designed to protect the interests and welfare of animals (Assael, 2005). In the early twentieth century, particularly after World War I, British trainers in the circus were very critical of foreign trainers, especially German, as using methods that were far too cruel to animals captured, accommodated, transported, trained, and later used for performance. Germany, along with other countries, did not have well-established animal welfare legislation, and so animal trainers may have been less sensitive to the standards of treatment of animals than their counterparts in Britain. Furthermore, residual ill feelings between Britons and foreigners because of the war prompted homeland trainers and managers to strive to enact policy to boycott 'alien acts' (Wilson, 2009).

Recognizing the ethical issues tied to the circus, P.T. Barnum used moral and educational values to suppress any misgivings that the public had towards the keeping and presenting of animals on the stage. When in 1861 the first hippopotamus to come to America was advertised to the US public, it was advertised as 'the behemoth of the Scriptures', suggesting that the event would be nothing short of a religious experience (Kreger, 2008). Yet it was a well-established fact that P.T. Barnum used prods, hot irons, and other instruments of influence to control the unpredictable behaviours of many of the large animals in his shows (Kreger, 2008). The claim that the circus industry maintained proper, humane training practices with performing animals was as unfounded then as it is now. Animals are 'encouraged' to perform using very draconian methods.

Apes that entertain us at circuses do so under conditions of extreme stress. While animals may appear to be happy and energetic, they must often do so to avoid being beaten with fists, bats, clubs, and other items to keep them in fear of their trainers. In some cases jaws are wired shut, and in others the animals must endure remote-controlled electric shockers to keep them in line (Sorenson, 2009). (See Zoocheck Canada (n.d.) for a detailed list of all jurisdictions around the world that have prohibited or severely restricted performing wild animal acts.)

In the highly publicized 2002 undercover investigation of the Carson and Barnes Circus in the USA, 'animal care' director Tim Frisco was videotaped instructing would-be handlers how to train elephants:

> Frisco to would-be elephant trainer: *'Tear that foot off! Sink it [sharp, metal bullhook] in the foot! Tear it off! Make 'em scream!'*
>
> Frisco to elephant: *'Becky! Becky!! You motherf—er!'* Frisco attacks Becky. Becky recoils and screams.
>
> Frisco to trainers: *'Don't touch 'em – hurt 'em. Hurt 'em. Don't touch 'em – make 'em scream. If you're scared to hurt 'em, don't come in the barn. When I say rip his head off [and] rip his f—ing foot off, it's very important that you do it. When he starts squirming too f—ing much, both f—ing hands – BOOM! – right under the chin!'* Frisco then swings the bullhook like a baseball bat.
>
> *'When he f—s around too much, you f—ing sink that hook and give it everything you got.'* Frisco demonstrates by twisting the bullhook back and forth. *'Sink that hook into 'em. When you hear that screaming, then you know you got their attention.'*
>
> Frisco explains that the abuse must be kept secret: *'Right here in the barn. You can't do it on the road. I'm not gonna touch her in front of a thousand people. She's gonna f—ing do what I want, and that's just f—ing the way it is. Make 'em holler, let 'em run from ya.'*

Box 4.2 Elephant attacks

15 May 1999
Timmons, Ontario, Canada

A 23-year-old American circus worker died after an elephant backstage at a circus performance attacked him. Police say the man, who assisted the trainers with the animals in the Leonardo Circus, was kicked in the head.

<http://www.gan.ca/old/en/campaigns/entertainment/circus/factsheets/elephant_attacks.htm>, accessed 21 April 2011

The relationship between zoos and circuses started to fall apart during the 1980s, Kreger (2008) adds, because of the former's concerns about the presentation of animals in anthropomorphic and non-educational ways as well as the lack of standards the circuses followed in regards to the welfare of animals. Accepting circus animals in the zoo environment was damaging to the reputation of the latter. This, coupled with shifts in societal attitudes, necessitated the implementation of changes in practice. While some of the changes are of a voluntary nature through the production of standards and guidelines, others are more stringent. Finland, Sweden, and Denmark, for example, have banned some animal acts altogether. In the UK, the number of circuses with animals dropped from 23 in 1997 to 12 in 2002, while the number of animal-free circuses rose from 10 to 21 in the same time period. An editorial on 5 April 2005 in the *Philadelphia Daily News* is representative of this changing sentiment: 'The circus elephants are coming to town next week, bringing an outmoded and problematic form of entertainment to all Philadelphians. Here's hoping that this is the last year such an antiquated spectacle is welcomed within our city limits' (Zoocheck Canada, 2006: 21).

Studies have confirmed how welfare has been compromised in circus animals. Conducting the first of these studies, Iossa *et al.* (2009) found no evidence suggesting that the conditions that such animals experience in the circus are anything close to the needs they have satisfied in the wild. The animals were found to spend only 1 to 9 per cent of their time in performing or training, and spent the rest of the day in exercise pens much smaller than minimum sizes as advocated in zoo standards. Given the fact that the circus remains mobile for much of the year, there is little opportunity to establish a complex 'home' environment. The result is an impoverished life for the animal, with the conclusion that the types of species most often used in circuses (elephants and tigers) are the ones least suited to circus life. Schmid (1995) found that even in captive environments differences in behaviour were found among elephants when shackled compared with those kept in paddocks. Paddocks offered elephants more freedom and comfort with social play observed more than under conditions where elephants were shackled. The freedom from chains or ropes seems to have physical and psychological benefits.

What is also problematic is the unregulated system of using and obtaining animals for entertainment in the circus. This is demonstrated in the following excerpt from Zoocheck Canada:

> Many performing animals have been taken from the wild, despite claims to the contrary. According to the 1994 Traffic Europe-World Wildlife Fund report *CITES and the Regulation of Wildlife Trade for European Circuses*, there is a limited but consistent circus trade in wild-caught apes, bears, elephants and other species which has escaped the attention of wildlife trade enforcement authorities. The report states that '... *wildlife trade related to circuses is highly unregulated*' and circuses succeed in evading enforcement efforts.

Circus operations and trade in performing animals are difficult to monitor because circuses change names, animal acts, and locations continuously. In addition, enforcement officers are simply overwhelmed by the vast number of operating circuses. An estimated 500 to 1,000 circuses exist in Europe alone. Similar numbers are estimated for Central and South America while it is thought that North America has more than 300 circuses and traveling acts.

(Zoocheck Canada, 2006: 18)

Circuses are morally questionable for two main reasons. The first is entertainment. Making animals perform tricks outside their normal range of behaviour for human pleasure is said by Garner (2004) to be morally dubious. Second, the level of fear generated by training and the amount of suffering animals have to endure through deprivation and remaining shackled or caged for long periods of time is said to make this enterprise morally illegitimate (Garner, 2004). For Stokes (2004), what really seals the fate of the circus is that there is no reconciliation, the animals do not get to go home like spectators or even domesticated animals like dogs and cats – where home is with us. Once their on-stage performance is done, they retreat to their cages alone, and the reality is that the illusion of nature masks the fact that their real homes can never be shared with us, nor can they be experienced by these animal performers.

In recent years the circus has reinvented itself as an institution in the most radical way possible. The Cirque de Soleil is perhaps the best example of this evolution, where animals are not used but rather may be depicted through what may be classified as art in the form of the ballet. Jurisdictions are also changing by banning performing animal acts, and China is said to be taking a lead role in this (Rob Laidlaw, Zoocheck Canada, personal communication, 29 January 2011).

Aquaria

Prior to 1970, there was little moral concern over the killing of cetaceans (Scarff, 1980). During this time, oceanaria and aquaria started purchasing dolphins and whales to train in their shows, and the acceptability of this was hinged on popular media. Shows like *Flipper* did much to instil a sense of confidence in the general public as to the moral acceptability of these practices. A case in point is Sea World, San Diego, California, which translated much of the emerging fascination with marine life into huge corporate success. In its formative years, Sea World management saw fit to hire women in bikinis to sit beside dolphins who were required to wear bikinis for an adoring public. The attraction during these years was primarily based on entertainment, and the influence of corporate privatization and mass media created a constellation of meanings that redefine people, culture, and the image of nature. Local and national corporate sponsors helped to subsidize construction of many of the exhibits and in return were given exclusive rights to move their products inside the park. The buy-in from corporate America helped to reinforce the importance of Sea World to the local and regional economy, thus serving to deflect any criticisms brought forward by animal rights activists who frequented the attraction. Hidden amongst all the glitz and glamour was the fact that Sea World relied on a network of animal traders to maintain a constant supply of animals for shows and displays (Davis, 1997). Furthermore, a culture of acceptance was ingrained in the officers of Sea World, who were taught to believe that as long as the animals were healthy, monitored, well fed, swimming in water that was clean and the proper temperature, and reproducing, their well-being was secured. Interviewees frequently mentioned to Davis in reference to captivity vs wild conditions that: 'Hey, that's a big, cold, vicious, polluted ocean out there!' (Davis, 1997: 106).

This mindset was challenged as research on cetaceans advanced. Studies demonstrated the cognitive abilities of cetaceans, showing a range of capacities or functions that were not unlike those in humans. This was taking place during a time of changing values in regards to the environment, and heightened public scrutiny over the use of these animals in shows and of whaling in general (Scarff, 1980). As the industry matured, still more research revealed that dolphins in captivity die young and there are few examples where they have been able to breed successfully. In this shortened lifespan dolphins show a spectrum of abnormal behaviours, not least of which is the propensity to ram against the sides of concrete pools until they die (Garner, 2004). And according to Regan (2004), the whole enterprise is simply wrong because of the fact that dolphins swim upwards of forty miles a day and dive to depths of almost a kilometre. They are one of the most social of the mammals, thrive in extended social groups, and use an advanced echolocation mechanism to navigate their way through an ever-changing, challenging environment. Killer whales live on average 11 years in captivity, but live as long as humans if left alone in the wild (see Box 4.3 overleaf).

Despite claims by the profession that animals are trained through positive reinforcement and cheerful dispositions, the harsh reality is that, as in the well-documented past, animals are physically assaulted and intimidated into performing their manoeuvres through 'whips, bullhooks, metal bars, chains, electric prods, muzzles, human fists' (Regan, 2004: 130). There is thus a significant power imbalance between trainer and dolphin, and deprivation is the key tool used in persuasion. All of the tricks performed – basketball, jumping through hoops, 'walking' on their tail, etc. – have no other meaning than the procurement of a meal. Marine park training strips away the wild nature of cetaceans and other animals and they become instruments of human enjoyment and entertainment rather than wild animals, although they are constructed as such (Regan, 2004). As Jean-Michael Cousteau writes, marine parks are nothing more than lucrative business ventures – 'circuses of the sea' (Regan, 2004: 139).

With the arrival of new data on cetacean intelligence and the welfare implications of practices at places like Sea World, these institutions evolved to include newer educational programmes – not unlike zoos. Sea World was no longer based just on entertainment, but also, and just as importantly, it built an identity as a public educational resource, attracting school groups – particularly students from

---

Box 4.3 Lolita: Slave to Entertainment

This provocative and revealing must-see documentary uniquely addresses the human relationship with wildlife. It speaks not only to animal lovers and activists, but to anyone at all who may have been duped by marine theme park propaganda. In fact, this is the film that an entire industry would rather you not see. And whether you like it or not, *Lolita: Slave to Entertainment* is assured to ignite conversation – if not heated debate.

When Two Species Collide in the Icy Waters of Puget Sound a Storm of Epic Proportions is Unleashed. Man versus nature; in the summer of 1970 a barbaric hunt kills five orca whales and destroys the lives of countless others. Six young orcas are ripped away from their family, sold to marine parks, and shipped across the world to enter into a life of slavery. Three decades later only one survives. And she just so happens to be Miami's biggest performer.

Lolita: Slave to Entertainment is a stirring wake-up call. For those who have visited a marine park, for those who think they might do so in the future, and for those who simply wish to know the truth about performing marine mammals, this film is a 'must see' (James Laveck Tribe of Heart, Producer of the award winning doc *The Witness*).

Since that fateful day in 1970, waves of controversy have pounded both shores of the US as freedom fighters from across the globe battle for her liberation. It is a story of beauty, grace, passion, respect, exploitation, greed, prejudice, and domination. Disturbing footage of marine mammal captures and alarming interviews with former *Flipper* trainer Ric O'Barry, marine mammal specialist Ken Balcomb, animal sociologist Howard Garrett, animal advocate and President of *Ocean Drive Magazine* Jerry Powers, and former whale hunter John Crowe.

<https://www.createspace.com/Customer/EStore.do%3bjsessionid=92EF451ADBDB2359FF57E001E8C566A2.cspworker01?id=205154&rewrite=true>, accessed 11 February 2011

---

under-funded districts – which the organization was able to use in bolstering support. Shows like 'Shamu Goes to College' and 'Yankee Doodle Whale' were abandoned because these were seen to be too humiliating to the animals.

In response to these problems and in line with the educational mandate of aquaria, newer programmes have evolved, referred to as Dolphin Interaction Programmes (DIP). Some researchers have discovered that these have been found not to have a deleterious effect on the welfare of dolphins. To test this general finding, Trone *et al.* (2005) examined the daily and monthly behavioural repertoires of three dolphins at the Marine Life Oceanarium in Gulfport, Mississippi, involved in such a programme over a period of six months. Up to three paying visitors, under the guidance of a trainer, were able to pet the back, fins, and belly of dolphins for approximately 15 minutes. Data was collected for three social behaviour categories (solitary, dolphin–human, and dolphin–dolphin) as well as for four behavioural event categories. The authors found that there was no alteration in the frequency of social behaviours and no long-term alteration in the frequency of behavioural events. Data for short-term (daily) behaviours demonstrated an increase in the frequency of play following participation in the DIP, and even the propensity to play with park visitors not involved in the DIP directly. The authors conclude by suggesting that the welfare of the dolphins in these programmes was not compromised, nor was it in jeopardy. Following Hediger (1964), the authors observe that the willingness to interact with humans corresponds to an 'assimilation tendency', where other species interact with humans and treat them as conspecifics, treating these others as surrogates of their normal social existence. While this study comments on the impact of these programmes, there are other broader questions that need to be considered in regards to captivity and well-being.

In other cases the animal protection lobby has been so strong in certain jurisdictions that major structural changes have taken place. Such has been the case in the UK, where lobbyists were successful in closing a dolphinarium through communication with tourists and local authorities. What has enabled this change is the opportunity to view dolphins in the wild (Hughes, 2001; and see The Dolphin Project (n.d.), which is dedicated to abolishing the marine mammal entertainment business).

Ethics in action

Although Eastern nations have often been criticized for their treatment of animals, attitudes appear to be changing. The BBC ran a story in 2005 based on a study by the International Fund for Animal Welfare, which found that 90 per cent of respondents in China, South Korea, and Vietnam said that humans have 'a moral duty to minimize suffering in animals', and most responded positively towards legislation that would help to ensure this duty – percentages not much lower than a similar study conducted in 'animal-loving' Britain. The story goes on to illustrate that current laws in these countries are well behind public senti- ment (BBC News, 2005; also see Davey's study (2007a) of the public perceptions in urban China toward zoos and animal welfare based on three populations: uni- versity students, the general public, and zoo visitors). Box 4.4 overleaf points to a different side of the zoo as an institution designed with the welfare interests of its inhabitants in mind.

The contractarianist approach is used to examine in more detail the ethical nuances of Box 4.4. Contractarianism is based on agreements between rational, self-interested individuals. The key question, according to Taylor (2003), is what sort of deal must I strike with others in order to get what I want? The protection of animals occurs only because humans feel it is in our current best interests to do so. Taylor illustrates this with an example: 'I shouldn't kick your dog because that

Box 4.4 Animals torn to pieces by lions in front of baying crowds: the spectator sport China DOESN'T want you to see

By Danny Penman
Daily Mail, 5 January 2008

The children giggled as they patted the young goat on its head and tickled it behind the ears. It could have been a happy scene from a family zoo anywhere in the world but for what happened next.

A man hoisted up the goat and nonchalantly threw it over a wall into a pit full of lions. The poor goat tried to run for its life, but it didn't stand a chance. The lions surrounded it and started tearing at its flesh. 'Oohs' and 'aahs' filled the air as the children watched the goat being ripped limb from limb.

Badaling is in many ways a typical Chinese zoo. Next to the main slaughter arena is a restaurant where families dine on braised dog while watching domesticated animals disembowelled by lions. The zoo encourages visitors to 'fish' for lions using live chickens as bait. For just £2, visitors tie chickens onto bamboo rods and dangle them in front of the lions. Tourist buses have specially designed chutes down which you can push live chickens and watch as they are torn to shreds.

East of Badaling lies the equally horrific Qingdao zoo. Here, visitors can take part in China's latest craze: tortoise baiting. Legend has it that if you hit a tortoise on the head with a coin and make a wish, then your heart's desire will come true. When giggling tourists begin hurling coins at them, they desperately try to protect themselves by withdrawing into their shells. But Chinese zoo keepers have discovered a way round this: they wrap elastic bands around the animals' necks to stop them retracting their heads.

At Xiongsen Bear and Tiger Mountain Village near Guilin, live cows are fed to tigers to amuse crowds. During a recent visit, I watched in horror as a cow was stalked and caught. Its screams filled the air as it struggled to escape. A wild tiger would dispatch its prey within moments, but these beasts' natural killing skills have been blunted by years of living in cages. The tiger tried to kill, tearing at the cow's body, but it simply didn't know how. Eventually, the keepers broke up the contest and slaughtered the cow themselves, much to the disappointment of the crowd.

Read more: <http://www.dailymail.co.uk/news/article-506153/Animals-torn-pieces-lions-baying-crowds-spectator-sport-China-DOESNT-want-see.html#ixzz1FTTjdApd> (accessed 4 August 2011)

would upset you, and you are another human being, one with whom I have an understanding about how to behave' (Taylor, 2003). As such, animals are not afforded direct rights, only indirect rights, because they are not rational agents. Recall from Chapter 3 that, because contracts can only be agreed upon by rational agents, even the killing of another's animal is only a sin because it involves the destruction of someone else's property. The ox is not a subject but rather an object such as a cart or a shovel (Fudge, 2005).

Fishing for lions using chickens and throwing live goats over a wall (also to lions) represents the idea that animals are not afforded direct rights. There is an implicit contract developed between zoo management and tourists, and the 'deal' that is struck between both stakeholders is that tourists get the thrill of participating in the act of seeing live animals ripped to shreds by predators, and management secures a steady stream of visitors who find this act appealing. It would seem logical to assume therefore that the tourist has a direct right to participate in this activity, and any denial of such would be an infringement upon this right. The other side of the contractarianist perspective is derived from Kantian ethics. If one is found to take pleasure in cruelty towards animals, like the tourists and the zoo management in this scenario, this may be deemed wrong not because of the cruelty extended to the animals, but rather because of the damage to the reputation of the perpetrator. If people are prone to such cruelty with animals they may be judged to be capable of similar actions towards humans.

Conclusion

Frost (2011), in his edited compendium on zoos and tourism, cites the figure of 27 per cent of those in a study conducted in the 1990s who believed that zoos should be abolished altogether (based on Shackley, 1996). Given the date of this study, or the report on this study, it is not inconceivable to think that this figure might be higher 15 or more years after the fact. But somehow this does not enter into the mindset of tourism scholars who place more weight on the notion of 'everything as attraction'. Indeed, Frost comments later in his introduction to the volume that 'Our aim is to get people rethinking zoos and aquaria, questioning, reflecting and improving them and the way they operate' (Frost, 2011: 8). There is no hint towards the other option of perhaps abolishing zoos altogether – a call that is reoccurring from a number of scholars in fields outside of tourism, but which is tantamount to heresy in tourism. This is troubling because it obliterates any external way of thinking about the world – external in the sense that if it doesn't appear in our journals or books it really does not exist at all.

I should note that Frost has come across a similar finding in regards to zoos to what I have found with the much broader area of animal ethics: there are many studies conducted by scholars outside of our field on zoos and animal ethics, but very few of these have been conducted by tourism scholars. If you think that we have wandered far *off the path* in this regard, the analogy is probably more akin to *having just found the path*. This comment is substantiated by the fact that nonhuman animals represent a significant attraction base sought after by tourists, and presented by tourism providers, and this fact leads to the following conclusion: we have failed as a field in recognizing the inherent value of these animal others in both scholarly and applied aspects of our work.

5   Animals at work in the service of the tourism industry

Introduction

The previous chapter explored how animals taken off-site or away from their natural ecological context are used as 'workers' in the service of the tourism industry. These animals, like tigers and sea lions, are part of the entertainment package, which is the primary focus of our pleasure. In this chapter I investigate those species that have a long history as enablers or facilitators of our pleasure travel experiences *in situ*, or in the animal's natural habitat. Part of the novelty of the experience may in fact be the thrill or enjoyment of riding an animal like an elephant or a horse. Tourists may also take great pleasure in the opportunity to travel through wilderness environments powered by harness animals (as discussed in Chapter 1). Discussion of companion animals is included here as well because of the link to domestication, with a more specific focus on the increasing trend towards taking pets on vacation. The planning and organization of these trips is discussed along with some tourism industry responses to this emerging trend. Perhaps the biggest finding is the critical lack of tourism-related information here, with the suggestion that much more needs to be done in this area in tourism studies.

Domestication

Kaushik (1999) suggests that from the dawn of humanity animals have been used to work for their human masters in aiding agriculture production or to enhance social status. The better we could control these animals the more efficiently they could work for our specific purposes. This course of change is referred to as domestication, which can be defined as 'the keeping of animals in captivity by a human community that maintains total control over their breeding, organization of territory, and food supply' (Clutton-Brock, 2007). Domestication involves a blend of cultural and biological processes. Animals are removed from the wild species group and are bred for the purpose of creating a founder group, which changes by natural selection as well as by a process of artificial selection at the hands of economic, cultural, and aesthetic procedures. The breed is the end product of domestication (Clutton-Brock, 2007). While most view domestication as basically a one-way process, some theorists argue that emphasis should be placed not only on the behaviour of humans toward animals, but also of animals toward humans. None of this has been the subject of extensive scientific endeavour (see Bökönyi, 1989).

Anderson (1997) suggests that domestication is a process of heredity change control into new forms according to the interests of humans. Changes to animals occurred behaviourally, genetically, and morphologically. Control over animals also meant control over nature more broadly, as illustrated by Anderson: 'trees were cleared, crops were planted and commercialized, animals were raised as livestock, soils were fertilized and habitats for human settlement were made' (1997: 464). In this regard, other species were brought into the fold of human influence and activity ('*domus*'), improved under conditions and terms valued by humans, and stripped of their former wild state. Important in this process, beyond the economic advantages of having domesticated animals, Anderson adds, was the cultural and political significance of the act of domestication – the ability to refine other life forms as a marker for humanness. Practices such as domestication, therefore, were benchmarks or signifiers of culture itself, which in early European times meant to tend to or cultivate something, like plants or animals (see Williams, 1983). During the eighteenth century, it was argued that domestication was best for animals in that it afforded them the opportunity to increase in numbers and have a much more enjoyable life in the absence of predation (see Thomas, 1983).

Conventional wisdom posits that wolves were the first animals to be subjected to the process of domestication in their transformation into dogs some 15,000 years ago. Vilà *et al.* (1997), however, used mitochondrial DNA control sequences of 162 wolves and 140 dogs representing many breeds to confirm that the latter evolved from the former, but that instead of 15,000 years ago, the separation took place over 100,000 years ago (see also Savolainen *et al.*, 2002, and Leonard *et al.*, 2002).

In Western Asia, because of cultural and environmental conditions, domestication of a number of species was initiated for the purpose of building the economies of newly developed city-states like Babylon. Clutton-Brock (2007) writes that goats and sheep were domesticated from indigenous wild species around 9,000 years ago; cattle and pigs about 8,000 years ago; and horses were domesticated from the wild herds in north-central Asia approximately 6,000 years ago. The wild cat, *Felis silvestris*, so important in the lives of Egyptians, was domesticated about 8,000 years ago (Clutton-Brock, 2007), and revered and used in mummification rituals (millions of cats have been found in excavated necropolises).

Diamond illustrates that 14 big animals (over 100 pounds) were domesticated before the twentieth century, and these can be subdivided into major and minor categories. The major five include the cow, pig, sheep, goat, and horse. These are considered major because they became widespread and important around the world. The minor nine were those that became important to people in limited space and include the Arabian camel, Bactrian camel, llama/alpaca, donkey, reindeer, water buffalo, yak, banteng (wild cattle of South East Asia also known as Bali cattle), and gaur. Elephants are not included in this list because these animals can be tamed but not domesticated. The capture and taming of elephants appears to have started some 4,000 years ago in the Indus Valley and reached a peak during the Mauryan times (Sukumar, 2008). Their use in the armies of India was widespread, and peaked during the late fourth century BC when the army of Chandragupta Maurya included approximately 9,000 elephants. (See Rodrigue (2005) for a detailed analysis of the evolution of domestication in the Near East.)

Tuan (1984) argues that domestication is synonymous with dominance, or the mastery of one over another: the bringing of one into another's domain. Domesticated animals were managed and manipulated to be small for ease of control. In reference to the human–animal interface during the time of the Bible, Preece (2003) argues that there were 'injunctions to treat domesticated food animals with diligent care and concern. They will then be healthier and more productive animals, and will thereby improve the quality of human life. Caring for them is thus in part instrumental to human ends' (p. 4).

Domesticated animals provided advantages to human communities in many ways, including the provision of meat, milk, fertilizer, and by pulling ploughs, but also by furnishing humans with materials and skins. Leather and fibres such as wool were useful for clothes and other items like saddles, while bones were used for hunting and as domestic wares like pots and utensils (see Diamond, 2005). More specifically, Noske (1997) writes that there are two main themes emerging in the literature in reference to the evolution of domestication. The first is symbiosis, marked by mutual benefit but not necessarily equality between partners. In this theme animals and humans came in close contact via the provisioning of food, with animals proving effective at getting rid of the waste. Noske says that it was typically young animals that were taken in by human groups for such purposes and these animals made good pets for members of these human groups. Symbiosis also includes the use of animals as totems with religious functions and significance (e.g., cattle), as well as the use of cats to rid fields of mice and other pests. A second theme includes social parasitism on the part of humans in the day-to-day functioning of animal populations. A case in point includes the use of tame reindeer as bait while hunting wild reindeer. Another type of relation paving the way toward domestication is referred to as crop-robbing. In this case, the early agriculturalists may have come into conflict with certain species that would have fed on these crops, and controlling these species through domestication would have served a dual purpose. They could use the animals as labourers and feed them in a way that was not detrimental to their crop yield.

Knight (2005) argues that although domesticated animals have a utilitarian function as sources of food or as workers, the relationship between animal and farmer is said to be much deeper and can border on something like the relationships that humans have with each other. We should therefore not be focused on *outcome* (the slaughter of animals for meat) but rather on *process* involving nurturance, mutuality, care, co-existence, and intimacy that precede the use of animals for sustenance. If, as Knight (2005: 2) contends, a person has been defined as one with a 'living soul or self-conscious being' who has 'rights and duties under the law', then animals should qualify as persons because many philosophers argue for moral inclusion based on legal status.

The same relationship cannot be forged with prey animals, although indigenous people are said to have a certain level of reverence and trust between hunters and hunted, because prey animals demonstrate flight behaviour in the presence of humans. The nurturance or care that is possible in the domesticated animal–human bond is unattainable, and the interaction itself is episodic and unrepeated – basically one-off encounters. Domestication, therefore, is the divide between wild and tame that affords the opportunity to forge these more intimate relationships. This applies not only to livestock but also to companion animals.

In the case of domestication, Theodossopoulos (2005) discusses the care that Greek island farmers place into their livestock in the possession of a double occupational identity: farmers and small-scale tourism entrepreneurs. Although tourism represents the larger percentage of the income for these island dwellers, their attitude of self-sufficiency has situated small-scale farming as complementary to tourism. Visitors and other entrepreneurs discuss openly the care, reciprocity, and responsibility that farmers have toward their animals. By contrast, there is a one-way relationship between wild animals and the members of these communities, as these animals are persecuted with anger and resentment because of the damage that they inflict on domesticated animals or other aspects of the farm enterprise.

While Serpell (1996) has shown that animal owners may place the care of their animals over the care of fellow human beings, such behaviour is not restricted to domesticated animals. There is a critical tension among the Tamang of Nepal, because water buffalo are afforded higher standing and are worthy of greater degrees of care than dependents (like mothers).

Animals used for their strength

Draught animals

Draught animals are those animals that work for humans for subsistence and livelihood purposes. Draught animals include equines such as horses, donkeys, and mules, but many other animals such as camels and llamas, water buffalo, sheep, goats, elephants, pigs, and dogs are also included in this classification. Over 50 per cent of the world's population is dependent on draught animals, and the work that these animals perform would require approximately 20 million tons of petroleum at a value of US$6 billion (Kaushik, 1999). These animals operate on over 50 per cent of the world's cultivated lands (Wilson, 2003). Table 5.1 illustrates the changes in domesticated animal numbers ($\times 10^3$) over the past four decades in developed and developing countries. Working animals like elephants, horses, and cattle need approximately twice as much energy intake while working than when they are at rest (Pearson and Dijkman, 1994).

During medieval times in Europe, the Middle East, and Asia, travellers used mainly the ass, horse, mule, camel, elephant, ox, goat, and sheep to aid their

Table 5.1 Use of draught animals worldwide

Animals	Developed countries		Developing countries	
	1961	*1997*	*1961*	*1997*
Cattle	340,441	355,238	601,004	968,723
Buffaloes	917	674	87,509	152,405
Horses	26,576	17,018	35,505	45,112
Asses	3,735	1,427	33,226	41,968
Mules	2,069	287	8,409	14,414
Camels	2.9	0.4	12,651	19,041
Other camelids	–	–	5,295	5,450
Sheep	540,123	419,065	453,949	653,503
Goats	31,919	31,089	315,898	664,902
Pigs	235,273	293,150	170,836	645,794
Rabbits	79,573	243,436	21,441	165,088
Chickens	2,275,891	4,028,622	1,624,354	9,355,942
Ducks	30,238	58,712	164,687	676,899
Geese	14,228	15,398	22,413	192,163
Turkeys	119,201	206,067	11,773	2,636

Source: Kaushik, 1999: 146

movement. Ohler (2000) says that goats and sheep were useful for travel because they could be used as pack animals and could be killed as needed for food on long journeys. Ohler provides the following description of the characteristics of each:

> The ass: native to the warmer regions of Arabia and North Africa, and domesticated in the fourth century BC, this animal was mainly used as a pack animal and to ride. Its capacity was said to be approximately 150kg, and it was ridden by adults carrying limited baggage. The donkey was associated with humility and lowliness.
>
> The horse: Domesticated by the end of the third century BC, the horse was much stronger and faster than the donkey, and capable of pulling more than 1,000kg and carrying approximately 170kg. The pulling capacity of the horse was important in the transport of travellers by coach or wagon, which enabled humans to move quicker between places and also to carry perishable foods from the countryside to urban areas before they would spoil. Horses were far more expensive to keep than donkeys, equalling in cost (oats, hay, stables, etc.) as much as the traveller himself (room and board and other costs).
>
> The mule (progeny of he-ass and mare) and hinny (progeny of she-ass and stallion): Strong as a horse, placid and patient, with a longer working life than a horse, with great endurance in completing heavy tasks. Excellent animal for carrying loads, especially over uneven terrain.
>
> The camel: Possessed many excellent qualities to aid the traveller, including being well adapted to dry and hot climates, providing meat and milk, as well as dung for fires, and camelhair for the making of garments.

Plate 5.1 Camel riding at Naples Zoo, Florida

Domesticated in the second century BC, camels could travel upwards of 100 miles per day, and carry a load of 270kg as a mount or pack. The camel could go for a week without water, drawing on water and fat stored in its one or two humps, depending on species, and a day without food. A 2007 edition of the *Travel Trade Gazette* says that in Australia, these animals are worth 200 pounds to an abattoir, but 1,200 pounds as trained tourist animals. There is a thriving business in Alice Springs, where tourists can ride camels during the day and eat them at night.

The elephant: Slower than the ass, mule or horse, and used in India for travel and for warfare.

Oxen: Used most frequently as a draught animal, but much slower than other animals used for travel, with less endurance (up to 9 miles per day). Remained as a central driver of the agricultural economy in Europe up until the twentieth century.

The extent to which these animals were regarded by their human controllers may be found in the Theodosian Code – a compilation of the laws, edicts and decrees of the Roman Empire undertaken by Emperor Theodosius II between the years AD 429 and 438. It was published in the eastern half of the Roman Empire in 438, and introduced in the western Roman Empire in 439 by Emperor Valentinian III. The Code was developed for purposes of practical utility – to eliminate ambiguity and confusion in Roman law and to replace these with brevity and clarity – and to enforce Roman eastern ascendancy (i.e. the eastern Mediterranean) (Lee, 2002). The code covers enactments in reference to all facets of Roman life including religion, economics, politics, and culture (see Burford, 1960). Clutten-Brock (2007: 89) writes that a number of the decrees in the code are laid down for the protection of animals used in the service of work and commerce: 'Eight mules shall be yoked to a carriage, in the summer season, of course, but ten in winter. We judge that three mules are sufficient for a two-wheeled conveyance' (8.5.8. Title 31). Rules and principles were established for shared agricultural practices in Welsh Laws of Hywel Dda, dated from 945 CE.

Riding animals

Animals that are used for the purpose of riding include elephants, equines, and camels primarily, but may also include ostrich, yaks, and various other species. The focus of this brief section is on the elephant as an example of this type of riding experience. The Asian elephant has been used in warfare and industry (logging), but because of the fascination and perhaps reverence that tourists have toward the elephant, an important industry has emerged both in Asia and in Africa. Of course, elephant-back riding occurs in other areas around the world that keep elephants, but the elephant is not indigenous to these areas.

Duffy and Moore (2010) explain that elephant-back tourism in Thailand and Botswana is another way that tourism has neoliberalized nature – neoliberalism defined as 'a specific form of capitalism which is privatization, marketization, deregulation and various forms of re-regulation' (p. 744). Tourism is an industry that has benefited from neoliberal policies from the 1970s onward through decentralization and less 'big stick' government, along with greater confidence in markets. Socio-economic shifts in the most developed countries, in step with increasing wealth, have contributed to sustained growth in tourism as well as a series of new markets to diversify product offerings. Elephant-back tourism has evolved out of these patterns of growth and development. In Botswana, for example, elephants that once lived in zoos have been trained and repackaged (and re-regulated) as privately owned resources for use as elephant-back attractions. These animals are especially useful because they have a familiarity with people. The authors suggest that these trained elephants are completely neoliberalized because their sole purpose in the workforce, at least in Botswana, is to serve international tourism.

The use of elephants in these types of programmes and experiences has raised a number of concerns. The methods of training elephants used for labour, such as chaining the animal for weeks on end and depriving them of the ability to build social networks, are problematic. In response to these concerns the African Conservation Foundation has initiated the Elephant Management and Owners Association, with the mission 'to promote and monitor the conservation, protection and welfare of the African elephant' (African Conservation Foundation, 2011). Duffy and Moore (2010) argue that mahouts (persons who 'drive' an elephant) are not cruel to elephants because these animals are typically their sole source of income, forging a relationship that lasts for several decades. The authors argue that 'Elephant trekking in Botswana has created a completely different way in which their elephants can be valued since they can now be valued as a source of labour' (p. 761). They further suggest that captive elephants in Botswana 'only exist as safari elephants because there is a market demand for them …' (p. 761). One wonders what would be the fate of these animals if this market did not exist.

But while some call into question the usage of elephants for tourism purposes, others argue that it really boils down to a matter of degree. Kontogeorgopoulos (2009), for example, found that the use of elephants in semi-captive camps for tourism purposes was the least of many evils for these animals. Because the elephants have economic value in the form of tourism demand (elephant riding, painting, shows, etc.), their lives are not nearly as bad. Formerly used in transportation, logging, and for military purposes, tourism presents itself as the only legal option for those who own elephants, and is said to have higher welfare standards than these other uses. Despite any gains in well-being, elephants are prevented from establishing natural herds, are frequently injured, live in artificial environments, show signs of stress, are unable to reproduce, eat non-natural foods, and endure harsh training conditions through confinement and torture (of the young) into submission.

Although the focus is not on horses in this section, it should be noted that the use of horses for many purposes, both historical and contemporary, is indeed significant. A key attraction for visitors to many cities around the world is the opportunity to take in city sights via a horse-drawn wagon tour down cobblestone streets, harkening back to earlier times. The horse, like the elephant, was used to allow its owners to travel faster and further than others on foot, making the horse an ideal companion in times of war (Diamond, 2005). Horses have been used by humans in a number of ways including transportation, warfare, sport, art, and for riding in tourism (Helgadottir, 2006).

The Brooke is an international not-for-profit organization that is dedicated to the improvement of lives of working equines (horses, donkeys, and mules) through direct veterinary treatment and community programmes for animal health and well-being (The Brooke, 2011). This organization works in a number of countries, particularly less developed ones, recognizing that over 100 million equines work long hours under often extreme conditions of temperature and weather and must often endure deprivation of proper food and a sufficient amount of water for the purpose of transporting people (tourists) or carrying supplies to support the tourism industry. Many tourism workers use these animals for tourism as their sole source of income in sustaining their families. In lean times animals are deprived of proper food (or enough food) as these families struggle to survive. More specifically, these animals often suffer from a range of health conditions that compromise their well-being. These include lameness, sore feet and hoof deterioration, heat distress and dehydration, serious injuries, weakness and loss of body condition, body lesions, lip and mouth wounds, eye abnormalities, fear, depression, distress and pain, and other secondary conditions like parasites and tetanus (see Wells, 2009). Figure 5.1 illustrates how the Brooke initiates action on improving equine welfare now and for the long term.

What's the problem?	What does the Brooke do?
The bigger picture	
The important role of horses, donkeys and mules in the developing world is often unrecognized or underrated by the individuals, organizations and institutions that allocate resources and make policies, laws and practices.	We are working to increase national and international recognition of the role of working animals in poverty alleviation, livelihoods and the global economy.
Secondary risks	
Owners, users and carers of working animals make choices about the living and working conditions of their animals based on the demands affecting their own lives and livelihoods.	The Brooke helps communities to analyse how the welfare of their working animals is affected and how practical welfare improvements can be made within these livelihood contexts.
Primary risks	
The living/working conditions of an animal will have the greatest direct effect on its welfare. Without basic health care small wounds, infections or mild illnesses become bigger, more painful problems. Poor diet, inadequate housing, rough handling or a heavy workload can mean animals suffer pain, exhaustion or collapse.	We work with communities to make sure that the animal's living and working conditions are the best they can practically be and we provide direct treatment through our vet and animal health teams and/or build-up treatment alternatives in communities.
Animal factors	
An animal may be too young or old to work or too small or weak for certain types of work. Sometimes an animal may have been born with a recognisable physical problem, like a misshapen leg, that may make certain movements difficult or painful.	The Brooke discusses with owners what they look for when buying a working animal and the use of specially adapted tools such as 'Practice Gap Analysis', which help owners to match the strengths of their animal to the work it can reasonably do.

Figure 5.1 Improving equine welfare now and for the long term

Pack animals

Animals that are used as pack animals include equines, camels, llamas, and yaks. The following section focuses on the yak.

The male yak has a working life of between 10 and 12 years, yak crosses slightly longer, and can carry weights of between 50 and 100kg depending on the health of the animal, feed conditions, and time of year – summer has better grazing conditions enabling the carrying of heavier loads (Kharel *et al.*, 2008). This longevity and carrying ability, along with its ability to operate at high altitudes, has made the yak particularly attractive to those working in the tourism industry in Asia, where yaks are being bred in larger numbers as these animals earn twice the income of a human porter. Female cattle numbers are decreasing because these animals make less money. This has disrupted the gender base of the yak population, but also the number of livestock in general. Livestock numbers are decreasing (other breeds such as goats, sheep, and horses) in favour of the yak because of the monetary returns generated by the flow of tourists in the region (Sherpa and Kayastha, 2009). The foregoing has disrupted more traditional products including hard cheese, milk, and butter, which are now considered much less profitable than the use of yaks as pack animals and meat, both of which are in high demand from tourists. Yaks used for tourism purposes generate five times the amount of income – during only five months of the year – than traditional uses (Shaha, 2002). Tambe and Rawat (2009) found that in the Khangchendzonga National Park, a region of India, recommendations for the reduction of yaks have been proposed in an effort to support alternative livelihood initiatives in spreading the benefits of tourism. Relatively few yak herders earn substantial sums of money by maintaining large herds, while sheep and pack animal herders earn far less.

Gurung and Seeland (2009) found that 64 per cent of residents in Chomolhari, Bhutan, receive economic benefits from trekking tourism, and most of this income comes from hiring out yaks and ponies to tourists. Farmers are able to earn 100,000 Bhutanese ngultrum per year (US$2,028), which is far more than the per capita income of $834 in 2003. Gurung and Seeland also found that farmers with yaks and horses enter into informal agreements with tourism operators, thus securing long-term benefits. Farmers without animals are excluded from the business and unable to benefit from tourism in the region. Adams (1992) found that of 141 village households in Khumjung, Nepal, 43 of these used animal or human portering services to make money from the tourism industry. Nepal has seen increasing mobility of people to Kathmandu because of limited economic opportunities in peripheral areas. Yet in Khumjung, this process has been lessened by the tourism. Those who own lodges or stores, or who own, raise, and rent out pack animals stay because the money made provides upward social mobility not found in the city (Linnard, 2007).

Not unlike other species that work in the service of the tourism industry, the increasing use of the yak has associated environmental impacts. In the Ladakh region of the Indian Himalaya, Geneletti and Dawa (2009) found that overgrazing is the main environmental impact caused by pack animals, especially on slopes providing easy access to nearby grasses. The reliance on pack animals is significant. The authors found that trekking expeditions rely on about seven pack animals and five porters for every ten tourists. Similarly, pack animals in Nepal (yak and horse, mainly) are responsible for overgrazing and heavy erosion of paths and trails (see Brown *et al.*, 1997).

In the US, research has been much more intensive in regards to the impacts of packstock on wilderness areas. The use of horses for wilderness travel has a degree of impact many times that of regular hiking. In Montana, Cole and Spildie (1998) found that shod horses apply force in the order of 1,000 tonnes/m^2 on trail systems (see also Monz *et al.*, 2000). The percentage of vegetation cover (shrubs and herbs) after trampling was diminished by approximately 40 per cent for shrubs and 10 per cent for herbs from horse riding. The percentage cover remaining was much higher for llama and human hikers in the same environment. Even relatively small numbers of horses (between 20 and 30) can contribute to excessive soil compaction, soil erosion, and vegetation changes in alpine environments (Harris, 1993). An investigation of 108 wilderness areas found significant variance in regards to packstock limits (Monz *et al.*, 2000). Limits ranged from 5 to 35, with a median of 15 and mode of 25. The authors conclude by suggesting that in light of the impacts that horses have on soil and vegetation ecology, these numbers are too high and should be lowered to numbers lower than hikers. Even at low intensities (a few hours per year) pack animals cause decreases in productivity. Over a four-year period shorthair sedge meadow productivity decreased by 18 per cent, Brewer's reed grass meadow by 17 per cent, and tufted hairgrass meadow by 22 per cent (Cole *et al.*, 2004).

Harness animals

Animals that are harnessed in the service of the tourism industry include dogs (the focus of the following section), equines, and reindeer, and there are many examples that demonstrate how product offerings have broadened in reference to these types of experiences. In Lapland, for example, those who farm reindeer have experienced a tremendous increase in visitation in recent years. Tied to this is the increase in interest in reindeer safaris, where tourists are pulled down trails while sitting in sleighs.

The bond between human and dog is likely the most complex of any human–animal relationship, with a rich and varied 'contact zone' that ranges from the symbolic to the utilitarian and the playful (Madden, 2010). While the playful (companionship) aspect will be explored later in the book, the utilitarian role assumed by dogs will be discussed here as well as briefly in the following section.

Dog sledding is an important outdoor activity in many countries including the USA, Canada, and many of the Nordic countries (see Mehmetoglu, 2005, who studied dog sledding as a form of nature-based tourism; see also Chapter 1). Dogs and dog sledding have been an important part of traditional life in the Arctic for about 1,000 years as the archaeological record supports (Morey and Aaris-Sørensen, 2002). In Canada it is an activity undertaken for pleasure but also to help emphasize the philosophical underpinnings of outdoor adventure education (Henderson and Potter, 2001). It has also been used as a form of wilderness family therapy, whereby family members use sledding, with the inherent risk and stress-related components of this activity, to deepen family self-knowledge, self-esteem, and intimacy (Mason, 1987).

Furthermore, dog sledding is based on contrasting values (Kemp, 1999). Although the sport is intensely competitive, emphasizing individualism, fame, and reward, it is also found to be cooperative. In her analysis of the Beargrease sled race, Kemp observes that the cooperative side often comes to the fore as competitors frequently sacrifice their position to help others and treat their dogs well. There is a tradition in this race that the mushers who honour these values are given the highest round of applause at the concluding banquet. The feeling is that, like rodeo, there are external conditions that weigh heavily on the success of the participant, like animals, weather, and temperature – elements outside the realm of control – and it is the shared connection between competitor and the elements where this cooperation initiates. Kemp likens this to a state of *communitas*, where the emergence of an unconventional moral order (i.e., cooperation and kinship) emerges to suppress the dominant values of competition, fame, and fortune.

The more conventional moral order in dog sledding is represented in Alaska's Iditarod. The world's longest and most grueling sled dog event, it is a 1,151-mile race along the Iditarod Trail (a National Historic Trail) from Willow to Nome that takes between 8 and 14 days. This race, started in 1973 to test the abilities of mushers and dog teams, is similar in distance to a race from New York City to Miami, Florida, and has evolved into a highly competitive event with a total purse in 2010 of over US$500,000. Dogs run about 125 miles per day, six hours at a time, and with little sleep, losing ten pounds over the course of the event. The demands of the race for both musher and dog are extreme, and while mushers can decide if they want to participate, the dogs cannot.

The Sled Dog Action Coalition has a mandate of 'improving the lives of Iditarod sled dogs and providing truthful information about their treatment'. Although there are no complete records of dog deaths, especially from the early years, an unofficial statistic for deaths is 142. The Iditarod committee is proud to announce, however, that no humans have died while competing in this race. The Coalition web site (www.helpsleddogs.org) shows pictures of a dog being dragged along the ice while the other dogs run, and while the musher is asleep.

Media reports are persistent in casting light on the abuses that have continued to take place over the years. George Diaz (2000) of the *Orlando Sentinel*, for example, wrote that dogs have been 'strangled in towlines, gouged by sleds, suffered liver injury, heart failure, pneumonia and "external myopathy", a condition in which a dog's muscles and organs deteriorate during extreme or prolonged exercise'. Diaz found that dogs were often kept in unsupervised kennels and shot in the head if they showed signs that they could not keep an acceptable pace. Saraceno (2004), citing a study in the *American Journal of Respiratory and Critical Care Medicine*, wrote that dogs suffer from abnormal accumulations of mucus in their lower air passageways, fluid on the lungs, bleeding stomach ulcers, cramping, dislocations, fractures, tendon and muscle tears, tendonitis, dehydration, hypothermia, raw paws, penile frostbite, and viral infections (see Davis *et al.*, 2002). In 2009, six dogs died, two with excessive fluid on the lungs (Viegas, 2009). The reason the 'Ihurtadog' persists, Saraceno adds, is because of corporate greed. Companies like Coca-Cola, Chevron, ExxonMobil, and Wells Fargo, benefit from their association with the event. Furthermore, the economic impact from tourism to cities like Anchorage is huge. In 2010, Hopkins reports, no dogs died in the Iditarod race, which is the only time that this has ever happened (see Box 5.1).

The IditArod is not the only event where dog sledding practices have come into question. The Associated Press (2005), following from an article by the *Aspen*

Daily News, reported that in Snowmass Village, Colorado, the Krabloonik kennel houses approximately 250 sled dogs, and over a period of nine years has shot upwards of 35 dogs for not performing well in their efforts to pull tourists around the backcountry, and to cull the herd. Many of the dogs killed were young and healthy, and the remains were buried in a pit near the kennel.

Box 5.1 Iditarod Rules, 2009

Rule 42 – Expired Dog

All dog deaths are regrettable, but there are some that may be considered unpreventable.

Any dog that expires on the trail must be taken by the musher to a checkpoint. The musher may transport the dog to either the checkpoint just passed, or the upcoming checkpoint. An expired dog report must be completed by the musher and presented to a race official along with the dog.

All dog deaths will be treated as a priority, with every effort being made to determine the cause of death in a thorough and reliable manner.

- The race marshal or his/her appointed judges, will determine whether the musher should continue or be disqualified.
- The chief veterinarian will cause a necropsy to be carried out by a board certified pathologist at the earliest opportunity and shall make every attempt to determine the cause of death.
- If a board certified pathologist is not available to perform the necropsy within the time frame to preserve the tissues appropriately (as determined by the race marshal), the gross necropsy and tissue collection will be performed by a trail veterinarian following the guidelines in the *Musher and Veterinary Handbook*.
- These tissues will then be examined by a board certified pathologist.

A musher will remain at the initial reporting checkpoint for up to, but no longer than, eight hours to commence the investigation. The musher and or his/her representative has the option to be present during the trail evaluation and necropsy. This period is not to be used as a penalty. A musher will also make him/herself available at all future checkpoints to assist in the investigation. The race marshal or his/her appointed judges may release a musher before the eight hours have expired if the judge is satisfied that the musher is no longer needed to further the investigation. Dog deaths resulting in disqualification are:

- Signs of cruel, inhumane or abusive treatment.
- Cause of death is heat stress, hyperthermia.
- A musher will be disqualified if he/she had been advised in writing by a race veterinarian or judge to drop the dog at a previous checkpoint, but

opted not to do so, unless the cause of death is clearly unrelated to this written recommendation.

The musher will not be penalized and may continue the race if:

- Cause of death cannot be determined.
- The cause of death is due to a circumstance, nature of trail, or force beyond the control of the musher.
- Cause of death is from some unpreventable or previously undiagnosed medical condition.

It is the policy of the ITC to report a dog death to the public by:

- The race marshal shall immediately issue a press release to members of the media identifying the dog's death.
- Immediately following the gross necropsy, the race marshal will notify the musher of the results and will issue a press release containing the findings and the circumstances of the death.

< http://www.iditarod.com/pdfs/2009/2009RulesFinal.pdf>, accessed 25 February 2011

Plate 5.2 Shanghai monkey working the streets for money

Animals used for their senses

Animals have provided many services for human beings and these are of the direct and indirect variety. Indirect include the ecological services that animals provide for the health and well-being of the planet (e.g., bee pollination), and direct include the work that animals do for humans – the focus of this chapter. The work that animals perform for humans through the use of their senses provides further opportunity to highlight the impressiveness of the many breeds of dog and the specialized nature of their various capabilities. John Caius's influential work entitled *Of Englishe Dogges* (1576) illustrates the rich diversity of dog capabilities through his taxonomy based on the type of work dogs perform. The three main categories of English dog include: 'A gentle kinde, seruing the game; A homely kind, apt for sundry necessary vses; A currishe kinde, meete for many toyes' (p. 2). Further sectioning includes: (1) hunting dogs like bloodhounds, greyhounds, terriers, stealers, and tumblers; (2) gentle dogs securing the hawk (spaniels, setters, and fishers); (3) delicate, neat, and pretty dogs (spaniel gentle); (4) dogs of a course kind for many uses (shepherds); and (5) dogs of the mongrel and rascal sort (bitch and a wolf). Nobler dogs were associated with the hunt, while courser dogs provided more menial services like guarding, herding, or pulling (Boehrer, 2007). Dogs – and of course the people who owned them – were also given higher standing based on the type of activity the animal was bred for (Boehrer, 2007).

The ability of dogs to understand human postural language is a function of the social nature of the dog's progenitor – the wolf – which is one of the most highly communal species in the animal kingdom. The social learning capacity of dogs has been refined in the domestication process through the selection of some social-cognitive skills that enable dogs to communicate well with man in preferential ways (Hare *et al.*, 2002). This has been examined from a sociological standpoint by Arluke and Sanders (1996), who find that communication with a dog is quite similar to communication with a small child. This entails the ability to speak for the nonhuman animal through an empathetic determination of feelings, preferences, and thoughts. In essence, this is tantamount to incorporating one's dog into a language community – a demonstration of a special type of intimacy such that the owner knows what is on the mind of the dog, which helps further define and enrich the relationship. Caring for animals is not only a physiological requirement, but may broadcast itself into the psychological realm at such a deep level.

Dogs make ideal working companions because of their capacity for communication, ease in training, and their highly refined senses. Dogs have thus been trained for a number of important roles in human society including guide, guard, patrol, service, assistance, therapy, those that search for explosives, drugs, plants or other animals, and those that search for and rescue people in recreation and in disasters (Olson, 2002; see also Hall *et al.*, 2004).

The Swiss Alpine Club took over the training and use of dogs (German shepherds) to search for victims in avalanche sites in the 1940s, according to Fogle (1988). Before that St Bernards were used by the Swiss army and before that by monks of the Great St Bernard Pass in the western Alps between Switzerland and Italy as early as the eighteenth century to search for and rescue lost travellers. The

---

Box 5.2 The first rescue dogs

The history of the rescue dog begins in the St Bernard Pass, a route in the Alps between Italy and Switzerland. It is named after the Augustine monk St Bernard de Menthon, who founded a hospice and monastery there sometime between 980 and 1050. The hospice has remained in operation ever since, and sometime between 1660 and 1670 the monks received their first dogs. They were the St Bernard dogs of today, only smaller and directly descended from the Asiatic mastiffs from Rome. While originally used as guard dogs, they were quickly switched to a search-and-rescue function.

At the turn of the eighteenth century, the monks of St Bernard Pass were regularly training St Bernards to rescue travellers who were lost in the pass. Marroniers, who were servants that accompanied people travelling through the pass, often brought dogs along with them and found their great sense of smell could help them find people trapped under snow a huge help. These marroniers used the rescue dogs often to save many lives in the pass. Between 1790 and 1810, more than 250,000 of Napoleon's troops trekked through St Bernard's Pass. Not one lost his life, and many of the soldiers told of how they were saved by rescue dogs, who dug them up when they were trapped under snow and laid on them to warm them until help came. Rescue dogs would work here for over 150 years.

Read more: 'The history of rescue dogs', eHow.com, <http://www.ehow.com/about_5384924_history-rescue-dogs.html#ixzz1EuMe4ddl>, accessed 4 August 2011

---

breeding stock was diminished and the dogs were later crossed with Newfoundland dogs, giving the breed a heavier coat but rendering them less useful for search and rescue because their coats would freeze and weigh them down. Fogle (1988) says the German shepherds were ideal because they were effective at working in close proximity to their trainers (see Box 5.2).

The International Commission for Alpine Rescue (ICAR) was formed in 1948 from representatives of the alpine countries of Europe. At present ICAR encompasses 33 organizations from 22 different countries, for the purpose of coordinating materials, techniques, strategies, and knowledge in regards to alpine rescue operations. Etter *et al.* (2005) found that over a 20-year period from 1983 to 2003, there were 138 avalanche fatalities, on average, per year in these countries. ICAR pioneered the use of dogs early in its development, and the first rescue of a living victim by a dog took place in 1954. This method is still an essential strategy used in optimizing the chances for successful search and rescue.

In a study of volunteer search and rescue (SAR) teams in the USA, Denver *et al.* (2007) found that there were 1,150 teams in total, ranging from one team in a state to 79 in California alone. The most frequently cited capability of these teams was their canine unit. One-third (33 per cent) of these teams had canine units because dogs could be used in just about any emergency, from wilderness missions and avalanches to collapsed buildings in urban environments. Four hundred dogs were used in the immediate wake of the September 11 terrorist attacks for search and rescue operations, to find the living and dead, but also to provide comfort to people who had been traumatized by the event (Hall *et al.*, 2004).

Dogs have also been used in wildlife management to detect the scat of grizzly and black bears over large parcels of land. This method was used as a management tool in order to better understand the range and behaviour of bears but also their stress, gender, and reproductive activity. Bears were found in areas of the region where there was most food abundance, but also where there was a high level of poaching (Wasser *et al.*, 2004).

Box 5.3 German airports use honeybees to sniff out air quality

By Boonsri Dickinson
1 July 2010

If you are at an airport in Germany and see honeybees flying around, don't worry. The bees have been enlisted as 'biodetectives' to inspect air pollution.

Airplanes, taxi, bus, and car emissions leave a chemical signature in the air, but also leave their mark on nearby plants. If honeybees are exposed to the tainted plants, then pollutants can eventually end up in the honey.

After 200,000 bees were deployed in June at Düsseldorf International Airport, scientists tested the honey samples for pollutants normally found in the air such as hydrocarbons. The scientists compared those samples with honey produced away from industry. The good news? The samples were similar.

It's the ultra-fine particles in air that are most worrisome – the small particles clog your arteries and the plaque build-up makes you more susceptible to a heart attack and stroke. Scientists know that people who live near highways have health risks associated with car emissions, but have not really studied what the health risk is for people living near airports.

Using honey to indicate air pollution is certainly a new way of monitoring air quality, *New York Times* reports.

Assessing environmental health using bees as 'terrestrial bioindicators' is a fairly new undertaking, said Jamie Ellis, assistant professor of entomology at the Honey Bee Research and Extension Laboratory, University of Florida in Gainesville. 'We all believe it can be done, but translating the results into real-world solutions or answers may be a little premature.' Still, similar work with insects to gauge water quality has long been successful.

Seven German airports also use the bees to monitor air pollution. Although if other airports around the world begin to use bees too, they might have trouble recruiting the ever disappearing honeybees.

<http://www.smartplanet.com/technology/blog/science-scope/german-airports-use-honeybees-to-sniff-out-air-quality/2688/>, accessed 12 April 2011.

Companion animals and tourism

Serpell (1989) argues that the keeping of pets or companion animals is thought to be a middle-class, Western expression of material affluence and sentimentality. The fact is that indigenous societies have shown a predisposition toward keeping pets for non-utilitarian purposes. Australian Aborigines kept dingoes, wallabies, possums, and other animals as companion animals; in South East Asia, indigenous people kept dogs, cats, pigs, monkeys, and other animals; while in North America, aboriginal people kept moose, deer, bison, wolves, raccoons, and many other animals (Serpell, 1989). In these cases, pets are 'raised, suckled if necessary, and cherished like children. They are protected, named, and cared for during life and, after death, they are often mourned' (p. 14).

Pet keeping is said to be a rather recent enterprise for the masses. Ritvo (2008) argues that, although certain members of the upper class, such as church leaders and members of the aristocracy, have possessed pets for hundreds of years, it is only in the last two centuries that the practice has thrived. Ritvo's research suggests that up until such time those who owned pets were held in low esteem by their contemporaries and ridiculed. Hogarth's paintings seem to point to this fact as pet animals like dogs and cats are placed in positions that represent vulgarity, bestiality, and subversion (Ritvo, 2008; see Chapter 2). During medieval times, because of the masculine traits tied to hunting, the ownership of dogs was a male domain, whereas the possession of dogs as pets was largely a feminine practice (Resl, 2007).

Carnivores like cats and dogs were a good choice as a companion because at the time of the onset of the agricultural revolution they served good utilitarian purposes (Kruuk, 2002). Cats catch mice and other rodents, while dogs take on a number of tasks according to how they are bred (for hunting, protecting sheep, finding lost persons, pulling sleds, and so on). They are also easily trained, and synchronize their daily patterns according to ours, with benefits uniformly outweighing costs (Bryant, 1990), including the amount of time they are active, which Kruuk (2002) says is between four and six hours. Any longer, and they would need constant surveillance and attention. Herzog (2002) offers a very different perspective in arguing that a theory exists in regards to the dog as parasite. Dogs take advantage of our willingness to nurture others, especially children, as a selective benefit in ensuring their own comfort, fitness, and survival.

Thomas (1983) argues that urbanization played an important role in a new type of sensitivity to animals – one that was driven by a non-utilitarian relationship between human and animal in the form of pet keeping. The practice helped to fix in the mind's eye the human complement that animals in fact had personalities, which helped to open the door for widening the circle of morality to include animal others. Pet keeping

> encouraged the middle classes to form optimistic conclusions about animals' intelligence; it gave rise to innumerable anecdotes about animal sagacity; it stimulated the notion that animals could have character and individual

personality; and it created the psychological foundation for the view that some animals at least were entitled to moral consideration.

(Thomas, 1983: 119)

Rollin (2005), in his work on partiality and animal ethics, spends considerable time discussing the bond between pet owners and their companions. To be sure, this is a relationship based on the giving of love and the receiving of love and friendship, which makes the relationship a reciprocal one. This bond may be defined as 'the mutually beneficial and dynamic relationship between people and other animals that is influenced by behaviours essential to the health and well-being of both' (Olson, 2002: 353), and it explains why we are so willing to keep companion animals.

The case of so many pets requires an industry that by all accounts is huge, encompassing trade in pets, pet food, equipment, veterinarian care, pet shows, grooming, literature and media, kennels, graveyards, insurance, and so on (Kruuk, 2002). There are more than 200 million domestic cats worldwide, for example, and in many countries the cat is the most populous companion animal (Bernstein, 2005). Serpell (1989) writes that about half of all households in Britain have at least one pet, with per capita pet ownership in some other western countries including France and the US being higher. Marx *et al.* (1988) found that 60 per cent of households in the US contain pets, and that 99 per cent of these owners consider their pet to be a member of the family (Voith, 1985; American Veterinary Medical Association, 2003). The American Veterinary Medical Association in 2007 provided the estimates on US companion animal ownership shown in Table 5.2.

Table 5.2 illustrates that dogs and cats are the companion animals owned most, by a large margin, over birds and horses. While more households own dogs over cats, the average number of cats (2.2) per household is larger than the 1.7 for dogs. Dog owners reported taking their pet to the veterinarian more than cat owners, and spending more per visit than on cats, birds, and even horses. In the late 1990s, there were approximately 56,000 veterinarians in the US, half of which focused solely on companion animals (Kaushik, 1999).

Table 5.2 Companion animals owned in US population, 2007 (cost in US$)

	Dogs	*Cats*	*Birds*	*Horses*
Percent of households owning (%)	37.2	32.4	3.9	1.8
No. of households owning (million)	43.0	37.5	4.5	2.1
Ave. number owned/house	1.7	2.2	2.5	3.5
Total number in the US (million)	72.1	81.7	11.2	7.3
Vet. visits per household/year	2.6	1.7	0.3	2.2
Vet. expenditure/animal (mean)	200	81	9	92

Source: American Veterinary Medical Association, <http://www.avma.org/reference/marketstats/ownership.asp>, accessed 29 September 2010.

It has often been suggested that 'we are what we eat'. Theorists in consumer behaviour might adapt this adage in suggesting that 'we are what we possess', and pets are just as much commodities as other goods, like cars or clothes, which people use to build and affirm their identities (Mullin, 1999). This type of human behaviour has been explained by Belk (1988) as the extended self theory, and it is based on the premise that the things we possess are very much a reflection of who we see ourselves as, such that there is an intricate relationship between what we own and our sense of self. By owning pets (possession) we might argue that these individuals see themselves as both social and nurturing. It has been the case, however, that the ownership of animals serves other utilitarian ends. The American Football quarterback Michael Vick's sentencing for the establishment of a dog-fighting ring at his house in Atlanta is a case in point. The extended-self theory might provide inroads to some rather negative characteristics of individuals who choose to use animals in such a damaging capacity.

The possession of animals like apes has as much to do with domination, control and power. Exotic pets, a $20 billion per year trade contributing to the endangered status of 130 primate species alone (Sorenson, 2009), fulfil fantasies and provide the owner with power and status over others who do not own similar creatures. The unfortunate consequence of this is that abuse towards the animal usually follows when it expresses its animal nature in ways that do not conform to our expectations. Owners may beat the animal, chain it up, remove teeth, isolate it, or use other measures in bringing the animal under control. Other measures include selling the animal to a zoo, giving it away to others, or releasing the animal into the wild. Such has been the case in Florida, where non-native python species have been released, left to reproduce and are now having a significant impact on the balance of nature there.

The bond between pet owners and their companions is said to be a relationship based on the giving of love and the receiving of love and friendship, which makes the relationship a reciprocal one (Rollin, 2005). But it has also been referred to as a type of 'kindness toward only a few favored animals' (Kete, 2007: 15), and exists in a world where other animals are used for work and food. We say that we are animal lovers but we really just love our pets (Saloña Bordas, 2004). This means that we can show love and compassion for those animals that we have chosen to be close with, whilst at the same time using and consuming other animals as a matter of daily practice and process. Oftentimes the pets we consider as our children are actually de-animalized – stripped of their identity and made to be something symbolic to us. Thus we see an element of fantasy in the pet-keeping culture. This has impelled Scruton (2002) to observe that in regards to animal companions, 'duties spread out with diminishing force across the surrounding sea of need' (p. 544), his way of saying we have a higher degree of responsibility to those things that are ours, like pets and children, than to other entities like wild animals and other peoples' children.

This element of responsibility has been the focus of much attention from Burgess-Jackson (1998), who advances a forceful argument emphasizing two types of responsibility in the care of companion animals. The first is meta-responsibility, which is the overarching responsibility we as humans have for the discharge of responsibilities for these nonhuman others. That is, 'The objects of meta-responsibility are themselves responsibilities' (Burgess-Jackson, 1998: 179). The second form of responsibility is referred to as primary responsibility, and this includes taking care of the needs (e.g., fresh water, shelter, good nutrition, medical care, and exercise) of animals. While the latter form of responsibility is quite easy to imagine, the former demands a bit more discussion.

Burgess-Jackson uses two examples to describe the nature of the meta-responsibility that humans have toward nonhuman companions, the first of which deals with reproduction. If one's dog reproduces, or is allowed to reproduce, one must be prepared to take care of the needs of the resultant puppies. The meta-responsibility here is to prevent this if one cannot take primary responsibility for the puppies. In this way both meta-responsibility and primary responsibility are mutually reinforcing. In the second example, Burgess-Jackson argues that taking in more animals than one can adequately care for (primary responsibility) is an example of meta-irresponsibility because one cannot assume primary responsibility for the needs of all the others collectively.

The love and care that we extend to our companions has reciprocal therapeutic benefits, as alluded to above, and this has been the topic of much recent study leading to a broad range of interdisciplinary studies referred to as animal-assisted therapies. There is now wide documentation about the social, psychological, and physiological benefits that have been stimulated by the keeping of animals (Brodie and Biley, 1999; see also Jorgenson, 1997), which helps to substantiate the belief that we are genetically predisposed to have a bond with other organisms, as we have discussed earlier in reference to Wilson's biophilia hypothesis. For example, Horowitz (2008) reports that companion pet interaction lowers blood pressure and heart rate and reduces anxiety. Using attachment theory, several authors (including Sable, 1995) argue that, just as the bond between mother and child has security and protection functions, so too does the relationship between animal and human that leads to the reduction of stress throughout the life cycle. We derive these benefits through pleasurable activity, facilitation of exercise, play and laughter, care for the other, feelings of security, a comfort to touch, and a pleasure to watch (Katcher and Friedmann, 1980).

While there is substantive social, psychological, and health work on the benefits derived from the interaction with companion animals, there is decidedly less physiological research that examines the human–animal bond. This dearth of knowledge changed in an innovative study designed by Odendaal and Meintjes (2002), who investigated neurophysiological changes in both humans (n = 18) and dogs (n = 18) based on a period of positive interaction. Pre- and post-test analyses included the measurement of blood pressure and blood chemistry with a focus on plasma β-endorphin, oxytocin, and dopamine. Results indicated decreases in blood pressure of both humans and dogs after positive interactions, as well as increases in levels of plasma β-endorphin, oxytocin and dopamine. Plasma β-endorphin is important in learning and memory, as well as blood pressure regulation and feeding behaviour. The hormone oxytocin is linked to intimate bonding and affiliative, joyous behaviours. Dopamine, on the other hand, is linked to pleasurable sensations that are derived from certain experiences and interactions (see Fennell, 2009 in a tourism context). Odendaal and Meintjes conclude by suggesting that interaction between both species may be described as a social symbiotic relationship, with dogs acting as prototypical companions that also have their needs met by humans. Subsequent work by Nagasawa *et al.* (2009) found that a dog's gaze at its owner increases urinary oxytocin concentrations in the latter, and that a longer duration gaze from the dog directed toward its owner brings forth higher concentrations of oxytocin than shorter duration gazes. These findings help to explain why dogs and humans demonstrate attachment behaviours. (See Verga and Michelazzi (2009) for a description of behavioural and physiological measures of reduced welfare in pets due to poor management and unsatisfactory environmental conditions.)

While the term pet therapy was used in the past, its generic basis has been replaced by more specific terms as the body of theoretical and applied knowledge in this area has expanded. Animal Assisted Activity (AAA), Animal Assisted Therapy (AAT), and Animal Assisted Education (AAE) all describe targeted interventions with specific therapeutic plans in mind (Fine, 2002) for the purpose of inducing physical, social, emotional, and cognitive improvements in humans (Corson and Corson, 1981).

Companion animals and travel

Figures suggest that there are over 30 million people worldwide who travel with their pets (Bailey Knows Travel, 2004), and they do so for a number of reasons (Leggat and Speare, 2000). The primary reason, and the one closest to the theme of this book, is for emotional reasons. The pet is considered an important part of the family and therefore is afforded the same type of benefits as other members of the family. Research confirms that having pets around reduces stress, so there is the belief on the part of the tourist that including the pet on a trip reduces stress and anxiety in humans, but also perhaps that stress may be reduced in the animal if it is not left at home (i.e., the animal misses or pines after its owners in their absence). There are also economic reasons for taking one's pet on a trip. In such cases, there is the elimination of boarding or kennel costs, which can be substantial. Pedigree pets may also be taken on trips for genetic reasons. The animal may be used to contribute to the gene pool in a different location, or females may need to travel in order to be impregnated. Pets may also need specialist veterinary care, which may not be available at home. These pets represent a high-risk group among travelling pets and so precautions need to be exercised in ensuring the well-being of the animal in transit.

There is evidence pointing to an increasing prevalence of parasitic diseases in pets because of travel to endemic areas (Irwin, 2002). The problem is the introduction of exotic diseases into the origin country and associated risks of passing these on to vulnerable populations, including children, the elderly, and those with compromised immune systems. Veterinarians are pressed to diagnose these diseases, and there is a larger public health risk of the introduction of these agents into new locations. The main problem, according to Irwin, is with tick-borne pathogens, which include a broad base of bacteria, viruses, and parasites. Canine babesiosis, canine hepatozoonosis, and canine ehrlichiosis appear to be most prevalent in dogs, in addition to Leishmaniasis. Giardia, Neosporosis and Dirofilariasis (canine heartworm) have also been found in companion animals. In a study of dogs accompanying their German owners to countries of the Mediterranean, for example, Menn *et al.* (2010) found that there was a significant risk of the dog acquiring an arthropod-borne disease. The recommendation is that pet owners seek advice from a veterinarian prior to travel, especially as some pathogens like *Leishmania infantum* are non-endemic in Germany.

Proper pet documentation is essential in streamlining the process of taking an animal on a plane, especially to countries with strict regulations. The International Air Transport Association (IATA) maintains regulations on the size of containers that hold pets, and owners should be familiar with the quarantine requirements, which may be published by animal clinics or embassies. Furthermore, a record of vaccinations should be taken along on the trip, which may be included in a 'pet passport', including a colour photograph of the pet, species, breed description, markings, registration number, and information on the owner, as detailed by Leggat and Speare (2000). The owner should also consider bringing along a travel veterinary kit in destinations that may not have the same level of service found at home. Aspects of this kit can be found in Table 5.3. In some regions, authorities have relaxed quarantine laws that require animals to be kept for extended periods of time due to public and political pressures (Irwin, 2002). The introduction of the pet passport has been helpful in streamlining the process of movement between regions.

In addition to the market of people who travel with their companion animals for leisure purposes, some have chosen to travel for the purpose of experiencing and helping animals in need. An industry example of each is included below. A main finding here is that, given the increasing significance of travelling with one's own pet, this remains an area that is vastly underrepresented in the tourism literature.

The travel company Bailey Knows Travel ('Why leave your best friend home?') recognizes that many pet owners have an interest in comfortably travelling with their pets. This company specializes in those looking for a one-of-a-kind travel experience (Bailey Knows Travel, 2004). Their 'Dog Adventures' product includes the following options: walking tours in historic cities; skijoring in the snow;

Table 5.3 The travel veterinary kit

Pet's usual medications: heartworm pills, oral antiflea drugs, drugs for other diseases.
Rectal thermometer.
Eye ointment.
Broad spectrum antibiotics.
Flagyl (eliminates parasites like *Giardia*).
Insecticidal treatment for fleas, ticks, or lice.
Broad spectrum anthelmintic treatment (drugs that expel parasitic worms).

mountain hikes; off-leash beaches and areas for dogs to romp; pet-friendly establishments; pet psychics; workshops on alternative holistic pet care; massages (both people and dogs); private breakfasts and meals where your pups can attend along with you; seminars on pet nutrition and training techniques; fly ball, agility courses, grooming; and doga (yoga for both you and your dog). Bailey Knows Travel is a supporter of Companion Air, the world's first pet-specific airline, providing 'specialized transportation to pet lovers who view their pets as family members rather than simply animals' (Companion Air, 2011). At the time of press, Companion Air had not booked their first flight.

Your Time Travels is a travel company that is designed specifically for animal lovers. The president of the company, Liz Longacre, feels there is a market for people who are motivated to volunteer with animal welfare projects and at the same time enjoy countries where volunteer help is needed. She feels that tourists will feel alive, engaged, and inspired about the sorts of travel experiences that aid animals who are in desperate need of help. Your Time Travels offers a spectrum of different opportunities including safaris, work at animal sanctuaries, and work at farm sanctuaries, along with vegan and vegetarian trips. The company also provides information on specific animal-friendly products that can be used while on vacation and at home (Box 5.4).

Finally, The Working Traveller is a supplement to the Overseas Job Centre and provides information on working and travelling throughout the world. In 2010 they posted a story on 12 cheap ways to volunteer with animals (Working Traveller, 2010). These are:

- Bats: The Tolga Bat Hospital, Australia, <http://www.tolgabathospital.org>
- Bears: American Bear Association, USA, <www.americanbear.org>
- Birds: RSPB, UK, <www.rspb.org.uk>
- Cats: Torre Argentina Cat Sanctuary, Italy, <www.romancats.com>
- Chinchillas: Save the Wild Chinchillas, Chile, <www.wildchinchillas.org>
- Dogs: Saga Humane Society, Belize, <www.sagahumanesociety.org>
- Farm Animals: Farm Sanctuary Internships, USA, <www.farmsanctuary.org>
- Horses: Sabine Smiling Horses, Costa Rica, <www.horseback-riding-tour.com>
- Insects: Monteverde Butterfly Garden, Costa Rica, <www.monteverdebutterflygarden.com>
- Monkeys: The Monkey Sanctuary, UK, <www.monkeysanctuary.org>
- Turtles: Proyecto Karumbe, Uruguay, <www.karumbe.org>
- Wolves: Wolf Park, USA, <www.wolfpark.org>

Zoophilia

Stephanie Feldstein of Change.org reports on a very different type of animal companionship in the tourism industry: bestiality tourism. This is a type of tourism where animals on farms in the US are victims of sexual abuse from paying customers. There is evidently a small segment of the population that participates

Box 5.4 Your Time Travels

I DIG ANIMALS. I think they are amazing, majestic and magnificent. They are the essence of nature. They are powerful, emotional, instinctual and full of sixth sense wisdom, but they are so vulnerable. They deserve so much more than they are given by our world. I've felt an unspoken connection to our furry and feathered friends and an instinct to protect them basically since birth. But I took a different career path and spent six years working as a transactional attorney at a big New York corporate law firm. That career was not my destiny.

I was inspired to start this company after the things I witnessed during my volunteer work abroad at an elephant sanctuary (see my launch video below for more details!) and since then I've been following my heart and living for my passion – animal welfare. Everyone can play their own unique role in spreading a message of compassion for animals. I've decided to do so through creating a travel company because unique mind blowing vacations with a purpose rock my own inner animal and I want to give them to as many people as possible.

Your Time Travels definition of a vacation = culture, adventure, hotels (suited to your budget), relaxation, etc. PLUS doing cool, unique, out of the ordinary stuff to learn about, interact with and respect animals. Zero exploitation allowed. If you want an ordinary, run of the mill vacation, exit this browser immediately.

So whether you want to volunteer abroad with animal welfare projects (while mixing in amazing sightseeing, adventure and cultural activities and hotel stays!), observe animals in their natural habitats through safari adventures, enjoy amazing vegetarian/vegan resorts, visit animal sanctuaries, or travel in the US with your own adorable pets, I can help you get you there.

I want it to be clear, with my trips you get EVERYTHING you would typically want out of a vacation – fun sightseeing, adventure and cultural activities, amazing hotel stays, all the luxury you want, etc. BUT you make your vacation EXTRA special and truly memorable by engaging in activities that do right by animals. It's this unique spin that will transform your ordinary vacation into an UNFORGETTABLE experience.

Let's work together to make the world a better place for animals. I am powerful and so are you.

Happy and humane travels!

<http://www.yourtimetravels.com>, accessed 18 February 2011.

in this practice and not all of the states in the union have made bestiality illegal (see Box 5.5).

This is not unlike the Tijuana Donkey Show, an industry that has been in existence for some 25 years. Tourists are offered rides to bars in the red light district of the city (cabbies are offered a cut of profits), and later entertained by a theatre show or burlesque (burlesco) involving a Latina woman who is charged with the responsibility of arousing a restrained donkey. Two men bring the donkey out on to the stage floor, knock the animal down, and restrain it by grabbing hold of two legs each. There is some degree of reservation on the actual existence of

---

Box 5.5 Animal sex tourism

by Stephanie Feldstein
17 April 2010

Douglas Spink is a convicted drug smuggler, a one-time dot-com millionaire, a horse trainer, and an alleged animal sex trafficker. His latest twisted business plan to let people come to his farm to have sex with animals was apparently hatched with a man in jail in Tennessee named James Tait, who already had a history of bestiality convictions. According to the county sheriff, 'They were promoting tourism of this nature.'

People who have sex with animals don't go around advertising their fetish, but since the general public would rather not believe that bestiality exists, most people aren't looking too hard for the signs. Spink and Tait were not smart men. They were caught because of phone conversations when Tait was in prison — just two felons chatting about sex with animals on recorded jail lines.

Bestiality is one of the most disturbing, taboo topics out there. It's a combination of so many things outside of people's comfort zones – animal abuse, rape of helpless victims, unnatural fetishes – that the only way people can deal with it is by turning it into a cheap joke. Sexual abuse of animals is very real, and there's nothing remotely funny about it.

Several animals, including horses, dogs, and mice, were taken from Spink's property. The search also uncovered videotapes of a man having sex with several large breed dogs. That bit of evidence helped authorities make another arrest, but at this point, they have no idea how many people visited this sick tourist attraction.

Back in January, Tait pleaded guilty to having sex with animals in Tennessee and was released on probation. He's more famously known for the 2005 Enumclaw case, outside of Seattle, where he was allowing people onto his rental farm to have sex with the neighbor's horses. One of his customers died due to related injuries. Tait was given a one-year suspended sentence.

After the Enumclaw case, Washington became the 34th state to prohibit bestiality, and one of 21 states to consider it a felony. Yes, that means sex with animals is still technically legal in 16 states, although injuries caused if practiced with smaller animals would fall under animal cruelty laws.

<http://animals.change.org/blog/view/animal_sex_tourism>, accessed 2 June 2010

these shows in Tijuana, where tourists are often promised entrance into these shows but robbed on the way instead. The original show is said to have started in Boy's Town, Nuevo Laredo, where the show is performed daily and prostitution is legal (Greensboring, 2011).

Ethics in action

The use of sled dogs for the Iditarod competition is used here as an example of how the welfare of dogs can be severely compromised for human ends – in this case sport. The unofficial death count of 142 dogs killed in the Iditarod race over the years is testament to the extreme stress that these dogs must endure. One witness of the 2010 Iditarod, herself a dog kennel employee, submitted a letter to the *Whitehorse Star* on 23 February 2011 commenting on the violent beating of a dog by one the race's highest-profile mushers. She wrote:

> After viewing an individual sled dog repeatedly booted with full force, the male person doing the beating jumping back and forth like a pendulum with his full body weight to gain full momentum and impact. He then alternated his beating technique with full-ranging, hard and fast, closed-fist punches like a piston to the dog as it was held by its harness splayed onto the ground. He then staggeringly lifted the dog by the harness with two arms above waist height, then slammed the dog into the ground with full force, again repeatedly, all of this repeatedly. The other dogs harnessed into the team were barking loudly and excitedly, jumping and running around frenzied in their harnesses. The attack was sustained, continuing for several minutes perhaps over four minutes, within view at least, until the all-terrain vehicle I was a passenger on turned a curve on the converging trails, and the scene disappeared from view.

If welfare is the humane treatment of animals, the foregoing example is anything but humane, especially in light of the fact that this dog would have likely been pushed to its physical and emotional limits. The indicators of good welfare – including if the dog is healthy, comfortable, well nourished, safe, able to express innate behaviour, and is not suffering from unpleasant states such as pain, fear, and distress – are all in jeopardy here.

Korte *et al.* (2007) argue that the freedom from all of these compromising conditions, above, is not representative of the complex conditions that dogs would encounter in the natural environment (acknowledging that domestication has redefined the nature of 'natural' in these animals). Good animal welfare should not be premised on the notion that animals ought to be exposed to a limited range of environmental challenges that fail to take the animal outside a limited comfort range. Korte and colleagues use the example of the freedom from fear. Fear is said to have fitness value in how it enables the organism to negotiate its environment, survive, and pass this 'knowledge' on to successive generations. Any attempt to suppress these fear-orientated stimuli would in fact be detrimental to the individual. The other example used by the authors is the freedom from pain, injury, and disease, which they say is utopian. The experience of pain allows animals to build resilience against further threats with eventual fitness implications. In addition, freedom from hunger and thirst is also problematic because hunger is one of a number of different challenges confronted on a daily, weekly, or monthly basis.

The problem with accepting the rationale of Korte *et al.* (2007) in this case is that the animals in the sled dog scenario have little to no freedom to exercise actions that would allow them to negotiate these challenging conditions. The animals are forced to run, eat, sleep, socialize, etc., according to the needs of the musher. Furthermore, the resilience and endurance thresholds of these animals would not be the same. Pushing the team of dogs according to the threshold values of the least conditioned dog is not a scenario that a musher would tolerate – quite the opposite. When humans control or push animals to such a great extent and, in doing so, deny species-specific response behaviours to cope with extreme conditions, we can argue that these are prime conditions that lead to compromised welfare.

Conclusion

Domestication, or the keeping of animals in captivity by a human community that maintains total control over physiology, behaviour, and breeding, has provided many advantages and opportunities for those employing the use of animals in the tourism industry. We use pack and harness animals to experience many of the most extreme environments that the tourism industry has to offer, and search and rescue dogs are called into action when these adventures turn into disasters. We enjoy the experience of horseback riding or elephant riding without full knowledge of the conditions under which these animals are kept and utilized. Organizations such as The Brooke have been instrumental in calling into question the ethics of using animals, particularly equines, for these purposes. The Brooke has also been useful in providing appropriate veterinary care when animals have been used too much. This chapter has also discussed what appears to be an expanding market of tourists wishing to take their companion animals with them on vacation. In recognition of this trend, many industry support systems have been put into place to facilitate these types of experiences, including travel agents that target this market almost exclusively as well as forms of transportation that strive to make the experience for pets, and tourists, more enjoyable.

6   Animal combat and competition
Blood, bravado, and betting

Introduction

The topic of the previous chapter explored the various roles that animals play as workers in the service of the tourism industry. In this chapter the focus is not on animals as labourers in the working or toiling sense of the word, but rather on the tremendous effort and stress animals must endure as 'players' in blood sports. There is historical precedence for the use of animals as such, most clearly emphasized in the Roman games, and the continuity of this surfaces in a number of blood sports like baiting, fighting, and so on. Many of these will be discussed here, with clear links to the contemporary tourism industry. These sports are practised as part of the cultural tradition and ritual of many places, but the inclusion of the tourism industry has provided clear economic benefits that help to substantiate the value of these activities.

Historical reference points

The Roman games

The spectacle of the Roman games, so well documented in our own age, was played out through multiple circuits of social power (Whatmore and Thorne, 1998). The games themselves were signatory of the imperial power and geographical reach of the Roman Empire itself. Intensive training was involved in these events for humans and animals alike, with forms ranging from animals pitted against each other, animals against humans (specialized animal fighters), to executions of slaves, criminals, deserters, or enemy captives. By forcing these marginalized groups to participate in such events, the Romans were demonstrating their superior status over these others who were considered closer to the animals they fought.

Whatmore and Thorne suggest that the performances that excited patrons most in the amphitheatres of the Roman Empire were the *venationes* or wild animal combats. *Venationes* were animal fights and staged hunts introduced early in the second century BC and held for over 500 years thereafter. Professional hunters involved in these events were called *venators* (Lindstrom, 2010). The literature is rich with accounts of these games, and noteworthy is the extent to which animals were sacrificed. The most animals killed in a Roman games appears to be 11,000 over a 123-day period after Trajan's victory in 109–108 BC. An enormous amount of money was spent on obtaining highly sought after species of wild animals from around the world in staging these spectacles.

Hopkins (1983) observes that the activities of the arena were sanctioned by the people of Rome because of a mob psychology. The individual was divorced from personal responsibility by being part of the collective, and this was reinforced through a type of primitive militarism that was played out through animal sacrifice and through a relief of collective tensions through arena games. But as Lindstrom (2010) argues, there was a binary operating in Roman civilization. On one hand, the Romans were clearly willing to watch and enjoy these games and sanction the use of animals in a way that can only be referred to as carnage. On the other hand, the people of Rome showed and practised an advanced form of care towards animals that was represented through the use of animals as pets and the application of veterinary services to care for these companions. More specifically, Lindstrom has documented a number of reasons why the games were both endured and enjoyed by the Roman populace:

1. Hunter insensitivity: Romans were hunters by nature, and may have assumed a cool, compassionless mental state at the moment the animal was taken.
2. The lust of killing, aggression, and horror: The connection between pain, blood, and death during the hunt is mediated by the release of dopamine in the blood system that leads to arousal, joy, and pleasure, which may have acted as a reward for participation in the event.
3. Desensitization: Repeated exposure to events, even horrifying events like the games, may have reduced the emotional response in the audience.
4. Curiosity: The belief that these animals came from an infinite supply outside the realm may have suppressed any concern over the death of the animal.
5. Altered state of mind through identifications and emotional turmoil: It may have been that spectators, many of whom were lower-class individuals, found the death of animals to be an emotional outlet for their pent-up feelings of humiliation. The *venator* served the purpose of revenge against society by proxy.

The diversity of uses

The Roman *venationes* stand as an extreme example of the extent to which humans have gone to exercise power and control over the natural world. Part of the motivation for participation in this type of killing, outlined above, is pleasure – both socially and psychologically derived. This pleasure at the expense of animals has remained a consistent theme over time. The diversity of different expressions of this mastery, power, or control is further wrapped up in a number of different forms of animal combat and competition that are practised either legally or illegally even today. It is not the purpose of this section to fully explain the history,

Table 6.1 Types of blood sports

Baiting	Fighting	Hunting	Fishing	Throwing	Other
Badger	Betta	Fox	Freshwater species	Cock	Camel
Bear	Canary	Wolf	Salt water species		wrestling
Bull	Cock				Coursing
Donkey	Cricket				Fox tossing
Duck	Dog				Dogging
Hog	Insect				
Hyena	Spider				
Lion					
Monkey					
Rat					

sociology, and various subtleties of blood sports, but merely to make mention of these according to the tradition of cruelty towards animals.

Opportunities for leisure for all the classes increased in Europe during the mid-seventeenth century as a result of the decline of authoritarian religion and the increase in material wealth (Cross, 1990). These were activities not restricted by class or vocation, but rather participated in by young and old, rich and poor, urban and rural. While rough sports such as cudgelling, wrestling, and boxing were increasing in popularity, so too were sports that involved a significant degree of cruelty towards animals. Table 6.1 categorizes a number of different blood sports mentioned in the literature and the animals used in these contests. While a few of these will be touched on briefly, bull and badger baiting, fox hunting, cockfighting, bullfighting, rodeo, and greyhound racing will be given more attention.

Baiting

Baiting refers to forcing an animal that is chained or tethered to fight a succession of other animals, usually dogs. An episode of baiting almost always leads to the death of the target animal, and often to the injury or death of the dog(s). William de Warenne, 6th Earl of Surrey, developed animal baiting during the early 1200s, upon finding entertainment in watching two bulls fight and soon after be pursued by local dogs (Kalof, 2007b). He encouraged the event to take place more regularly and even purchased and donated land where the events originally took place. Animal baiting as a gambling event began in 1562, after which it evolved into a desired leisure activity (Brownstein, 1969). Blood sports later became important social events linked to the consumption of alcohol, which included church houses that, in addition to holding special events designed to raise money for the church, evolved into drinking houses where blood sports would take place (Kalof, 2007b).

The sport of bull-baiting was functional for about 600 years, lasting up until the early nineteenth century. The object of the sport involved betting on the abilities of individual dogs in the process of bringing the bull down, as well as on the ability of the bull to dispatch dogs with its horns. Boddice (2008: 205) describes the activity:

It involved tethering a bull to a stake set in the ground, allowing it a certain amount of freedom. Trained dogs would then be set upon the bull, their aim being to attach themselves to the bull's nose, or other tender parts, and bring the bull to its knees.

While bull-baiting had social and psychological benefits to spectators, it also had specific culinary advantages. The setting of dogs upon the bull just prior to its slaughter was said to improve the taste of the meat, presumably because of the release of hormones and associated increase in blood supply to areas of the organism in making the meat tender (Griffin, 2005).

A baiting sport with a long-standing tradition in the UK is badger-baiting. Although outlawed for over 170 years in Britain, this activity appears to be on the rise once more. *The Times Online* offers the following description of the sport, in an article exposing the re-emergence of this form of blood sport (Mooney, 2009).

> The cry of the terrified badger as it fights for its life is heart-rending. The animal screeches in terror as it attempts to defend itself against the terriers, which have been set upon it by a gang of badger baiters in a field in Co Down. One of the dogs, a cross between a lurcher and a pit bull terrier, moves forward and locks its jaws around the badger's head and pulls it from its underground sett. That allows the other dogs to join in the attack. Frenzied, they latch on to the badger's rump and rear legs and begin tearing it limb from limb. Nothing is off limits in this illegal blood sport. One of the spectators rushes forward and urges the dogs to bite harder in order to kill the quarry. He is careful not to get bitten by the badger; it could inflict a serious injury were it to lock on to his leg. Another pit bull-type dog begins to shake the struggling badger, while the other dogs continue to pull and tear at the creature's rear legs. Outnumbered and injured, the badger falls limp and offers no resistance. It is dying from internal injuries, an horrific end for a species supposedly protected by law.

Just like bull-baiting it is not only the badger that suffers incredibly in the sport, but also the dogs (see Box 6.1). The Campaign for the Abolition of Terrier Work (CATW) has as its mission the move to expose the cruelty that terriers have to endure in digging out foxes and badgers – 10,000 badgers alone per year – for the entertainment of people. (See also the practice of 'ratting', where entertainment was derived by placing dogs in a pit with a number of rats. The object of the sport was to see how many rats a dog could kill over a given time.)

Fighting

Animal fighting emerges in a number of forms including betta fish, canaries, cocks, crickets and other insects, spiders, and dogs. The recent media frenzy over dogfighting at the home of the high-profile US NFL football player Michael Vick demonstrates the intensity of the sympathy that can be levelled over these types of

Box 6.1 Crackdown appeal after swoops on badger-baiting ring

Belfast Telegraph
23 February 2009

New legislation to crack down on badger baiting was demanded last night following a major operation against those involved in Northern Ireland.

Raids were carried out across Co Armagh throughout the weekend following a six-month investigation stretching across the Irish border and as far afield as France and the USA.

A website especially set up as part of a sting drew those involved in the badger baiting towards the investigation and helped identify them.

The Ulster Society for the Prevention of Cruelty to Animals (USPCA) said the investigation uncovered 'glaring shortcomings' in the policing of laws which were supposed to protect the badger and its habitat.

Successful prosecutions by the agencies charged with protecting badgers in Northern Ireland were virtually unheard of despite hundreds of the animals being torn apart each year, said the charity.

During the weekend swoops several dogs were seized in a joint operation by the PSNI and the USPCA.

The PSNI said: 'Police working in partnership with the USPCA attended a number of premises in the Armagh area following reports of animal cruelty.

'In one incident a number of dogs were removed. No arrests were made and investigations are continuing.'

Three pit-bull type terriers were among those seized and taken into care by the USPCA.

The chief executive of the USPCA said the scale of the persecution of both dogs and badgers shocked everyone involved in the investigation mounted by his organisation and the *Sunday Times*.

Demanding action, he said: 'If the evil of badger persecution is to be eradicated from our countryside it is the responsibility of landowners as custodians of the environment, the statutory agencies, whose remit is to protect this valuable creature, and the rural community to be vigilant.'

He added: 'Gangs of men with dogs and shovels are not invisible. The PSNI needs information and they need to act on it.

'Northern Ireland remains the only country within the UK that still tolerates hunting with dogs.

'It is our view the Stormont Assembly should now introduce legislation to ban an activity that offers nothing but suffering to our native wildlife.'

He said information uncovered during the USPCA investigation into dog fighting had drawn them into 'the murky world of badger persecution; the nauseating destruction of both a valued member of our native wildlife and of the dogs used in a vile activity that defiles our countryside.'

'Hundreds of our badgers perish each year to satisfy the bloodlust of common criminals.'

Belfast Telegraph (2009)

Plate 6.1 Badger baiting, 1824

practices. This sentiment is captured in a study by Lee *et al.* (2010), who discuss the predictors of sympathy toward the bait dog seen in film clips of the Michael Vick dogfighting case in 2007 based on personality trait theory. Although dogfighting is illegal in all 50 states of the US, it continues as a 'depraved' form of amusement and as a form of gambling (Sullivan *et al.*, 2008). The rationalization of dogmen (those who fight their pit bulls against other pit bulls) has been studied by Forsyth and Evans (1998). They demonstrate that these individuals use a number of neutralization techniques to justify their deviance (see Sykes and Matza, 1957). These include:

1. Denial of injury: 'We're not hurting anybody and the dogs love to fight, so what's the harm?'.
2. The condemnation of condemners: 'Cockfighting is legal, but not dogfighting. What's the difference?'.
3. Appeal to higher authorities: 'Dogfighting around this part of the country is a tradition … It's something that's been here so long, if it wasn't here it just wouldn't be Louisiana'.
4. Special people: 'The old-timers know all the champions and the great bloodlines. They have produced most of the champion dogs. If they don't like you, you are not going anywhere in dogfighting. You have got to show them the respect they deserve'.
5. We are good people: 'We are respectable people who pay taxes and salute the flag, we work at honest jobs. If we are bending their rules a little, then that's okay if that's the way they want it. But 99 per cent of our lives consists of

following the rules and being good people. You don't penalize good respectable people for jaywalking'.

The authors observe that much of the dogmen's rationalization is based on the denial of bad behaviour on a balance sheet. Because their good vastly outweighs their evil, participation in the activity is felt to be morally acceptable.

One of the most abundantly researched examples of animal–animal combat is cockfighting, which comes packaged with a rich history of meaning between animal and handler. It is an example of a type of blood sport involving animals matched against animals of their own kind, like dog fighting above, according to beauty, strength, or speed. For cockfighting, all three of these characteristics are deemed important. In its present-day form, roosters are born, bred, and trained to be fighters. The inferior ones are killed. Breeders train these birds by attaching weights to their legs and forcing them to engage in practice fights. They also pluck certain feathers and cut off wattles and/or combs to prevent these from being torn during fights. Spurs are removed, replaced by ones of metal. Fighting continues until one bird is incapacitated or dead, discarded in barrels close to the pit even if still alive (PETA, 2011b).

Cockfighting, at 6,000 years old, is said to be the world's oldest spectator sport and, at least during the 1600s, an activity where people from all stations of life, from parliamentarians to butchers, were immersed in the same event (Boddice, 2008). Hamill (2009) follows two main themes in his historical account of cockfighting, which he in turn follows from George Wilson's 1607 treatise entitled *The Commendation of Cockes, and Cockfighting. Wherein is shewed, that Cockefighting was before the coming of Christ*. The justification for cockfighting in early modern England comes from the Bible and the divinely appointed authority over the animals, whereby God's creatures can be used for any number of human ends, including:

> For clothing and sustenance for his bodie, but also ... for recreation and pastime, to delight his minde: as with Cocke-fighting, Hawking, Hunting, and such like. For honest recreation is not prohibited by the word of God: but rather tolerated and allowed.
>
> (Wilson, 1607, as cited in Hamill, 2009: 375)

The second theme discussed by Hamill is the metaphorical transformation of man's idealized self as represented through the courage and toughness of the cock in battle. Hamill once again uses sources and stories narrated by Wilson to validate his perspective. The Greek general Themistocles, in preparation for his siege upon Dalmatia, used cockfighting as a method to prepare his troops. Before any of the battles took place the general set down two cocks who immediately engaged in battle, sustaining many wounds and never stopping until both were exhausted and soon after died. Themistocles had hoped

> that the sight of the courage which [the cocks] shewed in this quarrel, might pierce into their hearts, and make a deepe impression in your discreet

considerations, that thereby you might be the more emboldened and encouraged, than you could haue beene by all the words of comfort that I can relate, or by all the examples of former accidents that may be repeated.

(Wilson, 1607: B2r-v; cited in Hamill, 2009: 376)

This fight to the death was to be a template for how soldiers needed to engage the enemy. No better example and no better words could have been used to kindle the type of courage needed to be victorious in battle.

Even though Eastern religions have been lauded for their reverence of animals, cockfighting continues in Hindu and Muslim countries (Preece, 2005). In fact, one of the landmark studies of cockfighting and culture comes to us from Geertz (2005) and his work in Bali, Indonesia. Geertz argues that cockfighting is about status and identity in the community and, although it is the cocks themselves who do the fighting, it is more about the owners of the cocks telling a narrative about themselves. In a subsequent publication Geertz (2005) explains that 'the fact that they [cocks] are masculine symbols *par excellence* is about as indubitable, and to the Balinese about as evident, as the fact that water runs downhill' (p. 60). And while the word 'cock' is used metaphorically as 'hero', 'warrior', 'champion', 'man of parts', 'tough guy', among others, the bird itself commands a great deal of attention from its owner, who grooms, discusses, feeds, trains, and gazes upon it with wonder and awe (Geertz, 2005). For Dundes (1994: 245–6), the connection between cocks and cockfighting is the symbol of male genitalia, suggesting that the cockfight might even be a form of public masturbation with 'grown men playing with their cocks in public' (Dundes, 1993: 53). (See Del Sesto (1975) for a discussion of customs and traditions in cockfighting.)

Cockfighting, like hunting, appears to be a man's business with very few women in attendance. Furthermore, the inclusiveness of cockfighting continues to be a theme that is shared amongst the participants of other blood sports. Even the poorest members of society often become actively involved in the contests, losing money that might otherwise be used to feed their families (Boddice, 2008) – a theme explored at length by Maunula (2007). Maunula argues that as one of the last strongholds of cockfighting in America's south, the game as tradition continues in Louisiana. There is a clannishness about the game that is important to the folks of the isolated rural south that involves socialization, entertainment, gossip, drinking, and a dynamic that includes a brotherhood of those inside the pit and a disregard for those outside the pit, i.e., for those who do not share the same values. Maunula explains that

The game's inclusiveness is mostly a reflection of the ingroup–outgroup dynamics that often tie members of an oppressed or deviant group together, resulting in a close-knit and cohesive community, regardless of the participant's social status outside the group.

(Maunula, 2007: 79)

The tournament season is upwards of nine months long, so the committed cocker must breed scores of birds in order to sustain himself throughout the year. Maunula writes that in response to a question about cruelty, one participant said that 'Our fowl is much better taken care of than those chickens you eat at KFC. We pamper our chickens with free-range living and good feed' (p. 78). While the practice was banned throughout the UK in 2005, it still persists in other locations including Ireland, Spain, Russia, and parts of the USA.

Hunting and fishing

As most of Chapter 7 is devoted to hunting and fishing as blood sports, these activities will not be discussed here. Instead fox hunting is included briefly as an example that follows from the forms outlined in Table 6.1.

In his 1893 play, *A Woman of No Importance*, Oscar Wilde, through the character of Lord Illingworth speaking on the topic of health, quips that the day's popular idea of health for English gentlemen involves galloping after a fox: 'the unspeakable in full pursuit of the uneatable.' Fox hunting is highly ritualized, as explained by Marvin (2007). This includes the metaphor of the man (hound) chasing down the feminized hare (pussy) (Bronner, 2008). It is not just the killing of a fox, an animal thought to be highly disruptive to inhabitants of the countryside, but an activity where animal identities – those of the fox, the horse, and dogs – 'are created *for* this event and *as a result* of this event' (p. 105):

> Here, the relationship between human and fox is highly complex and highly ritualised. It is mediated through other animals – horses and hounds – there are formal rules governing the encounter, and rules of etiquette covering everything from proper clothing and forms of address between people to acceptable and unacceptable forms of behaviour. In foxhunting, humans do not engage with foxes quietly, efficiently and unobtrusively. They announce their presence in the countryside, they expect (and require) the fox to flee, to be difficult to find and to capture.
>
> (Bronner, 2008: 93)

Marvin (2007) writes that the sport had become so popular by the mid-1800s that not only was England mapped according to foxhunt counties, but a detailed set of rules was established in regards to fair play and acceptable standards. Even further, it had evolved into an elitist, formal activity that had fused meaning on socio-cultural and ecological levels. As such, the killing of foxes was not the central concern here; rather, it was the meaning tied to the way these deaths came about based on the complexity of the relationships between environment and culture (Marvin, 2002). Fox hunting was banned in Scotland in 2002 and in England and Wales in 2005. It remains legal in Northern Ireland.

Cock throwing

This blood sport was widely practised in England until the latter part of the eighteenth century. In this sport, cocks were tied with a short lead to a post, at which point people would take turns throwing weighted sticks known as coksteles at the bird until it was dead (see Kete, 2007).

Other blood sports

The sport of camel wrestling originated in Turkey approximately 2,400 years ago. It stems from a time when camels were heavily used as beasts of burden, and wrestling was designed to demonstrate the breeding ability of competing caravan owners. It involves two male camels placed in the vicinity of a female camel in heat, and the subsequent battle between the males over the female. A winner is declared when one camel is knocked down or runs away from the encounter. Camel wrestling is an activity that carries with it a tremendous amount of cultural memory (Donlon *et al.*, 2010). But while some blood sports are inherently cruel, Donlon *et al.* argue that the muzzling of camels and the quick intervention of handlers after an animal has been declared a winner serve to protect the animals from injury (see also Kaushik, 1999).

The tradition has been kept on through festivals that communicate group membership and group values – a celebration of heritage – not unlike many other sports that utilize animals. In this capacity, recent years have firmly instituted camel wrestling as an important tourist attraction with a focus on the activity and its heritage value rather than the health of the camels (Donlon *et al.*, 2010). Camel wrestling events are advertised in the mainstream media and in tourist guidebooks alike. Orbiting the event are a number of small-scale entrepreneurs offering handicrafts, clothes, and music. The same small-scale commercial activity has been documented in reference to cockfighting, where suppliers of cockfighting equipment have been joined by a number of peddlers selling T-shirts, hats, and a range of other items that people need at these events or wish to take home as souvenirs (Maunula, 2007; see Box 6.2). Table 6.1 also mentions fox tossing, which was a popular activity in Europe during the seventeenth and eighteenth centuries. Participants would throw foxes as high as they could by aid of a long rope. Another activity, hare coursing, is discussed below as part of the section on greyhound racing.

Blood sports began to fall out of favour in the UK due to humanitarian sentiment, religious piety, modernization, and urbanization. After 1790, blood sports ceased to be advertised in local newspapers, and were found to be a barbarous custom, with societal interests declining. It was not newsworthy and the activity seems not to have generated much in the way of controversy, according to Griffin (2005). Advertisements in sporting magazines appear to have waned significantly during the early 1800s, based on increasing complaints about the unfairness of the sport. Legislation against bull-baiting first commenced in 1800 and later in 1802 (both unsuccessful), with a more broadly based animal bill introduced in 1809, which also failed. Although Martin's Bill of 1822 protected horses and cattle from acts of cruelty, bulls were not mentioned in the act. Bulls were, however, explicitly mentioned in that of 1835. In the Netherlands, prohibitions against blood sports prior to 1800, such as decapitating a goose by pulling off its head, cockfighting, and cat clubbing (clubs thrown at a cat in a barrel), were not necessarily instituted

Box 6.2 Turkey: tradition of camel wrestling making a comeback

In its 2,400-year history, the tradition of camel wrestling in Turkey has seen many winners and losers. But owner Ismail Egilmez had reason this year to celebrate a totally new kind of triumph. His beloved camel had just won the first-ever beauty pageant of its kind.

The pageant featured a procession of drooling, half-ton males decked out in bright decorations, bells and bobbles, strutting before a panel of judges.

The spectacle marked the latest effort by camel wrestling organizers to reinvigorate an ancient custom that has been making a comeback over the past three decades. The day after the beauty pageant, 20,000 people gathered in a natural amphitheatre to watch the wrestling tournament, a turnout that countered the impression that the tradition is fading.

One owner, Rifki Sendur, 50, brought his camel, Cheerful Outlaw, about three years ago from Afghanistan after paying 20,000 Turkish lira ($12,800). Along with Iran, Afghanistan is the main source of wrestling camels, which are bred specially for the Turkish market, and are hybrids of the one-humped dromedary and two-humped Bactrian.

Wrestling camels, all male, fight when the females are in heat, and are fitted with tight halters to prevent them biting each other. A victory is declared when one camel is either forced to the ground, or flees his opponent.

During the early years of the Turkish republic, the sport was discouraged since it did not tally with the modern, European image to which the state aspired. But in 1983 it was revived as a tourist attraction, and since then the number of camel owners has risen from 200 to more than 2,000 today.

Camel wrestling is a rich man's game, according to Vedat Caliskan, an assistant professor of Geography at Canakkale University and an expert on the sport. Other than serving as occasional tourist attraction, wrestling camels have no practical uses. They cannot be bred, and the sport itself brings no financial rewards: the prize at the Selcuk tournament for a champion camel is a machine-made rug. 'It is just the family interest that goes on and keeps the tradition going,' Caliskan said. 'If . . . a new generation loses interest, it can die out.'

Caliskan and others also fear that the sport may become disconnected from its grassroots supporters due to the rising cost of buying and keeping the animals, and it could end up being merely a show for tourists.

For Metin Citak, the main organizer of the Selcuk tournament, the sport is about keeping alive the bond between Turks and the animal that served their nomadic ancestors for centuries, and which he sees as an integral part of Turkish heritage. 'In the past, a camel was something you couldn't live without, the lives of the camels and the humans were in symmetry,' he said. 'Now technology and transportation have developed, but camel wrestling is important for the culture to remain.'

Christie-Miller (2011)

Plate 6.2 Fox tossing, 1719

over compassion for the animal but rather because these celebrations often involved excessive alcohol consumption and thus social deviance (Dijkstra, 2004).

A theme that is not well covered in the literature on blood sports is the environmental impacts of these activities on the regions where they are practised (Jones, 2009). Jones uses fox hunting, angling, and other forms of animal abuse to examine how practitioners of these activities had intended or unintended consequences on landscape, wildlife, and agricultural lands. For example, in order to secure good populations of trout for fishing, otter, pike, perch, heron, kingfisher, and many other species were thinned out because these were thought to prey on or compete with trout, reducing their numbers for human enjoyment.

Blood: bullfighting

Earlier in the chapter the Roman games were discussed as an event that was distinguishable by the magnitude of cruelty extended towards animals. The present-day manifestation of this cruelty may be found in the bullfight and rodeo (Jamieson, 2006), both of which are discussed in more detail below.

Bullfighting, although said to be part of the Spanish culture, soul, and pagan past, is really a manifestation of the late eighteenth century (Bailey 2007), and

Plate 6.3 Mounted bullfighting, Seville, *c.* 1850

from its inception primarily a way to make money (Shubert, 1999). Mounted bullfighting or lancing bulls from horseback was practised up until the beginning of the eighteenth century, at which time it was replaced by footed bullfighting because of the preferences of a French king who held the Spanish throne. Footed bullfighting, the kind that prevails today, evolved to use directly the helpers who provided traditional assistance to those on horseback (K. Thompson, 2010).

Every year approximately 40,000 bulls are killed around the world in this spectacle – 30,000 in Spain alone (Hall and Brown, 2006). Although the event is advertised to tourists as a fair competition, it is anything but fair. Before the event, bulls are weakened by severe beatings with sandbags, debilitated with laxatives, and drugged. Horns are shaved to alter balance and navigation, and their vision is impaired because handlers rub petroleum jelly in the bull's eyes (PETA, 2011a). Increasingly it has become a commercial enterprise and promoted to lure in tourists for a taste of the exotic in efforts to bolster local economies. Not unlike many other types of human–animal forms of combat, there are a large number of small vendors making their products available to tourists.

Similar to a play, the bullfight is divided into specific acts. Act One involves the release of the bull into the ring; Act Two involves the entrance of the picadors (horsemen who stab bulls with a lance) and the insertion of large poles into the neck of the beast; Act Three involves the stabbing of the charging bull with banderillas (decorated barbed darts); and in the final act the matador (matador comes from Latin *matare*, 'to subdue or kill') finishes the bull off with a sword (Acquaroni, 1966). The whole spectacle, from releasing the bull to dragging it out of the stadium, takes a mere 20 minutes (Belmonte, 1937). The comparison to a play is not an exaggeration as many commentators find it elegant, beautiful, and full of tragedy (McCormick, 1997).

Many have tried to deconstruct the bullfight for a deeper understanding of its essence. Marvin (1994) provides a detailed description of the meaning and spectacle of the bullfight in Spain. He argues that the bullfight is symbolic of the differences between human and nature. What it means to be civilized is both to control and to rise above the unpredictability of the natural world through the conflict between man and beast. I say 'man' specifically because the bullfight is a representation of what it means to be 'male' in Spanish, and, more particularly, Andalusian culture. 'The ideas of masculinity, sexual potency, wilfulness, assertiveness and independence are all closely associated in this culture' (Marvin, 1994: x; see also McCormick (1997), who observes that women's liberation in Spain is decades behind other movements in Europe and North America). The success of the matador is premised on his ability to make the bull act the way he wants it to, thus breaking the will of the animal and exercising his ability to control nature (the bull) through brains over brawn. In fact, the control and manipulation of the animal and the removal of its will are symbolic of bringing the bull into a state of domestication.

In this process of control, the animal is not killed quickly but rather slowly to demonstrate this denaturing of the animal. The placing of banderillas in the neck and shoulders of the bull is important in balancing the strength of the bull with its slow demise. The colour of the banderillas is a sign of the imposition of domestication and culture on the beast. As such, the killing of the animal is tied to tradition, and so must be done properly in order to honour culture and to signify the skill of the matador at certain risk to himself. After the bull has been sufficiently dominated there is a time at which point the crowd and the matador insist upon this culturally charged death:

> There are special rules which stipulate how the killing must be performed and the types of implement to be used … The matador must approach the bull from the front and the sword must pass though the lower part of the neck of the bull. This means that at the moment the sword goes in, the body of the matador ought to pass over the bull's horns (or to be precise, over the right horn), a movement which involves great risk because if the bull lifts its head at this moment the man is almost certain to be gored.
>
> (Marvin, 1994: x)

In recent years the bullfight has become gentrified because of a mix of different and changing conditions in Spain. Where once bulls were bred with pride, expertise, and as part of the Spanish way of life, increasingly this has given way to the use of bulls that are 100kg overweight and have their horns clipped to make it safer for the matador, which is patently unacceptable to a knowledgeable crowd. But even the crowd has changed. McCormick (1997) argues that where once there was a healthy mix of all walks of society, the bullfight is now for tourists looking for a glimpse of the exotic, businessmen on mobile phones, young girls, and wives.

The changing cohort of spectators has run concurrent to changing perceptions within Spanish society as well as internationally in reference to the moral acceptability of bullfighting. Bailey (2007) reports that the bullfight (polls suggest that 70 per cent of Spaniards have little or no interest in bullfighting) is so contemptible to many that it is viewed consistently as the lowest form of abuse of any and all acts of human cruelty towards animals. This stems from the fact that the animal's demise is a pre-planned, sanctioned, and regulated form of abuse that has at its core the entertainment of hundreds or thousands of spectators. As one commentator has argued, bullfighting makes 'immorality moral, [and turns] illegality into justice, vice into virtue, brutal cruelty into civility' (Costa, as cited by Bailey, 2007: 28).

More specifically, resistance inside Spain has been mounted from two main sources. The first includes Spaniards who have come to identify more strongly with the new Europe, and the second includes Catalan nationalists who feel marginalized linguistically, culturally, and economically from the Spanish central state. Oppositional tactics by the Catalonians surround the notion that as a key symbol of Spain's national heritage, the bull is useful as a symbol of Castile or the despised Spanish centrist state. The use of a number of different faunal mascots like cows and sheep in different regions is significant because this represents a move away from the bull as a Spanish national symbol towards another personality. The recent ban on bullfighting in Catalonia is another step towards the removal of centrist authority in the Catalonia region (see Box 6.3).

It is not too much a stretch to imagine that the ban on bullfighting is really not so much about the rights of bulls, but rather very much about political posturing. The right-of-centre national coalition used the ban on bullfighting as a means by which to claim a stronger association to the rest of Europe than to Spain; not so much an attack against Spain as an opportunity to express values that are shared with these European others. For Black (2010) this has stirred up the ghost of the great chain of being, 'in which the species *homo catalan* is revealed (through the ban) to be closer to the "more advanced" *homo europeus* than to the more primitive *homo hispanense*' (p. 236).

The debate over bullfighting has also stimulated broader discussions on the use of cattle for consumption (Bailey, 2007). While opponents argue against the brutality of bullfighting, what they fail to do is consider that millions of livestock die in North America and Europe under the most dreadful of conditions. When asked about the comparisons between the bullfighting and meat-processing industries, advocates suggest that meat processing *en masse* is legitimized by the fact that eating meat is a matter of sustenance and bullfighting a matter of pleasure. We can condone one while not the other. What separates the two, according to Bailey, is matters of degree. The bullfighting spectator is uncomfortable with the act because there is no separation between the act itself and the spectator, who is in full view of the event. By contrast, meat processing involves someone else who is paid to torture and kill the pig. This form of lying to ourselves, this hypocrisy, illustrates a lack of moral integration whereby 'The left hand doesn't have to or want to know what the right is doing' (Bailey, 2007: 30), in efforts to secure a civilized state of being.

Plate 6.4 Protest against bullfighting

Bravado: rodeo

Rodeo includes events such as calf roping, steer roping, steer wrestling, bareback horse riding, bareback bull riding, saddle bronco riding, and barrel racing, and is an example of a practice that supports the animal welfare platform of the acceptable use of animals with responsibility for humane treatment. The popularity of rodeo is growing, with some 5,000 rodeos taking place in the US annually, and over 25 million in attendance. It is another event that relies on the entertainment value of the human–animal encounter. Part of the interest lies in the hardship that humans must endure in mastering the animal: horses buck, calves race from riders at top speed, and staying atop a bull is no easy feat (Regan, 2004).

The intent is to make cowboys look brave and in order to do this the animal must be provoked into displaying wild behaviour. While many of these animals are used continuously, provoking wild behaviour comes in the form of the use of certain devices, which include electric prods or 'hotshots' that induce pain, fear,

Box 6.3 Bullfighting ban a first for Spain

By Vanessa Romeo
Barcelona
28 July 2010

The Catalan parliament dealt the death blow to bullfighting in the region on Wednesday, outlawing the centuries-old spectacle for the first time on mainland Spain.

The result of 68 in favour, 55 against the ban was expected, after Catalonia's parliament in December accepted a petition by citizens to stop bullfighting, as activists concerned about animal cruelty battled devotees of the Spanish tradition.

Some lawmakers cited the declining popularity of bullfighting in Spain, where fewer people go each year to the arena to watch toreros in their elaborate 'suits of lights' engage enraged bulls at close range with red capes and swords.

'There are some traditions that can't remain frozen in time as society changes. We don't have to ban everything, but the most degrading things should be banned,' said Josep Rull, member of parliament for the Catalonian nationalist party (CiU).

Animal rights activists have pledged to spread the ban from the autonomy-minded region throughout the rest of the country, which would be difficult because some regions have passed laws protecting bullfighting as their heritage.

Anti-bullfighting groups gathered signatures from 180,000 Catalans, which forced parliament to vote on the tradition which dates back to 711, when the first bullfight took place in celebration for the crowning of King Alfonso VIII.

'They have heard the outcry of a society that is reinventing its traditions,' said Anna Mula, of the group Prou! (Enough!).

Before the vote, animal rights activists, one drenched in red paint, and bullfighting aficionados gathered outside parliament to hear the result.

Highly ritualised bullfighting, in which the matador and his entourage use capes, lances and darts to subdue the bull which is killed at close quarters with a sword, was made illegal in Spain's Canary islands in 1991.

For fans, who shout 'Ole' in chorus at the bullring to appreciate a daring or stylish move, the showdown is a moving display of fear and courage.

'It's not a cruel show. Completely the opposite. It's a show that creates art: where you get feelings and a fight between a bull and person, where the person or the bull can lose their life,' bullfighter Serafin Marin told Reuters.

In Spanish newspapers, bullfighting reviews are found not in the sports pages, but in the arts and culture sections.

Romeo (2010)

or anger. While cowboys choose or volunteer to participate in these activities, animals have no choice. Veterinarians have reported various types of trauma in animals forced to participate in the rodeo, including broken ribs, backs, and legs, punctured lungs, deep internal organ bruising, haemorrhaging, ripped tendons, torn ligaments and muscles, and snapped necks (PETA, 2011c).

With 50 per cent of the points awarded on the basis of how hard the broncos buck, it is in the rider's best interests, as well as the fans', for the horse and rider to put on a good show. The problem is that horses are used again and again in these shows, and there is little motivation to buck on command. Inducement is provided by electric prods just as the gate is opened and the use of a flank strap that is tightened just below the ribcage. Further inducement is provided by the rider him/ herself by spurring: the use of dulled metal spurs to dig into the side of the animal, which, when done repeatedly through the event and subsequent events, creates a great deal of discomfort.

The effects of the roping of calves are by most accounts worse. After attempting to escape a rider at 30mph, the calf is abruptly halted in its tracks by rope around the neck. The rider then dismounts, drops the calf, ropes three legs together, mounts his horse again, and then waits six seconds to see if the calf frees itself from its ties. E.J. Finocchio, as a former veterinarian, wrote a letter to the Rhode Island State Legislature in support of the banning of calf roping:

> As a large animal veterinarian for 20 years ... I have witnessed firsthand the instant death of calves after their spinal cords were severed from the abrupt stop at the end of a rope when travelling up to 30mph. I have also witnessed and tended calves who became paralyzed ... and whose tracheas were totally or partially severed ... Slamming to the ground has caused rupture of several internal organs leading to a slow, agonizing death for some of these calves.
>
> (cited in Regan, 2004: 152–3)

The world's largest rodeo, the Calgary Stampede, a ten-day event held in July with over one million people in attendance, came under fire in 2010 because of the death of six horses. The main cause of injury and death to horses occurs in the chuckwagon races, which pit four teams of horse-drawn wagons against each other (each team has four wagon horses and four horses carrying outriders). Injuries leading to deaths included cardiac arrest, broken shoulders, abdominal rupture, and a broken front leg (Raia, 2010). The number of deaths in the year 2010 is not inconsistent with other years. In 1986, 12 horses died during the stampede, and on 3 July 2005 nine horses died after plunging into the Bow River on a trail ride. These deaths have renewed discussion by animal welfare groups over the unnecessary stress placed on horses and other animals at the Stampede, not only in reference to chuckwagon races but also bull riding, steer wrestling, and tie down roping (the Australian government has developed standards for the care and treatment of rodeo livestock, including sections on responsibilities for rodeo personnel, rules for the care of livestock, equipment specifications, and stock and arena selection (Australian Government, 2010)).

Rollin's (1996) face-to-face discussions with rodeo participants provide a rich and detailed account of the social world of these athletes, where individuals are raised and socialized in the values and norms deemed acceptable in this activity, particularly 'what is the west'. These values include how to manage animals appropriately, how to survive in a harsh environment, the skill set that makes survival possible, and unique western American pride. Attacks against these values are taken as attacks against the individual and his or her culture, which only serves to illustrate the divide that exists between the urban east and the frontier west. The former sees animals as pets, nature as the good and worthy of protection, violent sports as morally objectionable, and the cowboy himself as ambivalent at best and a redneck at worst. The stronger this belief gets on the part of easterners, the more the westerners show resolve in protecting this unique lifestyle in the face of the criticism.

Rollin further observes that, as industrial factory farming fell into place, cowboys and the ranching way of life remained the last stronghold of animal husbandry. This ethic of care meant that human handlers provided the best possible environment for animals to be raised, from providing protection from inclement weather to the provision of food and water and the protection from predators and ill health. As young adults, participants recalled that the only times when physical punishment was issued from their parents was when animals were not fed and watered and otherwise taken care of. What is particularly revealing about this group is that after a discussion of the animal abuse problems taking place in rodeo, the participants acknowledged that there was a great deal wrong with the sport. And because the sport was important as an activity and as an identity, there was an expression of interest among the cowboys about how the rodeo could persist without compromising this firmly entrenched ethic of care.

The Mexican rodeo or *charreada* is similar to the model of the mainstream rodeo, discussed above, except for a few other ritualized aspects that make it distinctive (Nájera-Ramírez, 1996). The rodeos take place on Sundays between May and October in Mexico and the southern US states, beginning at noon with a parade of participants, with music played throughout the event, and culminating with a dance that finishes about 9.00pm. People participate in the event according to family unity, pride in Mexican culture, and the continual practice of a time-honoured tradition. The practice of the *charreada* as a positive representation of Mexican culture in the US has come under scrutiny, however, because of the abuse of animals in the name of tradition. American news personnel were met head-on with violence in any attempt to document the events of the *charreada*. Media coverage was successful at generating public support over animal welfare issues, but coverage was found to be racially charged according to proponents of the *charreada*, with the upshot contributing to the polarization of Mexican and Caucasian communities.

Betting: greyhound racing

An entrenched narrative in the literature on the greyhound is that it is an ancient and noble breed (Madden, 2010). The greyhound is said to be the world's oldest purebred dog, with records tracing back to 6000 BC to ancient Turkey. Since this time they have been revered as a religious icon, a hunter of animals and people (Finch and Nash (2001) note that British and French explorers used greyhounds to hunt and slaughter indigenous people of the Caribbean and southern Americas), and a companion (Barnes, 1994). But it is the sport of greyhound racing that is the topic of consideration here.

Greyhound racing is adapted from hare coursing, established in the 1830s, which is a form of hunting and recreation that requires the set-up of a course or enclosed area where greyhounds and a few other breeds (e.g., whippets) chase down hares by sense of sight, not smell. The dogs, unlike other types, are bred for speed, not stamina. It is unlike a fox hunt where animals hunt the fox in unison, but instead a competition between two, three, or sometimes four dogs, with people standing and watching. It is accompanied by gambling over which dog can turn and subdue the hare during the event. A specially developed collar called a slip, a double-collared leash that releases both dogs simultaneously, restrains dogs. The person in charge of releasing the dogs is called the 'slipper'. After an 80-yard lead, the dogs are slipped and the event commences. The most famous of the coursing events was the Waterloo Cup, run from 1836 to 2005 in Lancashire, England, spanning three days in a 64-dog competition. Even though hares are the most common animals coursed, other animals include foxes, deer, coyotes, gazelle, antelopes, and even wolves.

Coursing, the precursor to modern-day greyhound racing, is a blood sport that is likened to a form of killing by proxy (Atkinson and Young, 2005). It is a form of memesis – there is imitation of a real-life situation but without having to endure the danger or risk. The real-life situation is a war-like competition, with all the trappings of excitement and the unknown of who will live and who will die, without risk to the spectator. There may also be awe in the sheer speed at which the event takes place, and likely the imagination of how quickly the pursuit might translate into a kill. Although coursing initially held status as a genteel activity in the same vein as fox hunting, it has fallen out of favour for two main reasons. First, a series of several management transgressions (e.g., poking the eyes out of rabbits so they would run in certain directions, thereby securing wins for judges) eroded the sense of fair play. Second, it required too much space, which opened the door to the more contemporary form of greyhound racing, which first started in California in 1919, despite several other attempts to get it up and running in other US states and in the UK (Madden, 2010). Coursing was made illegal in the UK in 2005.

In its early years greyhound racing was tremendously popular. In the UK attendance increased from 6.5 million in 1928 to over 9 million in 1932, despite the impact of the depression (Jones, 1986). Totalizer gambling on greyhound racing reached 39 million pounds in 1938, 75 million in 1944, 138 million in 1945 and 2,000 million in 1946, with 60,000 attending the White City Derby in 1947 (Baker, 1996). The reason for such a climb in interest was evidently because of the rise in disposable income after World War II and a shortage of consumer goods on which to spend this money otherwise (Baker, 1996).

Greyhound racing was also enjoyed by both upper- and working-class folks, as other blood sports had been. And just like these other activities, it developed a social stigma that rendered it crass and corrupt and not appropriate for the more privileged classes. In the UK, the regular fixing of races and various other scandals induced riots, and there was concern that such forms of passive leisure were leading to moral decline and physical softness (Baker, 1996). In South Africa, greyhound racing suffered because of the social problems created by too many poor people investing too much of their hard-earned money into an activity that yielded little besides entertainment. During the 1940s, church leaders combined forces with the help of youth groups, welfare bodies, school principals, and city councils for the purpose of putting an end to the activity (Grundlingh, 2003). However, what is revealing, according to Grundlingh, is that in the debate over the legitimacy of greyhound racing, the issue of cruelty was never the main point of contention. Instead it was cultural identity and how best to use leisure time.

Over 20 countries around the world sanction greyhound racing, the main players being the US, Ireland, New Zealand, Great Britain, and Australia. In the US, 16 states sanction the sport, Florida having the most tracks and generating the most interest. Over 34,000 greyhounds are bred for the industry each year, and the vast majority of these are deemed unsuitable – upwards of 20,000 – and killed through clubbing, electrocution, or lethal injection. The dogs begin running at 18 months and retire at five years. Those that survive to race are subjected to very harsh conditions. The food they are given is of the poorest quality, and often this food is injected with steroids to make the animals faster. Many of the dogs are seriously deprived of food, and may remain muzzled and in small crates (nine square feet) for up to 22 hours at a time on days when they are not racing (Regan, 2004). The violence against greyhounds that is so prevalent in this industry has been placed into four categories by Atkinson and Young:

1. Breeding: One in every ten dogs bred for racing is culled because it simply does not have the stuff or substance to be a potential winner. Those dogs that are deemed worthy are isolated from human contact and kept in crammed cages without proper care.
2. Training and racing: Dogs are forced to race up to three times the recommended level, and this overuse leads to a variety of injuries including broken bones, torn muscles and ligaments, spinal cord injuries, lacerations, abrasions, and so on. The dogs are also fed meat characterized as 4-D: dead, dying, downed, and diseased, purchased for pennies a pound. The nutritional value of this meat is not enough to sustain the physiological needs of the dogs.
3. Housing: Upwards of 1,000 dogs may be kept in a kennel in rows of stacked cages. The dogs are let out up to four times per day to stretch, perform bodily functions, and to eat. Otherwise they are kept in these cages 22 hours per day. Music is blasted in the kennels to drown out the sound of the dogs barking and wailing.

4.   Release: Dogs, based on performance, are downwardly discarded through the system to tracks of lesser importance, and when they lose continuously they are fostered through adoption agencies or simply killed.

The intensity of the schedule often means that dogs sustain a range of different injuries, including broken bones and cardiac arrest. Dogs that cannot run any more or are too old are often sold to laboratories for testing. Regan reports that Colorado State University alone used 2,650 greyhounds between 1995 and 1998. In other cases, dogs are simply slaughtered. In Lillian, Alabama, during 2002, the *New York Times* reported on the discovery of a mass grave containing thousands of greyhounds. These had been sold to a man, R.L. Rhodes, who took responsibility for their termination. He killed them with a single gunshot to the head, and is reported as saying 'They didn't feel a thing' (Regan, 2004: 156). This type of treatment is not just restricted to the US. Regan writes that in Madrid in the year 2000, the magazine *Interviú* reported that hundreds of dogs had been strung up in trees because they were no longer of service to the racing industry.

Ethics in action

In Chapter 3, virtue ethics was described as a relative newcomer on the scene of animal ethics. The focus of this perspective is not on following normative rules,

Plate 6.5 Showing the dogs before a race in Fort Myers, Florida

but rather on the type of person one should be. I continue the discussion here through the use of two sides of an issue related to blood sports, according to Scruton (1996) and Hursthouse (2000).

Scruton's position is that the morality of fox hunting, angling, and other blood sports is a function of the motives tied to participation in these activities. If participants take joy or pleasure in the tearing apart of the fox or the slow, agonizing death of the bull they are not acting in a virtuous manner – they are deemed cruel. By contrast, if there is no enjoyment in the pain and suffering of these animals, i.e., pain and suffering are by-products of the activity, and if participation in these activities demonstrates other characteristics or traits like courage, the activity might be deemed virtuous. This analysis is rejected by Hursthouse, who claims that Scruton's use of the word 'cruelty' is incomplete. We may, as Rowlands (2009) suggests, subject animals to painful medical procedures if in the end these will provide a benefit to their well-being and longevity. Hursthouse would thus consider the use of callousness (although these activities might surely be considered cruel) in suggesting that both participants and spectators would be acting callously in choosing to ignore the fact that these activities inflict pain and suffering – they are essentially and conveniently turning a blind eye to these facts, and this is not what a virtuous person does.

In mediating this dispute, Rowlands returns to the three main objections against virtue ethics for help. First, in his attempts to deflect criticism away from this perspective, Scruton focuses on cruelty to the exclusion of other vices and virtues – like callousness. So even *if* protagonists are found not to be guilty of cruelty, they might certainly be guilty of callousness. There is subjectivity involved in defining the nature of these terms and how they apply to specific situations like blood sport participation. Rowlands argues that in our under- standing of virtue ethics, we should take into consideration how these traits or characteristics 'are embedded in an appropriate surrounding milieu of judgement and emotions' (2009: 99). Second, Rowlands argues that both Scruton and Hursthouse may be guilty of being vague in their use of terms like cruelty and callousness, especially because these uses serve to substantiate arguments on both sides of the table. Third, and perhaps most importantly, there is a conflict of vices and virtues, and the interpretation of these (and here we go back to the importance of motives for participation) that confounds the argument. Even though we could argue that bullfighting and fox hunting are callous, Rowlands explains, they happen to be fun and this type of outcome should outweigh the callousness of the event. However, one of the basic tenets of virtue ethics, according to Rowlands, is that virtues trump vices. In cases where there is a conflict over which trait should apply in a given situation, the recognition of callousness over fun should reign supreme. As Rowlands observes: 'The problem of conflict for virtue ethics arises not when virtues conflict with other things that might be thought beneficial, but when virtues conflict with other virtues' (2009: 105). How these virtues get prioritized is a function of many things, not least self-interest and circumstance, as noted above.

Conclusion

Historical reference points have been used in this chapter, including for example the Roman games and cockfighting, to situate contemporary practices that use animals for purposes of blood, bravado, and betting. The motivation for partici-pation in these activities then, as now, appears to be the pursuit of psychological and social pleasure. Theorists have discussed the denial of any deviance in the participation of these events at length, and the dogfighting case involving Michael Vick is a case in point. Participants use a number of neutralization techniques to justify this deviance, which allows for the degree of social acceptance that allows these events to carry on. This is akin to a type of clannishness that involves socialization, ritual, entertainment, gossip, drinking, and a dynamic that includes a brotherhood for those who share the same values and a disregard for those who do not. Clannishness, socialization, and ritual in relation to the use of animals are carried forward in the following chapter in reference to hunting and fishing. These too are blood sports, and because of the volume of material on these two activities, much of which includes questions of a moral nature on the reasons for participation, they are highlighted in a chapter of their own.

7   Animals pursued for sport and subsistence

Introduction

This chapter examines moral questions surrounding the acceptability of hunting and fishing as forms of consumptive tourism. In the case of hunting, philosophers continue to debate the merits of this activity along the lines of animal rights versus ecological holism. Rights-based advocates argue that it is never acceptable to kill animals for pleasure because these animals, not unlike humans, have inherent value. By contrast, the ecological holists, stemming from the Aldo Leopold camp, argue that killing an animal is morally justifiable if the integrity and stability of the ecosystem is maintained. Although fishing and hunting are often placed in the same category, there are other questions that need to be considered. The literature on fishing appears to be more interdisciplinary because of the quasi-consumptive nature of some forms of fishing, i.e., catch and release. Much of the debate surrounds the welfare issues tied to catch and release and the moral acceptability of catching, stressing, and suffering for the purposes of human pleasure alone.

Hunting

History

At the outset, the reader must recognize that hunting is not an activity that was invented at some point in time in the past for purposes of sustenance and recreation. Techniques may have been invented, but the act itself is evolutionary. Hunting is part of the fabric of who we are and how we evolved. In this we should also recognize that we have gone from Stone Age to Space Age only in the last five seconds of a 24-hour evolutionary clock. This suggests from an evolutionary standpoint that we are very much creatures of this other dominant temporal domain. In the western world particularly we do not need to hunt in this day and age. But if we did not have the luxury of supermarkets and other food retailers, many would surely feel compelled to hunt for survival, even if this was designed to supplement a largely agrarian lifestyle.

Historical accounts illustrate that hunting for some was about obtaining food for survival and for others a matter of training and fun. In the first case, Resl (2007) observes that hunting for food was a pursuit of the lower classes – the activity was undertaken out of necessity for survival. In the latter case, wealthy elites hunted for purposes of military training, exercise, entertainment, or to demonstrate their socio-economic status. This appears to be the case at least as far back as 2446 BCE, where hunting was taking place in Egypt. Lions were released and moved along pre-established paths by attendants for royal hunters to slay. These hunting displays were instrumental in demonstrating the power of the king both as a hunter and as a ruler (Houlihan, 1996). The military function of hunting has been discussed by Boehrer (2007), who has referred to this function as the 'armigerous gentry's traditional *raison d'être*' (p. 14). It was embraced by those of rank in society because of the associated breeding of fine horses both for war and hunting, which might only be secured by those of higher social standing. What further separated men of quality from others was represented in the earliest printed manual on hunting in England, *The Boke of Saint Albans* (1486), which had three main sections: hawking, hunting, and heraldry – this last concept dealing with duties and responsibilities. Hawking and hunting were signifiers of standing because these duties and responsibilities separated gentlemen from 'ungentlemen' (Boehrer, 2007).

The emergence of poaching in the United Kingdom had much to do with this disconnect between the poor and the wealthy, according to Boehrer (2007). Poaching was as much about risk as it was about eating. Story has it that Shakespeare was taken from the property of Sir Thomas Lucy for poaching his deer, but this is disputed (like much surrounding Shakespeare himself). But as Greenblat and other scholars observe, there is little doubt that poaching represented resentment towards those who owned large parcels of land and who were privileged as such: 'For Elizabethans deer poaching was not understood principally as having to do with hunger; it was a story not about desperation but about risk ... It was a skillful assault upon property, a symbolic violation of the social order, a coded challenge to authority' (Greenblat, 2004: 151–2). The emergence of Britain's Game Act of 1671 was designed to extend the right to hunt to the social class of men who owned country estates (the landed gentry), where previous to this it was the sovereign who was sole owner of game. Further reforms came about in 1831 through the Game Reform Act, extending hunting rights to everyone in Britain in possession of a permit (Munsche, 1981).

The years following the US Revolutionary War catalysed a change in the relationship between man and the frontier. Hunting underwent a massive change in American society, as soldiers became 'lionized' figures on the frontier, and where 'the myth of the frontiersman became an attractive icon to be emulated among middle and upper class males' (Herda-Rapp and Goedeke, 2005: 150). This perspective is followed by Midgley (2002), who writes that the Victorian hunter assumed that every animal he came across would attack him or was noxious, and so was required to dispatch them on sight. There was really no thought about eating the animal, but stuffing it was viewed as conquering the great beast and written up accordingly in one's memoirs. And during the Age of Empire (1875–1914) the narratives of hunters in the Canadian west demonstrate not a need to convey meaning about empire, but rather a focus on the character traits of the individual, including masculinity and conquest of beasts (Wonders, 2005). As urbanization and industrialization continued to force a disconnect between men and nature, hunting was pursued as a manner by which to forge a reconnection (Brower, 2005); an act that would remedy the ills of civilization (Haraway, 1989).

This mindset is represented in a number of personal accounts that are well documented in the literature on hunting. In his book, *Ape*, Sorenson (2009) illustrates how nineteenth-century hunters and naturalists alike felt about killing animals for their own purposes. Paul Belloni du Chaillu wrote of his explorations in equatorial Africa as perhaps the first white man to see and kill the gorillas of the region. His stories tell of slaughtering animal after animal, explaining that he was never so happy as when shooting one, further noting that he almost felt like a murderer when hearing their cries of distress. This was a time when accounts of big game hunters in pursuit of the 'Big Five' (lion, elephant, leopard, rhinoceros, and water buffalo) served to emphasize the romantic and iconic nature of man versus beast (Carruthers, 2005). Evolutionary biologist Alfred Russel Wallace shot large numbers of orang-utans in Indonesia, Sorenson writes, orphaning one intentionally for the purpose of keeping it as a pet. Like the public in general, these individuals showed little concern for the suffering of others taken for pleasure.

One of the motivations of removing the great herds of bison from the American west was to supplant this species with more marketable herds of livestock (Cronen, 1991). Upwards of 40 million bison were eliminated in decades, with heightened depletions after the Civil War when the railroads continued deep into the west. There are myriad accounts of hunters never getting off the trains at all, firing at will, killing dozens, and continuing on into the west. Cronen argues that perhaps the biggest threat to the bison population was the perfection in tanning of hides, and the subsequent creation of a market for leather fashions. The year following, Cronen explains, all hell broke loose. Three to five animals died for every hide that made it back east as more and more hunting parties descended on the west. In Kansas, the slaughter reached a peak between the years 1870 and 1873, and thereafter completely collapsed. As hunters moved from state to state, and even up into Canada, there was nothing left to take a decade later.

The etiquette of hunting changed during the latter part of the ninteenth century according to Brower (2005). The massive kills of buffalo became regarded as vulgar and wasteful, replaced by a sporting ethic that held central the belief in fairness and stylishness. The Fair Chase Statement written by the US-based Boone and Crockett Club (established in 1887) is representative of this changing mindset:

> FAIR CHASE, as defined by the Boone and Crockett Club, is the ethical, sportsmanlike, and lawful pursuit and taking of any free-ranging wild, native North American big game animal in a manner that does not give the hunter an improper advantage over such animals.
>
> (Boone and Crockett Club, 2008)

The implementation of fair chase rules and principles was designed not only to conserve the resource (animals) but also to maintain social acceptability of hunting among hunters and within the public in general (more on this below). The interest in hunting remained high throughout the 1950s. In 1955, for example, at least one person in one out of every three households in the US hunted (Clarke, 1958).

Theorists argue that hunting is no longer as attractive as it was at the turn of the twentieth century and onwards into the 1960s. This is the result of sweeping changes in the attitudes of people towards the environment and towards hunters, coupled with the recognition that with precise forms of technology and other human-induced interventions (e.g., GPS units), there is really very little sport left in the activity (Regan, 2004). And the numbers exist to confirm this trend. As of 2004, only 5 per cent of Americans possessed a hunting licence (Regan, 2004). What has replaced the larger numbers of hunters and anglers of the past is the opportunity to continue to enjoy nature as a wildlife viewer, not a wildlife taker. The 2006 US National Survey of Fishing, Hunting, and Wildlife-Associated Recreation reports that wildlife-associated recreation includes anglers, hunters, and wildlife watchers, with sportsmen defined as those who fish, hunt, or both. The report illustrates that although 6 per cent more people (16 years and older) participated in wildlife-associated recreation over the previous census, representing 5.2 million people, the number of anglers and hunters fell from 37.8 million people in 2001 to 33.9 million in 2006, with $3 billion less spent in 2006 than in 2001 (see Table 7.1).

Table 7.1 Total wildlife-related recreation

Participants	87.5 million
Expenditures (US$)	122.3 billion
Sportspersons	
Total participants	33.9 million
Fishers	30.0 million
Hunters	12.5 million
Total days	737 million
Fishing	517 million
Hunting	220 million
Total expenditures (US$)	76.7 billion
Fishing	42.0 billion
Hunting	22.9 billion
Unspecified	11.7 billion
Wildlife watchers	
Total participants	71.1 million
Around the home	67.8 million
Away from home	23.0 million
Total expenditures (US$)	45.7 billion

Source: US National Survey of Fishing, Hunting, and Wildlife-Associated Recreation (2006)

Even though numbers of hunters have declined in recent decades, it is interesting to see the extent to which hunting operators are getting the message out to a market, still rather robust, which spends a significant amount of time and money on this activity. Bauer and Herr (2004) found that 29 per cent of all tourism websites were fishing and/or hunting related (this represented six million Google hits), and that some hunters are willing to pay tens of thousands of dollars for a hunting trip abroad that targets species that they are highly motivated to pursue. The resilience of hunting, despite lower numbers of participants, may be found in the number of animals killed annually. In the US, this amounts to 134 million (Regan, 2004), with approximately six million wild ungulates killed each year in the northern hemisphere, 1.2 million of these in Germany alone (Bauer and Giles, 2002).

In remote or marginal areas, like Canada's High Arctic, hunting exists as an important part of the economy. Gregoire (2008) writes that 450 polar bears were shot in Nunavut in the 2006–7 season, 120 of these by sport hunters and 330 by subsistence hunters, the former of whom contribute CDN\$2.5 million in revenue to Nunavut, with 75 per cent of this money staying in the territory. It is not uncommon for a sport hunter to pay upwards of CDN\$30,000 to a local guide for the opportunity to hunt a polar bear (this fee does not include airfare, permits, or other fees). The costs associated with hunting over other forms of nature-based tourism are borne out in other regions. For example, in Namibia, Barnes and Novelli (2008) report that although anglers are twice as numerous as hunters, the latter group pays almost nine times more per trip (N\$54,120) than the former (N\$6,270). Part of the reason for the difference in economic impact is that hunting

Plate 7.1 Hunting dogs with a day off, Griffith Island, Ontario

works through outfitters, while fishing is non-guided. Lindsey *et al.* (2006) find that the revenues from hunting can often play an important role in community development as well as in the rehabilitation of habitat. Hunting tourists are willing to hunt in areas that have depleted numbers of animals and where ecotourism is not an option, and are hesitant to hunt in areas where conservation goals are compromised. The authors suggest that these attitudes are potential drivers for positive changes in the hunting industry in Africa.

The hunter

There are three general categories of hunting according to Luke (1997; see also Causey, 1989), with the first two central to the discussion below: sport hunting, done for its own sake; subsistence hunting, done as a means of survival; and market hunting, done for the purpose of selling animal parts. An example of market hunting is offered by Brashares *et al.* (2004), who discuss the multi-billion dollar trade in bushmeat that is a central contributor to the economies of developing countries, but which threatens the persistence of tropical vertebrates. Kümpel *et al.* (2010) write that, although bushmeat is both a source of food protein for families and income, it is this latter function that concerns conservationists who fear that this unsustainable practice is contributing to the extinction of large mammal species. In the absence of preferable livelihood opportunities, hunting is

Plate 7.2 Market hunting in ivory

an important stand-in income for many men as there are virtually no barriers to participation, including little capital investment for involvement.

The discourse on hunting and hunters is voluminous, with several authors developing typologies of hunters based on a number of criteria. I have selected one by the ecofeminist Kheel (1995), who categorizes hunters according to six different types, with the first three of these given more depth here because of their link to the discussion that follows.

1. The happy hunter: Unabashed sport hunter who hunts for purposes of psychological need along with character development. Although rules are developed for fair play, masculine instincts are demonstrated along with superiority over the animal world.
2. The holist hunter: Hunts in order to maintain the balance in nature (ecological need). Instead of recreation and sport, hunters use terms like sustainable yield, population density, culling, and harvesting in acting as managers of the ecological world. The world of science and business acts as a safe harbour in the storm of popular criticism over hunting.
3. The holy hunter: Here religious needs are sought in attaining a state of spirituality. Reverence and respect for the animal are demonstrated and in return the hunter gains an almost transcendental state via a merger with the animal. While hunters often say a prayer for the animal before it is killed, and believe that the animal gives itself to the hunter (in the tradition of indigenous cultures), these feelings align more with feelings of guilt than anything else.
4. Hired hunter: commercial profit.
5. Hungry hunter: to eat.
6. Hostile hunter: to eradicate pests.

Hunting for the first three of these groups is said to be instinctive, sexually charged, and primeval in nature. Masculinity is a sought-after state in men that is fed by violence and death. Alienation from nature happens naturally in a man's life, and the act of hunting restores this balance. Kheel takes up the argument brought forward by Dinnerstein (1987), who argues that at birth the child's identity is indistinct from other factions of the world, and in the search for self-identity boys construct opposition both to women and to nature. This identity-searching comes packaged with fear and rage as well as the need to return to a primordial state – a return to the original coexistent self. Furthermore, the transition from boy to man involves a rite of passage thought to be similar in intent around the world, many of which involve violence towards women and the environment (including animals). Linking these themes together, Kheel argues that

> Violence becomes the only way in which the hunter can experience this sense of oneness while asserting his masculine status as an autonomous human being. By killing the animal, the hunter ritually enacts the death of his longing for a return to a primordial female/animal world, a world to which he cannot return.
>
> (Kheel, 1995: 106)

These various hunter types may target specific species or they may choose to hunt in certain more convenient ways (Regan, 2004). List hunters collect animals in the same way that birdwatchers list birds that they have observed. This includes the African Big Five (leopard, lion, elephant, Cape buffalo, and rhinoceros) and the Arctic Grand Slam (caribou, musk ox, polar bear, and walrus). By contrast, canned hunting (about 1,000 facilities in the US alone) is a type of hunting that takes place within the fences of 'preserves'. In Texas alone, the industry is worth over one billion dollars annually (Kluger, 2002), and there are almost 8,000 breeders in the US breeding animals with the biggest rack of antlers possible for the walls of high-paying clients (Nicholls, 2007). The animals in these enclosures are more docile than wild animals since they have been exposed to humans as exotic pets or kept on farms, producing a level of familiarity and perhaps even trust. Furthermore, many of these exotic animals come from zoos, where there are often surplus animals that the zoo administration can no longer afford to keep. Despite the fact that the Association of Zoos and Aquariums (AZA) has policies prohibiting the sale of excess animals to canned hunt companies, zoos are able to skirt regulations by selling them to animal dealers as middle-men. Of 19,361 animals leaving American zoos between 1992 and 1998, 38 per cent went to dealers, auctions, hunt camps, or other places that would not provide the welfare conditions that a zoo might offer. As Regan notes, the hypocrisy of zoo administrators, those who should look to the best interests of their stocks, should not be overlooked.

All of the various forms of hunting entail a contest between the hunted and the hunter. Hunting for meat, for example, might be considered a contest between the hunter's skills and the animal's ability to use its wits and the natural environment to elude the hunter. However, it is sport hunting where the contest is the central feature of the experience – the competition is an end in itself (Marvin, 2007). It is the encounter, pleasure, and satisfaction of the pursuit and the matching of abilities within the rules of the game that are deemed most important. Donald (2006) suggests that it is important to maintain a sense (perhaps more like an illusion) of excitement and adventure in what is supposed to be an elemental battle between human will and intelligence over the animal's ability to negotiate its environment in its will to survive. The development of the sporting code, according to Donald (2005), legitimized fairness in the practice of hunting. For example, in Britain there developed a general distaste for broad-scale animal drives, where members of a species were driven or corralled into enclosures and easily shot while in a state of panic. Donald observes that this move away from mass slaughter was in large part symptomatic of the need to avoid killing females of the species – the breeding stock – for the purpose of ensuring a stable population. How the abilities of hunter and hunted are matched in the face of advanced modes of transportation and technology (guns) is an important consideration.

The excitement brought on by the pursuit of game for sport includes an odd mix of differing emotions according to Donald. It includes sheer blood lust or the joy of killing and domination of nature, possibly coexistent with veneration for the beast pursued. Hunting has been connected with erotic urges, where the pursuit of the animal is paralleled to the pursuit, conquest, and possession of a woman – as noted by Kheel above. Hunting provides a sense of catharsis for the hunter, while in other cases it provides a connection between the hunter and the rhythms of nature, including death and regeneration. In such cases the hunter plays out predator–prey relationships that are simply part of our instinctive natures.

In Africa, the big game trophy hunting that emerged alongside colonial rule in the 1890s and continued in intensity from 1900 to 1945 acted as a major symbol of this dominance over local people and the natural resources of the land. As Akama (2008) writes, the face of big game hunting in the early years was US President Teddy Roosevelt who shot, had stuffed, and sent to America some 3,000 African specimens. A type of violent and heroic imperialism according to Ritvo, that involved 'rows of horns and hides, mounted heads and stuffed bodies' (1987: 248) was favoured over subsistence hunting (Akama, 2008; Sukumar, 2008).

For Carruthers (2005), sport hunting in Africa was attractive because it represented freedom from the restrictive chains of Western society, and because it was an antidote to the crowded, industrialized, and private property landscapes of English society. He feels that the early hunter-visitors to Africa were 'the first wildlife ecotourists of southern Africa', and this consumption of nature was an import–export form of trade involving the international market, with the commodity being experience (citing Nash, 1979). But this sentiment is far from universal. Carruthers later cites Gray (1979), who felt that these visitors were more concerned about themselves, extracting personal worth in the form of the slaughter of animals. The aim was entertainment, and because these people had no stake in the future of the countries they were exploiting, they felt no need for reciprocal exchange.

In recent decades, as the foregoing discussion suggests, trophy hunting has fallen upon hard times. Studies suggest that trophy hunting is on the decline because the pursuit of a trophy appears to be the least important reason, set against a range of other motivations including the enjoyment of nature, excitement, opportunity, challenge, society, meat, and solitude (Boulanger *et al.*, 2006). In a study of Montana residents and non-resident outfitter-sponsored elk hunters, Eliason (2008) found that the latter group were more likely to seek trophy-class animals than the former, although this number was still not strong. On a ten-point scale of importance of harvesting a trophy animal (10 being extremely important), the mean score of non-resident hunters was 4.8, while the resident score was 3.6. One of the main reasons for the decline in trophy hunting over hunting for meat is explained by Swan (1995), who argues that since most Americans eat meat, it would be somewhat embarrassing for these people to oppose those fellow meat-eaters who choose to hunt for their own meals.

The attractiveness of hunting as an activity is wrapped up in a few consistent themes. Theorists argue that hunting is a learned activity based on socialization theory, where family and friends are the key drivers of this socialization, especially in rural areas. Stedman and Heberlein (2001) found that rural males whose fathers did not hunt were more likely to hunt than urban males whose fathers did not hunt, suggesting that hunting is more a way of life in rural communities than urban. People in rural communities often define themselves in terms of their connection to hunting (Kete, 2002). This fits well with constructionist theory, or the idea that we have perceptions about nature that are culturally embedded – based on cultural values and beliefs as well as how we attach meaning to these experiences in this cultural milieu (Herda-Rapp and Goedeke, 2005). Individuals raised in an environment where deer hunting is valued will have differences of opinion about this activity, and deer, than those raised in an urban environment. Both socially construct deer in ways that reflect differences in their cultural values and beliefs. The constructivist approach is important and has provided the theoretical foundation for research in human dimensions of wildlife research because it allows theorists to closely examine the differences that exist in how such groups define nature.

Differences in how communities define or construct nature are evident in work by Ericsson *et al.* (2004) on the support for hunting as a mechanism to control the expanding wolf population in Sweden. These authors looked at four rather discrete entities within Swedish society: the general public, hunters, the public living in wolf areas, and wolf area hunters. These groups were presented with the question of whether it is acceptable to hunt wolves to control their numbers and distribution under four different circumstances, including: (1) to reduce the risk to domestic animals being killed; (2) if wolves lose their natural fear of humans and come into populated areas; (3) because people are afraid of wolves; and (4) because wolves compete with humans over game. Respondents were given three response options: support, neutral, oppose. Table 7.2 shows the percentage of each of the groups in support of each of the four options. The first two statements, 'reduce risk to domestic animals' and 'if wolves lose fear of humans', show the greatest support among the four groups. The wolf area hunters had the highest response percentage for each of the four statements on the conditions in support of hunting.

Table 7.2 Percentage of Swedish groups in support of hunting option

Option	General public	Hunters	WA public[a]	WA hunters
Reduce risk to domestic animals	53[b]	83	68	91
If wolves lose fear of humans	54	80	65	86
Because people are afraid of wolves	24	56	37	70
Because wolves compete with humans over game	11	35	18	45

[a] WA refers to 'wolf area'
[b] Each percentage value represents just one value (support) of three reported in the article. Neutral and opposition values are not included which, if included, would otherwise amount to 100% for each option and stakeholder group.

Another major theme is the rite of passage for young boys (Kheel, 1996) and the masculinity of the activity in general. Much of the narrative surrounds the coming of age or rite of passage of boys to men, and the more recent decline in hunting and lack of interest on the part of young males due to many competing interests (technology, laziness, and so on) and the animal rights movement. Those boys who do choose to participate share in the narrative of the transformation from a boy raised and nurtured by his mother, to a male-dominated social world dominated by masculinity. And those boys who are lucky enough to shoot their first buck are, at dinner, presented with the testicles of the buck, with men offering words of encouragement along the lines of the aphrodisiacal properties of the food.

The hunting-as-masculine theme is explored by Kalof and Fitzgerald (2003) in their analysis of the display (photographs) of dead animals in 14 hunting magazines. Working from a hypothesis that these animals would be displayed in a way that demonstrates reverence and respect – the manner in which the hunting agenda is currently framed – the authors found quite different representations. Animals in the photographs were marginalized and objectified (e.g., animals positioned under weapons). The dominance of this activity by white males was also found to hold true in regards to these photographs. None of the photos ever depicted a female or person of colour holding a gun if a white male was also included in the picture. The prevalence of males was evident in Eliason's (2008) study, mentioned above, with 90.8 per cent (n=255) of residents and 100 per cent (n=281) of non-residents as male. The dominance of whites involved in hunting was also a factor in this study, with 98.8 per cent of all resident hunters and 98.9 per cent of non-residents Caucasian.

Still another theme surrounds the notion of ritual, which may play heavily into both rite of passage and socialization, as discussed above. As Luke (1996: 92) contends, 'It is not that men hunt to get meat, just the reverse, they eat the meat in order to hunt – that is, in order to gain *ex post facto* legitimization for the hunt itself'. While ritual is explained as behaviours that are repeatable, structured, expressive, performed, and symbolic (Rappaport, 1992: 249, as cited in Bronner, 2004), rites connote 'a scared or magical connection to sacrifice and transformation' (Bronner, 2004: 18). To suggest that these rituals and rites may have masculine undercurrents would be a gross under-representation. Activities like shirt-cutting for missing one's shot at an open buck are meant to symbolically castrate the offender in front of his peers, rendering him emasculated and feminized. Hunting is therefore a drama played out between two physically impressive foes, where sentiment for the hunted is repressed, and the gun as a phallic symbol is used to emerge victorious. Buck fever, or missing a shot because of psychological factors, is a sign of mental and physical weakness, and, further, the testing of oneself against another male (the buck), and failing, is a sign of inferior sexual prowess, according to Bronner.

> shirttail cutting (for a missed shot at a buck), blood smearing (on the face after a kill), blood drinking, and the 'hunter's dish' (eating of the deer's heart and

liver by person who shot him) ... 'buck fever' (missing a shot because of psychosomatic symptoms), lucky objects (e.g., rabbit's foot), refraining from shaving, the last bite (feeding the deer grass after the kill), cutting the throat to bleed the animal, cutting the tarsal glands to prevent ruining the meat, observation of dangerous behavior of bucks, narrating stories of 'ghost' bucks, relating the aphrodisiacal powers of antlers, taking a 'trophy' (usually the tail), the obligatory photograph with the hung buck, and so on.

(Bronner, 2004: 13)

Taking things a step further, however, other theorists argue that the ritual and socialization at hunt camps have just as much to do with gender dominance as with other expressed motivations. Adams (2003), for example, argues that the conquest of the deer is more akin to the violation of women when she says that 'The sexual conquest of the object, identifying and stalking the prey, the thrill of capture, degrading, ejaculating in, or killing the victim – with this narrative, one could be reading pornography, the testimony of a victim of sexual assault, a hunting story – or all three' (Adams, 2003: 90).

Not unlike the cockfights discussed in Chapter 6, pigeon shoots – a spectator contest that involves betting – are an activity that has been contested in the US on the basis of tradition and ritual, and changing moral standards. Bronner (2005) writes that those who support the shoot argue that pigeons are dirty pests that foul the landscape and hence need to have their numbers controlled. On the other hand, protesters argue that those who participate in the shoot – who kill upwards of 7,000 birds in a day – are violent, predatory, phallocentric, abusive, and patriarchal. Bronner writes that animal welfare groups are challenged in attempting to eliminate these contests because tradition acts as a social force and even a moral system. These traditions help to define a community according to what the unit deems to be right and wrong. The arrival of different value systems, as those from opposing bodies like animal welfare groups, disrupts the system, prompting all members of the community, not just participants, with new ways of looking at the world to greatly broaden the moral universe of those living in the community. Opponents and supporters of the bear hunt in New Jersey have adopted the same rhetoric. Opponents argue that bears are benevolent and peaceful animals, while supporters suggest that bears are a threat to humans (Harker and Bates, 2007).

Literature tied to ritual and hunting has also dealt with the sensitivities that tourists must have when travelling abroad. Bauer and Herr (2004) use the example of hunting ethics in Germany – *Jagdliches Brauchtum* – drawing upon time-tested ritual and tradition as a means by which to protect the resource base. Like the case in the US, there are mock trials for failure to abide by these customs, as part of the practice of hunting. Tourists who abide by these practices and rituals are more seamlessly accepted into the community.

Another theme emergent in the literature is embodiment, which, in the nature-based tourism sense, might mean the closer and much more intense bodily or sensual connection between the tourist and the object of pursuit and enjoyment.

Franklin (2001) discusses two types of embodiment in hunting and fishing. The first is in reference to Isaak Walton's *The Compleat Angler* (1653), where nature was essentially an antidote to city life, which had increasingly become industrialized and commercialized. Fishing was a therapeutic exercise that was enhanced through the association of like-minded individuals. The angler was thus 'someone who rejected the modern world in some way and belonged to a fraternity, a leisure cult that worked in order to angle' (Franklin, 2001: 62). The second embodied a consumptive recreationist type, called the 'Darwin and the "Killer Ape" Legacy', which was shaped according to the belief that the need to hunt was a function of our animal ancestry, which otherwise has been diluted by an urban existence. Humans had to exercise this killer ape ancestry through frequent trips to the backcountry, and carry out epic battles with impressive predators, or risk deterioration in the cityscape.

What Franklin found through reference to other theorists (see for example Cartmill, 1993) was more of an inclination of hunters towards the first type, Isaak Walton, than the second type, the killer ape. Following from Macnaghten and Urry's (1998) *Contested Natures* and overreliance on the visual gaze in distancing or disembodying humans from the natural world, hunting and fishing by contrast are activities that re-engage the senses in a 'fully sensed engagement with the natural world' (Franklin, 2001: 67); hearing, touch, and smell in a coordination of all of the senses. Franklin takes the discussion one step further in suggesting that natural areas visited by tourists – and the implication is groups of tourists who frequent some places on a regular basis – is self-defeating because the end result is a sterilized product devoid of animal activity beyond what is provided at visitor centres or perhaps animals that have been habituated. By contrast, hunters in smaller numbers dispersed in space and time with knowledge of habitat and behaviour of their quarry, not to mention their tracks and sounds, make the experience more sensual and intimate than other forms of animal-based outdoor recreation. Wildlife viewing is simply that – watching wildlife. By contrast, hunting taps into just about all of the human senses, including sight, sound, touch, smell, and taste. Hunting is an act that binds together predator and prey in the great chain of being, with an intensity unmatched in the wildlife watching experience. In hunting the animal is watched and eaten, according to Farnham (1992).

In defence of hunting

Philosophers have developed a number of arguments in favour of hunting and these have been structured on practical and philosophical grounds. A number of these arguments are listed below and follow from Comninou (1995), Vitali (1990), and Luke (1997). Many of the arguments listed below will be examined in more detail to follow.

1. Animals are placed on earth for our own personal consumptive needs.
2. Hunting is justifiable because animals are lower than humans on the great chain of being.

3. Hunters claim a higher moral platform because of the responsibility in finding and killing their own food.
4. Hunting has cultural meaning attached to it and it is justifiable because of the application of a unique human skill in the procurement of meat.
5. Only persons have rights, not ecosystems. If the plants and animals that compose the ecosystem do not have rights, then the entire system does not have rights.
6. Hunting is part of our ancestral lineage (evolutionary argument on basis of atavism).
7. Hunting contributes to conservation through hunters' fees.
8. Hunting is a part of wildlife management in the absence of natural predators for ecosystem balance.

The perspective that animals exist to fulfil our own personal consumptive needs is advocated by Clarke (1958), who says that hunting is a form of play that gives the hunter satisfaction. Hunting is partly aesthetic but it also has a deeper function, that being the maintenance of a harmonious relationship between humans and nature, 'for wildlife is truly his prey as it is that of any other predator' (Clarke, 1958: 425). Added to this is the belief that

> ... I can see no blame in the hunter, so long as his conscience, ruled by respect for nature, governs his actions. This respect is an emotion, and it must be admitted that the true climax of the hunt is, for most hunting, death. Personally I feel the same way about killing game as I do about felling a tree.
>
> (Clarke, 1958: 425)

Hunting is part of our genetic make-up defined through evolution (Bauer and Herr, 2004). It is who we are and what we have done for millennia. To many hunters the purpose of animals is to fulfil human interests. There is no doubt to the fact that the mindset is one of belief that these are willing victims. The hunter and writer Archibald Rutledge commented that 'certain game birds and animals are apparently made to be hunted, because of their peculiar food value and because their character lends zest to the pursuit of them' (Luke, 1996: 96).

   This argument corresponds well to the idea that animals should not be extended moral consideration because they are simply not as important as humans according to their placement on the great chain of being. Rolston (1988) accepts a value chain in regards to members of the ecological community, with humans given priority over animals and animals given priority over plants. He argues for the ethical justification of hunting on the grounds that this activity (predation through hunting) is a normal and integral part of human functioning within the ecosystem. Hunting for sustenance is morally justifiable, but hunting for cultural reasons i.e., religious purposes, sport, and recreation, is not. In this, Rolston supports the principle of nonaddition of suffering, whereby we share a duty to avoid inflicting more pain on the hunted than they would experience in the natural world.

Accordingly, when an act follows evolution (nature), one can support it from a moral standpoint.

Philosophers have also attacked non-hunters using the position of hypocrisy. Hunters are far less hypocritical than meat purchasers and consumers, and it is the latter who must come to grips with the tacit support of the factory farming industries (Franklin, 2001). Hunters thus claim a higher moral platform because they have an active hand not only in the choices of where and when and which animals are to die, but also a responsibility as to how the dead animals are handled and consumed. This moral platform has facilitated the development of a different environmentalism according to Franklin, 'with humans *in* the landscape, not skirting nervously around its edges as "organized tourists"' (2001: 75). Cahoone (2009) has also argued for this position in suggesting that contemporary hunting is actually not a sport but rather a 'neo-traditional trophic practice whereby agro-industrialists elect to approximate the pre-agrarian skill of procuring meat by taking individual wild prey. This is no pretended primitivism, but a practical approximation of an archaic activity' (pp. 72–3). When hunting is regulated and responsible, hunters exemplify trophic responsibility, knowledge of the food hunted, killed, and eaten, and self-sufficiency. They employ ecological expertise, experience a type of interdependence with animals, and are honest about the meat they eat and the manner in which they procure it. By contrast, meat-eaters who purchase their food in the store are hypocritical. Even vegetarians, Cahoone adds, cannot claim moral superiority based on a higher form of responsible land stewardship, because farming kills animals in the following ways:

1. Clearing land kills animals outright and reduces habitat and therefore diversity.
2. Pesticides and fertilizers pollute water on which animals depend.
3. Heavy machinery kills ground-nesting amphibians, reptiles, birds, and small mammals.
4. Deer are often killed to protect crops from opportunistic wildlife.
5. Supporting technologies contribute a series of indirect harms to wildlife.

Added to this is that the amount of fossil fuel used in the act of killing one elk (the production of the gun, ammunition, driving to the field, etc.) is only marginally higher than the fossil fuel required to produce an equivalent amount of local vegetables. The production of non-local produce, however, is far more costly than the elk.

Innumerable works have argued that indigenous people maintain a close interpersonal relationship with animals and nature. Rabb (2002), for example, argues that meat eating is not a necessary evil amongst indigenous people, but rather a cultural process that defines identity, and that kinship between humans and animals means that sometimes animals have to be eaten. The manner in which indigenous people obtain meat has also been debated. Traditional hunting to many Aboriginal groups does not necessarily mean traditional approaches to hunting. This is the case with the Hope Vale Aboriginal community in the Great Barrier Reef World Heritage area, Australia. Using discourse analysis, Nursey-Bray *et al.* (2010) found that 'traditional' meant a cultural right of a prehistoric tradition, which should not be weakened by the fact that people of the community do not now need meat to survive, meat is now in shorter supply, and killing methods and technologies have changed over time. The community argues that the traditional hunting culture is premised on relationships with country, places, and people. The discourse analysis further showed that land managers were concerned over biodiversity issues in regards to aboriginal hunting practices and patterns. Concern was shown not for individual animal rights, but rather for ecosystem health, demonstrating an ecocentric approach in line with Leopold and others rather than an animal rights approach (Nursey-Bray *et al.*, 2010). Moriarty and Woods (1997) discuss whether indigenous societies should be exempt from the argument against hunting. From this it would be interesting to observe whether there have been any indigenous societies in history that have refrained from consuming meat, as a guide which might help us to determine whether our contemporary predisposition to consume meat is morally problematic. If there is no record of any society not eating meat (following what Rolston argues above), would this be further justification for the consumption of meat along these ecological lines? (Fox (1999: 129) contends that 'Most of the world's indigenous peoples have depended, to some extent at least, on meat-eating'.)

While Singer has argued that the shooting of a duck does not lead to its replacement, the argument levied by the sport hunting platform is that it in fact replaces ducks severalfold through the use of monies for habitat protection and other conservation measures, not to mention the benefits to other species on those lands not hunted (Loftin, 1984). After several years of discrediting hunting, the conservationist movement appears to be embracing this land use in places like Africa where it is said to be saving wildlife (see Akama, 2008). While conservation fees help to create habitat for animals, the wildlife management approach constructs a strong defence of hunting according to the proper balance of members of the ecological community:

> Unless animals are hunted they will breed to excess and overpopulate the range beyond its carrying capacity. This will degrade the habitat through overuse and the game will be subject to starvation, parasitism, and disease inflicting an equal or greater amount of suffering on the animals. Under natural conditions, populations were controlled by predators, but the predators are now rare. Many predators do not coexist well with man, and some of them are dangerous. Therefore, reintroduction of predators, while it has a romantic appeal, is impractical except on a very limited basis. Thus, human hunters must occupy the niche of the absent predators and cull the game herds. This actually benefits the species by improving the gene pool. It also benefits individual specimens, since it is no less painful and terrifying (indeed, it may be significantly more so) for an animal to be hunted and killed by a natural

predator or to die of starvation, disease, or old age in the wild than to be
hunted and killed by a man.

(Loftin, 1984: 243–4)

There is the recognition that predators should never be hunted because they do not
overpopulate a region and degrade a range, but there is the question of why one

Plate 7.3 Legal hunting and its benefits

species of animal is deemed more important than another. Killing certain animals to preserve others that are endangered is seen as virtuous (List, 1997).

What has also helped to nourish the hunting platform is the use of terminology that has contributed to its social acceptance. The movement away from 'sport' and 'trophy' (as above) and the use of 'ethics' and 'sustainability' in advertisements and brochures has proven helpful. There is also the link to ecotourism that has been difficult for certain markets to comprehend according to the meaning of consumptiveness and non-consumptiveness (see Chapter 8). A review of the hunting literature by Luke (1997) has generated consensus concerning the meaning of specific aspects of the sportsman's code according to anthropocentrism, sustainability, and other concepts. The six guidelines of the code include:

SC1: Safety first
SC2: Obey the law
SC3: Give fair chase
SC4: Harvest the game
SC5: Aim for quick kills
SC6: Retrieve the wounded.

Luke argues that SC1 and SC2 are anthropocentric because their purpose is to facilitate the hunting experience in a safe and sustainable manner. SC3, Luke says, is a bit more ambiguous. It perpetuates an air of fairness by eliminating hunting practices that place the animal at a disadvantage. This includes the use of fences or other barriers to restrict the movement of animals or the use of automatic weapons, motorized vehicles, or electronic devices to track the animal. The guideline is giving the hunted animal a chance to escape under fair conditions and so levelling the playing field. It is also designed, however, to preserve the experience for the hunter in generating levels of competence and satisfaction. SC4, although an action that takes place after the kill, still has implications regarding what is killed in respect of what is seen to be distasteful in an animal or species (e.g., I want to shoot a bigger animal or another type of duck that is more palatable). But it also means that the hunter needs to make good use of the body of the animal and not just specific bits like the head or antlers (in the case of ungulates). SC5 may also be looked at from two sides. The first includes the belief that taking a good shot and missing does not mean that the hunter should shoot again when the chances of a direct kill are not high. This opens the door for injury and escape of the animal, prolonging its agony. The other side includes the hunter's self-interest in obtaining the animal through the challenge (and enjoyment) of a very difficult shot. Taking the animal down under less than ideal conditions might be met with praise from counterparts. It may also, however, be met with disdain in the event that the animal is shot and escapes injured. SC6 demonstrates the sense of personal responsibility toward the animal. It is the responsibility of the hunter to pursue an animal that has been shot and to make every effort to find it and minimize its pain. In general SC1 to SC3 may be interpreted anthropocentrically, while the rest of the codes should be taken to recognize the intrinsic value of the hunted and the responsibility to limit pain and suffering.

Luke's comprehensive evaluation of the sportsman's code has given way to a paradox: the more faithful the hunter is in following the code, the stronger the possibility that in doing so it makes it very difficult to justify continued participation. This line of thinking would be helpful as an extension to the rich base of literature on Bryan's (1977) specialization index in regards to trout fishing.

In opposition to hunting

Clark (1997) says that hunters and experimentalists are easy targets for public scrutiny, despite the fact that they are not the biggest cause of animal exploitation or employment. Perhaps it is the individualistic relationship between the experimenter and the animal or the hunter and the animal that makes this so. To be sure, however, the capture and consumption of animals for the purpose of meeting physiological needs may be placed on a different pedestal than the capture and consumption of animals for our own pleasure.

The problem with sport hunting, according to Caras (1970), is that there is no qualifying the underlying motivation of hunters: the object is to pursue an animal by any means for the purpose of ending its life. It matters not the station that one occupies in life or the manner of killing the animal. It is also worth bearing in mind that judging the moral acceptability of hunting needs to boil down to the essential basis of hunting, and to Causey (1989) this includes the kill and the pleasure experienced in this act (see also Lopez, 1986). What compounds the problem is that hunters, according to Causey, have been found to be not fully able to articulate or justify the pleasure derived from taking the life of an animal. In the absence of this, of real authenticity, hunting becomes a cheap imitation of the real thing (Ortega y Gasset, as cited in Causey, 1989).

One of the most damning indictments against hunting for sport comes from Kheel (1996), who argues that even though sport hunters are trading in their 'sport' label for other more socially acceptable labels, those who hunt out of desire, not necessity, engage in an act of violence. There is deliberate pursuit of the animal in an effort to create a contest, despite the fact that the game lacks symmetry. Because most animals hunted are noncarniverous, there is no reciprocity of attack on the part of the animal, whose only recourse is simply to flee. The only real danger posed to hunters is the possibility of shooting each other. Sport, in the sense we view it today, pits one willing foe against another, both of whom freely chose to participate in the activity. It is not so in hunting, where one is willing while the other is not given an opportunity to choose. Kheel also refers to hunting as non-productive or non-instrumental, where many hunters argue that it is not really the killing of animals that is most important but rather the experience of hunting or convening with nature. The development of rules of good conduct or fairness in the activity reflects the institutionalization that each and every sport enjoys. This has provided a safe haven for hunters, who argue that such rules make the sport ethically legitimate. Kheel argues that sports do not have predetermined outcomes, but those hunting products such as canned hunts where animals are trained to frequent eating and drinking spots at predetermined times eliminate the opportunity for one side to 'win' over the other.

The rights position on sport hunting is centred on self-defence. We all have the right to defend ourselves, and hunting *for sport* is a violation of the animal's right not to be harmed by another, especially one in pursuit of pleasure (Taylor, 2003). Most arguments on the acceptability of hunting, however, boil down to discussions based on utilitarianism: whether benefits outweigh the costs of the activity. The costs, according to Causey (1989), are: (1) fear, pain, suffering, and loss of life on the part of animals; (2) indirect costs to humans according to the depletion of hunted populations, especially predators; and (3) travel, equipment, and damage to property. The benefits, Causey argues, are not so clearly delimited. Are there benefits to the hunted, or merely benefits to the hunter? To Loftin (1984), benefits are realized by species and the environment in general from hunting, which may be greater than the costs borne by individuals of the species who must die for the greater good. This greater good comes in the form of more habitat and greater numbers of the member species. A more specific example is provided by Kruuk (2002), who observes that the downing of a lion is still one of the ultimate tests of manhood, bringing enhancement of status in just about any social group. But he says that there is nothing utilitarian – in the sense of direct use – about hunting for sport. The hunter seeks not fur for warmth or trade, nor does he or she hunt in order to eliminate cattle raiders or maneaters. It is done purely for sport, fun, or for the trophy that is the reward or product of the experience.

While rights and utilitarianism offer guidance in decisions about the ethical merits of hunting, Scruton (2002) deepens the debate by suggesting that it is not utilitarianism or rights that should be the focus of our deliberations but rather intentionality. In the case of utilitarianism, moral judgement ought not to be a calculation of utility of interests. Morality, Scruton argues, 'is not so much a matter of calculation, as a matter of setting the boundaries where calculation stops' (2002: 544). The first course of action is to establish duties and the boundaries for these duties. We have greater duty for our companion animals than for animals in the wild, just as we have greater duty for our own children than the children of others. As for rights, Scruton argues that it is persons who have rights and not animals, because the former can recognize the rights of others. Animals cannot. We accept children and idiots (his term) into a 'community of self-governing moral beings' because they gain membership by association. Granting rights to animals is to violate the principle of ontological parsimony, i.e., ascribing to animals the ability to express practical reasons and to adopt or refute social or moral norms.

Scruton further argues that our definition of unacceptable suffering should not be premised on the rights of animal victims, but rather on the duties and virtues of the perpetrator. What this suggests is that intention is central to an understanding of what passes as morally good and morally unjustifiable. If the hunter is the instigator of suffering it means that suffering is not so much a matter of something that happens, but rather that it is something that is inflicted purposefully. He argues this point on two levels and the combination of these two (Scruton, 2002: 562):

1. Cause: Suffering inflicted deliberately and for its own sake may be regarded as unacceptable because of the sadistic motive of the one who inflicts it. To condemn his action is to condemn the vice that is revealed in it. Suffering inflicted negligently or carelessly on an animal towards which you have a duty of care is also unacceptable, since this is a violation of duty and also ... a vice.
2. Effect: Suffering ... becomes unacceptable when an animal is driven beyond its natural capacity to return to homeostasis (this is in reference to Bateson and Bradshaw's 1997 work on the stress caused to red deer in Exmoor National Park, UK). Under natural conditions, deer are killed by ambush relatively quickly. Hunting with hounds, however, promotes long chases that the deer are not genetically equipped to deal with and cannot return to a state of homeostasis.

In the end Scruton argues for both perspectives in that hunting, and other forms of animal domination, might be wrong. Perhaps his most forceful point is that as rational beings we have the ability to decide on what is the best attitude to take towards the rest of creation. If we admire animals, love them, and respect them, we may express the Roman idea of piety, which encompasses the belief that the world is not ours for the taking and that as part of nature there ought to be respect for the order of things. Consequently,

> Our primary duties to wild animals are quite independent of any duty of care that we may assume when we set out to manage them. For they are duties of piety. This is how we should approach the idea of unacceptable suffering. Piety requires us to respect the life of a wild animal, to relate to it as it naturally is, and not to drive it beyond the limits that its nature can accommodate.
>
> (Scruton, 2002: 563)

If we treat the animal as a *machine à chasser*, Scruton adds, we not only disrespect the animal as a sentient being, but we also debase ourselves as individuals who reside outside of the realm of piety because the animal is simply a recreational resource to satisfy our pleasure.

Other theorists, including Moriarty and Woods (1997), contend that hunting is not justifiable using the ecological niche rationale as above, because meat eating and hunting are not natural events; they are cultural events. Even though human culture is a product of evolution, we are so far removed from ecosystems and nonhuman animals as to render any direct continuity as useless. Moriarty and Woods (1997: 399–400) construct the following two scenarios to demonstrate their rationale:

1. A mountain lion has not eaten anything substantial for some time. She searches her territory and uses her senses to lead her to several deer. The lion ambushes one of the deer, knocking out its back legs, leaping onto its back, biting into its neck, and breaking the neck. She eats a substantial portion of the deer carcass, including the viscera. She then drags some of the carcass to her den and eats the remains over the next several days.
2. A deer hunter travels to a designated area for which he or she has a license to hunt a specific type of deer (usually whitetail or mule deer) and sex (male or female) during a specified time period. The hunter travels to the designated area in a vehicle and spends several days walking around in orange-colored clothing (to prevent getting shot by other deer hunters) looking for deer. The hunter sees a deer a hundred yards away that appears to be the correct deer as specified on the license. He or she shoots and kills the deer with a high-powered rifle, guts the deer (leaving the viscera as waste), tags it, hauls it to his or her vehicle, transports the deer home, carves it up in his or her garage, freezes the meat, and spends the next several months eating the deer after cooking it on a barbecue grill or stove.

What is different from these two scenarios is that the latter is a cultural event, through every step, that differs significantly from the former, i.e., when, why, where, how, etc., to hunt. The argument that Moriarty and Woods (1997) construct is that the deer-hunting scenario is not a natural form of predation. So '*That* we eat may be determined naturally; *what* and *how* we eat is determined culturally' (p. 401).

Following the strand of reasoning about our separation from nature, the sheer magnitude of human population, in the absence of predators (aside from war and famine), has irreversibly tipped the balance: too many of us, too much technology, with an unfair advantage in the absence of anything close to an ecological balance. Imagine if all 6.9 billion people on the planet suddenly decided to hunt for food? Aside from the moral question, there is a biological reality here that would have implications not only for the source of food (animals becoming extinct quickly) but also the human population dynamic, with several million people dying in the absence of animal or plant sustenance.

The most damning bit of evidence against hunting is the pain and prolonged agony in the process, according to Loftin (1984). Even though hunters may be conscientious in their attempts to take down animals, the stark reality is that more often than not animals are crippled, and die a slow, painful death. This means enduring the terror of predation as well as dealing with being crippled by an arrow or bullet. Furthermore, hunting does not cull the population in the right way, according to Loftin. Predators are useful in killing the old and sick members of a population, making it genetically more robust. Such is not the case with hunting.

Tackling sentiency: fish pain science and philosophy

Fishing or angling (in reference to the use of an angled fishhook) includes subsistence, recreational, competition, and tournament forms. While subsistence makes a general relationship to fishing for the well-being of oneself, commercial fishing refers to the industry that captures fish in large numbers using a number of methods for profit. Recreational fishing, the focus here, is defined as 'fishing where the catch is not intended for sale' (Paulrud and Waldo, 2010: 163), and a recreational fishing company is a company that 'delivers goods and services to fishers during part of a fishing trip' (p. 163), and may include the use of a guide, food, accommodation, or equipment rentals.

In the late 1990s, there were 20 million fishing licences issued in Europe, which represented 6 per cent of the population. In France some three million anglers were generating about US$3 billion of revenue (Kaushik, 1999). In Sweden there were 1,310 fishing outfitters as of 2006. In terms of revenue generation, Connelly and Brown (2010) found that fishing contributed US$60 million to the shoreline communities of Lake Ontario in New York State and the creation of over 1,000 jobs. However, these same communities can expect to lose approximately $19 million in five years time due to declining interest in the salmon fishery specifically as well as the decline in fishing generally.

Fishing is subject to many of the same principles and philosophies of conservation as hunting. Fees collected by managing authorities from participants are often used in trust to improve the environmental and physical conditions for fishing but also for other recreational uses and for environmental integrity in general. In New South Wales, Australia, Bauer and Herr (2004) found that the purchase of fishing licences went towards buying out commercial fishing licences, creating recreational fishing areas, protecting and restoring fish habitat, promoting responsible fishing, stocking from fish hatcheries, and investing in more research.

Fishing, like hunting, is considered to be a consumptive activity. Apart from the practice of catch-and-release fishing, participants catch and remove fish from their environment for personal consumption. The difference between hunting and fishing is that the former tries to reduce pain and suffering, while the latter purposefully subjects animals (fish) to painful conditions because of the nature of the activity itself (Dionys de Leeuw, 1996). Håstein *et al.* (2005) argue that while good progress has been made on the welfare conditions for terrestrial animals, optimal humane care standards for aquatic beings are less well defined. Part of the problem, they argue, is that public understanding of the ethical and physiological issues of aquatic animals is not as high a priority as those of terrestrial animals. The exclusion of fish from the welfare debate is in large part due to the fact that they have been denied sentience by the academic and lay communities (Soo and Todd, 2009; see also Schwab, 2003). What follows is a discussion on the topic of fish pain from the perspective of science and philosophy, the purpose of which is to deepen our understanding of the potential welfare issues created in the pursuit of pleasure (NB: I have drawn liberally from Fennell and Nowaczek (2010) in this section).

Science

Many studies on catch-and-release focus on the negative impacts on fish populations and on improving the angling techniques and hook types to decrease mortality rates after releasing the fish. Some authors compare commercial and recreational fishing in playing a major role in global declines of fish stock (Cooke and Cowx, 2006). For instance, a study of bonefish showed 39 per cent mortality within 30 minutes when fish were released in areas of high abundance of sharks (Cooke and Philipp, 2004). Fish exposure to air showed behavioural changes for the first 30 minutes after release and later problems in regaining stability. A study of striped marlin by Domeier *et al.* (2003) demonstrated mortality rates of 26.2 per cent within five days of release, where injury was the predictor of mortality. All fish bleeding from the gill cavity died, followed by 63 per cent of deeply hooked fish, and 9 per cent released in good condition. The Oklahoma Department of Wildlife Conservation (1997) found that 43 per cent of fish released after being caught died within six days. Alós (2009) evaluated post-release mortality of main target species of north-western Mediterranean recreational fisheries, pointing to the anatomical position of the hook (deep-hooking) as the key mortality factor in larger fish which increased with passive angling (rod not in hand).

A recent study on consequences of catch-and-release angling on northern pike indicated that angling-related stressors result in both physiological and behavioural disturbances to pike, which generally seem to be resilient to catch-and-release, compared with other fish (Arlinghaus *et al.*, 2009). Effects of catch-and-release on ascending Atlantic salmon during various stages of their spawning migration also point to some troubling facts. According to Thorstad *et al.* (2007), the time salmon spent travelling upstream during migration was longer than natural resting periods, while 31 per cent of fish showed unusual downstream movement immediately after release. The growing body of literature demonstrates that many human activities harm fish, and the degree of impact depends on the species, their life history stage, and context (Huntingford *et al.*, 2006).

Alongside the issue of mortality, stress and injury, as above, is the question of whether fish in fact feel pain – a question that has eluded empirical confirmation until recently. It is an important question because it has physical implications as well as moral ones. While some theorists categorically reject the idea that fish have the capacity to experience pain (e.g., Rose, 2003), there has been a tremendous influx of research in the last few years to call this into question. New techniques and technologies are now able to deliver the empirical evidence that fish display species-specific behavioural and physiological responses to painful stimuli, which are not simple reflexes (Sneddon *et al.* 2003; Chandroo *et al.*, 2004; Cooke and Sneddon, 2007; Davie and Kopf, 2006; Dawkins, 2006, 2008; Reilly *et al.*, 2008; see also Braithwaite, 2006; Braithwaite and Boulcott, 2007; Davis *et al.*, 1976; Dunlop *et al.*, 2006; and Yue *et al.*, 2004).

In 2003, long-awaited empirical evidence surfaced on fish sentience. Sneddon *et al.* (2003) found that when rainbow trout were injected in the snout with bee venom or acetic acid solution, they performed anomalous behaviours not recorded in fish injected with saline or the control group. Those fish injected with venom or acid performed a rocking motion for about 1.5 hours after injection, while the group injected with acid commenced rubbing of the lips against the gravel at the bottom of the tanks. This to the authors represented behaviour reminiscent of higher order vertebrates who have experienced pain. Furthermore, the acid- and venom-injected fish took approximately three hours to resume feeding, while the saline and control groups resumed feeding after just one hour. This study has been criticized by Rose (2003), who argues that because of the amount of toxin injected into the fish (the equivalent of 100ml of bee venom injected into a human lip), the trout demonstrated a remarkable resistance to trauma. Fish lack specialized regions of a neocortex and there is no alternative system in the brain of a fish as a substitute for performing similar functions. The neuro-behavioural functions of fish had been widely discussed in previous work by Rose (2002), who argued that although it is improbable that fish experience pain or emotions, they might still display physiological stress responses to noxious stimuli, and that this is still an important consideration in the welfare of fish.

Subsequent work has shown that there is a growing interest in solving this debate. Yue *et al.* (2004) investigated the capacity of rainbow trout to experience fear through an avoidance-learning task. Fish were placed into a two-chambered tank and subjected to a plunging dip net where they could escape into a second chamber. Later they were presented with a light stimulus 10 seconds prior to the net being plunged into the water. Over a period of 5 days, all 13 fish learned to avoid the dip net at the onset of the light (fear), and the fish also demonstrated the capacity for longer-term learning. Portavella *et al.* (2002) found that when shocked, goldfish display avoidance responses that are processed in three different areas of the forebrain. The authors concluded that avoidance of noxious stimuli such as shock does not represent simple reflexive responses, but rather demonstrates attributes that characterize cognition and affect (see also Braithwaite and Boulcott, 2007). Similar findings have been reported by Chandroo *et al.* (2004), who argue, on the basis of anatomical, pharmacological, and behavioural data, that fish have the capacity to suffer in similar ways to tetrapods (vertebrates with four feet or legs). Fish undergo a range of physiological changes under conditions of stress. Primary responses include the release of stress hormones into circulation. Secondary responses include the activation of metabolic pathways, which alter blood chemistry. Tertiary responses may include changes to the whole animal in response to a combination of stressors, including decreased reproductive capacity, growth of the individual, and immune functioning (Iwama, 2007).

Similar evidence on the perception of pain by fish has been published by Cooke and Sneddon (2007), who identified exact locations of the nociceptors (a sensory receptor that responds to pain) and chemical receptors on the head of trout, which allow the fish to sense all stimuli including pain. More recently, a study by Nordgreen *et al.* (2009) has made further inroads on fish sentience. These scientists exposed goldfish to controlled, localized heat increments under the assumption that increasing heat would prompt escape responses. Two experiments were conducted, with the first involving the injection of half the sample (n=8) with 40mg of morphine and the other half with a similar volume of saline. The second test was identical, but involved injection of 50mg of morphine and saline respectively. The researchers confirmed the results of previous studies suggesting that goldfish perceive heat as noxious, but that the administration of morphine did not have an analgesic effect, i.e., the fish given morphine did not take longer to react to the heat. Initially this prompted the researchers to conclude that the goldfish do not experience pain, but they later observed other interesting behaviours. When the temperature of the tank was returned to normal, goldfish given morphine displayed normal behaviours. However, fish subjected to saline acted more defensively. The researchers concluded that this latter group felt pain and this experience led to changing behaviour characterized as wariness, fear, or anxiety. Fish treated with morphine were said to have had the experience of pain blocked, but their reaction to the heat at the same level of the fish treated with saline was a reflexive response to hotter water. These fish could detect the noxious effect of heat without actually experiencing the same level of pain as the saline-treated fish. (See Appel and Elwood, 2009, who found that hermit crabs experience pain when subjected to abdominal electrical shock, and trade off this pain according to preferred or unpreferred shell housings. Those in preferred shell housings evacuated at higher voltages than those in poorer quality shells.)

The difficulty in coming to grips with the issue of fish sentiency lies in the inability to fully understand the nature of consciousness in fish, according to Arlinghaus *et al.* (2007). A lack of science in understanding the nature of suffering in fish means that a feelings-based approach to welfare should be replaced by an approach involving a welfare system hinged on good health, a properly functioning biological system, and not being forced outside its normal range of biological functioning (e.g., stress). In response, Huntingford *et al.* (2007) argue that a feelings-based approach (i.e., the absence of suffering) is essential because it captures the broader societal sentiment about how humans adversely impact animals, and the associated and burgeoning current debate on the welfare of animals (including fish) more generally. They argue that:

> If biologists working in the field of animal welfare limit their consideration to the empirical study of functional aspects of welfare only, they are at risk of producing information irrelevant to the ethical concerns that provide a major justification for research into fish welfare.
>
> (Huntingford *et al.*, 2007: 278)

While objective science is absolutely critical in this debate, the absence of absolute knowledge on consciousness, including pain and suffering, forces us into the moral province (see Arlinghaus *et al.* (2009) for an updated perspective on the pragmatic- and suffering-based approaches to fish welfare).

Philosophy

Theorists in both philosophy and science have argued that, in order for a species to be ascribed moral consideration, the species must possess characteristics that are deemed morally relevant. The most important characteristic, according to Lund *et al.* (2007), is sentience – having the power of sense perception, such as the ability to detect sensations of pain and pleasure. Lund *et al.* advance the following reasoning in regards to fish: (1) If a being is sentient, then it deserves serious moral consideration; (2) Fish are likely to be sentient; (3) Therefore, fish deserve serious moral consideration (2007: 112). The foregoing discussion has made significant progress in our understanding of points 2 and 3, above.

Just like the example used above in regards to the moral permissibility of hunting to feed one's family, the same holds true for fishing. We can perhaps justify fishing if it means that a family is fed, but not if fishing amounts to the pleasure of playing with the animal and releasing it in a compromised state. This reasoning has been supported by Håstein *et al.*, (2005), who argue that fishing for subsistence is morally justifiable, whereas fishing for pleasure is morally objectionable because of needless harm. The argument has also been supported by Balon (2000), who observes that the debate on sport fishing has more to do with human morality than animal rights. Balon supports fishing for food and subsistence, aquiculture, sustainable commercial fishing, and recreational angling as a supplement to family nutrition. What he is at odds with is sport and recreational fishing, especially competitions, where the focus is not on fishing for food but rather for pleasure, as well as the manipulation of the natural environment to facilitate these activities. His argument rests on the belief that there is simply no respect for the animal, which must endure stress in the process of being hooked and released while the angler's main concern is with speed and winning the competition (see also de Leeuw, 1996). There is also the issue of intentionality built into this broader discussion. The decision of what is cruel and what is not boils down to a matter of intentions. While an act may be cruel, the agent performing the act may not be because of his or her intentions (Olsen, 2003).

To help prioritize the use of fish in the context of various forms of nature-based tourism, Fennell and Nowaczek (2010) propose a holistic framework (Figure 7.1). Compared to an ethical perspective, a philosophical outlook, or even factual scientific evidence, this practical framework considers the type of angling, motivations, and outcomes (catch-and-release or killing). Each type is organized according to three aspects of priority along a continuum: (1) whether the action is consumptive (essential and non-essential) or non-consumptive; (2) the action's positioning in relation to nature-based tourism in general or ecotourism more specifically; and (3) whether it is deemed anthropocentric or biocentric considering the ethical characteristics of each action (following from Taylor, 1986).

Action 'a' in Figure 7.1, groups fishing for sport in competition, is felt to be the most consumptive and non-essential, the most anthropocentric, and as far away from what we view as ecotourism in comparison to the other types of interaction with fish. Fennell and Nowaczek argue in support of Balon (2000), who felt that fishing for sport in competitions offers no respect for the animal and this is compounded by the sheer number of participants in these activities. Conversely, type 'h', viewing of fish, which is marked by learning and appreciation with no direct physical handling of fish, is deemed non-consumptive and the most biocentric of all types, rendering representative of the ethical archetype of ecotourism (the topic of Chapter 8). The focus on learning as the product of the

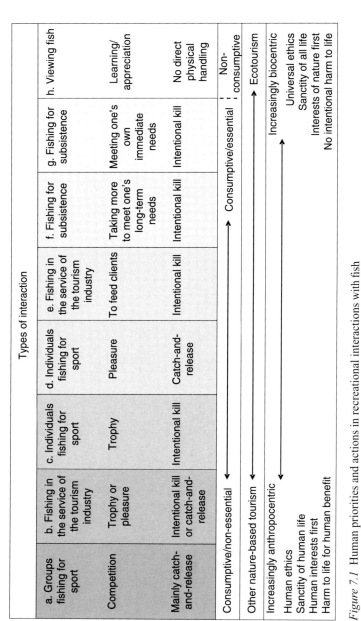

Figure 7.1 Human priorities and actions in recreational interactions with fish

experience in ecotourism separates ecotourism from many other nature-based tourism (NBT) forms. The line of separation between non-consumptive and consumptive is dashed, indicating that although ecotourism is thought to be non-consumptive in principle and practice, there may be associated indirect impacts on the resource or there may be differences in how sustainable and ethically managed operators are in regards to this type of interaction. It is argued that fishing for subsistence (subtypes 'f' and 'g') is more ethical than angling for purposes of catch-and-release and for trophy (subtypes 'c' and 'd') because these latter forms represent non-essential consumptive practices (outcomes include stress, injury, and quite possibly death in the case of catch-and-release) that have more to do with individual pleasure than meeting subsistence needs. Subtypes 'b' and 'e' involve angling in the service of the tourism industry, and care has been exercised in differentiating these two types. Group fishing for pleasure or trophy ('b') is deemed less ethical according to the three aspects of priority than angling for the purpose of feeding tourism clients ('e'). Additionally, some ecotour operators could use the conservation motive for catch-and-release angling as a green marketing tactic to entice new clients who lack knowledge of the mortality rates of released fish (e.g., no-take reserves addressed by Bartholomew and Bohnsack, 2005; Cooke and Cowx, 2006; Cooke and Philipp, 2004; Cooke and Suski, 2005; Lindsey *et al.*, 2006). However, much more work needs to be undertaken in understanding how this action corresponds to values and beliefs of ecotourists in comparison to other nature-based tourists.

In consideration of the empirical research above on fish sentiency it is encouraging to see a practical application of this knowledge. Cooke and Sneddon (2007) use the Recreational Anglers Code of Conduct developed by the New South Wales Council of Freshwater Anglers for its members and other anglers, which demonstrates recognition of the conscious experience of pain and fear by fish. This understanding promotes policies to improve the welfare of fish, which results in improved management and conservation efforts (Box 7.1).

Ethics in action

The rightness or wrongness of hunting can be argued on the basis of utilitarianism, as above, but also on the basis of the debate between animal rights and ecocentrism. What is the difference? O'Neill (2000) explains that an animal rights activist would assign moral value on the basis of individuality (see Regan (2004) and Wise (2000), for example). An animal rights activist would always argue that hunting could never be morally justifiable because animals have a right not to be harmed or killed. A right, therefore, is like a protective shield based on moral or legal principles for the individual, whereby the alleged good of the community is not enough to override the protection of the individual (Taylor, 2003). By contrast, ecocentrists assign moral value on the basis of systems and collections, i.e., species and ecosystems. This latter perspective stems from Aldo Leopold's land

---

Box 7.1 New South Wales Council of Anglers Code of Conduct

Fish should be landed quickly to minimize damage and stress.

Dispatching a caught fish should be undertaken quickly and humanely by a blow to the head or spiking through the brain just behind the eye.

Tethering of fish for any purposes is an unacceptable practice The use of small barbless hooks is recommended for use where fish are to be released.

Soft knotless landing nets are recommended for use where fish are to be released.

When releasing a fish, keep it in the water, handle as little as possible with wet hands, carefully remove the hook, and walk the fish upright to regain its balance before allowing it to swim off.

All fish bleeding from hooked gills should be killed as they will not survive.

If lifting a fish to be released is unavoidable, support the fish's body weight with a horizontal lift using wet hands.

Do not lift by the gills or tail.

Where internal damage may result in hook removal from a fish to be released, the hook should be left undisturbed and the line cut as close as possible to the fish's mouth.

The use of non-stainless steel hooks which rust and break down quickly is recommended.

Gaffs should only be used in circumstances where a net is not suitable due to the fish size and the fish is then quickly dispatched.

Adapted from Cooke and Sneddon (2007)

---

ethic, whereby something is deemed good, like hunting, if it secures benefits for the entire system, and bad if it tends otherwise (Varner, 1998). Sport hunting is not immoral, therefore, if it serves to maximize biotic good (see Callicott, 1980, 1989; and Rolston, 1988, 1994, for example).

This philosophical divide has led to incompatibility between the two groups, with the suggestion that one could never be the other. The problem, according to O'Neill, stems from the interpretation of moral standing and intrinsic value: environmentalists wrongly feel that objects in the natural world such as rocks and trees have moral standing, but moral standing is only extended to an agent if that agent can be harmed or benefited – if their interests are of consideration. Only sentient beings would thus have moral standing. Rocks and trees do not because they are not part of the moral community, as they 'do not qualify as possible recipients of beneficent actions' (O'Neill, 2000: 186). An object such as a rock or tree may possess intrinsic value without having moral standing 'if its existence is a good thing in itself, apart from its role as a means to other goods' (p. 185). O'Neill uses the example of a beautiful painting which is said to hold intrinsic value in as much as we view it as a good thing regardless of the pleasure it generates. Few, he argues, would suggest that it has interests deserving of the status of moral standing (see also Warren (1983), who argues that there can be a reconciliation between environmental ethics (holism) and animal rights (atomism) by recognizing that the rights of animals are not of the same magnitude as the rights of humans, and further that the value of a sentient being ought to be weighted more heavily than the value of a non-sentient being).

Westra (1989) has composed a provocative critique of Callicott's (1986) work on merging animal ethics and the broader land ethic. Callicott has argued for sympathy as an essential characteristic of human nature, which might be extended across the species border in how we deal with animals but also the natural world in general. Contrary to this standpoint, in fact nearly opposite to this, Westra suggests that hostility grounded in respect, following from war morality, should be the starting point. A just war involves the acknowledgement that 'it is you or me', involving normatively accepted practices, while a morally unjust war involves indiscriminate killing with torturing weaponry. Westra's argument advances according to the belief that sympathy does not transcend the species boundary, i.e., it may only be found in humans and is not the guiding principle of the law of nature – the nature of wild nature. So the immediate threat of hostility in a war (kill or be killed) can be likened to a respectful hostility in the natural world through the killing of animals for the immediate survival needs of humans. In reference to the *means* of the expression of this hostility, all methods that employ indiscriminate procedures and involve pain must be forbidden. As such, it would be morally unjustifiable to kill more deer in sport than one needs for one's personal or one's family's immediate survival. This view also incorporates the belief that other species do not have an absolute right to life or even the avoidance of innocent or minimal suffering, as this would appropriately mirror the conditions of nature according to the condition of respect. To Westra,

> This entails limiting our hostility toward animals to our use of them for food, prohibiting unnecessary suffering, poor living conditions, and methods of killing far worse or in excess of what is normal in natural habitats, and accepting special responsibility for those animals that we have deliberately brought into being for human purposes.
>
> (Westra, 1989: 229)

What Westra fails to take into consideration, according to Taylor (1996a), is that humans do not have to kill animals to satisfy their nutritional needs. We can survive quite easily without killing animals – although this is perhaps more easily accomplished in the more developed countries of the world.

Conclusion

The focus in this chapter, bridging from Chapter 6, has been on the depth of the moral debate in reference to the acceptability of sport hunting and sport fishing for purposes of human enjoyment. Most of the focus was placed on hunting because of the volume of material devoted to this theme along utilitarian, rights, and ecocentric lines. A different approach was used in the debate on fishing, and this followed a trajectory based on sentiency. The reason for this surrounds the debate on the moral acceptability of catch-and-release fishing. Science has revealed that fish do in fact feel pain and that a large percentage of fish caught, depending on how they are caught, actually end up dying. This knowledge would be helpful in informing tourism operators and tourists about the consequences of their actions, which in turn would play a part in the decisions to fish or not. A conceptual framework illustrating the human priorities and actions in recreational interactions with fish was included for the purpose of breaking down the moral acceptability of a variety of different types of fishing. Ecotourism was included in this framework as an option, and described as a more acceptable form of interaction with fish because of non-consumptive qualities and its focus on biocentrism (see Taylor, 1986a). It offers an introduction to the concept of ecotourism and wildlife viewing, which is the topic of the next chapter.

8 Wildlife viewing

Introduction

In the previous chapter the focus was on tourist activities that place more of an emphasis on the extraction of animals (as resources) from the wild. In this chapter the spotlight is placed on a form of tourism that places value in the preservation of animals in the wild. As Knight argues, 'Wildlife tourists *watch* the lives of wild animals, whereas hunters *take* the lives of wild animals' (2009: 168). The watching of animals for recreational purposes is not new. Although the Romans enjoyed the spectacle of animal struggle and death in the arena, they also enjoyed viewing animals in a number of different vivaria, including aviaries, fishponds, and parks (Kalof, 2007b). The enjoyment of nature on nature's terms or for nature's sake corresponds to a different type of relationship – a different type of consumption – between animals and humans. Finding the care for nature waning in contemporary man during the 1950s, Machura (1954) wrote that tourism could be a way of arousing the love for and protection of nature. Over 50 years later, thriving ecotourism and wildlife tourism industries spread their tentacles all over the globe in the arrangement of products for an ever-expanding market of interested tourists (see TAMS, 2006a; TAMS, 2006b; WTO, 2002 for figures on the importance of wildlife viewing).

Important to many destinations is the fact that this type of tourist spends more money, stays longer, engages in more activities, and spreads his/her expenditures more widely throughout the country as compared to more general interest tourists (Pearce and Wilson, 1995). And just as important is the fact that the wildlife tourism sector is dominated by a number of small enterprises, which are located in remote and rural regions, thus contributing economically to these more peripheral regions (Catlin *et al.*, 2010a).

Classification complexities

The consumptive debate

The literature on nature-based tourism (NBT) suggests that there are differences in how we consume wildlife, with ecotourism generally viewed as non-consumptive, and other forms of NBT, such as hunting and fishing, said to be more consumptive (Duffus and Dearden, 1990; Goodwin, 1996; Reynolds and Braithwaite, 2001; Weaver, 2001; Tisdell, 2003; Wilson and Tisdell, 2001; Newsome, Dowling and Moore, 2005; Fennell, 2008a). Although this seems rather straightforward, Lovelock (2008b) observes that no other form of tourism, save for sex tourism, is more controversial than consumptiveness tied to wildlife tourism, given the nature of the activity: killing for sport and conservation or for other purposes is an era of heightened concern over the welfare and rights of nonhuman animals.

Consumptiveness is used as manner to separate activities that use the environment in different ways. By *consume* it is meant that, in the case of hunting, an animal is shot and removed from the environment altogether. Fishing can present itself as a form of consumptive recreation if anglers catch, kill, and consume the fish itself, thus removing it from the environment. Fishing might also be viewed as a non-consumptive form of recreation, however, if anglers catch fish and release them back into the environment, stress and injury aside (see Lovelock's work on consumptive wildlife tourism (2008b)).

The following definition serves to illustrate the importance of use and supply in an understanding of consumptiveness in environmental and resource management contexts: 'Consumptive use is the use of a resource that reduces the supply (e.g., removing water from a source like a river, lake or aquifer without returning an equal amount)' (Mimi, 2011). Non-consumptive use may be taken as use of a resource that does not reduce the supply of the target species or feature of the environment, i.e., there is no net loss to the environment as a result of our actions. A couple of examples may further aid in understanding what may be viewed as consumptive or not in tourism.

Turtle riding on the Great Barrier Reef during the early twentieth century was a popular activity for tourists. I use it here as an example of changing values – how these values are relative to a period of time and to other instrumental uses of an animal. Pocock (2006) constructs turtle riding as a form of non-consumptive outdoor recreational fun, where the visitors did not regard the activity as offensive to the animal, and where the 'hilarity and thrill is at the expense of the human rider' (Pocock, 2006: 137). The activity blossomed during the 1920s, when turtle canneries were established along the reef islands. Turtle riding was contrasted with the cruelty of the canneries (tipping turtles over and letting them die in the sun, which took long periods of time), and involved standing or sitting on the back of the turtle on land and hoping to stay on the back of the turtle as it entered the water. Pocock found evidence of turtle riding in written documents into the 1950s, with a decline in the 1960s due to new environmental concerns, but also due to the development of newer ways to engage with marine life, including scuba diving, underwater viewing chambers, and snorkelling. Before that time, the turtle played a vital role in the procurement of knowledge about the marine environment – and offered the first forays for many from the terrestrial to the marine realm. Although there was a power imbalance between human and animal, the transformation from land to sea was said to tip the competition (sport) in the favour of the turtle as the two entered the sea. Turtle riding would be viewed as non-consumptive with no reduction in supply, whereas turtle canneries would be consumptive because of the reduction in the supply of turtles.

How we value animals and their use is central to the idea of consumptiveness. The use of whales for human instrumental ends is a case in point. Parsons and Rawles (2003) found that 91.4 per cent of whale watchers (non-consumptive) would not think of participating in this activity in a country that practised whaling (consumptive). This has prompted the World Wildlife Fund (1993) to observe that whale watching and whaling are like oil and water. One is definitely not good for the other, and for the tourism industry in general – such as the case of Iceland, where in 2003 the whaling industry was reinstated by the government. In a study on the environmental values of sea kayakers and fishing tourists by Dawson and Lovelock (2008), sea kayakers were found to participate in activities that were deemed to be more environmentally sensitive and maintained higher environmental value and environmental behaviour levels than their fisher counterparts, despite the fact that they both reported valuing the environment to the same level. This latter example demonstrates that we may *say* we value the natural environment, but what we *do* in our lifestyle preferences may be antithetical to these statements, and this disconnect has spilled over into the consumptive and non-consumptive realms.

Tremblay (2001) argues that it is tempting to consider non-consumptive forms of tourism as being morally superior, because there is evidence to suggest that non-consumptive experiences lead to increased education (see the section on zoos in Chapter 4). Furthermore, profitability of the non-consumptive sector often means that higher numbers of individuals are required to match the economic gains realized through consumptive forms like hunting. Individual hunters contribute more to local economies than individual ecotourists, and the higher numbers of the latter contribute to crowding, habitat disruptions, and the need for more infrastructure. Tremblay echoes the sentiments expressed by other theorists who would rather see consumptive and non-consumptive activities exist in a state of complementarity for commercial and environmental sustainability.

Further complicating the issue of what is consumptive and non-consumptive is the measurement of impacts. Activities like birdwatching, labelled as non-consumptive, have been found to have a range of effects (see Lovelock, 2008; see also Newsome *et al.*, 2005). In a comprehensive overview of 166 documents containing original data, Boyle and Samson (1985) found that non-consumptive forms of outdoor recreation and tourism have significant impacts on fauna. The authors reported effects on fauna from hiking and camping (52 reports), boating (37), wildlife viewing and photography (27), all-terrain vehicle (ATV) use (20), snowmobile use (12), shore recreation (8), and rock climbing (7). Birds were subjects affected most often (61 per cent), followed by mammals (42 per cent) and reptiles and amphibians (4 per cent). Specific examples reported include trampling of habitat; disturbance of large mammal movement patterns by hikers and campers; habituated animals more susceptible to poaching; tourist visits to waterfowl nests leading to nest and egg loss due to predation; and photographers being more disruptive to wildlife than recreationists who accidentally encounter wildlife, because the former are more frequent in their quest and stay for a longer period of time. The issue has been further compounded by the fact that newer forms of tourism like wildlife tourism encompass both consumptive (e.g., hunting) and non-consumptive (e.g., birdwatching) forms of wildlife use.

The one nature-based tourism activity that seems irrefutable as consumptive is hunting. The killing of animals reduces supply. But Craig-Smith and Dryden (2008) illustrate that not all hunting, including trophy hunting, is consumptive. Recent additions to the sport have included the shooting of animals with tranquillizing darts, whereby tourists get to measure the animal and photograph it before it returns to a cogent state. The authors argue that 'If the animal is permanently removed from the environment this is consumptive hunting; if it is released back into the wild unharmed this is non-consumptive hunting' (Craig-Smith and Dryden, 2008: 268–9). The fact that the animal has not been killed is a fact that is without question; whether or not the animal is unharmed is a question that requires further investigation. Added to this is the broader issue of ecosystem integrity, especially when introduced species have devastating effects on native flora and fauna (Lovelock, 2008a). The removal of these animals may in fact be the best course of action in terms of the long-term health of the system. There is also the issue of the importance of activities like hunting to the economies of lesser developed countries. If local people are to have some connection to their land, they must be able to hunt for subsistence in order to avoid conflict, and the money that is generated from hunting tourism is so substantial that it is able to support a number of other development initiatives to allow for the structure of a more balanced economy in these localities and broader regions. This is the case in Africa in Zimbabwe, Botswana and South Africa (Mbaiwa, 2008), and in Namibia (Barnes and Novelli, 2008). It is becoming clear that successful consumptive wildlife tourism might only be achievable through collaborative interactions in the communities in which they take place (Cohen and Sanyal, 2008). Wildlife tourism in its consumptive form justifies its use of wildlife according to similar factors: (1) direct wildlife management and supporting research, (2) providing funding for conservation, (3) providing education about conservation, (4) political lobbying in support of conservation, and (5) providing socio-economic incentives for conservation (Higginbottom *et al.*, 2003; see Fennell, 2000 in reference to why billfishing is not a form of ecotourism based in part on issues tied to economic impact and consumptiveness).

An interesting sidebar to this discussion is reference to zoos as representative of non-consumptive wildlife tourism (Higginbottom *et al.*, 2003). We read in Chapter 4 that zoos are basically repositories of captive wildlife that serve recreational, educational, and conservation mandates. Based on the definition above, i.e., use of a resource that reduces supply, it is difficult to imagine zoos as anything but consumptive. Animals are captured and taken out of their natural environments and forced to live in conditions that compromise their ability to live a full, natural life and, in many cases, to reproduce. It is not the tourists themselves who are acting in a consumptive manner directly, as in other examples of wildlife tourism, but rather the zoo organization that facilitates the experience.

Box 8.1 Going anywhere nice this year?

Visitors to Norway will be invited to liven up their holiday with a spot of seal hunting. Conservationists are appalled, but it's not the first time the tourist industry has been accused of bad taste.

The antics of British holidaymakers are called into question almost as often as a plane load of hormonal teens touches down on some hapless Mediterranean isle.

But as the last stragglers on Europe's sun-kissed beaches travel home for the winter, a new source of moral outrage has emerged to take its place.

Come January, Norway will allow tourists to take part in its annual seal cull as part of their break. It's not going down well with animal lovers, who claim the idea is 'sadistic'.

It's one of several examples . . . of thrill-seeking vacationers stretching the limits of just what is acceptable.

For about £110 amateur hunters will be offered a day out and one seal. Those wanting a longer break, or more animals, can pay £650 for four days' hunting and two seals.

It's all part of an attempt to meet the government quota of killing 2,100 animals a year. Norway considers seals a pest, but local hunters have not been able to meet the target.

Shrugging off criticism of the decision, fisheries minister Svein Ludvigsen said the idea was 'not to step up seal hunting, or render the species extinct. All we're doing is allowing foreigners to take part'.

The visitors will be allowed to shoot the seals and will have to adhere to strict guidelines, says the government. But environmental group Greenpeace has warned Norway it may appear 'barbaric' and drive other tourists away.

Source: BBC News, Friday 8 October 2004, <http://news.bbc.co.uk/2/hi/uk_news/magazine/3713360.stm>, accessed 25 April 2011

Nature-based tourisms

The need to develop and use new terms in tourism at the expense of others has complicated the landscape in nature-based tourism, particularly ecotourism and wildlife tourism. While any number of papers might be used to discuss the overlap between these concepts, a paper by Rodger *et al.* (2007) is useful in illustrating the issues in identity between these related forms:

> Nature-based tourism occurs in natural settings but includes emphasis on fostering understanding and conservation. Ecotourism is similar to nature-based tourism but includes education and interpretation while aiming to be ecologically sustainable . . . Wildlife tourism is distinct to both of these as it is

where tourists are specifically interested in seeing wildlife. Although the term wildlife often refers to both fauna and flora, in common usage and the tourism industry it is generally understood to mean only fauna (animals) ... However it must be noted that while ecotourism, nature-based tourism and wildlife tourism are not one and the same, neither are they exclusive as there is a good deal of overlap between them.

(Rodger *et al.*, 2007: 161)

There are a few elements built into this quote that are worthy of further discussion. First, although many nature-based tourism operations may be categorized differently than other operations said to be sustainable (as in the Nature and Ecotourism Accreditation Program (NEAP) in Australia), the simple fact of the matter is that in practice there are often small degrees of difference separating these products that have fulfilled criteria like sustainability over those that have not (generally speaking). Several publications have assessed the implicit problems and issues of the certification/accreditation and ecolabelling processes (see for example Jamal *et al.*, 2006).

Second, I would argue against the above statement that wildlife tourism is distinct from ecotourism as 'tourists are specifically interested in seeing wildlife'. The genesis of ecotourism grew out of this need to focus on animals and remains one of the most important attraction-based interests of ecotourists today: Lepidoptera in China, birds in Costa Rica, penguins in Antarctica, bears in Alaska, and so on. Further, I would suggest that sustainability, interpretation, and education are just as important to wildlife tourism (WT) as they are to NBT or ecotourism, although these elements are not tied to WT in the quote above.

Third, a basic review of definitions of wildlife found almost equal weighting on the inclusion or exclusion of 'flora' as a key component. For example, the Forestry Commission of the UK government defines wildlife as: 'Anything living, both plants and animals, which is not domesticated' (UK Forestry Commission, 2011). The Government of South Africa defines wildlife as 'animal and plant species occurring within natural ecosystems and habitats'. The Wildlife Society is a non-profit science and education-based organization with the goal of improving wildlife stewardship and conservation in North America. As ecology is the primary scientific discipline of the wildlife profession, the interests of the Society hold the interactions of all organisms in their natural environment as a primary focus. The Wildlife Society emblem contains both plants and animals. In light of the foregoing, perhaps a better moniker for wildlife tourism is animal-based tourism or wild animal tourism, the latter being more appropriate as it eliminates the domesticated animal contingency. I say this because Rodger *et al.* note that 'In the year ending December 2004 there were 2.21 million domestic wildlife tourism visitors to Australia (wildlife tourism is visitors who engage in the activities of whale and dolphin watching or visit wildlife parks, zoos and aquariums ...)' (2007: 161). If WT is to encompass ecotourism-like activities, as above, in addition to activities like visiting zoos and aquaria, then we should understand that there are vastly different markets inherent in this umbrella term that wander the continuum of WT. The motivations, attitudes, and beliefs of zoo tourists might be vastly different than the attributes of a hard-core ecotourist. An ecotourist might never visit a zoo because of the ethical issues tied to this institution (staying away from the consumptive market is the point being raised here). It might very well be that the keeping of animals in zoos is a form of deprivation that might be considered even less praiseworthy than hunting. These questions have not been raised adequately enough in the literature on WT.

Finally, it is noteworthy again that many of the findings of Rodger *et al.* (2007) point to more similarities between ecotourism and WT than differences. For example, the wildlife tourism operators included in Rodger *et al.* report that for the question: 'Which of the following [pre-identified response categories] do you consider to be important parts of the tourism experience you offer?' 'viewing scenery' (80 per cent of respondents), broadly with the inclusion of plants, was more important than seeing wildlife in a natural state (78 per cent) and watching wildlife without binoculars (55 per cent). Viewing wildflowers (39 per cent of respondents) was said to be more important to operators than watching wildlife with binoculars (27 per cent). The authors conclude by suggesting that

> Not surprisingly the results from this study emphasise a number of similarities between wildlife tourism and ecotourism, including tour size and destinations, activities undertaken, and measures taken to protect the features of interest, whether wildlife or the natural environment more generally.
>
> (Rodger *et al.*, 2007: 170)

The heterogeneity of the WT market has been supported in the literature, as it has been in ecotourism. In a study of stingray viewing tourists, Semeniuk *et al.* (2009b) were able to establish two general groups. The first, a pro-management group (approximately two-thirds of all tourists), was in support of conservation fees, measures to protect stingrays from injury, and the reduction of congestion. The second group, pro-current, was in favour of a small access fee as well as management decisions that allowed for continued handling of the stingrays even though this might contribute to injury. One of these groups could be defined as ecotourists, while the other would be more akin to a general tourism population more concerned with the novelty of the activity than the welfare of the animals.

Curtin and Wilkes (2005) found that the UK outbound wildlife tourism market has experienced a shift in recent years from a specialized market offering programmes geared towards certain species, with higher physical demands and on-site involvement, to a broader and more general market of people looking for comfort and relaxation in interesting environments. This is perhaps fuelled by a greater need to experience different types of vacations based on heightened interests in the natural world, and less elitist-style pricing for these experiences, such that demand and supply have evolved in a lockstep pattern. What this suggests to Curtin and Wilkes is a wider range of products to suit the needs of both markets.

Amante-Helweg (1996) tested the knowledge base of swim-with-dolphin tourists by asking them to answer 15 questions on the taxonomy, biology, and social structure of dolphins, and found that correct answers ranged from 2 to 12 (median of 8). Although 58 per cent of respondents said that they had a great deal of knowledge on animals, less than 5 per cent replied to questions in a way that was suggestive of expert knowledge. This prompted Amante-Helweg to suggest that this programme is in a latter stage of development, moving from a clientele that is expert to one that could better be characterized as general knowledge or general public. It can be argued that these forms of ecotourism go through a cycle of evolution from a highly engaged and knowledgeable tourist base in the earliest stages of development toward a more general population later as the activity becomes perceived as safe, and so on (see Butler, 1980; Cohen, 1972). A study by Boshoff *et al.* (2007) found that visitors and residents reported the 'Big Five' as 'not important' and 'fairly important' over 'very important' in a study of South African protected areas. This is contrary to the belief that these charismatic megafauna, along with the legacy of the categorization of these animals as a group, are the main focus of such trips.

What the foregoing suggests is that there appears to be a difference in degree and not necessarily in kind in regards to forms of tourism where animals are a central feature. This degree appears to be diminishing with increasing intensity over time as the base of products matures. This blending of type we saw with the discussion on consumptiveness, where there has emerged a significant amount of grey area in terms of what is viewed as consumptive or not.

Valuing animals

Monetarily

There is a theme in ecotourism, especially among the policy decision-makers of the lesser developed countries, that since 'wildlife pays, wildlife stays'. Hunting was an attractive option to these jurisdictions because it brought the promise of large sums of money that could be gained at the expense of the wildlife resource. The ability for ecotourism to use wildlife for commercial purposes became another very attractive option because wildlife had direct value in view of the fact that these animals could be used again and again in a rather sustainable fashion.

Wildlife use values have been discussed at length by Barnes *et al.* (1992). Direct use values include, for example, the experience of viewing elephants in Kenya. This value can be measured by two different approaches, including the travel cost method and contingent valuation (willingness to pay), with both approaches yielding comparable results in reference to the value of viewing elephants, at approximately US$25 million per year (each humpback whale in the Hervey Bay region of Queensland, Australia is estimated to be worth $100,000 according to Brook, 2001). The authors also discuss estimates of other values that relate to elephant viewing. These include (a) the option value of individuals who wish to preserve the elephants as a viewing option in the future; (b) the bequest value, which includes individuals who have no intention of viewing elephants but understand that future generations may value the opportunity to view elephants;

and (c) the existence value, which includes individuals who benefit from knowing that the elephants are and will be preserved. Indirect values attached to the preservation of elephants relate to the biological services or functions that these animals perform within the community. These include seed dispersal, expanding grasslands, and eating certain vegetation that might otherwise outcompete other varieties.

An example of the direct use value of wildlife is provided by Walpole and Leader-Williams (2002), who argue that the most important role that a flagship species plays is not its ecological function in the ecosystem (i.e., niche fulfilment), but rather its contribution to the socio-economic fabric of the overall community. Animals like tigers, gorillas, rhinos, or dolphins induce visitors to pay large sums of money to see them, which in turn aids their conservation and that of other species. Second, the local community may support conservation efforts if they see some benefits from living with these species. Walpole and Leader-Williams (2002) use the example of the Komodo dragon (*Varanus komodoensis*) as an example of the importance of the flagship to tourism and local communities. If not for this species, very few western tourists would visit the remote islands of eastern Indonesia, and there might be little incentive to preserve the animal. In 1995–6, tourists spent over US$1 million in the surrounding community and this industry supported over 600 jobs (Walpole and Goodwin, 2000). The money generated from this wildlife attraction also provided many other park management benefits, including funds to support law enforcement in Komodo National Park.

The relationship between keystone species or charismatic megafauna and tourism can be examined further through the work of Walpole (2001) using the same species. Supplementary feeding programmes on Komodo encouraged the development of an economic system that supported not only the dragons (goats slaughtered and tied to a tree to attract dragons) but also the park and local people. When the supplementary feeding programme was eliminated due to behavioural and physiological changes to the animals, there was a ripple effect throughout the community. The decline in viewing quality (not being able to see the dragons) contributed to fewer tourists venturing to the islands as word of the changes spread. Furthermore, the sale of goats to the park was lost, and fewer tourists were available to purchase wooden dragon carvings, along with fewer visitors using the boat shuttle service. The case study demonstrates that there are trade-offs that occur in the effort to ensure the well-being of animals for tourism purposes. In such cases, biological decisions on population fitness should take precedence over economic decisions, although these may be met with frustration by local people and other stakeholders.

Issues tied to human well-being and livelihood are thus central to the discussion of how best to use animals. Lindsey *et al.* (2005) write that improvements in the conservation of wild dogs in Africa will not occur on ranchland if there continues to be a lack of economic incentives for landowners. The authors argue that ecotourism dollars may be used to offset some or even all of the predation costs, i.e., the value of keeping wild dogs on ranches for ecotourism offsets any loss of livestock that might occur because of the dogs. Willingness to pay studies confirm that tourists are prepared to pay large sums of money to experience this form of wildlife in South Africa, making ecotourism a viable option.

When conservation limits the ability of those living in or adjacent to protected areas from feeding their families or earning a living, it is often the animals that take the brunt of this frustration in the form of illegal poaching in the absence of any incentive to place value in conservation. This issue continues to surface in regions around the world (see Hill, 2002; Sekhar, 2003; Evans, 2009). In Mgahinga National Park, Uganda, for example, the creation of the park in 1991 necessitated the removal of a local population of inhabitants who were in turn compensated financially for their removal (on average US$27 per person). But although the competition amongst the community for funds generated by gorilla tourism is one way to offset the discomfort of having to be removed from the region of the park, there are other issues that have surfaced in the absence of appropriate institutions and revenue-sharing programmes that should be designed to take care of the needs of local people (Adams and Infield, 2002). Although the international appeal of the gorillas is enormous, local people may be more concerned with livelihood issues than the appeal of the animals to external parties.

Still, there are deeper philosophical questions tied to the conservation of animals and their economic value to humans. The notion that these animals are worth more to us alive than dead encapsulates the broader problem. We have not really progressed much further than the discourses tied to the value of dead whales measured in blubber and oil. These animals are still being evaluated according to their worth to us. Peace (2005) says that it is still our 'volition to consume' that is given highest priority.

Marketing animal icons: making something out of nothing

The thylacine or 'Tassie tiger', although extinct (or rather thought to be extinct), remains one of the most iconic themes in Tasmania. The level of reverence and nostalgia surrounding the animal is such that it has been recently selected as Tasmania's brand logo. Turner (2009) provides an interesting glimpse into the rhetoricity of thylacine representation in Tasmanian tourism, and suggests that there are three polarities at work in this representation: the thylacine as wild or domesticated, present yet absent, and national yet regional.

The first polarity, wild versus domesticated, has generated a number of contemporary representations of the thylacine that range from reverence to trivialization. Reverence includes artwork that elevates the animal, while trivialization includes the 'Disneyfication' of the thylacine: said to be the result of a saturation of images that are devoid of true meaning in efforts to be distinctive. The risk to Tasmanian tourism, Turner writes, is that the thylacine becomes decontextualized from Tasmanian history in rendering images of what the thylacine should look like in the eyes of the tourist.

Although not as extensive, Turner's second polarity on the present yet absent thylacine is important as it creates something out of nothing: the presence of an absence – in the same capacity as the Loch Ness Monster. What is really impressive about this phenomenon is that history becomes a central theme in the attraction and also the glimmer of hope that the animal still does actually exist (although the last 'Tasmanian tiger' died in a zoo in the capital, Hobart in 1936). Tourism Tasmania authorities are quick to note that the animal is technically extinct, but with a number of unsubstantiated sightings that keep the dream of the thylacine alive. The tourism industry has capitalized on this by offering a number of tours that venture along routes where people have sighted the animal as well as places where the animal was captured and the conditions of capture. Maps have been created to graphically situate these sightings and captures, which provide rich fodder for the imagination. The creation of maps touches on the third polarity identified by Turner as the national versus regional identity of the tiger. The many sightings that have taken place on mainland Australia serve to challenge the image in the mind of the tourist that the animal is uniquely Tasmanian. But recent exhibits have shown the complicated relationship that exists between people and environment. National/regional polarity has paired the thylacine with Tasmanian aborigines, both of whom were rendered extinct by anthropogenic causes. In two centuries its greatest predator and its native population both disappeared and it is left to tourism promoters and tourists alike to recreate the Tasmanian tiger in the cultural imaginary.

The taniwha of New Zealand is another case in point. The Maori hold this mythical beast in high regard, and this is evidenced by the fact that the Maori community successfully had a small section of motorway re-routed around a wetland that is said to be the ancestral home of this beast. The construction of a highway is largely a matter of cost–benefit calculation, given the needs of the human population to move quickly and efficiently through the countryside. The attainment of this goal needs to be balanced against cost, and these projects are completed at a cost of millions of dollars. Environmentalists would argue that there are numerous issues to take into consideration in a road's construction, including for example sewer design, drainage, the control of hazardous materials, erosion, deforestation, and so on. But what of ritual and mysticism, which are rarely if ever given consideration in these cost–benefit calculations? Is this a case of the rights of a mythical beast? Is it a case of the rights of Maori tradition and culture being upheld? Is it a testament to the impressiveness of an evolving relationship between indigenous and Western peoples? Maybe it is all of these.

Although we use animals frequently as wildlife icons for the marketing of wildlife tourism, Tremblay (2002) observes that little is known about the traits of the types of species used. He discusses a number of characteristics or dimensions that might be more attractive, including human likeness (the extent to which an animals reflects human characteristics), large size (larger animals and birds preferred over smaller mammals and birds), visibility, and aesthetic appeal. Furthermore, charisma is seen to be important and goes beyond animals just being cute (like koalas) to include approachability and playfulness. Tremblay says that negative charisma prevents an animal from being used as an icon, which refers to an animal's unsavoury traits, including unappealing aesthetics (the animals is seen to be ugly), behaviour (scavenging), danger to humans, or the perception that the animal is dirty (rats) or scary (spiders) (see Chapter 2). When asked about animal icons in the Northern Territory, Australia, tourists identified most strongly with the

Plate 8.1 Taniwha rock carving, Lake Taupo, New Zealand

saltwater crocodile as a symbol not only of flora and fauna but also of culture. Yet tourism marketers might struggle with the image of a 'man-eater', finding it too controversial as the primary symbol of a land that is much more than simply one large predator. In other research, Ryan (1998) found that the crocodile did not immediately come to mind as a descriptor or symbol of the 'Top End' of Australia in eliciting general comments about the region. Instead, tourists described this region as 'hot', 'humid', 'awesome', 'spacious', 'vast', 'different', 'big', 'lush', and 'barren'. Only when prompted did tourists begin to associate crocodiles as meaningful in the description of the Top End.

Animals that are endangered or scarce have also not been the topic of discussion in tourism research, according to Tremblay, although in practice (i.e., in marketing itself) this must surely be of consideration. Professional sports teams have used endangered animals as emblems. A case in point is the Florida Panthers of the National Hockey League, who use the highly threatened panther as the key symbol of their team. Experts suggest that there are only about 100 of these animals left in the wild.

Like humans

Some animals, such as whales or gorillas, garner more interest than others because of their size, aesthetic appeal, visibility in the media, or difficulty in being found in the wild (see Tremblay, 2002). What is dealt with much less in tourism is the discourse, alluded to above, on interest based on the sharing of human characteristics – a topic that is afforded much higher value in animal ethics (see Sunquist and Sunquist, 2002; Woods, 2000). Notwithstanding, there are a few tourism studies that broach the topic and provide a good base of understanding.

The main problem with whale watching in contemporary society, according to Peace (2005), is that tourists are told not only that whales are 'like us' as humans, but more specifically that they are like 'you' or 'me'. This is problematic because tourists are made to think that whales have specific identities and characteristics in the same way that we as humans use to differentiate one human from another. The second critique follows from the first in that the attribution of human qualities to whales separates these animals from the broader ecological system of which they are part. Focusing on superficial comparisons to humans is to fail to underscore the processes of significant transformation in the southern hemisphere or the broader global changes that affect us all.

The 'like humans' discourse is followed by Cater and Cater (2007), who observe that we can relate to some animals over others because of the crossover of certain actions and behaviours, e.g., child rearing. These animals are constructed as near to us, while others that are different remain in the realm of the 'other'. This type of anthropomorphism is rampant in the tourism industry, and Cater and Cater use the aquarium as an example where tourists are asked to 'bring your family to meet ours' (2007: 163). But even though anthropomorphism can be used as the great divider, it should not be vilified completely as misrepresenting animals. A more enlightened anthropomorphism can break down the walls of speciesism (Cater and Cater, 2007), and according to Clark (1997), a particular characteristic of an animal that appears to be part of the human behaviour domain does not always smack of anthropomorphism.

The dimensions of this 'like human' discourse have been more formally outlined by Ryan (1998), who has developed a classification of wildlife appeal based on perceived safety and danger, and the degree of human similarity (see Figure 8.1).

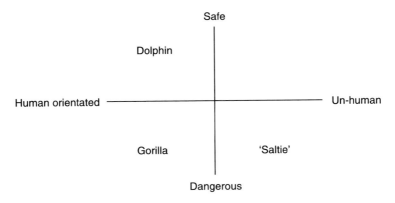

Figure 8.1 Classification of wildlife appeal

It may very well be that an animal's acceptance is contingent upon where it falls in this matrix. This is a theme that has been explored in the literature. However, from a fascination point of view, and this is where tourism enters the equation, those animals that are dangerous and un-human may still garner a significant amount of interest from the travelling public.

Proximity

The preceding section on 'like human' provides a good introduction to the present section on proximity. The argument here is that the increasing interest in human–wild animal interaction is a function not only of qualities and traits of animals that are thought to be human, but also curiosity in regards to physical and behavioural characteristics of the animals sought, their status in regards to vulnerability, as well as their place in the film and entertainment pantheon (Harvey, 2007). There is a keen desire to be close to animals, which also means the opportunity to touch. This form of interaction has not been dealt with at any length in the literature, according to Curtin (2005), especially the emotional, cognitive, and physical benefits from these interactions. Bulbeck (2005) finds that the desire to touch animals is part of the human condition, which allows people to gain a more complete experience with the animal. Children often get the opportunity to touch animals in petting zoos, and the opportunity to feed animals seems almost as important as touching them. A positive experience for these children demands that animals like goats and sheep willingly tolerate attempts to make contact (Anderson *et al.*, 2002). For Franklin (1999), while modernity is based on curiosity and the spectacle of the other, a move to the postmodern is characterized by a heightened emotional bond with animals that is couched in a broader moral context: the search for a more intimate or embodied experience (Franklin, 1996, 2008; see also Mordue, 2009; Baker, 2005); a move from watching to doing, which involves tapping into all the senses beyond vision alone (see also Carvalhedo Reis, 2009 in regards to the rich and meaningful ways hunters should engage with animals; and Baker, 2005, in terms of how people want the satisfaction of looking into the eyes of the beast – of seeing and being seen).

During the late 1800s, photography emerged as a way to get close to animals as an alternative to hunting. Brower (2005) illustrates that early wildlife photography was referred to as camera hunting. George Shiras published the first nonhuman animal photograph in an 1892 edition of *Forest and Stream*, of a doe as a roundel to give the effect that the animal had in fact been hunted (as though seen through the scope of a rifle). Brower tells us that these early images were as much trophies as the dead carcasses of animals, because of the sport required to capture them on film. The camera hunter had to be as much a woodsman as the conventional hunter, perhaps even more so because of the skill required in getting close to the animal given the limited technology in cameras of the time. The concept of camera hunting was developed by the editor of *Forest and Stream*, George Bird Grinnell, who argued that camera hunting was a superior form of sport to hunting with a gun, as it left prey intact, while at the same time obtaining a trophy. As quoted in Brower (2005: 17):

His trophies the moth may not assail. His game touches a finer sense than his palate possesses, satisfies a nobler appetite than the stomach's craving, and furnishes forth a feast that, ever spread, ever invites, and never palls upon the taste.

(Grinnell, 1892: 287)

The need to get closer has been catalysed by what Bulbeck (2005) calls the 'Attenborough effect', named after the famed naturalist and documentary maker David Attenborough. Television viewers are privileged to view animals up close and personal (after hundreds of hours of cinematography), and expect to be able to do the same in their travels to places of interest. When this fails, there is an erosion of satisfaction that results from the failure of guides and operators to do the same. Lemelin (2006) observed aspects of the Attenborough effect in his work on the ocular consumption of polar bears in Churchill, Manitoba, Canada. Television viewers often get digitally enhanced films that manipulate the aggressive or predatory nature of polar bears, as something different than natural behaviour demonstrated at the time of filming. The upshot of this is that tourists find themselves attempting to mimic these exceptional films such that the motivation is not really to fully 'see' the bears, but rather to place more emphasis on the collection of trophy photographs taken home and shared with friends and family. Tourists, according to Lemelin, don't want to purchase postcards; they want their own trophy snaps of the exotic and the remote – and in this case the charismatic. What further complicates the situation is that even though ecotourists are able to penetrate into quite remote regions, a range of management imperatives that formalize the relationship between humans and nature often mediate their experience. Paths, trails, boardwalks, fences, viewing platforms, glass, metal, and so on act as boundaries that reinforce nature as the 'other' (Markwell, 2001).

The need for 'closer as better' has necessitated the implementation of regulations to control the physical touching of animals in wildlife tourism. The whale shark industry is a case in point. The singular nature of the whale shark experience allows operators to charge individual tourists upwards of A\$300 per outing (Cater and Cater, 2007). Catlin *et al.* (2010b) estimate that approximately 8,000 to 10,000 whale shark tourists spent about A\$6 million in the Ningaloo Coast region of Western Australia in 2006, with 15 licences distributed amongst a few operators. In a study by Davis *et al.* (1997) on whale shark tourism, numerous tourists actually touched a whale shark despite the potential of a fine of A\$10,000. However, Davis *et al.* (1997) discovered that getting closer did not affect the overall experience. Tourists a metre away from the sharks did not have an appreciably more satisfying experience than tourists one to three metres, or more than three metres from the sharks.

Australia is not the only place in the world where whale sharks are a tourist attraction. In Belize, whale sharks visit Gladden Spit to feed on the spawn of aggregations of snappers – the relationship between snappers and sharks has prompted officials to declare the region a marine reserve (Gladden Spit and Silk Cayes marine reserve), helping to heighten tourist interest in the whale sharks during certain parts of the year. In an effort to mitigate any impacts that might occur between sharks and humans, a number of guidelines have been drafted to regulate the increasing number of whale shark tours, as seen in Box 8.2.

In the case of swim-with-dwarf minke whale excursions, passengers reported higher levels of satisfaction the closer the whales swam to the tourists, and higher levels of satisfaction with longer periods of time interacting with the whales (Valentine *et al.*, 2004). Amante-Helweg (1996) found that even though 96 per cent of tourists on a swim-with-dolphin tour got to actually touch a dolphin, 100 per cent of all participants reported that they enjoyed the activity regardless of the chance to touch the dolphins or not. By contrast, Schänzel and McIntosh (2000) found that proximity was especially important in viewing penguins in the South Island of New Zealand. Higher degrees of enjoyment were expressed the closer the tourists got to the penguins – enjoyment that was higher than expected. A number of cognitive benefits were reported from the experience, including knowledge, awareness, and pleasurable memories, but a key aspect of Schänzel and McIntosh's work was the emotive response from participation in this activity. Respondents reported feelings of pleasure, curiosity, amazement, and fascination, with the suggestion that the affective domain is one which is deserving of more research in this area.

The extent to which wildlife tourists cross the line in their efforts to get closer has been documented by Markwell (2001) in his work on orang-utan tourism in

---

Box 8.2 Whale shark tourism: tour guides, boatmen, and fishermen

- All whale shark tour guides must hold a valid whale shark license.
- Only 8 snorkelers per snorkel guide permitted.
- Only 8 divers per licensed divemaster.
- All boats should approach whale sharks at idle speed or no more than 2 knots/hour, and remain at least 50 feet (15 m) away from the animal(s).
- Do not block the whale shark's path with the boat.
- Discharge your passengers 50 feet (15 m) from the whale shark.
- To avoid harassing the sharks and to maximize safety, tour boats should keep a distance of 200ft (60m) away from each other during a whale shark tour with snorkelers/divers in the water.
- When the whale shark(s) has gone, have all snorkelers/ divers on the surface get back into the boat.
- When divers and snorkelers have returned to the boat, please leave the area to give other tour guides and guests an opportunity with a whale shark.
- All snorkelers and divers on whale shark tours must be out of the water by 5:30pm.

Florida Museum of Natural History (2011)

Borneo. Tourists crossed the line by touching baby orang-utans even though this was strictly forbidden. Interviews conducted by Markwell (2001) on these events confirm that tourists who touched the apes were well aware of the restrictions, but felt compelled to do so in enhancing their overall experience:

> ... probably because we were doing something naughty. And, oh, you'd never get to see them that close-up and in such a natural surrounding and then the fact that you were doing something you weren't supposed to do. It was a bit more adventurous when you were actually touching one, real interaction.
>
> (Markwell, 2001: 51)

The event presented itself as an ethical issue for another participant:

> Oh, and I can still feel its touch and I remember it was me saying to be careful about the Rid (insect repellant) we had put all over our arms and hands, and I thought well, what about it and its health, but I still got this sense of yeah we were human beings, we're just that tiny bit superior, so I can let this orang-utan lick me and possibly get ill, you know, it was almost too precious a moment to give up.
>
> (Markwell, 2001: 51)

One can well imagine the cognitive dissonance of the offending agent here:

> I wonder what the others will think if I touch the ape?
> I wonder if others want to touch the ape as much as me?
> If somebody goes first, everyone else will fall in line. They just need someone, like me, to lead them off.
> Will I get in trouble?
> This trip is expensive, and we deserve the opportunity to have some 'extras'.
> The guide won't care. He seems pretty relaxed.
> Just think what my friends at home will say when I tell them I actually got to pet an orang-utan!

The hierarchy between human and beast is unmistakable in the second of the quotes above. As superior beings we have the authority, the right, to do as we please in our interactions with inferior others, even if this means compromising their well-being. Markwell describes this event as both the transgression of the boundary between tourist and animal, to the point where the safety of the animal was jeopardized, and the need for closer, more embodied experiences. It should be noted that not all of the tour participants shared the need to interact with the orang-utans from a tactile standpoint, but the orang-utans were still not extended the dignity of being considered more than just a 'thing':

> To see some of the group sort of carrying on with the orang-utan, like 'this little baby' and all that nonsense, you know, things shouldn't be touched or

handled by anybody other than the people who are supposed to be looking after them, and to sort of use animals like that for self-gratification, and that's what I think it is, just gratification of your own feelings, is wrong. At the time I said to them, 'Oh leave the bloody thing alone.'

(Markwell, 2001: 51)

Part of the problem is that ecotourists are either not aware of the problems created by contact that is too close, or that they simply do not care (as above). In a study of hikers and mountain bikers at Antelope Island, Utah, Taylor and Knight (2003) found that about 50 per cent of the sample felt that their participation did not adversely affect wildlife in any way, and further that it was acceptable to approach wildlife more closely than wildlife would allow. Finally, recreationists tended not to take responsibility for stress on wildlife and chose rather to fix blame on other users.

The disconnect between knowledge provision and knowledge application has been investigated by Moscardo and Saltzer (2004), who employed the social psychological theory of mindfulness in analysing visitor satisfaction in wildlife tourism experiences. The theory posits that individuals enter into a situation in either a mindful or mindless state, the former characterized by an active cognitive state where individuals are synthesizing the informational and environmental cues around them. These mindful people are open to learning and may, as a result, achieve higher levels of satisfaction. Moscardo and Saltzer expand upon this idea as shown in Figure 8.2, which incorporates setting conditions, visitor characteristics, visitor–wildlife experience, wildlife characteristics, and outcomes. The authors argue that variety (e.g., more than just one species) and interactive participation (e.g., handling wildlife) provide the tourist with a multisensory encounter, thus enhancing the overall experience. The implications of this model for interpretation management are far-reaching (see Moscardo, Woods and Saltzer, 2004, in the same volume).

Habituation and provisioning

The main challenge to wildlife viewers, according to Knight (2009), is the reluctance of animals to show themselves – the legacy of hunting just about every type of animal over millennia. Animals use a variety of physical and behavioural adaptations, including flight, to disappear into the natural environment, and this makes the job of tracking and seeing animals extremely difficult. There is even more pressure on operators and guides to get as close as possible, because proximity sells and distance does not. Knight argues that there are essentially two ways of making wildlife viewing easier. The first is habituation, or the removal of the animal's need to escape, replaced by tolerance of humans. The problem with this approach is that it often takes extensive amounts of time to habituate animals in the wild. The more highly favoured approach is to attract animals through provisioning, which is providing food and water at fixed locations in order to facilitate watching for tourists who are often short of time. Knight stresses that

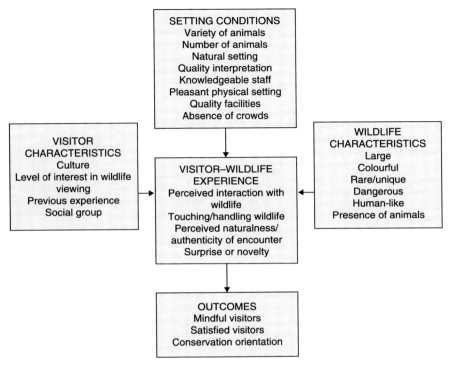

Figure 8.2 A mindfulness model of wildlife-based tourist experiences

these strategies have the consequence of changing the wild quality of the behaviour of animals, but this is necessary in order for wildlife viewing to exist at its present scale. Wildlife, simply stated, needs to be made available to the consumer.

Habituation is defined as 'the acceptance by wild animals of a human observer as a neutral element in their environment' (Johns, 1996: 258). The manner in which to measure or assess habituation in animals can be based on behaviour or physiology. Examples of the former include charge reactions in chimpanzees. These reactions decreased over a sixteen-month period of time, whereas ignore reactions increased (Johns, 1996). For gorillas, habituation is a process that takes between 3 and 24 months of daily contact (Butynski and Kalina, 1998). Van Polanen Petel *et al.* (2008) found that lactating Weddell seals showed evidence of rapid habituation over a short period of time after repeated exposure to pedestrians causing no overt harm. Two-thirds of the seals looked up at pedestrians during the first approach with only 18 per cent looking up during the tenth approach. Furthermore, there was an associated decrease in time spent looking at the pedestrian with repeated contact between seals and humans. Reduced aggressiveness of skuas in Antarctica is a sign of habituation (Pfeiffer and Peter, 2004).

Physiological habituation in marine iguanas of the Galápagos Islands, Ecuador, has been measured by Romero and Wikelski (2002). These authors analyzed corticosterone concentrations of animals in tourist-frequented sites and in places where tourists are not allowed. In situations involving handling and release of iguanas, animals in tourist-exposed sites had lower corticosterone levels after 30 minutes of stress than animals in tourist-free zones. The authors speculate that iguanas are down-regulating corticosterone levels in response to the presence of tourists as part of the process of habituation. Although iguanas are not stressed, the authors argue that higher levels of corticosterone are required to optimize energy regulation – and this may be compromised in tourist-exposed areas where handling of animals may take place. Habituated bears also show lower levels of stress than non-habituated bears (Herrero, 1989). Fowler (1999) found that Magellanic penguins have lower stress responses behaviourally and physiologically when they learn that frequent interaction with tourists along a path does not present a threat. Finally, de Villiers *et al.* (2006) found that 40 metres appeared to be the threshold at which heart rate would start to increase for giant petrels when approached by humans. The resting heart rate of these birds was 80 beats per minute, and this started to increase at about 40 metres and continued to increase during approach to 5 metres, with a maximum increase of 204 per cent over the resting heart rate.

Research on human–bear interaction by Smith *et al.* (2005) has shown that there are three different types of habituation, with the first two benefiting bears as habituation lessens energy expenditures, and the third benefiting humans, who do not have to respond to bears that are not threatening. These include bear-to-bear habituation, bear-to-human habituation, and human-to-bear habituation.

Bear-to-bear habituation

Facilitated by bear density. As bear numbers increase, bears interact more frequently with other bears, and bear-to-bear habituation is more likely to occur. The reason for this acceptance of conspecifics in such high density is the level of abundant food (e.g., salmon runs). There is enough food for all. Overt reaction distances are very short, in the order of two metres. The authors posit that the bear-to-bear habituation condition enables safe viewing of bears at relatively close distance because this habituation to other bears is thought to be generalized to people, eliminating the perception of surprise. Furthermore, food-defending behaviours are suppressed, eliminating this particular cause of human attack.

Bear-to-human habituation

This type may be facilitated by bear-to-bear habituation. In high-density bear regions the authors expect this form of habituation to be more prevalent than in low-density areas. Bears in high-density areas have small overt reaction distances. This form is the most frequently cited type in tourism research on human–animal interactions, and studies on parks and protected areas, where hunting is eliminated, tend to emphasize this point. The potential benefits and risks (costs) of bear-to-human habituation are found in more detail in Table 8.1.

Human-to-bear habituation

Facilitated by the degree of bear-to-human habituation in an area. When people spend time around bears with small overt reaction distances, these people show a tendency toward habituation to these bears, losing their wariness of these animals and giving way to behaviours that may be classified as careless or casual. This form of habituation has been observed at Katmai National Park, Alaska:

> Humans habituate to bears at Brooks. This results from repeated encounters with bears at close range ... Such bears are often described as 'cute' by people and these people tend to lose their common sense by getting too close. There is a need to identify ways to lessen habituation in visitors.
>
> (Servheen and Schoen, 1998, as cited in Smith *et al.*, 2005)

Human density is a factor in many of the studies discussed above. For those people living adjacent to parks and protected areas in Tanzania, Newmark and Manyanza (2002) report that they continue to have problems with wildlife because of higher densities of people. The authors recommend the implementation of land use practices that are conducive to low human density and that are unattractive to wildlife on lands that are adjacent to parks and protected areas.

Table 8.1 The potential benefits and risks (costs) of bear-to-human habituation

Benefits primarily to humans	*Costs primarily to humans*
Safe bear viewing and photography. Economic benefits to communities. Habituation decreases the chance of bear attack to humans. Habituation and roadside habitat may increase capacity for protected areas.	Conflicts with fishing and hunting. Close proximity may encourage ignorant or illegal acts. Increasing odds of injury with more interaction. Habituated bears have a higher tendency to approach humans, and people may respond inappropriately. Habituated bears may cause traffic jams and collision injuries. It costs money to manage habituated bears, especially if they are food-conditioned.
Benefits primarily to bears	*Costs primarily to bears*
Bears better able to access natural foods near centres of human activity. Bears may use presence of humans to avoid encounters with other bears. Bears promote bear viewing, which, in turn, may promote bear conservation.	Bears near roadsides or railways are more likely to be injured or killed. Bears more likely to be killed if outside protected areas. Bears near roads are more likely to be fed by people, get people's food, and become food-conditioned. Bears more likely to be approached by people for photographs, increasing risk of human injury and bear removal.

Adapted from Herrero *et al.*, 2005

In reference to provisioning, the second major factor of proximity, Knight identifies many different environments where this activity takes place, including garbage dumps in North American parks (see Schullery, 1980), the attraction of lions and leopards in Africa with carcases (Edington and Edington, 1986), the use of dead buffalo in India to attract tigers (see McDougal, 1980), and the killing of goats up until 1994 to attract Komodo dragons in Indonesia (Walpole, 2001). The regularity and predictability factors are controlled and both animals and humans are supposedly happy with the arrangement. Close proximity through provisioning provides for greater intimacy and contact, and the behaviour allows provisioned animals to 'become positively attracted to humans, whom they associate with food. The giving of food to wild animals may be represented positively as an expression of kindness, intimacy, friendship, or trust across the species barrier' (Knight, 2009: 177). And further, under certain very intimate circumstances such as play, 'visitors cease to be simply viewers of the animals but become interactants with them as well' (p. 178).

This move towards the sharing of food with animals has also been discussed by Orams (2002), who feels that this behaviour is part of our human nature practised for millennia (as cultural and religious ritual). It comes as no surprise, therefore, that tourists would want to share food with animals.

Impacts of proximity

The feeding of animals in captive, semi-captive, and wild environments, however popular, produces significant problems according to Orams (2002), including alteration of natural behaviours (e.g., less time foraging and hunting), dependency and habituation (e.g., learning to become less self-sufficient), aggression (intra-group and inter-group fighting), and poor health and injury (feeding of inappropriate food). These impacts correspond to the first of three categories of negative effects that stem from wildlife tourism according to Green and Higginbottom (2001): (1) disruption of activity, including noise, habituation, provisioning, fleeing, or hiding; (2) direct killing or injury, which may be intentional from activities like hunting and fishing, or unintentional such as stepping on eggs inadvertently or via road accidents; and (3) habitat disruption or alteration from off-road vehicle disturbances, the clearing of land for tourism developments, and the trampling of vegetation. As category 2 was the focus of the previous chapter, category 1 is given most attention below (with more of a focus on the marine tourism industry), with some examples of category 3.

Category 1

The maturity of the cetacean watching industry has come packaged with a shift in the proximity of tourists to animals. There has been a move from passive viewing at a distance, to a more recent move to get close and interactive, according to Spradlin *et al.* (2001):

For example, commercial tours offer the public the chance to: swim with humpback whale cow/calf pairs in their breeding/nursery habitat in the Caribbean; pet grey whales in their breeding/nursery habitat in Baja, Mexico; pet and 'cuddle' harp seal pups on ice floes in Canada; walk amongst seals or sea lions in their rookeries in California and the Galapagos Islands; swim with dolphins in their resting or feeding areas in Hawaii, Florida, New Zealand, the Bahamas and Japan; swim with manatees in Florida and Belize; and feed wild dolphins in Australia.

(Spradlin *et al.*, 2001: 2)

Dolphin feeding programmes have been criticized for the onset of various health-related problems in the dolphin population. Cater and Cater (2007) observe high infant mortality, low juvenile survival, and behavioural changes from the provisioning of dolphins at Monkey Mia on the west coast of Australia, with heightened aggression towards humans displayed by dolphins at Tangalooma (see Orams, 1995). Reactions considered negative included dolphins abandoning their activity, changing direction, separating from the group, escape/avoidance, and altering dive times. Positive reactions included dolphins deliberately approaching the boat, dolphins observing the boat, surfing in the wake behind the boat, fishing next to the schooner, and following the schooner. Bottlenose dolphins in Doubtful Sound, New Zealand have been observed to change behaviour as a result of the tourism industry. Licensed and unlicensed craft intrusions have

Plate 8.2 Girl swimming with bottlenose dolphin, Hawaii

disrupted their resting periods and also their ability to socialize (Lusseau and Higham, 2004).

De Fatima Filla and De Araujo Monteiro-Filho (2009) found that when dolphin-observing schooners stuck to the correct regulations on separation between animal and craft, there was a positive reaction measured in the behaviour of the dolphins. By contrast, when boats approached to distances of less than 50 metres, classified as chasing, these resulted in 100 per cent negative reactions from the dolphins. The authors argue that there is a difference between observers moving towards dolphins, and dolphins moving towards observers. In the latter case, the dolphins seem to be in control of the situation, and in the former not in control, eliciting negative responses in these cases.

The absence of codes of ethics for whale watching has proven to have undesirable impacts on the behaviour of humpback whales. Whaley *et al.* (2007) found that whales displayed a range of agitated behaviours (breaching, tail slaps, dives, and so on) in an effort to avoid boats that were too close and in the path of the direction of travel of the whales (see Weinrich and Corbelli, 2009, who argue that whale watching in southern New England has had no effects on calf productivity and survival in that area).

The number of competing interests over certain resources means that there is sustained discussion over the use of these resources. For example, even though whale watching has been deemed more acceptable than killing whales, there is still the question of the degree of impact by virtue of human–animal interaction. Corkeron (2004) argues that even though whale watching is classified as ecotourism, anthropogenic noise leads to short-term behavioural changes in the whales with perhaps long-term consequences. Coastal dolphins living in discrete societies with limited home ranges are affected daily by tourist vessels, the extent of which we are only recently beginning to appreciate (Corkeron, 2004). For example, Henheffer (2010) writes that the increasing incidence of whale and dolphin beach strandings appears to be as a result of hearing loss. High-decibel noise from supertankers, oil exploration and military operations has doubled every ten years since the 1960s, and has disrupted the echolocation and communication abilities of these animals. Of 1,200 to 1,600 dolphins and whales stranded on US beaches annually, only about 17 per cent survive and new studies point to the fact that some 33 per cent of these cetaceans are found to be deaf or have severe hearing loss.

In the case of swimming with captive dolphins, Curtin and Wilkes (2007) found that although tourists chose to participate in such an activity because of a life ambition, the mythical appeal of dolphins and the desire for close proximity, the experience itself generated time-lapse cognitive dissonance after an immediate post-experience response. Immediate reactions included an appreciation of the size, grace, and power of these animals, and included excitement and thrills, but also a sense that the experience was too short, too expensive, and too staged. Later on, participants were able to reflect on their experience and these reflections included concerns about the size of enclosures, captivity, performing for tricks (rewards), and the cost–benefit calculation surrounding expense and unfulfilled expectations. These later reflections may come about as a result of knowledge of the stress and severely compromised quality of life, not to mention shorter life, that dolphins have to endure in the process (see Frohoff and Packard, 1995; Frohoff, 2004).

The types of problems and issues documented in dolphin and whale watching tourism have been reported in other forms of marine tourism. In Hamelin Bay, south-western Australia, stingray tourism is an industry growing in popularity with tourists given the opportunity to feed rays from shore (Newsome *et al.*, 2004). Peak visitation is during the middle of the day, and there is a corresponding peak of stingrays at this time. The authors found that there was a range of behavioural impacts including habituation to humans because of the food provisioning, and aggression towards other stingrays in an effort to secure food. There was potential for a number of other impacts, including injury from boats, overfeeding, eating the wrong foods, damage from fishing hooks, and the risk of disease from poor water conditions. Semeniuk *et al.* (2009a) argue that most studies of tourism's impact on wildlife focus on behavioural changes to target species. In a study of stingrays in the Cayman Islands, a group of rays exposed to tourists and another group from non-visited sites were compared with the former group, demonstrating haematological changes suggestive of physiological costs borne from tourist interventions. More specifically, those exposed to tourists were provided non-natural food, sustained higher injury from boats, conspecifics and predators, and had more parasites, leading to sub-optimal health, than the non-tourism group, based on a number of haematological measures.

In reference to seals, Kovacs and Innes (1990) report that the presence of ecotourists during the whelping season had an adverse effect on both mothers and seal pups. Females spent less time with their pups in the presence of tourists, and those that did stay spent far less time nursing and more time on alert, while pups were found to rest less and move to different locations more frequently. When tourists moved within three metres or got close enough to touch the pups, the animals displayed a freeze response, which was the only time that this behaviour was shown. All mothers and pups returned to typical behaviours within one hour of the departure of tourists.

A longitudinal study by Berman *et al.* (2007) provided near perfect conditions under which to investigate the impacts of tourism on Tibetan macaques. Over a period of 19 years – six years before the group was translocated for tourism purposes, twelve years during their management for tourism purposes, and one year when tourism was temporarily suspended – these time periods corresponded with changing behaviour. Observations confirm that infant mortality in the troop was low before the period of tourism, increased significantly during the tourism years, and fell to pre-management levels during the year that tourism was suspended. The reason for the increased mortality of infants was increases in adult aggression in the area where primates were fed due to intra-group competition for food. Tourism staff were found harassing the macaques by throwing rocks and shouting at them in attempts to have them enter the food provisioning area, which the authors feel contributed to this aggression. The conclusion drawn is that infant mortality may be a helpful indicator of the impacts to of tourism on some species of animals. In a study on the feeding of mountain sheep by Lott (1988), tourists wanted to know that the sheep trusted them, i.e., that animals are better judges of people than people, and being trusted by a sheep reflects well on the individual. What feeding sheep did establish, unfortunately, was a dominance hierarchy whereby one or a few would cut off access to the source point for food, intensifying aggression and stress amongst these animals.

Work has also been conducted on the type of mobility used to access different species and the type of response shown by these animals (Wolf and Croft, 2010). In their study of two species of kangaroo in South Australia, the authors found that kangaroos fled less often when approached in a vehicle than when tourists approached on foot, confirming the results of other studies comparing these two modes of travel. Other factors that were measured by Wolf and Croft included time of day of approach as well as density of cover and conditions of the day. Flight initiation distances were all lower during the evening, when there was more cover available for the kangaroos, and during calm days.

The use of motion sensors and GPS units in radio collars worn by 13 female elk yielded valuable data on the travel time responses to different recreational activity disturbances (Naylor *et al.*, 2009). Although travel time increased in response to the presence of all four activities, higher travel times were recorded for off-road vehicles, followed by mountain biking, hiking, and horseback riding. Feeding time decreased as a result of ATV exposure and resting also decreased. A control group not exposed to any recreational disturbance spent less time travelling, and more time resting and feeding.

The translocation of animals represents an event that forces an animal outside of its normal range of tolerance. Millspaugh *et al.* (2007) examined faecal glucocorticoid metabolite (FGM) levels as a measure of stress response in five working translocated elephants and five wild elephants. The authors found that the FGM levels were highest during the translocation period and up to one month after the event. Between one and two months after the event, FGM levels returned to a level comparable to wild elephants. The authors also found that FGM levels were higher during periods of human interaction and that the two highest recorded levels of FGM corresponded to transportation and episodic loud noises.

Category 2

Briefly, nature-based tourism has been shown to adversely affect the well-being of the common or European wall lizard, prevalent in Europe and North America (Amo *et al.*, 2006). The authors discovered that, although lizards did not modify their escape behaviours in response to tourist pressure (i.e., tourists were viewed as predators), other damaging impacts were observed. Those lizards forced to undertake anti-predatory behaviours suffered from lower body condition. In females, lower body condition has been linked to the production of offspring of a smaller size and thus a lower probability of survival. Furthermore, lower body condition was also linked to a higher likelihood of tick infestation, and those females parasitized by ticks had lower fat stores and produced smaller clutches.

This suggests that increased tourism to areas inhabited by these lizards contributes to lower body condition and higher incidences of parasite infestation. The authors argue that the management of nature-based tourism should take into consideration the design of trails in protected areas for the purpose of limiting the stress on this species.

Category 3

Davenport and Switalski's (2006) review of environmental impacts from tourism and leisure transport identifies many examples where the pursuit of pleasure and enjoyment through travel has significant impacts on the well-being of individual animals and their habitat. A few of these examples are summarized below.

All-terrain vehicles (ATVs) are said to be responsible for a 90 per cent decline in the gopher tortoise population (native to south-eastern USA), who get crushed under the wheels of these vehicles or have their burrows caved in under the pressure of the machines. The animals cannot exit their burrows under these conditions, nor can they enter them, and they later succumb to the heat of the region (see Burge, 1983). While smaller animals are more susceptible to collisions with ATVs (Wilkins, 1982), large animals are affected because hunters are able to gain access to more remote locations not otherwise frequented by humans. Indirect effects of ATVs on wildlife include stress, loss of hearing, altered movement patterns, disruption to nesting patterns, and avoidance (Davenport and Switalski, 2006). In winter, snowmobiles have been shown to have many of the same effects on wildlife as ATVs, but compounded by the cold weather and reduction in food with higher energy demands. Well cited in the literature is the finding that the subnivean layer, the layer between the ground and snow is often crushed, and animals with it including their tunnels for movement (see Romgstad, 1980). This has secondary effects on some predators, who must widen their range to find populations of prey that have not been disrupted by snowmobiles.

Personal watercraft are also said to have an impact on wildlife, especially surface-dwelling, air-breathing vertebrates such as seals, turtles, and dolphins. Davenport and Switalski (2006) illustrate cases of turtle decapitation and death by blunt trauma impact from personal watercraft. Nesting birds, sealions, elephant seals, and otters are among the many other species that are regularly disturbed by the noise and intrusion of personal watercraft.

Ethics in action

The concept of respect is used here as a manner by which to build more credibility into ecotourism and wildlife tourism over other forms of tourism that rely on the capture and presentation of animals, animals forced into combat and competition, as well as hunting and fishing. Taylor's (1986) work on biocentrism (discussed in Figure 7.1) offers a good start. Taylor argues that moral worth in the form of equal respect ought to be extended to living parts of nature, including plants and animals, but not non-living matter. Each individual has intrinsic or inherent worth because each is a teleological centre of life with the purpose of maintaining its own existence. Taylor rejects human superiority over other living things because animals contain abilities that make them unique and worthy of moral status.

But when we capture, hook, force, confine, deprive, or kill we prevent animals from realizing their capabilities and this, according to Nussbaum (2006), is a justice issue that infringes upon dignity and respect. What is attractive about ecotourism is not the denial of dignity and respect, but rather their celebration. The focus of the activity, even though this is not often articulated, is the recognition that animals possess innumerable needs, functions, abilities, and so on, and these are most efficiently expressed because they are left in the wild. By suggesting that forms of nature-based tourism like zoos and ecotourism ought to be categorized or labelled together is to miss this critical reality – in acknowledgement that ecotourism is not a tourism panacea, as noted above.

Furthermore, even though there is criticism over the idea of species egalitarianism, i.e., that all species should have equal moral standing, or that animals are more important than trees, there are still non-instrumental reasons for caring about these that have to do with respect and aesthetics (Schmidtz, 1998) that have much to do with the ecotourist's tool kit (the principled ecotourism culture as identified by Malloy and Fennell, 1998). By choosing to care about a tree, its size, age, colour, and so on, we entertain moral questions pertaining to if and how we ought to care for it. Assigning respect to other species provides us, as agents of the tourism industry, with the opportunity to express values that are not just tied to our own pleasure and enjoyment, but rather of a different nature and scale.

Conclusion

The foregoing discussion has identified a number of complexities that exist in the ecotourism and wildlife tourism sector along the lines of consumptiveness, defining characteristics, and proximity, and the impacts that go along with this closeness to animals. The literature supports the contention that wildlife tourists are more concerned with the minimal impact of their activities on a species (turtles in this case) than other considerations including their own experience and personal comfort (Ballantyne *et al.*, 2009). There is the expectation that certain behavioural restrictions are implemented, and tourists felt uneasy with the possibility that the animals would be suffering as a result of their involvement in the tour or presence in the vicinity. On the other hand, Bulbeck (2005) writes that ecotourism and wildlife tourism may be characterized as a guilty pleasure. We know we are playing a part in the disruption of habitats, populations, and individuals in the wild, but our own self-interested needs surface as being more important than the needs of the places we are so interested in visiting. This dilemma will continue to haunt these more ecologically sensitive forms of tourism as travel for nature-based purposes continues to rise alongside projections for annual increases in international travel. The animal response to the impacts discussed in this chapter is the focus of the following chapter, where there is a continuation of many of the same general themes.

9   The animal threat

Introduction

The frequency and severity of animal–human contact with negative consequences for the latter is the topic of this chapter. Databases on animal–human encounters for the general population are well organized, but there is what might be described as patchy data in tourism studies (Quigley and Herrero, 2005). This chapter focuses on negative encounters with terrestrial predators like bears, dingoes, and crocodiles, and then proceeds to discuss the situation in the marine environment with more attention on jellyfish stings and their effects. The extent to which arthropods, particularly mosquitoes, have an impact on tourists is discussed as well as various other microorganisms. In this capacity, and because of the magnitude of the problem, microrganisms are subsumed under a two-kingdom classification scheme of animals (including microbes) and plants for purposes of organization. The role that humans play as vectors of disease is briefly addressed and this is followed with another brief section on how the changing perception of the manatee has enabled Floridians to find a more animal-centred balance in their lives.

The animal threat

An example of the precision with which general encounters with wildlife are represented is poison control centres. From 2001 to 2005, the United States Poison Control Centers together reported 472,760 animal bites and stings (94,552 calls per year). Twenty-seven people died, with most of these as a result of snakebite (Langley, 2008). In New Mexico between the years of 1993 and 2004 animals caused 63 human deaths. Horses were responsible for 43 of these (humans thrown, crushed, dragged, or kicked), cattle nine deaths, dogs three, bees three, sheep two, snakes one, spiders one and a bear one. Lathrop (2007) found that medical examiners concluded that many of these deaths could have been prevented by a change in human behaviour, including the use of proper protective gear or the avoidance of alcohol. While these are not tourism numbers, the statistics demonstrate how frequently US citizens have negative encounters with wildlife.

In tourism this type of precision does not exist because of the absence of regional and local organizational frameworks with which to collect data. Added to this is the fact that the travelling public's knowledge of human injury from animals does little to bolster tourism visitation. In many cases there is simply anecdotal information at hand, pointing to the fact that animal injuries have taken place, and that these are a function of the proximity issues discussed in the previous chapter (Bauer, 2001). Good statistics are needed according to Pandey *et al.*, (2002), because tourists ought to know the risk factors of various illnesses, diseases, and injuries in the places they choose to travel. In their work on the risk travellers face of exposure to rabies in Nepal, Pandey and colleagues found that 1.2 per 1,000 tourists per year had possible exposure to rabies while trekking and that more women and younger travellers were in higher risk categories. The following few studies have examined *general* trends in these animal–human interactions. A more specific treatment follows according to terrestrial and marine environments, as well as zoonoses and humans as vectors.

A study by Moscardo *et al.* (2006) illustrates that the animals most commonly involved in a negative tourist–animal encounter, as reported by tourists, include kangaroos (15 per cent), monkeys (9 per cent), snakes (9 per cent), mosquitoes (6 per cent), elephants (5 per cent), jellyfish (5 per cent), crocodiles (4 per cent), komodo dragons (4 per cent), magpies (4 per cent), and monitor lizards (4 per cent). Given that this was an Australian study, the authors note that there is a bias towards Australian data, but the study also includes data from all other major world regions. Tourists reported feelings of fear, frustration over the lack of information available on how to deal with these encounters, that food (picnics) was often a precipitating factor in these encounters, as well as the impact that insects had on diminishing the travel experience.

In a study of 10,499 adventure travellers to Nepal, 3.3 per cent (423 cases) of all diagnoses were animal bites. Not included in this number were various other animal-related annoyances including arthropod bites, scratches, rabies, and one marine sting. The animal bite category was the third highest after injuries (e.g., fractures, burns) and altitude sickness, 6.1 per cent and 4.7 per cent of all diagnoses respectively (Boggild *et al.*, 2007).

Gautret *et al.* (2007) found that of 320 cases reported between 1998 and 2005 of animal-associated injuries to tourists from developed countries, the highest proportion was recorded in Asia, followed by Australia/New Zealand, Africa and Latin America. Dog bites were responsible for 51.3 per cent of injuries, followed by monkeys (21.2 per cent), cats (8.2 per cent) and bats (0.7 per cent). Males were more likely to be bitten by a dog, whereas females were more likely to be bitten by a monkey. Gender was the focus of a study involving 59,000 tourists by Schlagenhauf *et al.* (2010), using data from the GeoSentinel Network (GSN). They found that women were more likely than men to contract acute diarrhoea, chronic diarrhoea, irritable bowel syndrome, upper respiratory tract infections, dental conditions, and reactions to medications. Women were also found to seek pre-travel advice more than men. By contrast, men were more likely to be hospitalized than women and also to contract febrile illnesses, vector-borne diseases (e.g., malaria), sexually transmitted diseases, viral hepatitis, or other problems such as frostbite or acute mountain sickness.

The significance of microbes to the well-being of tourists has been investigated by Zell (1997), who finds that infection escalates in the summer months. Tourists involved in summer backpacking are at risk of waterborne diarrhoeal illnesses, tick and other zoonotic infections, and injuries from mammal/reptile bites. In freshwater rafting and kayaking, tourists are at risk from waterborne diarrhoea, while those participating in marine aquatic sports like scuba and snorkelling are exposed to marine envenomations from invertebrates (jellyfish), punctures and envenomations from vertebrates such as stingrays and fish, and bacterial infections from abrasions and lacerations. These threats will be discussed in more detail below.

Terrestrial threats

This section addresses terrestrial animal threats along with associated challenges that tourists face in the pursuit of chosen activities. As space precludes a more detailed treatment of this group of animals, bears and a few other predators will be discussed according to relevant aspects of the literature, over other animals that pose less of a threat but still account for a number of animal–human attacks. An example of this latter group includes Gibraltar macaques. Fa (1992) examined medical records between 1980 and 1989 to show that macaques had bitten 308 people over this period. But because of the large numbers of tourists visiting the area, these attacks represented only 0.0001156 bites per person. Fa observes that biting is a density-dependent phenomenon. Monkey aggression rates increased in the afternoon over other periods of the day, because of more tourists, and during the summer months.

Moscardo *et al.* (2006) found that large predators described as dangerous are species that many tourists would like to see in the wild (e.g., crocodiles and sharks). The fascination with these large predators translates into these animals being considered as major tourist attractions – and sometimes a major threat. In this capacity, Kaltenborn, Bjerke, and Nyahongo (2006) conducted a similar study on the self-reported fear of potentially dangerous animal species in the Serengeti region of Tanzania. On the basis of 593 responses from individuals living in eight separate communities, the authors found that females were more fearful of large predators than men, fear was much more prevalent for specific species (e.g., more fear of lions and leopards over hyenas and cheetahs) than general groupings, and the elderly were less fearful of potentially dangerous species than younger cohorts. A related study by Roskaft *et al.* (2003) of 4,300 people in Norway on patterns of self-reported fear towards four large carnivore species that inhabit the country (brown bears, wolves, lynx, and wolverines) found similar results. Women were more fearful of these animals than men, although this study found that fear increased with age for both sexes. Rural inhabitants living in the vicinity of one of the species were found to be less fearful of the animal than rural inhabitants living where the carnivore was absent. Furthermore, those with higher levels of education and those interested in outdoor pursuits were less fearful than those with less education and little or no interest in outdoor activities (see Chapter 2).

In North America, bears (black, brown or grizzly, and polar) are both revered and respected. Hunters and wildlife tourists actively pursue these animals for nature-based tourism purposes, and there are a number of operators who focus specifically on these species. Having conducted student wilderness trips in the northern regions of Canada myself, I know that the primary concern that students have is encounters with bears. Although the chances of injury and death from bear attacks are very low, it is the perception of the characteristics of the animal that remains foremost in the minds of students and other travellers.

Statistics indicate how slight the chances are of injury or death from bears. Floyd (1999) illustrates that, on average, ten people per year are attacked by bears with only one death, and the number of recorded deaths caused by black bears between the years 1900 and 2007 was only 52 (Wolfe, 2008), far fewer than deaths during outdoor activity as a result of bee stings, spider bites, or lightning strikes. Data on these encounters, whether fatal or not, has enabled researchers to identify different categories of attack. Quigley and Herrero (2005) suggest that unprovoked attacks on humans occur when the human is the attraction of interest as opposed to food or other items. These may be predatory and including stalking, because of disease (e.g., rabies), or for purposes of right of way (e.g., game trails). Provoked attacks occur when tourists enter the personal space of an animal, or intentionally try to interfere by touching, photographing, or trying to kill the animal – all of which translate to invasion of personal space. There is a real or perceived threat and the attack is the animal's manner of defence. Floyd (1999) illustrates that bear attacks are of three kinds:

1. Sudden encounters: These include instances where neither the bear nor the human is aware of each other until they share the same space. Black bears normally make brief eye contact, become frightened, and leave the area quickly. Brown bears, especially mothers with cubs, attack humans during a sudden encounter, but most of these attacks do not result in death. The attacks last less than two minutes (which seems a very long time). The motivation of the mother bear appears to be to neutralize the intruder, who is perceived as a threat and not a source of food.
2. Predation: The victim is treated as a food source. Black bear attacks, although not aggressive in comparison with the other two species, account for 90 per cent of attacks and are almost exclusively by males. Brown bear attacks are almost never predatory.
3. Provocation: These occur with increasing frequency as more people penetrate into the backcountry, especially with populations of bears on the increase. Provocative behaviour includes photographers coming too close to female bears with cubs, or hunters wounding a bear and later becoming prey. Gender appears to play no significant role in these scenarios.

The terminology used in describing bear–human interactions is said by Smith *et al.* (2005: 1) to be misleading. For purposes of clarity they offer definitions of related terms shown in Table 9.1. The relationship between interactions or

Table 9.1 Terms used in describing bear–human interactions

Term	Definition
Bear sighting	When a person sees a bear, but the bear is apparently unaware of the person.
Bear–human interaction	Occurs when a person(s) and bear(s) are mutually aware of one another.
Encounter	Synonymous with interaction
Incident	An interaction between a bear(s) and a person(s) in which the bear acts aggressively. Bear incidents are a subset of human–bear interactions and have outcomes ranging from benign to injury.
Attack	The intentional contact by a bear resulting in human injury. Bear attacks are a subset of incidents.
Overt reaction distance	The distance at which a bear overtly reacts to another bear or a person.

Source: Smith *et al.* (2005)

encounters, incidents, and attacks is represented in the figure, with circle sizes indicating lesser degrees of magnitude of occurrence (although these are certainly not representative of exact numbers of each).

The finding that bear attacks causing injury or death are increasing from decade to decade has caused much concern among researchers. Herrero and Higgins (1999) found that between 1960 and 1990 the average number of bear-inflicted injuries in British Columbia escalated in line with increases in the provincial population, which means more people in bear habitat. Eighty-eight per cent of injury or fatality by grizzly bear occurred to those hunting, hiking, or working in backcountry areas. By contrast, 77 per cent of black bear injuries or fatalities

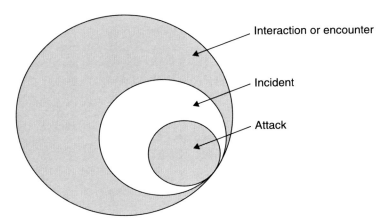

Figure 9.1 Relationship between various bear–human interactions

occurred to those hiking, bear viewing, working, or recreating in front-country regions. An examination of the spatial and temporal distribution of black bears in Colorado by Baruch-Mordo *et al.* (2008) revealed that over an 18-year period, bear–human conflicts continued to increase over time, and will continue to increase. In India, the higher incidence of sloth bear attacks is attributed to higher densities of human populations and a corresponding decline in habitat for bears. Bargail *et al.* (2005) report that between April 1998 and December 2000 there were 137 recorded attacks on humans by sloth bears, resulting in 11 deaths, in the North Bilaspur Forest Division alone. Most of these attacks (54 per cent) took place during the monsoon season and most occurred between four and eight o'clock in the morning.

Higher densities of people and the reduction of habitat are at the centre of animal–human interactions with other species. In Zimbabwe the redefinition of the Nile crocodile as an endangered species by commercial (skins and teeth) and conservationist interests has placed local fishers on Lake Kariba in a difficult position. As the population of crocodiles has expanded in recent years because of conservation efforts, so too has the number of interactions between humans and crocodiles. Hostility towards the crocodile is firmly entrenched within the social milieu of local communities living around the lake, linked to competition for fish, fear, loss of assets, harassment, and loss of life. But the problem is that the external sources that would not be happy in a world without the Nile crocodile are not the ones who must live together with this animal. Commercial and conservation bodies have developed policies and solutions in the absence of the opinions of local communities, who have been depicted as obstructive to these other interests. To assume that hostility will be abated through incentive programmes that promise revenue benefits to these communities through the implementation of sustainable practices is to underestimate the depth of the costs (often hidden) that these communities must endure in the face of commercial exploitation and conservation (McGregor, 2005). Similarly, density is said to be the main issue in terms of increases in numbers of cougar–human encounters since the mid-1990s on the West Coast Trail, British Columbia, as this region continues to generate higher visitor numbers. D.M. Thompson (2010) found that there were a few hotspots where these encounters typically took place, particularly campsites close to sources of water. The recommendation is to better understand the travel routes used by cougars in space and time, which include logging roads and hiking trails, and to direct tourists away from these routes through education and protocols that reduce the chance for interaction.

The perception that people have about bears, as noted above, is fuelled by media attention, possibly because of what Wolfe refers to as a 'culturally ingrained fear and loathing of large carnivores in western society' (citing Kellert *et al.*, 1996). Human injury or death from these large carnivorous animals makes for a better story. In response to public outcry over the death of an 11-year-old who was camping (asleep at the time) in the Uinta National Forest, Utah, Wolfe argues that, although sad, we have to assume some level of risk in the participation of these outdoor activities. Governmental agencies cannot and should not sterilize the backcountry experience of all potentially fatal hazards (improbable as they are) because some risk makes up part of the overall event. If problem bears are found to be in the area, these should be moved or eliminated in the eyes of Wolfe, and proper signage should be fixed so that recreationsists are made aware of the potential problems faced when interacting with dangerous animals. Apart from these measures, governmental agencies have no further responsibility (Wolfe, 2008).

The death of a nine-year-old boy, killed by a dingo in April of 2001 on Fraser Island, Australia, is another case in point (Peace, 2002). In the wake of this tragic death, decisions had to be made about how to mediate the human–animal interface on Fraser Island – decisions based on lengthy discussions that were heavily influenced by the media and that very quickly demonized the dingo as a 'natural born killer' and 'deadly stalker'. On one hand conservationists argued that the dingo herd was one of the finest representations of pure blood stock anywhere in Australia, and this fact was helpful in getting Fraser Island UNESCO World Heritage status. On the other hand, economic development (tourism) had to be protected, and the dingo had placed this in jeopardy. But what had not surfaced in the media was a series of other attacks on tourists that were suppressed in order to keep the wheels of development in motion. These attacks were said to be a function of higher levels of visitation – more people – and a correspondingly higher chance for interaction. But it is not only density but behaviour on the part of tourists too. Peace argues that the dingoes had become much more reliant on food hand-outs from tourists, citing commentators who felt that not only was the dingoes' ability to hunt diminishing but also there seemed to be fragmentation in their social structure, leading to 'an unnatural reliance on people which, when emboldened animals became hungry or frustrated, led them to attack vulnerable human beings' (Peace, 2002: 17). Weaker animals were surviving and pack leaders were no longer passing on hunting skills to younger animals of the pack.

The recommendations that surfaced not long after the death were devoid of any mention of economic development, according to Peace, and focused on the problem from a management perspective only. Tourists were to be educated on the threatening nature of dingoes, and fines were to be handed out to tourists and operators who were found to behave in inappropriate ways. A point made by Burns and Howard (2003) suggests that humans need to be managed as much as or more than dingoes (in Canada and I suspect the US, bear problems are really just people problems). As for the dingoes, conservation officers will use physical coercion, slingshots, high-frequency sound devices, pepper sprays, whips, and baits to make them sick, in order to control the dogs. A fence, keeping dogs out of some town sites on Fraser Island, was completed in October of 2008 (ABC News, 2008).

In reflection of this incident and the subsequent measures, Peace comments that:

> The dingoes are now fully circumscribed by an official mindset which demands they retreat to specified wilderness areas: they are currently the target of a panoptic regime which dictates that they exhibit and adhere to

certain behaviours and not others; they are already subject to a punitive system of surveillance and control which demands that specific kinds of boundary between themselves and people be strictly maintained. A final act of physical enclosure would be no more than that – the physical inscription on the island landscape of ways of thinking about dingoes which reveal not so much a genuinely humane concern for them as a profound degree of alienation from them.

(Peace, 2002: 19)

Burns and Howard (2003: 699) share one of the many voices on this complex issue:

It's all pretty straight forward really. The tourists are stupid. The residents short-sighted. The dogs starving. The rangers, who don't know how to look after the island, are over-worked and under-funded. And the government doesn't give a damn ... until somebody dies that is, and then they only give a damn about their political future.

Another emergent theme in the literature on predatory animal encounters with humans is the lack of information and preparedness on the part of the latter. Durrheim and Leggat (1999) found a lack of information on the risks to tourists posed by wild animals in South Africa, even after discussion with members of the South African Tourist Board, the Association of South African Travel Agencies, the Tourist Safety Task Group of the police service, and consultation with employees of the parks and game reserves. Employing a content analysis methodology of South African newspapers, the authors found that seven tourists had been killed and another 14 injured by wild mammals over a ten-year period from 1988 to 1997. Of the fatalities, four were killed by lions, two by hippos, and one by an elephant. In three of the cases involving lions, tourists left their vehicles and approached the pride on foot for closer photographs, and in the other case a lack of adequate fencing of lodge precincts was the contributing factor to death (the game reserve was fined). In one case involving hippos, a tourist breached rules by walking into a non-fenced area, and in the other case a tourist walked to within two metres of a hippo calf. The elephant apparently had a dental abscess, which prompted the tourist attack. With approximately a million tourists visiting the Kruger National Park alone in 1996, the number of attacks on tourists is surprisingly small according to the authors. They argue that tourists need to stay in their vehicles or in fenced parts of the reserves, observe park instructions and regulations, never approach animals that display abnormal behaviour, and demand adequately trained staff when using the trail systems.

In Chapter 2, snakes were described as one group of animals that humans have developed an innate fear of, and this fear has evolutionary origins. Travelling to remote areas of different countries provides the possibility of encounters with snakes, and good knowledge of the habitat and disposition characteristics of snakes should be known beforehand. In areas where poisonous snakes are endemic, this knowledge should include prevention and management of snakebite (Boyd *et al.*, 2007). With only 15 per cent of the world's 3,000 snake species venomous, the chances of encountering these snakes is not high, but it remains a risk because of adventure travel to remote regions of the world, where treatment and management of these bites becomes especially important. For example, fatality rates from pit viper bites in the US have improved from 5 to 25 per cent in the nineteenth century to 2.6 per cent currently because of antivenom and critical care techniques (case fatality rate is only 0.3 per cent in Europe and South Africa). In less developed countries the fatality rate remains much higher. Nepal, for example, has a fatality rate of 27 per cent owing to the remoteness of the regions in which tourists find themselves.

Although it is beyond the scope of this work to deal specifically with the management of snakebite, Boyd *et al.* (2007) provide a comprehensive set of recommendations for the management of bites based on a review of 3,500 documents (see Table 9.2).

The obvious benefit of reducing animal attacks on humans is the avoidance of human injury or death. But in addition there is the advantage of conserving wildlife populations, the promotion of goodwill towards animals, minimizing economic loss, and the improvement of quality of life for humans. Reducing the potential of an attack is therefore in the best interests of the human, the animal itself (which would otherwise be eliminated), and the species in general, which may otherwise be the subject of persecution through media reports. The best ways in which to reduce the chances of attack have been discussed by Quigley and Herrero (2005). These include:

- Prevention: Advertise your presence to avoid surprising the animal. Animals will almost always assume natural avoidance measures (except in diseased cases or unstable individuals).
- Avoid looking like prey by carrying children in a backpack or wearing clothing that makes you look larger. Wearing backward-facing masks has apparently helped in India and Bangladesh.
- Stay away from places with lots of cover. Animals will use these places in order to ambush prey. Stay in the open.
- Reduce or eliminate food as an attractant. This is said to be the most important element of prevention by the authors.

The foregoing discussion has centred on the frequency and type of encounter with predatory terrestrial animals. However, although far less well known, there are cases of attacks by herbivores such as hippos and zebras. In fact, hippos are a constant concern to local people in Africa who must compete with these animals for habitat – fishing in the case of the human population. Toovey *et al.* (2004) report a case where a zebra allowed to roam free on a South African private nature reserve attacked a tourist in her accommodation. The tourist came across the zebra in the doorway of her cabin. The animal proceeded to knock her over and direct a bite to the bottom portion of the back of her leg, resulting in a degloving type

Table 9.2 Some local and systemic symptoms and signs of venomous snakebite

Local

- Puncture wounds or scratches (due to fangs and/or accessory teeth); may be difficult to see
- Pain (may be early, burning, and severe or may be absent)
- Redness (erythema)
- Soft-tissue swelling (edema)
- Bruising (ecchymosis)
- Bloody oozing (sanguinous exudate) from fang marks
- Blistering (vesicles and bullae filled with serum or blood)
- Numbness or tingling at and around bite site
- Red streaks along lymph vessels and swollen tender lymph glands (lymphangitis and lymphadenitis)
- Tissue destruction (necrosis)

Systemic

- Early collapse
- Numbness or tingling remote from bite (e.g., around lips)
- Muscle twitching (fasciculations)
- Weakness (paralysis) of muscles
- Eyelid droop (ptosis)
- Difficulty speaking (dysarthria)
- Sweating and chills (diaphoresis)
- Nausea, vomiting
- Faintness or dizziness
- Breathing quickly (tachypnea) or slowly (respiratory depression)
- Blood pressure drop (hypotension)
- Abdominal pain
- Clotting disorders; clots and bleeding from any anatomic site
- Headache
- Stumbling (ataxia)
- Fixed dilated pupils (cranial nerve palsy [not necessarily indicative of death])
- Confusion
- Loss of consciousness (syncope, coma)
- Convulsions
- Heart toxicity (acute myocardial infarction, hypotension, pulmonary edema, cardiac dysrhythmias)
- Muscle toxicity with pain and tenderness (rhabdomyolysis, myoglobinuria, hyperkalemia, secondary cardiac dysrhythmias, and renal failure)

Source: Boyd *et al.* (2007)

wound. Extensive skin grafting was required, and complete healing was reported some six months later.

The marine environment threat

Fenner (1998b) places marine envenomation into two categories according to fatalities that species within these groups are responsible for. The first group includes the jellyfish and the other includes the marine vertebrates such as the blue-ringed octopus, cone shell, sea snakes, stingray, and the stonefish, each of which is summarized in Table 9.3 on p. 227 (after Fenner, 1998a). Jellyfish are discussed briefly below and this is followed by a discussion of some of the members of this second category of animals (marine vertebrates).

Jellyfish

Fenner (1998a) writes that there are three main classes of jellyfish that threaten humans: (1) Scyphozoans or true jellyfish; (2) Cubozoans, or the box jellyfish, including two families. The first, Chirodropids, have up to 15 tentacles in each of the four corners of the box, and Carybdeids (e.g., Irukandji) have just one tentacle in each corner. The third group (3) are the Hydrozoa, which are not really jellyfish yet resemble them. This last group includes the Portuguese man-o'-war. Boulware (2006) writes that there are an estimated 150 million jellyfish envenomations annually around the world, with 500,000 in Chesapeake Bay alone and a further 200,000 in Florida waters. The Chirodropids or multi-tentacled box jellyfish are the group that are responsible for the most human deaths, with 66 in Australia since 1884. It is likely, however, that in places like the Philippines this group of jellyfish has been responsible for thousands of unreported deaths over the years, according to Fenner, with annual death rates between 20 and 50. The distribution of this group of animals includes the east and west coasts of the Atlantic, the west coast of the Indian Ocean and the Indo-West Pacific. The encounter rate between jellyfish and human is high in this case because of the behaviour of both:

> Chirodropids swim into shallow water when the wind is light and hot, and the water is calm. Unsuspecting victims frequently walk, or run, into tentacles trailing behind the jellyfish bell. The bell is difficult to see in the water, and the tentacles are almost invisible.
>
> Pain is instant and savage; the victim will often scream with pain. Children often stand in the water, picking at the tentacles and getting stung on the hands and arms, increasing the envenomation, while adults frequently run out of the water and rub the tentacles. Most stings occur on the lower legs and body.
>
> Adherent tentacles, like sticky threads, usually adhere to the victim: tentacle marks look like the victim has been whipped, or branded with irons. If the victim lives, blistering and skin necrosis occur over the next few hours; scarring often occurs, and lasts for life. Victims may rapidly stop breathing, sometimes within a few minutes of the initial envenomation, with death occurring rapidly unless prompt first aid and medical aid is available.
>
> (Fenner, 1998a: 137)

A case report of a fatal jellyfish encounter in the Gulf of Siam documents the quickness with which the individual succumbed to the envenomation. After emerging from the water unsteadily and asking for water to drink, and presenting ladder-like marks across the neck, back, and chest, the individual collapsed within minutes and was unresponsive. The box jellyfish (*Chironex fleckeri*), felt to be one of the deadliest animals in the world, was responsible for the sting and has been responsible for deaths in Australia, Japan, and the Philippines (Suntrarachun *et al.*, 2001).

Irukandji jellyfish include a few very small but highly venomous box jellyfish species, including *Carukia barnesi*, named after its discoverer Jack Barnes, and *Malo kingi*, named after Robert King, a tourist from the United States who was killed by the species (see Gershwin, 2007). These species are responsible for a condition known as Irukandji syndrome, named after a tribe in northern Queensland, in which envenomation causes a collection of symptoms which may include abdominal cramps, back pain, leg cramps, chest tightness, hypertension, nausea and vomiting, headache, distress, sweating, extreme pain, or a feeling of impending death. In Australia the risk of Irukandji syndrome has significant implications for leisure and tourism, especially with increased numbers of visitors annually, despite the fact that a study confirmed that only 35 per cent of tourists visiting Western Australia were jellyfish aware (Macrokanis, Hall, and Mein, 2004). While Irukandji syndrome was thought to be endemic to Australia, recent evidence suggests that it is more widespread. De Pender *et al.* (2006) report Irukandji syndrome-like symptoms in a Dutch tourist swimming in Thailand, and Grady and Burnett (2003) found evidence of Irukandji syndrome in divers swimming off the coast of Florida. The first recorded death linked to Irukandji syndrome was of a 44-year-old male swimming in the waters of north-eastern Australia. The man rapidly developed symptoms of Irukandji syndrome followed by deterioration of consciousness because of intra-cerebral haemorrhage. He died 13 days later as a result of brain death (Pereira *et al.*, 2010).

In a study of the knowledge tourists had regarding the risk and contact with Irukandji jellyfish in Northern Queensland, Harrison *et al.* (2004) uncovered some disturbing results. They found that half of international tourists and 20 per cent of domestic visitors incorrectly assumed that it was safe to swim inside stinger-resistant nets, as compared to 3.9 per cent of locals. A series of other questions confirmed that international tourists had little knowledge about Irukandji. The authors concluded that a cooperative educational response was needed to inform tourists about jellyfish envenomation by Irukandji as well as the box jellyfish. Boulware (2006) has studied a product called Safe Sea, which is a sting inhibitor that is produced using the mucus of the clown fish (a fish that inhabits the tentacles and stinging cells of sea anemones). In laboratory tests, the lotion was able to prevent 85 per cent of jellyfish stings, and in controlled field testing prevented 82 per cent of stings with no side-effects.

Stingray

Diaz (2008b) reports that in the United States alone there are some 750 to 2,000 stingray injuries each year, with likely thousands worldwide as a result of freshwater species that come into contact with humans who are in search of recreation or fresh seafood. Those most at risk include waders, snorkellers, scuba divers, beach or wade fishers, bottom fishers, and spear fishers. Divers and waders receive predominantly lower extremity injuries, while fishers sustain upper extremity injuries from the removal of stingrays from nets or hooks. Stingrays do not contain venom glands in the same manner as other animals, but rather a unique

Table 9.3 Human fatalities and marine animal envenomation

Vertebrate	Characteristics
Blue-ringed octopus	*Location of fatalities*: Australia, Singapore *Distribution*: Indo-West Pacific, north to Okinawa, east to Philippines, west to India, south to New Zealand *Appearance*: 15–20 cm in diameter with tentacles extended; electric blue rings when disturbed. *Envenomation*: Painless minor bite from beak; numbness in lips, weakness in breathing, respiratory failure if not treated *Fatalities*: 2 in Australia, 1 in Singapore[1]
Cone shell (mollusc)	*Location of fatalities*: Australia, Fiji, India, New Caledonia, Okinawa (Japan), Vanuatu *Distribution*: Indian and Pacific Oceans east to Hawaii, north to Okinawa, and south to New Zealand *Appearance*: A cone shape with a slit-like aperture, up to 15cm in length *Envenomation*: Pain at the site, with a bluish tinge; followed by numbness and swelling; muscle weakness; swallowing and speech affected; nausea; respiratory paralysis Fatalities: Up to 50 deaths reported, index of mortality 25%[2]
Sea snakes	*Location of fatalities*: Burma, Malaysia, India, Java, Okinawa (Japan), Oman, Sri Lanka, Vietnam *Distribution*: All oceans except the Atlantic *Appearance*: Similar to terrestrial snakes, but with a flattened tail *Envenomation*: Only 10% of bites inject venom; painless; drowsiness, nausea, vomiting, weakness, visual disturbance, breathing problems, renal impairment *Fatalities*: Hundreds in these countries.
Stingray	*Location of fatalities*: Australia, California, Colombia, Fiji, New Zealand, Surinam, Texas *Distribution*: Worldwide *Appearance*: Large flat-shaped, with a whip tail *Envenomation*: Whip of tail when stepped on; tail has one or more sharp barbs that break off or cause lacerations; acutely painful; serious if barb penetrates chest or abdomen. The venom has cardiotoxic effects in humans *Fatalities*: Approximately 20 deaths worldwide
Stonefish	*Location of fatalities*: Australia, East Africa, Japan, Seychelles *Distribution*: Indian and Pacific Oceans north to China, east to Hawaii, south to Australia *Appearance*: Tough, warty fish 20–30 cm long. Colour of its surroundings, with 13 spines on the back *Envenomation*: Immediate, severe pain; bluish discolouration around puncture site; local limb paralysis, nausea, vomiting, faintness; deaths often not caused by the bite itself but from secondary causes (drowning) *Fatalities*: at least 5 cases

[1] Cavazzoni *et al.* (2008)
[2] Junior *et al.* (2006)

system has evolved in this animal group in regards to spine architecture and its venom delivery system, according to Diaz (2008b: 104):

> The flat spines are stiletto sharp, with backward-pointed barbs or serrations, and are composed of a strong bone-like cartilaginous material known as vasodentin. On the underside of the spine are two longitudinal grooves, which run the length of the spine and are filled with venom-secreting glandular cells. Both the vasodentin spine and its ventral glandular tissues are sheathed in an integument or epidermis, that tears open when the spine is plunged into a victim, unroofing glandular tissue to diffuse venom.

Hot water immersion appears to be the most effective therapy for patients reporting pain due to marine animal envenomation. In a study of 22 fish stings in tropical north Australia, hot water immersion was found to be wholly effective in 73 per cent of cases (Isbister, 2001; see also Atkinson *et al.*, 2006). Diaz says that as more tourists explore coastlines and tropical reefs in peripheral regions without easily accessible health care, there will be more stingray injuries with unpleasant outcomes (see Box 9.1).

Zoonoses

Zoonosis refers to an infectious disease in animals caused by bacteria, viruses, prions, fungi, or parasites, which may be passed on to humans. The reverse of this – humans passing on infectious diseases to animals – is referred to as anthroponosis. Examples of zoonoses include Babesiosis, Chagas disease, cholera, dengue fever, West Nile virus, and *Giardia lamblia*. Examples of carriers include cattle, bats, wolves, lice, rats, fleas, mosquitoes, ticks, monkeys, and snails. There are just over 1,400 pathogens known to affect humans and 61 per cent of these are zoonotic. Mavroidi (2008) argues that tourism exacerbates the problem because many diseases – SARS, West Nile fever, yellow fever – are spread to other regions through the migration of people. The occurrences of the following zoonoses per 100,000 travellers per month of stay are estimated as follows (Mavroidi, 2008: 654):

Diarrhoea: 30,000 to 80,000
Escherichia coli: 10,000
Malaria in West Africa without use of prophylaxis: 2,000 to 3,000
Dengue fever: 200
Typhoid fever in India, and north and north-west Africa: 30
Typhoid fever overall: 3
Japanese encephalitis: 0.1

Zoonoses may be categorized according to the mode of transmission or the host organism (Mavroidi, 2008: 652), all of which are discussed in more detail below:

- Arthropod vector-borne: malaria, dengue fever, etc.
- Food- or water-borne: salmonelloses, typhoid fever, brucellosis, amoebiasis, etc.
- Airborne or droplet-borne: SARS, avian influenza, etc.
- Animal host/reservoirs: plague, hanta fever, rabies, avian influenza, etc.

Box 9.1   How deadly are stingrays?

The numbers behind the Crocodile Hunter's death.

By Daniel Engber
Tuesday 5 September 2006

'Crocodile Hunter' Steve Irwin died as a result of a freak stingray attack on Monday. The animal's barbed tail delivers venom that causes excruciating pain, but it almost never kills. Several different figures for the number of recorded stingray-related fatalities have surfaced in the media, ranging from 'about 30' worldwide, to 'fewer than 20,' to 'only 17.' Well, which is it?

No one really knows. It's hard to keep track, and there isn't enough interest in stingray attacks to merit an international monitoring effort. The reported numbers come from best guesses and the few publications that have addressed the issue. (The 17 figure comes from a textbook first put out by an Australian organization more than 30 years ago.)

If someone did want to record stingray fatalities, they might follow the example of the International Shark Attack File, which has been tallying shark bites for more than 40 years. Staffers at the Florida-based Shark Attack File start each day by combing through online article databases. Any leads get referred to a network of hundreds of biologists, doctors, and other informants stationed near coastlines around the world. A local rep makes contact with the victim of the attack – or the authorities, in the case of a fatal bite – and gathers as much information as possible. A standard Shark Attack File questionnaire looks for data on the weather, the tides, and how both the shark and the victim behaved before, during, and after the attack.

Widespread fascination with shark attacks has kept the Shark Attack File afloat for many years, but there aren't many groups that keep track of other deadly animals. (Individual researchers have compiled records for some animals, like the mountain lions that have been causing problems out West.) It's relatively easy to get data on animal-related fatalities in the United States, where the Centers for Disease Control publish a database of information reported from death certificates. Epidemiologists can determine how many deaths occurred from a specific animal by plugging various codes into the CDC database – 'E-905.4', for example, corresponds to 'centipede and venomous millipede'.

Engber (2006)

Arthropod vector-borne

Arthropods have a tremendous range and are vectors of diseases in humans as well as animals. Examples include mosquitoes, blackflies, sandflies, midges, bed bugs, bees and wasps, houseflies, tsetse flies, fleshflies, blowflies, sucking lice, mites, spiders, and ticks. These little beasts contaminate food, and are allergens (dust from insect bodies, saliva, and venom) as well as disease vectors; they compromise the health of livestock in innumerable ways and are a nuisance to tourists who spend a great deal of time in backcountry settings (Okaeme, 1987). Insect pests also have a tremendous impact on the economies of certain regions. For example, desert locusts periodically invade northern Africa and the Sahal. The plague of 1986–9 cost in excess of $300 million to control, and a more recent invasion in 2004 in Mauritania, Mali, Senegal, and Niger damaged four million hectares of crops invaded by the locusts, leading to 2.5 million households at risk of food shortage. In Mauritania alone, 80 per cent of all crops were destroyed (UNEP, 2007).

While the focus of this section is on vectors, insect venom is important to discuss because of the magnitude of impact on humans. A study in the journal *Wilderness and Environmental Medicine* used Center for Disease Control data to find that 1,943 Americans died from interactions with animals between 1991 and 2001 (Engber, 2006). Hornets, bees, and wasps accounted for about a quarter of all deaths. In another study, a commercial expedition of two and a half months to the Amazon region of Brazil and Venezuela provided an opportunity for the team physician to record health and injury reports on the 26 personnel involved. Nineteen members of the team required medical assistance 78 times, recorded as such: 19 per cent ear, nose and throat disease; 15 per cent injuries; 15 per cent stings, bees, wasps, insect bites, ticks; 13 per cent respiratory; 12 per cent dermatological; 9 per cent gastroenterologic; 17 per cent other (Shaw and Leggat, 2003). The results indicate that threats and risks in international travel, especially to remote areas, come not from the large vertebrate species that we often worry about, but rather from the small and microscopic beasts that are so difficult to manage. Karatzanis *et al.* (2009) argue that the beach environment is perhaps the most hazardous because tourists are at risk to anaphylactic reactions from hymenoptera stings (bees and wasps), high-risk foods, and jellyfish stings.

The arthropod vector-borne disease that is perhaps most important by virtue of the number of deaths and illnesses caused is malaria. In 2008, there were 247 million cases of malaria, with nearly a million deaths. Half the world's population is at risk. In Africa alone, a child dies every 45 seconds from malaria (WHO Malaria Fact Sheet, 2010). International travellers represent a high-risk group for malaria because they lack immunity.

Travel agents are often not the answer in adequately preparing tourists for travel to malaria endemic areas. Grabowski and Behrens (1996) found that 61 per cent of 202 British travel agencies provided no spontaneous health warnings when a covert researcher approached them about travel to regions where malaria was endemic. Once prompted, 71 per cent of agents gave general health advice, 67 per cent suggested seeking advice from a health practitioner, and only 37 per cent suggested the need for malaria prophylaxis. This lack of information dissemination occurs even in destination regions. Maartens *et al.* (2007) found that, although there was a major reduction in malaria cases in northern KwaZulu-Natal, follow-up surveys of tourists and tourism facility owners indicated that both groups considered the perceived risk of malaria to be much higher than the actual risk.

A better option for travellers is the travel health clinic, which understands the transmission, prevention, and clinical features surrounding malaria. Teodósio *et al.* (2006) found that there was a considerable improvement in the knowledge gained by tourists in regards to a number of features of malaria after consultation with travel medicine experts: 98.5 per cent of tourists understood that malaria was transmitted by mosquito, 91.5 per cent knew that malaria could be prevented by prophylactic medication, and just over 90 per cent could identify early symptoms of the disease. However, about half of the post-consultation group did not know that there was not a vaccine available for preventing malaria, and only 53 per cent could give correct answers about malaria incubation time periods. While travel medical clinics increase the knowledge about particular diseases, it seems the more in-depth information beyond the most essential aspects of prevention and transmission is not internalized (see the study by Senn *et al.* (2007) on reasons for choosing one form of chemoprophylaxis over others on the basis of efficacy, profile, regimen, and price; see also Chen *et al.*, 2009 for a discussion of the willingness of long-term travellers to seek travel advice over short-term travellers).

A similar study was undertaken in Bangkok, Thailand, and involved the survey results of 434 backpackers, 55 per cent male with a median age of 28 (Piyaphanee *et al.*, 2009). The authors found that 94 per cent of backpackers were aware that there was a risk of malaria by travelling in the region. Twenty-two per cent took malaria chemoprophylaxis, 33 per cent used other measures to prevent the bite of mosquitoes, while 40 per cent used no prevention whatsoever. Based on ten true/false questions that sought to understand their knowledge of malaria, the mean score was 5.52 out of 10. Approximately 35 per cent thought that eating contaminated food could lead to malaria, and only 54 per cent of those travelling in forested areas used insect repellent on a regular basis. Almost one-third of respondents (30 per cent) using chemoprophylaxis stopped using these drugs prematurely.

A study by Sicard *et al.* (2009) documents an unusual case of 26 tourists travelling together from France to Burkina Faso, nine of whom contracted malaria, and the various malaria prevention devices and behaviours used by this group. The group stayed in a rustic settlement in a forested village, with an average length of stay of 17 days. Survey results indicate that all tourists used repellent, but only 17 used it every evening. Occasional use of clothing to cover the body was employed by 13 tourists, bed nets were used by 19 individuals (seven of the nets impregnated with insecticide), but only 13 used these every night. Nineteen tourists said they took chemoprophylaxis against malaria, with nine reporting that they used it adequately, and ten that they used it inadequately (see Prakash *et al.*, 2009, for the results of a study on the insecticidal efficacy of mosquito bed nets after successive wash cycles). The authors found that none of the nine tourists using chemoprophylaxis adequately contracted malaria, while three of ten using chemoprophylaxis inadequately suffered a malaria attack. All six of the individuals not using chemoprophylaxis contracted malaria. The study illustrates that tourists can contract malaria quickly in endemic areas and also that proper use of chemoprophylaxis provides adequate protection against the disease.

The mosquito is also responsible for the transmission of dengue fever. The disease is caused by a Flavivirus spread by two species of mosquito of the same genus: *Aedes aegypti* and *Aedes albopictus*. The disease symptoms may include fever, myalgia (muscle pain), rash, headache, nausea, and diarrhoea, in some cases nerve palsy (Chappuis *et al.*, 2004), and fatal haemorrhagic fever (DHF). It is a problem for tourists because the disease is now endemic in 100 countries, primarily in South East Asia, South America, Africa, and Central Asia (Sung *et al.*, 2003). Dengue represents the second most frequent reason for hospitalization in tourists returning from tropical countries, and is more frequently diagnosed than malaria in countries outside of Africa (Massad and Wilder-Smith, 2009). In the Americas, dengue is on the rise. A study by San Martín *et al.* (2010) found that cases increased over three periods of time: 1.03 million cases from 1980 to 1989 (242 deaths), 2.73 million from 1990 to 1999, and 4.76 million from 2000 to 2007 (1,291 deaths). The highest concentration of cases occurred in the Hispanic Caribbean during the 1980s, shifting to the Southern Cone during the 1990s and 2000s. Dengue, like many other tropical diseases, has seasonal oscillations, which makes pre-travel advice especially important for prospective travellers. Schwartz *et al.* (2008), in a review of 522 cases using the GeoSentinel Network (GSN), discovered region-specific spikes for South East Asia (June, September), South Central Asia (October), South America (March), and the Caribbean (August, October). In South East Asia, for example, the authors observed that in an epidemic year of dengue, 159 cases per 1,000 tourists were reported, as compared to 50 cases in non-epidemic years (see Box 9.2).

Mosquitoes are also responsible for encephalitis, West Nile virus, and yellow fever. An outbreak of yellow fever in the state of Rio Grande do Sul in Brazil from 2008 to 2009 took the lives of seven people and over 2,000 howler monkeys, illustrating how media sensationalism and biased information can place humans and animals on a collision course. The fear of the disease and the unfortunate tie between monkeys and people, along with the spread of incorrect information linking monkeys to the spread of the disease, prompted local efforts to try to exterminate the howlers. Although howlers and humans are the main hosts to the infectious agent, a *Flavivirus*, Bicca-Marques and Freitas (2010), experts on howler ecology and behaviour, suggest that howlers have dispersal limitations that prevent the disease from spreading over large areas. By contrast, mosquitoes are much more highly mobile, as dispersal can take place through any number of means including, for example, eggs or larvae inside trucks, buses, or aeroplanes. Humans may also have promoted the spread of yellow fever through the number of undiagnosed asymptomatic people in conjunction with our highly mobile tendencies. While howlers are said not to be the main conduit for disease transmission, the authors contend that they are excellent sentinels – early warning indicator organisms exhibiting the onset of yellow fever in a region. As such, we

Box 9.2 Dengue/DHF Press Release, WHO

WHO initiates bi-regional approach to tackle dengue fever in Asia Pacific

Dengue is emerging rapidly as one of the most important public health problems in countries of Asia-Pacific Region (nearly 1.8 billion people in the region are at risk as compared to an estimated total of 2.5 billion globally). The epidemics of dengue are being reported more frequently and in explosive manner, the disease is spreading to countries where it has not been reported earlier, and it is moving to rural areas.

Rapid spread of dengue in Asia-Pacific Region is attributed to globalization, rapid unplanned and unregulated urban development, poor water storage and unsatisfactory sanitary conditions. It is an integral part of urbanization because of increase in the breeding habitats of the vector. Dramatic increase in mobility of the people facilitated by rapid transport is increasing the risk of spread. The mosquito that spreads the disease *Aedes aegypti* is a domesticated species that breeds in artificial containers and waste where water accumulates. In short, dengue is primarily a man-made health problem.

Besides the risk of death, dengue causes ill health and serious adverse social and economic losses. The disease is oftentimes a prominent news. The currently available tools in prevention and control of dengue even though not perfect have been known to be effective for more than two decades. Dengue control efforts work if it becomes everyone's concern. Several countries have succeeded in controlling the growing menace of emergence of dengue. Examples are Singapore and Cuba. However, the present dengue control programmes in some countries are inadequately resourced.

World Health Organization (2007a)

should not be killing howlers in ignorance, but rather saving them for their own good as well as ours.

Another arthropod-borne protozoan infectious disease is Chagas disease. Endemic throughout most of the Americas, it is an illness caused by the trypanosome, *T. cruzi*, transmitted to humans via the kissing bug or assassin bug. The 130 species feed on vertebrate blood, but pass along the protozoan through fecal matter deposited near bite wounds (see Diaz, 2008a). Yet another is leishmaniasis, a disease caused by parasites of the genus *Leishmania*, transmitted by some species of sand flies. The disease is endemic in about 88 countries, and approximately 1.5 million new cases are documented each year (Stark *et al.*, 2008). There are three types: cutaneous leishmaniasis (CL), mucosal leishmaniasis (ML), and visceral leishmaniasis (the most severe). The former is one of the top ten presentation diseases among tourists visiting tropical nations (Blum and Hatz, 2009). After a bite by an infected sand fly, an ulcerous skin lesion develops, which heals after a

Plate 9.1 The female *Anopheles* mosquito

number of weeks. One parasite species, *Leishmania braziliensis*, can further complicate matters by causing the development of mucosal lesions in the nose and mouth, which may lead to disfigurement (Bauer, 2002).

The incidence of illness from ticks has also been increasing. Süss *et al.* (2008) discuss the physiological and environmental conditions that make ticks tick in relation to increasing public health problems in Europe and many other parts of the world due to higher incidences of tick-borne encephalitis (TBE) and Lyme borreliosis (LB). The authors illustrate that 90 to 95 per cent of all tick bites come from the genus *Ixodes*, with 100,000 to 150,000 of these resulting in LB and 10,000 to 15,000 in TBE. The increasing number of cases of these illnesses is attributed to global warming, where the environmental conditions for ticks are improving in Europe, including a humidity rate of over 85 per cent, temperatures greter than 7°C, and people in sufficient numbers to make feeding possible. The influx of tourists during the spring and summer months makes this latter condition that much more likely. Hosts are detected by four main primary factors: shadow, body heat, odour, and vibrations caused by movement. Süss *et al.* (2008) further observe that the duration of the blood meal is dependent on the tick's stage in its life cycle. Larvae require a meal of two days, whereas an adult female may feed for up to ten days. In the case of the female, her body may increase in size 200 times, requiring highly adapted physiological processes to prevent the body from bursting. Ingested blood is concentrated between three and five times, with water extracted from the blood passed back to the host. It is in this movement of water back to the host that bacteria from the gut of the infected tick move through the system and into the host (*Borrelia burgdorferi* in North America; *Borrelia garinii* and *Borrelia afzelii* in most European cases). Experts contend that there is a period of 24 hours before this movement of water into the human host occurs, thus minimizing the chances for infection.

Food- or waterborne

Foodborne illnesses are defined as diseases, usually either infectious or toxic in nature, caused by agents that enter the body through the ingestion of food. Every person is at risk of foodborne illness (World Health Organization, 2007b). Waterborne are defined as the same but transmitted through the consumption of fresh water.

Travellers' diarrhoea (TD) is the most common illness for those travelling from the developed world to the lesser developed countries. TD can be defined as 'three or more unformed stools per 24 hours starting during or shortly after a period of foreign travel, with at least one accompanying symptom, such as urgency, abdominal cramps, nausea, vomiting, fever' (von Sonnenburg *et al.*, 2000: 133). Some 1.8 million people die from diarrhoeal diseases every year (World Health Organization, 2011).

The topic of TD diseases has received increasing investigation because of its importance in tourism. Silva *et al.* (2009) studied a group of 174 Portuguese children travelling to Portuguese-speaking tropical destinations and found that 21.8 per cent of these travellers had at least one attack of TD. In a like manner, McIntosh, Reed and Power (1997) compared reports of diarrhoea in travelling and non-travelling residents of the United Kingdom. They found that 39 per cent of tourists reported having diarrhoea while travelling abroad, with just 6 per cent of the same sample reporting diarrhoea in the two weeks prior to their travel. Just under a tenth (9.7 per cent) of non-travellers reported diarrhoea in the two-week period prior to being questioned. The results of their study suggest that tourists were 6.5 times more likely to suffer an attack of diarrhoea while travelling than when spending a comparable amount of time at home. Further results suggest that because of the trend towards increased international travel, especially to high-risk destinations, a number of social, health, and economic costs will be incurred.

Knowledge and perceptions of the illness have also garnered the attention of researchers. In a study of the preferences for the treatment and prevention of acute TD, Ericsson *et al.* (2009) found that Canadian and US travellers were less cognizant of the risks associated with TD than their German and UK counterparts. Furthermore, the Europeans were less likely to take chemoprophylaxis than North Americans. Although the study was not designed to uncover why there was the choice for or against chemoprophylaxis, another study found that a sample of Canadians from Quebec (77 per cent) did not consider TD to be a serious illness and therefore did not consider the use of chemoprophylaxis as essential (Provost and Soto, 2002).

For further insight into the transmission of TD, Oundo *et al.* (2008) investigated the presence and risk factors of the carriage of enteroaggregative *E. coli* (EAEC) in 1,399 food handlers in three popular tourist destinations in Kenya over a one-year period. EAEC was detected on 29 subjects (2.1 per cent of the sample), and the use of pit latrines was associated with the isolation of EAEC. The authors concluded that food handlers are obvious reservoirs and possible transmission routes for the bacteria that cause TD, and food and water are the most important vehicles responsible for TD. Echeverria *et al.* (1994) explain that minor epidemics of food infections often take place in small villages in remote developing countries. This is because food is often obtained and transported under conditions that do not guarantee freshness. The authors obtained 820 food samples of six different uncooked foods (beef, pork, chicken, fish, vegetables, and fruit) from the markets of two villages just outside Bangkok, and tested these within two hours at a district hospital laboratory. Tests confirmed that 12 per cent of the samples contained enteric pathogens, including strains of *E. coli*, *salmonella*, and *V. cholerae*. Travellers should be aware that food purchased from these markets, either prepared by hosts or by tourists themselves, may contain pathogens, and therefore the careful, hygienic preparation of these foods is essential in avoiding illness. This information should be made available to the tourist either through guidebooks or other programmes designed to protect tourists and local people from illness.

A frequent cause of diarrhoea is some type of gastrointestinal (GI) infection. A global study of GI infection involving over 6,000 travellers between the years of 2000 and 2005 found significant differences between counties of the developed and underdeveloped world (Greenwood *et al.*, 2008). Travel to sub-Saharan Africa, South America, and South Asia (the very highest risk region) was marked by higher incidences of GI infection, followed by Oceania, the Middle East, North Africa, Central America, the Caribbean, and South East Asia, with moderate rates of infection. Low levels of infection included countries of western and northern Europe, North America, Central and Eastern Europe, Southern Europe, North East Asia, and Australasia.

Boulware (2004) investigated both water treatment and the more infrequently examined hygiene in a study of gastrointestinal illness of 280 Appalachian Trail (US) backpackers, who compiled almost 39,000 days of wilderness exposure. Fifty-six per cent of the respondents said that they experienced diarrhoea during the course of their travels, with differences in those who treated water and those who did not. Of those backpackers who inconsistently treated water, 69 per cent experienced diarrhoea. Of those who consistently treated water, 45 per cent suffered diarrhoea. Those who reported practising good hygiene (i.e., hand washing post defecation and cleaning cookware routinely) were less likely to ever experience diarrhoea.

The type of wilderness in reference to other land uses has been found to play heavily in the quality of drinking water in lakes and streams. Derlet (2008) assessed the water quality, using coliform bacteria counts as an indicator, of 72 sites in five different settings in wilderness areas in and around Yosemite National Park, US: (1) natural areas rarely visited by humans, (2) day use only sites, (3) high use by backpackers, (4) high use by pack animals, and (5) cattle- and sheep-grazed tracks. He found that 70 per cent of the pack animal sites and 100 per cent of the cattle and sheep sites grew coliform bacteria, indicating the presence of other pathogenic organisms of fecal origin. By contrast, natural area sites and day use sites contained no coliforms whatsoever, and only 17 per cent of the high use by backpackers sites contained coliforms. Wilderness travellers need to be aware of the risks associated with water consumption settings (4) and (5) especially, with diminishing risks in the other three areas.

Illnesses such as TD have monetary implications. Wang *et al.* (2008) estimated the economic costs of traveller's diarrhoea involving travellers both at the generating and destination regions. Consideration of costs is structured according to three stages:

1. Pre-travel
   a. costs for pre-travel health advice.
   b. costs for self-carried medication.
2. During travel
   a. loss of revenue for tourism countries due to incapacitation.
   b. costs for medical care and hospitalizations abroad.
   c. other costs (loss of business opportunities, etc.)
3. Post-travel
   a. healthcare costs due to ill-returned travellers who seek medical help at home.
   b. lost productivity costs due to workdays lost caused by ill-returned travellers.

The authors estimate that pre-travel costs for health service in the United States amount to approximately US$880 million, with costs for self-carried medications amounting to approximately US$145 million. Costs during travel are approximated at US$1 billion, while total lost productivity on the return home from TD amount to US$654 million. In high-risk regions the attack rate for travellers is 30 to 50 per cent, or more generally depending on the world region visited from 13.6 per cent to 54.6 per cent (Steffen *et al.*, 2004).

In terms of prevention, Ashley *et al.* (2004) found that knowledge transfer through training interventions can go a long way towards improving sanitary conditions for travellers. In 1996, 25 per cent of travellers to Jamaica were affected with traveller's diarrhoea. A structured programme for prevention and control of TD in the ensuing years based on technical assistance to nurses, training of food and beverage personnel, as well as environmental sanitation staff yielded greatly improved conditions by 2002. Over the six-year period, TD rates dropped by 72 per cent from levels in 1996. The authors conclude that increasing vigilance in this area is essential for visitor satisfaction and long-term regional success of the industry.

Airborne or droplet-borne

The SARS epidemic of 2001 had a crippling effect on the travel industry at international and local levels. The cancellation of the World Cancer Congress in

Toronto, and Canada's boycott of the women's world hockey championships accentuate how health and travel are linked at the broadest level; while the closure of schools and restaurants in Toronto is indicative of impacts at the local level. The frequency of these emergent issues compounds the traditional development challenges of an industry that can have devastating social and ecological effects on a destination.

Animal host

The following few examples illustrate the diversity of ways in which animals pass along infectious diseases to humans. The first two are examples from farming environments, the third an urban, the fourth a marine, and finally a karst environment.

Mad cow disease, or bovine spongiform encephalopathy (BSE), is a fatal neurodegenerative disease caused by an infectious protein called a prion. In cattle the infectious agent causes the brain and spinal cord to become spongy over a prolonged incubation period of up to eight years. In the UK, approximately 180,000 cattle were infected and over four million animals killed in efforts to eradicate the disease. The disease is passed on to humans if they consume parts of the brain or spinal cord. In humans the disease is called *Creutzfeldt–Jakob disease* (vCJD or nvCJD), and by October 2009 it had killed 166 people in Britain.

Heuvelink *et al.* (2002) present a case of haemolytic-uraemic syndrome (acute renal failure) involving a young child who had recently spent time at a petting zoo. The syndrome is caused by a strain of *Escherichia coli* (0157), which may be found in the faecal matter of goats and sheep. The infection is serious as there is a 5 to 10 per cent mortality rate. The zoo voluntarily shut down, and two of eleven other zoos tested positive for this strain of *E. coli*.

Although distinct from the farming environment discussed above, the animals of the urban milieu can pose as considerable a threat to humans. For example, tourists wearing open-toed shoes are at risk of exposure to rat bites. In one case, a man staying in a holiday resort in Vietnam was bitten on the toe by an urban rat, and later experienced relapsing fever, chills, and a lesion on the infected toe. Subsequent admittance to a tropical disease centre found that he had contracted rat-bite fever, which is caused by one of two bacteria (*Streptobacillus moniliformis* or *Spirillum minus*) transmitted by the bite or the faeces of rats, with an incidence pinnacle in Asia (Signorini *et al.*, 2002).

Infectious diseases can also be transmitted to humans in the marine environment. While stonefish have the potential to envenom people through spines, fish also have the potential to poison people through consumption. Ciguatera fish poisoning has been documented in tourists, particularly sport tourists, because of their consumption of predatory tropical fish such as barracuda, red snapper, amberjack, grouper, and mackerel. Ciguatera is an acute gastrointestinal intoxication that is characterized by watery diarrhoea, abdominal pain, nausea, and vomiting, usually lasting about 12 hours. This may also be followed by neurological symptoms, including numbness and tingling of the lip, tongue and limbs, severe itching and cold-to-hot temperature reversal (Bavastrelli *et al.*, 2000). Bavastrelli *et al.* (2000) report that Ciguatera is a toxin produced by marine microalgae that become attached to the epiphytes of larger algae, which are in turn consumed by herbivorous fish. These small herbivorous fish die from the toxin, and are soon after eaten by predatory fish as noted above. The toxin becomes bio-concentrated as it moves through the food chain, and while it is harmless in the host fish, the toxin produces illness in human consumers.

In this last example of animal hosts, histoplasmosis or 'cave disease' is discussed, which is a disease caused by the fungus *Histoplasma capsulatum*, endemic in the Americas, Africa, and East Asia (Manson *et al.*, 1981). The fungus exists in nature as a mycelium (vegetative part of the fungus) and can be found in soil containing bat and bird droppings. People who work in excavation or construction, and recreationists such as spelunkers who become exposed to fungal spores, are at high risk for infection. Nasta *et al.* (1997) reviewed the medical records of four Italian spelunkers returning from Peru after visiting caves (approximately 20 days in caves) with high humidity and with frequent contact with bat and bird droppings. Medical tests showed acute pulmonary disease (patchy lesions in the chest cavity) among the travellers, including high fever, headache, cough, nausea, liver and spleen enlargement, and myalgia. The risk to tourists becomes even higher, with new studies reporting that histoplasmosis can be transmitted at the entrance of caves, and not just inside the caves as previously thought. Two of three researchers studying bat echolocation just outside the entrance of Tamana cave in Trinidad contracted acute pulmonary histoplasmosis, illustrating that bats disperse enough of the fungal organisms in their droppings outside caves to be a threat to humans (Jülg *et al.*, 2008).

As a final note in this section, the Global Viral Forecasting Initiative (a network with the purpose of identifying viruses that have pandemic potential and to track their flow into human populations) has suggested that viruses generally move from animal populations into human populations in groups that come into close contact with animals. These groups include hunters and poachers. Equatorial regions are hotspots for virus transmission as these regions have high rates of poaching and higher levels of biodiversity (National Geographic, 2011).

Humans as vectors

The fungus that causes histoplasmosis or 'cave disease' is an example of a disease passed from animals (bats in this case) to humans. There are examples where the reverse is true: humans having a significant impact on bats. Fox Mayshark (2010) reports that white-nose syndrome is spreading rapidly in the United States (see Box 9.3). The fungus has been traced to Europe, where it is likely to have crossed the Atlantic on the shoes or clothes of a tourist visiting caves in Europe and returning home to the United States. Whereas the bats in Europe have built immunity to the fungus, bats in North America have not, with the result that millions of bats are being killed annually, and the fear that at least in Tennessee there may be total extinction of the state bat population. During hibernation the bats' immune systems are less robust, and the animals have to use their diminished stores of energy to fight off the infection. The animals are weakened to the point of starvation or are in some cases forced to feed in winter out of extreme anxiety or confusion. Bat experts in the US are suggesting that caves be closed to tourists in the hope of eliminating the transfer of the fungus between bat colonies (Fox Mayshark, 2010).

While tourist boots are implicated in the spread of white-nose disease in bats, Curry *et al.* (2002) speculated that, in a similar fashion, tourist boots could act as

---

Box 9.3 Killer bat disease closes Cadomin Cave

By Garret Kinjerski
Edmonton Sun
14 May 2010

A deadly bat disease has closed Cadomin Cave in Whitehorse Wildland Provincial Park near Hinton for the year.

Although not threatening to people, the disease called white-nose syndrome – after the white ring left on a dead, diseased bat's nose – could disrupt essential bat populations in Alberta.

It's estimated the disease has killed more than one million bats in the northeastern United States since 2006, said Camille Weleschuck, spokeswoman for Alberta Tourism, Parks and Recreation. The mortality rate is above 80%.

'Alberta is considered to be at risk,' she said.

Cadomin is considered one of Alberta's top caving sites, and she wants to keep the disease from spreading through tourists.

The fungal-based disease is believed to spread through people visiting the caves. Researchers in Ontario and Quebec are also monitoring increased mortality in their bat populations.

People are encouraged to take precautions like sterilizing clothes and shoes when entering a cave or mine.

'Anyone visiting caves or mines where bats occur should be aware of the basic precautions to avoid spreading this disease to new sites, and especially avoid bringing it to Alberta,' said Mel Knight, minister of sustainable resource development.

Bats play an important role in Alberta's ecosystem, contributing to the success of farmers' crops and also helping to control insects, like mosquitoes, according to an Alberta Park report on the long-term risk of the disease.

Access to Cadomin Cave will now be permitted only to Alberta researchers monitoring the situation. Posters are placed at the trailhead access for Cadomin.

Source: Kinjerski (2010)

vectors in the transmission of disease in Antarctica. Given the increasing rate of tourism in the Antarctic region, there is concern on the part of tourism operators and scientists alike that the introduction of pathogens could have a significant impact on wildlife colonies. The authors took swabs of the boots of tourists under three conditions: prior to landing (group A), on return to the ship (group B), and after the boots had been washed in seawater (group C). The researchers discovered 20 bacteria isolates from 15 of 72 pairs of swabs collected. Two were from group A, four from group B, and 14 from group C. The authors conclude that current best practice of boot decontamination is inadequate in ensuring that pathogens will not be transmitted to Antarctica. A possible solution to this is to insist that tourists only use boots provided for them and that stay in Antarctica, in eliminating the chance of introducing a pathogen that may have widespread effects on a population. In a study by Whinam *et al.* (2005), cargo, food, and expeditioners were all found to be vectors on trips to Antarctica. On cargo and food items, plant material, seeds, spiders, insects, soil, and fungi were found. On equipment such as cases, daypacks, and the cuffs of Velcro closures, mostly plant propagules were found: 981 propagules and five moss shoots collected from clothing and equipment from 64 expeditioners, many of whom had visited other overseas destinations in the previous six months.

Grimaldi *et al.* (2011) found that there are no known occurrences of infectious disease there that might be attributed to tourism or scientific research. This has been because of the implementation of strict regulations in the region. In a study of 233 faecal samples from eight species of birds at six localities, there was no evidence of *Campylobacter jejuni*, *Salmonella* spp. and *Yersina* spp. Measures such as washing boots in between landings, eliminating direct interaction with animals, using toilets only on boats, and leaving nothing at the landings have all been effective at controlling the movement of bacteria between humans and birds (Bonnedahl *et al.* 2005).

The care exercised in controlling the import of pathogens is very high in places like New Zealand. In 2006–7, the Ministry of Agriculture and Forestry Biosecurity of New Zealand made 116,700 seizures from 2 per cent of arriving air passengers. Contaminated equipment was the most frequently seized good (34 per cent), followed by fruit fly host material (23 per cent) and meat products (10 per cent). The seizure of a fruit fly contaminated mandarin at Dunedin airport served as a reminder for the importance of vigilance in protecting New Zealand's $2.5 billion fruit and vegetable export (McNeill *et al.*, 2008). The reader is urged to watch the video at National Geographic (2010), which shows how ecotourism is killing chimps in Mahale National Park in Africa, by the passing of infectious disease agents from ecotourists to the chimps.

There are four main sources of disease exposure that have potential to affect the health of the great apes: tourists; researchers and managers; guides and guards; and unintentional human contact (Woodford *et al.*, 2002). In the case of tourists, frequent contact with groups of apes and increased chances of disease because of the physical demands of travel tend to exacerbate the situation. Tourists know that their chances of visiting apes may decline if they have an infectious disease, so rely on medications that suppress the disease or mask symptoms, or they may simply say that they are not sick at the time of their tour. Pathogens have been categorized by Woodford *et al.* (2002) according to their mode of transmission, including aerosol/inhalation transmission, faecal/oral transmission, and indirect routes of transmission. Aerosol/inhalation transmission includes coughing, sneezing, and spitting, all of which have the potential of projecting infectious aerosols several metres, and these discharges contain viruses and bacteria of the common cold and flu as well as other diseases including polio, mumps, measles, and chicken pox. Woodford *et al.* (2002) document several cases where gorillas, chimpanzees, and other apes have died because of respiratory illnesses transmitted by humans. Cases of faecal/oral transmission have also been recorded by Woodford *et al.* (2002), who show that apes are susceptible to diseases passed on through the infected faeces of humans. Pathogens include bacterial groups responsible for diarrhoea, viruses such as hepatitis, protozoans such as *Giardia lamblia*, and intestinal worms. Finally, indirect routs of transmission include boots of tourists and other human groups, as well as vector-borne diseases passed on by arthropods, mainly mosquitoes (see Box 9.4).

Ethics in action: finding balance

The preceding discussion has summarized numerous examples of the extent to which humans are impacted through direct encounters with other species. These encounters are often the result of our travels in new places and the deliberate pursuit of some animals because of their charisma as tourist attractions. In other cases, the encounters are the result of unintended or chance encounters with consequences for tourists and animals alike. If we are to wander in to the territories of these animal others, humans need to take responsibility for their actions in the recognition that we cannot control all of the risks to backcountry travel, as Wolfe (2008) has noted above. We need to find balance, and part of this balance would presumably involve understanding the inherent value of these others, regardless of what we might think of them and their role within the systems that we cohabit. The last example included in this chapter highlights the evolution of thought and perception of the manatee that formerly was despised in Florida as an ugly monster capable of decimating fish supplies and lunging out of the water to bite boaters, only to become revered as a gentle animal icon with social and economic significance (Goedeke, 2004).

By the end of the nineteenth century, scientists were worried about the over-harvesting of manatees as a source of food as well as the general perception of the animal by the public. Manatees were regularly killed for amusement (local people and tourists), hooked by anglers to play them for sport, run over by boaters, and shot at for fun. The Center for Action on Endangered Species reported that:

> Manatees are molested regularly in Florida. Cement blocks have been dropped on their heads in the Miami Canals, one was seen with a garden rake embedded

Box 9.4 Recommendations for best practice in reducing disease transmission to great apes

Before the tourists reach the national park they should be made aware of the regulations for visiting, and the disease risks for the apes. The provision of facemasks would emphasise the latter point.

Rewards, in excess of tourist tips, should be offered to guards and guides for diligently enforcing the rules.

Information about local outbreaks of disease should be obtained from local health authorities.

Researchers and relevant park and project staff should be appropriately vaccinated and free from gastro-intestinal parasites. Vaccinations should include tuberculosis, measles, mumps, rubella, yellow fever and polio (killed injectable vaccine only).

Researchers, guards and guides should be tested annually for TB if they are not vaccinated (vaccination can produce false positive test results).

Faeces, vomit and other debris should be removed in disposable containers, or buried at least 50cm deep if deposited in the apes' habitat.

The frequency of ranger patrols around the apes' habitats should be increased to reduce illegal entries.

Autopsies should be performed on dead apes whenever possible, but only by veterinarians or other trained personnel who have access to protective clothing, facemasks, rubber gloves, disinfectants and equipment for specimen preservation and storage.

Guards, guides and other local people should be made aware of the dangers of handling, butchering and eating the flesh of dead apes.

All tourists proposing to visit habituated great apes should be required to undergo health screening and to produce an up-to-date vaccination certificate.

Source: Woodford *et al.* (2002: 158)

in its back, their eyes are poked out, and they are shot at by children and adults apparently for 'sport' or target practice. During 1975, several shooting incidents were reported, but apprehending violators is difficult.

(cited in Goedeke, 2004: 104)

Goedeke writes that even though a law was enacted in 1893 prohibiting harvest, public regard for the animal was so low that these molestations continued. The quote above does suggest, though, that by the mid-1970s things had started to change by virtue of the reporting by residents of manatee shootings. Changing perceptions were aided by scientific study on the manatee as well as by an organization called the Save the Manatee Club, started in the early 1980s aided by the singer/songwriter Jimmy Buffett and the Governor of Florida, Bob Graham, who had developed a childhood love of the animal because 'they were playful, with lots of human characteristics' (Goedeke, 2004: 106). New knowledge of the manatee as being harmless and endangered led to changing perceptions. No longer was the animal useless, grotesque, and ugly; it was viewed as charismatic and held social and economic value because of the emergence of an ecotourism industry based on its ability to draw sympathy from increasing numbers of tourists. Not only has the tourist public embraced the animal, but more importantly the local and regional public has reinvented the manatee as a symbol 'of everything gentle and beautiful in Florida waters' (p. 112); an icon that was worth preserving.

Shifting sentiment in regards to the manatee in Florida make this a good example of utilitarian reasoning. Recall that utilitarianism refers to the notion that a good choice among a number of options is the one that produces the most amount of pleasure and minimizes pain for all affected (Taylor, 2003). As Gruen (2010) suggests, it is sometimes a better option to impose harm or suffering in animals if this is the lesser of two evils: moderate suffering with a quick death is better in the mind of the utilitarianist than extreme suffering causing death. In its application to animals, utilitarianism is usually about the suffering animals bear against the benefits that humans gain from their use and the potency and nature of the interests at hand, i.e., whether the pleasure and pain of animals is as important as that of humans in weighing benefits and costs. A breakdown of these benefits and costs may amount to the following:

1. The continued harassment and killing of manatees for no reason has benefit to a few humans in regards to their enjoyment (sadism).
2. The fear, pain, suffering, and loss of life of the manatees are of less significance than the benefits derived from those participating in this activity.
3. The later recognition that the manatee has economic significance changes the balance of cost and benefit in the relationship that Floridians have with this animal.
4. Floridians recognize that the killing of manatees has broader significance not only for those that kill manatees but also for Florida in general. The balance of cost and benefit is thus calculated not only at an individual level but also, and more importantly, at a broader scale.
5. There is recognition that more benefits can come to individuals and society if the manatee is protected. These benefits come in the form of tourism revenue but also the chance for those who would otherwise think of harming the manatee to participate in commercial activities, either direct or indirect, that allow them to benefit financially. The reputation of Floridians also increases in the eyes of outsiders who may view this society as more virtuous because of their actions, inducing higher levels of visitation.

The evolution of changing social perceptions of the manatee in Florida is consistent with changing perceptions of other animals in North America (e.g., the wolf)

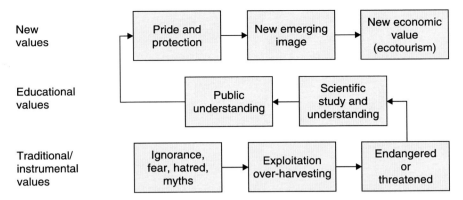

Figure 9.2 A process of species reinvention over time

and around the world (e.g., the tiger). There is a process or evolution that is similar in many of these cases and it has to do with changing values that are not only consistent with widening the moral concern we have for animal others, but also, more disconcerting, with populations on the brink. Figure 9.2 is designed to arrange a number of key factors in visually illustrating a process of reinvention.

Plate 9.2 Manatee tours, Florida

Plate 9.3 Manatee

Conclusion

With the increasing number of tourists travelling each year, tourist–animal encounters of a negative variety will likely grow proportionally. What is problematic for the tourism industry is that the media often sensationalizes these encounters, causing hesitation or unnecessary concern on the part of tourists. However, as the tourism industry is shown to be very resilient, a more devastating result is the worsening of relations and perceptions between humans and the species responsible for the human injury or death. The story intensifies according to the scale of the threat, with animals as the assailants and humans as the victims. Malamud (2007) argues that stories of swine flu, avian flu, killer bees, AIDS, and mad cow disease usually position the particular animal in question as the dangerous other, with little discussion of the human–animal interface which is the root cause of the issue. He says that the real problem is human intervention. When we grind up animals to feed other animals without consideration of the possible outcomes of this practice, as in the case of mad cow disease, there are bound to be problems. Finding balance is so vitally important, but this balance only comes when there is value extended to the animal other.

10 Conclusion

> True human goodness can manifest itself, in all its purity and liberty, only in regard to those who have no power. The true moral test of humanity (the most radical, situated on a level so profound that it escapes our notice) lies in its relations to those who are at its mercy: the animals. And it is here that exists the fundamental failing of man, so fundamental that all others follow from it.
>
> (Milan Kundera, *The Unbearable Lightness of Being*)

The preceding discussion has demonstrated a critical lack of involvement in the area of tourism and animal ethics. The emergence of animal ethics as a new interdisciplinary field of enquiry is said to offer guidance as a way forward; a manner by which to bring animals 'in'. The challenge inherent in this new emphasis has been identified by Hall and Brown (2006), who argue that the tourism industry has concern for the welfare of animals, but this concern rests primarily in the role that animals have in sustaining the viability of operations or of communities. This instrumental value set is so firmly entrenched – so pervasive in the system – that even when we have the best interests of animals in mind we cannot escape tourism's bottom line. For example, the Humane Society International (HSI) is an organization that provides animal welfare information around the world, including resources for the Caribbean tourism industry, where its mission is to 'encourage the Caribbean tourism industry to support animal welfare'. The group suggests that because

> animal-loving tourists often report discomfort with seeing hungry, homeless, sick or injured animals on their Caribbean vacations, the tourism industry can benefit directly by improving animal welfare in the Caribbean. Improved tourism experiences for Caribbean visitors will lead to a greater number of tourists spending more money.

The motives of this organization may be pure in helping to address the needs of sick and homeless animals, but the intended goal of making tourists feel better about their travels in the Caribbean is very clear in their message. Happy tourists (in the absence of diseased or injured animals) contribute more to needy Caribbean economies.

I have long felt that tourism, both in practice and theory, is a reactive industry: its success is contingent on the values that exist within society. Tourism does not change these values, but rather capitalizes upon what individuals and groups deem to be important. From this perspective there is much significance in Midgley's (2002) discussion of values. We can only properly address our values if we know something about our wants. And to Jameson (1984) these wants have added up to a contemporary society that is defined by a waning of emotion, depthlessness and affectlessness, and the commoditization of objects.

> As for expression and feelings or emotions, the liberation, in contemporary society, from the older *anomie* of the centred subject may also mean not merely a liberation from anxiety but a liberation from every other kind of feeling as well, since there is no longer a self present to do the feeling. This is not to say that the cultural products of the postmodern era are utterly devoid of feeling, but rather that such feelings – which it may be better and more accurate to call 'intensities' – are now free-floating and impersonal, and tend to be dominated by a peculiar kind of euphoria.
>
> (Jameson, 1984: 64).

This concept of self-centredness, this psychology of entitlement, becomes packaged in a lost sense of responsibility and identity. We almost seek out the comfort of the crowd because inside it we no longer have to take responsibility for decision-making and for the consequences of our actions. This is what Kierkegaard had in mind when he argued that 'A crowd ... in its very concept is the untruth, by reason of the fact that it renders the individual completely impenitent and irresponsible, or at least weakens his sense of responsibility by reducing it to a fraction' (Kierkegaard, 1859/1939: 114; see Fennell, 2008b). We do not want to ask questions about where our food comes from in an effort to avoid the personal anxiety this creates in deciding whether or not it is morally justifiable to comsume it. We do not want to probe deeper into questions about animal captivity because this unlocks a whole series of emotions that might not correspond with our pursuit of enjoyment. These questions are suppressed so we are able to enjoy what we might otherwise classify as wrong. We choose not to vilify these institutions (e.g., zoos) because in doing so we must certainly vilify ourselves.

Moving the relationship forward

A significant finding in this work is the existence of a torrent of research, coming from so many different disciplines, arguing for a change in how we regard the animal other. If the change from modernity to postmodernity is definable, at least in part, by a heightened emotional bond with animals that is couched in a broader moral context (Franklin, 1999), research has endeavoured to keep pace through the willingness to 'see the *new* animal on the frontier' and to revisit and reform our own inward ideas and habits (Malamud, 2007: 26). This entails a further willingness to sweep away animal and human identities in coming closer to each other's realities – a type of becoming-animal (Deleuze and Guattari, 1987). Carrying this idea forward, the Oxford Centre for Animal Ethics maintains that 'We cannot change the world for animals without changing our ideas about them.' New ideas about the use of animals for human instrumental ends need to be informed by (1) science that explores the boundaries of the complexity of animal systems, and (2) philosophers who have been so influential in framing the depth of the problem (Oxford Centre for Animal Ethics, 2011).

From the perspective of science, Bekoff argues that a paradigm shift is well under way; prestigious journals now publish material on animal empathy, joy, and play, in recognition that animals have 'rich and deep emotional lives' (2008: T8). Elephants have been shown to experience post-traumatic stress disorder over negative events in their lives that alter social relations and physiology (see Bradshaw *et al.*, 2005); zoo keepers are phasing out elephant exhibits because of the proven emotional needs, or distinctive personality traits, of elephants (Berger, 2006); spindle cells (the cells responsible in processing emotion in humans) have been found in many species of whales (Bekoff and Pierce, 2009); and mice suffer distress when they see their cage-mates encounter a painful event, becoming more sensitive themselves to painful stimuli (Langford *et al.*, 2006).

Keeping pace with science, and perhaps informing science, is a capacious base of philosophical work on animals and morality. Schalow (2000), for example, argues that if we are to move this animal ethics agenda forward we might do so by acknowledging that, although animals cannot speak for themselves, we have the opportunity to demonstrate benevolence and responsibility in speaking for them. Using Heiddegger's concept of dwelling on earth, Schalow argues that we have a unique power to communicate that is akin to a type of freedom, and we should choose to use this freedom wisely in our efforts to be stewards rather than masters. We are most human or authentic (built upon this concept of freedom and responsibility in the existential manner of thought, outlined above using Kierkegaard) when we demonstrate and display care towards others:

> Authentic freedom cultivates our place of dwelling on the earth, renouncing the drive of our human will rather than allowing it to fuel our domination of nature. Freedom in this radical sense concurs with the quest to rescue animals from technological exploitation, as exhibited in both medical experimentation and agriculture.
>
> (Schalow, 2000: 266)

Freedom, control, exploitation, and limits of our knowedge about animals are all themes explored by Wolfe (2003) in reference to what he feels is another major test for humanity. He begs us, through the ideas of Vicki Hearne (and others), and in the spirit of Stanley Cavell, to ask if we are indeed ready to understand the animal. But this can only take place if we are to 'underknow' animals by not standing above as master but rather below so as to suppress our humanism, which might only serve otherwise to narrow and flatten our options. Only when we can approach the question of the nonhuman animal 'not as the other-than-human but as the *infrahuman*, not as the primitive and pure other we rush to embrace as a way to cure our own existential malaise, but as part of us, *of* us' (Wolfe, 2003: 17) can we hope to make ethical strides in the relationship.

I wish to introduce the reader to one more way of looking at the issue of how best to consider our relationship with the animal other, based on two ways of positioning the just treatment of animals (Bryant, 2005). The first, a position that Bryant heavily critiques, is the similarity argument, whereby animals are akin to humans in certain capacities that afford them legal entitlements and, as a result, a society that is just would extend species-appropriate legal entitlements that might parallel entitlements extended to humans. The Great Ape project is one such initiative that is based on this perspective of justice. Bryant feels the similarity argument fails because it is difficult to claim similarity when obvious differences exist between animal and human. Efforts to prove similarity or dissimilarity are often based on the need for controlled scientific research in proving claims. The situation involving research on the capacity to feel pain is a case in point, especially when animals are already subjected to excessive amounts of pain in research procedures. As Bryant suggests, 'It is no small ethical problem for animals' advocates to create incentives for such research or to use such research in their advocacy' (2005: 57). An additional flaw of the similarity argument is that animals are characterized not by their diversity, but rather by what they may or may not possess in line with human capacities. Bryant argues that the ideological basis for justice in this approach is disrespectful to animals because evidence is sought to prove that the animal under scrutiny is in essence human, eliminating diversity and uniqueness in favour of human standards.

The second position, and one favoured by Bryant, is a model of justice built around anticipatory accommodation – anti-discrimination laws that stem from feminist and disability rights advocacy and which shed new light on the meaning of dissimilarity. If a building is constructed in anticipation of wheelchair users, then any wheelchair user is not any different in terms of his/her accessibility of the entire building space than any other user – there are no 'special' accommodations needed. Anticipatory accommodation incorporates values of inclusion and diversity, with the belief that differences would be incrementally naturalized over time as values within society evolve. Furthermore, anticipatory accommodation acts place the burden of justification on those who in the past were entitled to discriminate on the basis of dissimilarity. Using the example above, developers were allowed to build buildings without facilities geared towards disabled occupants until such laws were enacted, demonstrating how values have indeed changed over time.

Bryant takes this reasoning into the realm of animal advocacy by suggesting that an animal-respecting society is starting to emerge through initiatives that employ the anti-discrimination approach described above. An example is the construction of artificial wildlife corridors (see Banff National Park as an example), where animals are provided the opportunity to cross busy highways without the possibility of being hit by vehicular traffic. In this case, Bryant adds, the idea for such a development was not premised on the belief that animals and humans are similar, but rather according to diversity. The burden in these cases has also shifted from the animal advocacy groups to developers who must make these allowances as an accepted part of business.

The aspect of who bears the burden is important and serves to further distinguish the similarity argument from the anti-discrimination approach:

> The similarity argument requires advocates to bear the burden of justifying inclusion of animals' interests. Since the similarity argument requires proof of similarity to humans, that burden is all the greater because of the tremendous actual diversity of animals. Thus, the diversity of animals is a liability under the similarity argument. By contrast, diversity is not a liability under the anti-discrimination approach. Indeed, it sets the anti-discrimination approach in motion. The anti-discrimination approach presumes inclusion and requires justification for exclusion or discrimination. That burden may be relatively easy to overcome initially. However, over time, as values of inclusion and diversity are reinforced and developed, it should be more difficult to justify acting in opposition to those values.
>
> (Bryant, 2005: 62)

Bryant argues that the anti-discrimination approach is inductive in its orientation because, by working through many specific projects designed on what an animal-respecting society might look like, activists have the potential to map out how this goal might eventually be realized. One of the specific projects mentioned by Bryant is the opening of a vegan restaurant. As more people discover the culinary benefits of vegan food, they might also come to understand that factory farming causes massive suffering to innumerable animals, contributes significantly to environmental degradation, and has human health implications. As values in society slowly change, it is the meat-eaters who must justify their consumption patterns, not the vegans. In comparison, the similarity argument is a form of deductive activism, which starts with a broad, and difficult to define, first principle like 'animals are similar enough to humans as to relevant capacities and characteristics to be treated like humans' (Bryant, 2005: 61). Given the indecisiveness about how to define this first principle, there would be long-standing impediments about how to apply it and what species it has relevance to. In this vein, much might be realized for some species but little for others.

Because the anti-discrimination approach requires restraint by those in power who might cause harm to others, it demands that these individuals in positions of power bear the burden of justifying harm to the interests of others. This is a foundational concept inherent in the precautionary principle, which, in the case of animal protection, would provide assistance to animals via a mechanism that prevents harm to animals before it might take place. As Bryant argues, 'it requires anticipatory accommodation of animal interests' (2005: 6). For those who might cause harm to the environment, the precautionary principle requires these individuals 'to (1) refrain from potentially harmful acts, even if scientific research has not yet proved the exact nature of the potential harm or the degree of risk of harm, and (2) bear the burden of proving that potentially harmful acts are sufficiently safe before proceeding' (Bryant, 2005: 46, citing Geiser, 1999: xxi, xxiii). The fact that we do not know for sure whether animals think or reason, or feel pain for that matter, is not grounds to decide that they cannot – that they are inferior. We should err on the side of the animals in the absence of sound empirical evidence. We should take a precautionary approach (Fennell and Ebert, 2004).

It may also entail a way of thinking, not unlike the precautionary principle, that takes us beyond duty to what Singer (1972) has called supererogatory – the idea that we should do more than is required, even though doing less under the same circumstances would be morally acceptable. This term differs from duty. If we fail to do our duty, this is morally wrong. However, supererogation often refers payment beyond what is being asked, or more than duty requires. Singer (1972) used this concept to argue in the cause of extreme poverty, where members of developed countries hold a moral obligation to financially ease the pain and suffering of people under conditions of famine, war, and so on. The current normative course of duty suggests that it is not wrong not to contribute to these causes, but a supererogatory approach dictates that we should be extending ourselves beyond the call of duty for animals in all aspects of our relationship.

Moving tourism forward

The aim of this book has been to examine how animals are used in the service of the tourism industry, and the many associated ethical issues. In concluding, it is worth emphasizing the hope that this work represents a beginning, in acknowledgement of other worthy studies from tourism scholars on the topic. More forcefully, it is reasonable to argue that until we are prepared to ask more critical questions about animals and tourism we risk marginalization because of what others, i.e., scholars in other fields, might characterize as ignorance and/or arrogance.

What is exciting for those who embrace this nascent area of scholarship in tourism is the opportunity to build a sub-field of knowledge that has at its core the interests of animals, not humans. This common bond may unite stakeholders from all corners of the tourism field, theorists and practitioners alike. Box 10.1 is an example of how one organization, the World Society for the Protection of Animals, has recognized the magnitude of the problem in tourism, and why it is vitally important to institute positive change in the behaviour of tourism operators as well as tourists.

The following few points are offered to help move the tourism animal ethics research agenda forward:

- Tourism researchers have employed very few methods or approaches in their investigations that the field can use with confidence in drawing accurate assumptions about the problems and issues surrounding the use of animals in the tourism industry.
- There is an opportunity for tourism researchers to intensify work in the *tourism* and animal ethics area in keeping pace with other disciplines. This is

Box 10.1 World Society for the Protection of Animals: animal-friendly tourism

Animal cruelty can be a by-product of tourism. Animal circuses, bullfights, 'swim with dolphin' programmes and poor welfare zoos are all examples of animal exploitation in the name of entertainment. But if tourists choose to spend their money on cruelty-free attractions, rapid change can result. Ethical tourism has become a hot topic – the public expects the travel industry to set high standards for its activities. Ethical whale watching is one of the industries experiencing rapid growth as a result.

Make change happen

We are all responsible for ensuring that our actions abroad do not contribute to animal suffering. Here are some straightforward tips on how to make a difference to the way animals are treated all over the world.

Before you go: Check if your tour operator has an animal welfare policy. While you are away:

- Don't accept culture as an excuse for cruelty. Cockfights, bullfights and the use of animals in religious or other festivals can all be considered part of a local culture, but culture is no excuse for cruelty.
- Don't be tempted to try the local cuisine if it includes wild animals. Avoid food items that are produced through cruel practices, such as foie gras, or involve inhumane killing, such as bushmeat.
- It is best to view wildlife where it belongs: in the wild. Many zoos keep animals in poor conditions with their basic needs denied. If you decide to visit a zoo ask whether it adheres to the World Association of Zoos and Aquariums' Code of Ethics before you enter.
- Captivity cannot meet the welfare needs of marine mammals such as dolphins and whales. Facilities displaying captive marine mammals and activities like swimming with dolphins should be avoided – they may appear fun and educational but are unnatural and stressful for the animals involved.
- Never purchase souvenirs made from animals. Avoid all products and souvenirs made from animals, including all fur, ivory, shells, seahorses, teeth, rhino horn and turtle shell products.
- Never pay to have your picture taken posing with a wild animal. Many of these animals have been taken from the wild and their mothers killed. They may be drugged, harshly trained or have had their teeth removed to ensure they 'behave' around tourists.
- If travelling with a group, check the itinerary doesn't include activities that exploit animals. If it does, lodge a complaint with your travel agent or tour operator, who may be unaware of the cruelty involved with such activities.

- It is possible to find ethical and humane equine (horse and donkey) and camelid rides, during which animal welfare is protected. However, please avoid any ride that gives you cause for concern about the animal's welfare. At a minimum, check that animals have access to shade, water and rest.
- Compassionate travellers should avoid riding wild animals such as elephants for entertainment, because these animals are often captured from the wild, inadequately cared for and usually trained using inappropriate and cruel methods.
- Remember the farm animals. While free-range organic food may be hard to come by in some areas, it is worth checking – if restaurants recognise a demand for cruelty-free food they may stock it in future.

What can you do if you see an animal suffering?

Standards of animal welfare can differ greatly from region to region, but you don't have to feel powerless when you witness animals suffering abroad.

If you see an incident of animal cruelty, note the date, time, location, type and number of animals involved. If possible, record what you have seen on film. Photographs and video footage are invaluable evidence, but never pay to take them.

It is vital to lodge your protests locally in the first instance. Report the cruelty to: local tourist offices, local police, a local animal welfare society, your tour operator, the zoo or aquarium management and – if you have serious concerns – the zoo association for that country. When you return home, inform the country's embassy, your local politician, the World Association of Zoos and Aquariums (if relevant) and fill in our online cruelty form.

WSPA (2011)

an important matter because, in the absence of studies conducted by tourism researchers in tourism, theorists from outside our field will fill this niche. I'm not sure it is in our best interests to give way.

- In view of the previous statement, interdisciplinary work should be undertaken on tourism, animals, and ethics, drawing on several fields and disciplines of study for the purpose of making new theoretical and applied contributions to the field and the industry.
- Tourism research would benefit from the establishment of research networks designed to capture cross-cultural dynamics related to the use of animals in different regions.
- The pleasure we derive from tourism experiences is often contingent upon how close we can get to animals. There is, however, a lack of knowledge about the conditions in which these animals are presented to tourists, *in situ* or *ex situ*. The further development of standards for animal use, in all manner

of activities, would be a start in recognizing that animal rights, in some cases, or well-being, in others, are more important than tourist pleasure. There is simply too much at stake in light of new findings on animal sentience, fear, stress, suffering, and so on, that animals experience because of human instrumental use of such.

Building from this last point, it is important to recognize that the animals we train and use are beings that we have not ourselves created. These animals are not ours in a biological sense – they do not simply give away their identity or membership as part of a species solely to us so as to lose their personal autonomy (Clark, 1997). They may be ours economically, but they have intrinsic value unto themselves. And the burdens we place them under should not be trivialized. Animals do not freely consent to the innumerable ways that we use them. Humans have the right to refuse. Animals do not. This means that arguments for the use of animals in the tourism industry and the way we treat them should be the topic of heated discussion, despite the fact that at present they are not.

As we travel this path we can take solace in the fact that the circle of morality continues to widen (Singer, 2011). As Preece has commented, 'Compassion for our fellow beings derives from the very psychology of what it is to be truly human' (2005: 390). This takes us back to the words of Kundera cited at the outset of the chapter. The true test of a moral tourism industry exists not just in how we treat each other, which continues to challenge us on so many levels, but in how we treat the animals that have no other option but to serve our varied interests. If we measure success in tourism as a function of progress or development on this dimension, we have a very long way to go indeed.

References

Aaltola, E. (2005) 'Animal interests and interest conflicts', *Ethics & the Environment* 10(1): 19–48.

Aaltola, E. (2009) 'Animal ethics', in J. Baird Callicott and R. Frodeman (eds) *Encyclopedia of Environmental Ethics and Philosophy*, Detroit, MI: Gale, pp. 4–53.

ABC News (2008) 'Fraser Island dingo fence completed'. Online. Available at: <http://www.abc.net.au/news/stories/2008/10/24/2400820.htm> (accessed 11 May 2011).

Acampora, R.R. (1998) 'Extinction by exhibition', *Human Ecology Review*, 5(1): 1–4.

—— (2005) 'Zoos and eyes: contesting captivity and seeking successor practices', *Society & Animals*, 13(1): 69–88.

Acquaroni, J.L. (1966) *Bulls and Bullfighting*, trans. C.D. Ley, Barcelona: Editorial Noguer.

Adams, C.J. (1990) *The Sexual Politics of Meat: A Feminist Vegetarian Critical Theory*, New York: Continuum International Publishing Group.

Adams, C.J. (2003) *The Pornography of Meat*, New York: Continuum.

—— (2008) 'Post-meateating', in T. Tyler and M. Rossini (eds) *Animal Encounters*, Boston, MA: Brill, pp. 47–72.

Adams, V. (1992) 'Tourism and sherpas, Nepal: reconstruction of reciprocity', *Annals of Tourism Research*, 19(3): 534–54.

Adams, W.M. and Infield, M. (2002) 'Who is on the gorilla's payroll? Claims on tourist revenue from a Ugandan National Park', *World Development*, 31(1): 177–90.

ADAPTT (2011) '140 Billion Animals Slaughtered Every Year'. Online. Available at: <http://www.adaptt.org/killcounter.html> (accessed 11 May 2011).

African Conservation Foundation (2011) 'Elephant Management and Owners Association'. Online. Available at: <http://www.africanconservation.org/explorer/south-africa/89-elephant-management-and-owners-association-emoa/view-details.html> (accessed 3 March 2011).

Agoramoorthy, G. (2004) 'Ethics and welfare in Southeast Asian zoos', *Journal of Applied Animal Welfare Science*, 7(3): 189–95.

Agoramoorthy, G. and Harrison, B. (2002) 'Ethics and animal welfare evaluations in South East Asian zoos: a case study of Thailand', *Journal of Applied Animal Welfare Science*, 5(1): 1–13.

Agoramoorthy, G. and Hsu, M.J. (2005) 'Use of nonhuman primates in entertainment in Southeast Asia', *Journal of Applied Animal Welfare Science*, 8(2): 141–9.

Akama, J.S. (2008) 'Controversies surrounding the ban on wildlife hunting in Kenya', in B. Lovelock (ed.) *Tourism and the Consumption of Wildlife: Hunting, Shooting and Sport Fishing*, London: Routledge, pp. 73–86.

Allen, C. (2004) 'Animal pain', *Noûs*, 38(4): 617–43.

Allen, C. and Bekoff, M. (2007a) 'Animal consciousness', in M. Velmans and S. Schneider (eds) *The Blackwell Companion to Consciousness*, Oxford: Blackwell, pp. 58–71.

—— (2007b) 'Animal minds, cognitive ethology, and ethics', *Journal of Ethics*, 11(3): 299–317.

Almazan, R.R., Rubio, R.P. and Agoramoorthy, G. (2005) 'Welfare evaluations of nonhuman animals in selected zoos in the Philippines', *Journal of Applied Animal Welfare Science*, 8(1): 59–68.

Alós, J. (2009) 'Mortality impact of recreational angling techniques and hook types on *Trachynotus ovatus* (Linnaeus, 1758) following catch-and-release', *Fisheries Research*, 95, 365–9.

Altick, R.D. (1978) *The Shows of London*, Cambridge, MA: Belknap Press.

Amante-Helweg, V. (1996) 'Ecotourists' beliefs and knowledge about dolphins and the development of cetacean ecotourism', *Aquatic Animals*, 22(2): 131–40.

American Veterinary Medical Association (2003) 'Press release: The human-animal bond revisited across the globe', 19 July. Online. Available at: <www.avma.org/press/releases/030719_hab.asp> (accessed 20 February 2010).

Amo, L., López, P. and Martín, J. (2006) 'Nature-based tourism as a form of predation risk affects body condition and health state of *Podarcis muralis* lizards', *Biological Conservation*, 131(3): 402–9.

Anderson, K. (1995) 'Culture and nature at the Adelaide zoo: at the frontiers of human geography', *Transactions of the Institute of British Geographers*, 20(3): 275–94.

—— (1997) 'A walk on the wild side: a critical geography of domestication', *Progress in Human Geography*, 21(4): 463–85.

Anderson, U.S., Benne, M., Bloomsmith, M.A. and Maple, T.L. (2002) 'Retreat space and human visitor density moderate undesirable behavior in petting zoo animals', *Journal of Applied Animal Welfare Science*, 5(2): 125–37.

Anthony, R. (2003) 'The ethical implications of the human–animal bond on the farm', *Animal Welfare*, 12(4): 505–12.

Appel, M. and Elwood, R.W. (2009). 'Motivational trade-offs and potential pain experience in hermit crabs', *Applied Animal Behaviour Science*, 119(1/2): 120–4.

Arlinghaus, R., Cooke, S.J., Schwab, A. and Cowx, I.G. (2007) 'Fish welfare: a challenge to the feelings-based approach, with implications for recreational fishing', *Fish and Fisheries*, 8(1): 57–71.

Arlinghaus, R., Schwab, A., Cooke, S.J. and Cowx, I.G. (2009) 'Contrasting pragmatic and suffering-centred approaches to fish welfare in recreational angling', *Journal of Fish Biology*, 75(10): 2448–63.

Arluke, A. and Sanders, C.R. (1996) *Regarding Animals*, Philadelphia, PA: Temple University Press.

Arrindell, W.A. (2000) 'Phobic dimensions: IV. The structure of animal fears', *Behavior Research & Therapy*, 38(5): 509–30.

Arrindell, W.A., Pickersgill, M.J., Merckelbach, H., Ardon, A.M. and Cornet, F.C. (1991) 'Phobic dimensions: III. Factor analytic approaches to the study of common phobic fears: an updated review of findings obtained with adult subjects', *Advances in Behaviour Research and Therapy*, 13(2): 73–130.

Ashley, D.V.M., Walters, C., Dockery-Brown, C., McNab, A. and Ashley, D.E. (2004) 'Interventions to prevent and control food-borne diseases associated with a reduction in traveler's diarrhea in tourists to Jamaica', *Journal of Travel Medicine*, 11(6): 364–9.

Assael, B. (2005) *The Circus and Victorian Society*, London: University of Virginia Press.

Associated Press (2005) 'Killing techniques being questioned at dog sledding operation near Aspen', *Summit Daily News*, 5 April. Online. Available at: <http://www.summitdaily.com/article/20050405/NEWS/104050029> (accessed 25 February 2011).

Atkinson, M. and Young, K. (2005) 'Reservoir dogs: greyhound racing, mimesis and sports-related violence', *International Review for the Sociology of Sport*, 40(3): 335–56.

Atkinson, P.R.T., Boyle, A., Hartin, D. and McAuley, D. (2006) 'Is hot water immersion an effective treatment for marine envenomation?', *Emergency Medical Journal*, 23(7): 503–8.

Augustine of Hippo (2006) 'The Catholic Way of Life and the Manichean Way of Life', in J.E. Rotelle (ed.) *The Works of Saint Augustine: A Translation for the 21st Century*, part 3, New York: New York City Press, Augustinian Heritage Institute.

Australian Government (2010) 'Standards for the care and treatment of rodeo livestock'. Online. Available at: <http://www.daff.gov.au/animal-plant-health/welfare/nccaw/guidelines/display/rodeo> (accessed 28 October 2010).

Baars, B.J. (1993) *A Cognitive Theory of Consciousness*, Cambridge: Cambridge University Press.

Bahn, P.G. and Vertut, J. (1997) *Journey through the Ice Age*, Berkeley, CA: University of California Press.

Bailey, C. (2007) '"Africa begins at the Pyrenees": moral outrage, hypocrisy, and the Spanish bullfight', *Ethics & the Environment*, 12(1): 23–37.

Bailey Knows Travel (2004) 'Dog Adventures'. Online. Available at: <http://www.baileyknowstravel.com> (accessed 2 March 2010).

Baker, N. (1996) 'Going to the dogs – hostility to greyhound racing in Britain: puritanism, socialism and pragmaticism', *Journal of Sport History*, 23(2): 97–119.

Baker, S. (2000) *The Postmodern Animal*, London: Reaktion Books.

—— (2001) 'Guest editor's introduction: animals, representation, and reality', *Society & Animals*, 9(3): 189–201.

—— (2002) 'What does becoming-animal look like?', in N. Rothfels (ed.) *Representing Animals*, Indianapolis, IN: Indiana University Press, pp. 67–98.

—— (2005) '"You kill things to look at them": animal death in contemporary art', in The Animal Studies Group (eds) *Killing Animals*, Urbana, IL: University of Illinois Press, pp. 69–98.

Ballantyne, R., Packer, J., Hughes, K. and Dierking, L. (2007) 'Conservation learning in wildlife tourism settings: lessons from research in zoos and aquariums', *Environmental Education Research*, 13(3): 367–83.

Ballantyne, R., Packer, J. and Hughes, K. (2009) 'Tourists' support for conservation messages and sustainable management practices in wildlife tourism experiences', *Tourism Management*, 30(5): 658–64.

Balmford, A., Leader-Williams, N., Mace, G.M., Manica, A., Walter, O., West, C. and Zimmermann, A. (2007) 'Message received? Quantifying the impact of informal conservation education on adults visiting UK zoos', in A. Zimmermann, M. Hatchwell, L. Dickie and C. West (eds) *Zoos in the 21st Century: Catalysts for Conservation?*, Cambridge: Cambridge University Press, pp. 120–36.

Balon, E.K. (2000) 'Defending fishes against recreational fishing: an old problem to be solved in the new millennium', *Environmental Biology of Fishes*, 57(1), 1–8.

Baratay, E. and Hardouin-Fugier, E. (2002) *Zoo: A History of Zoological Gardens in the West*, London: Reaktion Books.

Barber, J.C.E. (2009) 'Programmatic approaches to assessing and improving animal welfare in zoos and aquariums', *Zoo Biology*, 28(6): 519–30.

Bargail, H.S., Akhtar, N. and Chauhan, N.P.S. (2005) 'Characteristics of sloth bear attacks and human casualties in North Bilaspur Forest Division, Chhattisgarh, India', *Ursus*, 16(2): 263–7.

Barker, K. and Grimaldi, J.V. (2003) 'Pattern of mistakes found in zoo deaths', *The Washington Post*. Online. Available at: <www.washingtonpost.com/wp-dyn/content/article/2006/07/26/AR2006072600621_pf.html> (accessed 21 June 2010).

Barnes, J. (1994) *The Complete Book of Greyhounds*, London: Howell.

Barnes, J.I. and Novelli, M. (2008) 'Trophy hunting and recreational angling in Namibia', in B. Lovelock (ed.) *Tourism and the Consumption of Wildlife: Hunting, Shooting and Sport Fishing*, London: Routledge, pp. 155–68.

Barnes, J., Burgess, J. and Pearce, D. (1992) 'Wildlife tourism', in T.M. Swanson and E.B. Barbier (eds) *Economics for the Wilds: Wildlife, Wildlands, Diversity and Development*, London: Earthscan, pp. 136–51.

Bartholomew, A. and Bohnsack, J.A. (2005) 'A review of catch-and-release angling mortality with implications for no-take reserves', *Reviews in Fish Biology and Fisheries*, 15, 129–54.

Baruch-Mordo, S., Breck, S.W., Wilson, K.R. and Theobald, D.M. (2008) 'Spatiotemporal distribution of black bear–human conflicts in Colorado, USA', *Journal of Wildlife Management*, 72(8): 1853–62.

Bashaw, M.L., Kelling, A.S., Bloomsmith, M.A. and Maple, T.L. (2007) 'Environmental effects on the behavior of zoo-housed lions and tigers, with a case study of the effects of a visual barrier on pacing', *Journal of Applied Animal Welfare*, 10(2): 95–109.

Bateson, P. and Bradshaw, E.L. (1997) 'Physiological effects of hunting red deer (*Cervus elaphus*)', *Proceedings of the Royal Society of London*, B264: 1707–14.

Bauer, I.L. (2001) 'Tourism and the environment, the other side of the coin: environmental impact on tourists' health', *Tourist Studies*, 1(3): 297–314.

—— (2002) 'Knowledge and behavior of tourists to Manu National Park, Peru, in relation to Leishmaniasis', *Journal of Travel Medicine*, 9(4): 173–9.

Bauer, J. and Giles, J. (2002) *Recreational Hunting: An International Perspective*, Wildlife Tourism Research Report Series No. 13, Sustainable Tourism Cooperative Research Centre, Gold Coast, Australia.

Bauer, J. and Herr, A. (2004) 'Hunting and fishing tourism', in K. Higginbottom (ed.) *Wildlife Tourism: Impacts, Management and Planning*, Altona, Victoria: Common Ground Publishing, pp. 57–75.

Bavastrelli, M. *et al.* (2000) 'Ciguatera fish poisoning: an emerging syndrome in Italian travelers', *Journal of Travel Medicine*, 8(3): 139–42.

BBC News (2005) 'Asia "wakes up" to animal welfare'. Online. Available at: <http://news.bbc.co.uk/2/hi/science/nature/4357527.stm> (accessed 15 September 2010).

Beardsworth, A. and Bryman, A. (2001) 'The wild animal in late modernity: the case of the Disneyization of zoos', *Tourist Studies*, 1(1): 83–104.

Beirnes, P. (1994) 'The law is an ass: reading E.P. Evans' *The Medieval Prosecution and Capital Punishment of Animals*', *Society and Animals*, 2(1): 27–46.

Bekoff, M. (1993) 'Common sense, cognitive ethology and evolution', in P. Cavalieri and P. Singer (eds) *The Great Ape Project: Equality beyond Humanity*, New York: St Martin's Press, pp.102–8.

—— (1998) 'Deep ethology, animal rights, and the great ape/animal project: resisting speciesism and expanding the community of equals', *Journal of Agricultural and Environmental Ethics*, 10(3): 269–96.

—— (2004) 'Wild justice and fair play: cooperation, forgiveness, and morality in animals', *Biology and Philosophy*, 19(4): 489–520.

—— (2008) 'Why "good welfare" isn't "good enough": minding animals and increasing our compassionate footprint', *Annual Review of Biomedical Sciences*. Online. Available at: <http://arbs.biblioteca.unesp.br/index.php/arbs/article/view/112> (accessed 2 March 2011).

Bekoff, M. and Pierce, J. (2009) *Wild Justice: Reflections on Empathy, Fair Play, and Morality in Animals*, Chicago, IL: University of Chicago Press.

Belfast Telegraph (2009) 'Crackdown appeal after swoops on badger-baiting ring', 23 February. Online. Available at: <http://www.belfasttelegraph.co.uk/news/local-national/crackdown-appeal-after-swoops-on-badgerbaiting-ring-14199372.html#ixzz1Lrz11vj V> (accessed 1 May 2011).

Belk, R.W. (1988) 'Possessions and the extended self', *Journal of Consumer Research*, 15(2): 139–68.

Belmonte, J. (1937) *Killer of Bulls: The Autobiography of a Matador*, Garden City: Doubleday, Doran and Co.

Belshaw, C. (2001) *Environmental Philosophy: Reason, Nature and Human Concern*, Chesham: Acumen Publishing.

Benton, T. and Redfearn, S. (1996) 'The Politics of Animal Rights – Where is the Left?', *New Left Review*, 215: 43–58.

Berger, J. (1980) *About Looking*, London: Writers and Readers.

—— (2006) 'Bronx zoo plans to end elephant exhibit', *The New York Times*, 7 February edn. Online. Available at: <http://www.nytimes.com/2006/02/07/nyregion/07elephants.html> (accessed 2 March 2011).

Berman, C.M., Li, J., Ogawa, H., Ionica, C. and Yin, H. (2007) 'Primate tourism, range restriction, and infant risk among *Macaca thibetana* at Mt. Huangshan, China', *International Journal of Primatology*, 28(5): 1123–41.

Bernstein, P. (2005) 'The human–cat relationship', in I. Rochlitz (ed.) *The Welfare of Cats*, Dordrecht: Springer, pp. 47–89.

Best, S. and Nocella, A.J. (2004) 'Defining Terrorism', *Animal Liberation Philosophy and Policy Journal*, 2(1): 1–18.

Bicca-Marques, J.C. and Freitas, D.S. (2010) 'The role of monkeys, mosquitoes, and humans in the occurrence of a yellow fever outbreak in a fragmented landscape in south Brazil: protecting howler monkeys is a matter of public health', *Tropical Conservation Science*, 3(1): 78–89.

Black, G.D. (2010) 'The ban and the bull: cultural studies, animal studies, and Spain', *Journal of Spanish Cultural Studies*, 11(3–4): 235–49.

Blake, A., Sinclair, M.T. and Sugiyarto, G. (2001) 'The economy-wide effects of foot and mouth disease in the UK economy'. Online. Available at: <http://www.saphastaligi.com/pdfler/fmd_in_the_UK_Economy_2001.pdf> (accessed 13 January 2011).

Block, G. (2003) 'The moral reasoning of believers in animal rights', *Society & Animals*, 11(2): 167–80.

Blum, J.A. and Hatz, C.F. (2009) 'Treatment of cutaneous Leishmaniasis in travelers 2009', *Journal of Travel Medicine*, 16(2): 123–31.

Boas, G. (1933/1966) *The Happy Beast in French Thought of the Seventeenth Century*, New York: Octagon Books.

Boddice, R. (2008) *A History of Attitudes and Behaviours Toward Animals in Eighteenth- and Nineteenth-Century Britain*, Lewiston, NY: The Edwin Mellen Press.

Boehrer, B. (2007) 'Introduction: The animal renaissance', in B. Boehrer (ed.) *A Cultural History of Animals in the Renaissance*, Oxford: Berg, pp. 1–26.

Boggild, A.K., Costiniuk, C., Kain, K.C. and Pandey, P. (2007) 'Environmental hazards in Nepal: altitude illness, environmental exposures, injuries, and bites in travellers and expatriates', *Journal of Travel Medicine*, 14(6): 361–8.

Bökönyi, S. (1989) 'Definitions of animal domestication', in J. Clutton-Brock (ed.) *The Walking Larder: Patterns of Domestication, Pastoralism, and Predation*, London: Unwin Hyman, pp. 22–7.

Boniface, P. (2003) *Tasting Tourism: Travelling for Food and Drink*, Aldershot: Ashgate.

Bonnedahl, J., Broman, T., Waldenström, J., Palmgren, H., Niskanen, T. and Olsen, B. (2005) 'In search of human-associated bacterial pathogens in Antarctic wildlife: report from six penguin colonies regularly visited by tourists', *Ambio*, 34(6): 430–2.

Boone and Crockett Club (2008) 'Fair chase statement'. Online. Available at: <http://www.boone-crockett.org/huntingEthics/ethics_fairchase.asp?area=huntingEthics> (accessed 6 April 2011).

Boonin-Vail, D. (1993) 'The vegetarian savage: Rousseau's critique of meat eating', *Environmental Ethics*, 15(1): 75–84.

—— (1994) 'Contractarianism gone wild: Carruthers and the moral status of animals', *Between the Species*, 10(1–2): 39–48.

Boshoff, A.F., Landman, M., Kerley, G.I.H. and Bradfield, M. (2007) 'Profiles, views and observations of visitors to the Addo Elephant National Park, Eastern Cape, South Africa', *South African Journal of Wildlife Research*, 37(2): 189–96.

Bostock, S.C. (1993) *Zoos and Animal Rights: The Ethics of Keeping Animals*, London: Routledge.

Boulanger, J.R., Hubbard, D.E., Jenks, J.A. and Gigliotti, L.M. (2006) 'A typology of South Dakota muzzleloader deer hunters', *Wildlife Society Bulletin*, 34(3): 691–7.

Boulware, D.R. (2004) 'Influence of hygiene on gastrointestinal illness among wilderness backpackers', *Journal of Travel Medicine*, 11(1): 27–33.

—— (2006) 'A randomized, controlled field trial for the prevention of jellyfish stings with a topical sting inhibitor', *Journal of Travel Medicine*, 13(3): 166–71.

Boyce, M.S., Haridas, C.V. and Lee, C.T. (2006) 'Demography in an increasingly variable world', *Trends in Ecology and Evolution*, 21(3): 141–8.

Boyd, J.J., Agazzi, G., Svada, D., Morgan, A.J., Ferrandis, S. and Norris, R.L. (2007) 'Venomous snakebite in mountainous terrain: prevention and management', *Wilderness and Environmental Medicine*, 18(3): 190–202.

Boyle, S.A. and Samson, F.B. (1985) 'Effects of nonconsumptive recreation on wildlife: a review', *Wildlife Society Bulletin*, 13(2): 110–6.

Bradshaw, G.A. and Bekoff, M. (2001) 'Ecology and social responsibility: the re-embodiment of science', *Trends in Ecology and Evolution*, 16(8): 460–5.

Bradshaw, G.A. and Lindner, L. (2009) 'Post-traumatic stress and elephants in captivity'. Online. Available at: <www.elephants.com/ptsd.php> (accessed 4 December 2009).

Bradshaw, G.A., Schore, A.N., Brown, J.L., Poole, J.H., and Moss, C.J. (2005) 'Elephant breakdown', *Nature*, 433: 807.

Braithwaite, V.A. (2006) 'Cognition in fish', *Behavioural Physiology of Fish*, 24: 1–37.

Braithwaite, V.A. and Boulcott, P. (2007) 'Pain perception, aversion and fear in fish', *Diseases of Aquatic Organisms*, 75(2), 131–8.

Brandes, S. (2009) 'Torophiles and torophobes: the politics of bulls and bullfights in contemporary Spain', *Anthropological Quarterly*, 82(3): 779–94.

Brantingham, P.J. (1998) 'Hominid–carnivore coevolution and invasion of the predatory guild', *Journal of Anthropological Archaeology*, 17(4): 327–53.

Brashares, J.S., Arcese, P., Sam, M.K., Coppolillo, P.B., Sinclair, A.R.E. and Balmford, A. (2004) 'Bushmeat hunting, wildlife declines, and fish supply in West Africa', *Science*, 306(5699): 1180–3.

Britain's Finest (2011) 'Wildlife Parks, Zoos and Animal Attractions in the UK'. Online. Available at: <http://www.britainsfinest.co.uk/attractions/search_results.cfm/searchclasscode/77> (accessed 3 May 2011).

Brodie, S.J. and Biley, F.C. (1999) 'An exploration of the potential benefits of pet-facilitated therapy', *Journal of Clinical Nursing*, 8(4): 329–37.

Bronner, S.J. (2004) '"This is why we hunt": social-psychological meanings of the traditions and rituals of deer camp', *Western Folklore*, 63(1/2): 11–50.

—— (2005) 'Contesting tradition: the deep play and protest of pigeon shoots', *Journal of American Folklore*, 118(470): 409–52.

—— (2008) *Killing Tradition: Inside Hunting and Animal Rights Controversies*, Lexington, KY: The University Press of Kentucky.

Brook, S. (2001) 'Breaking down the whaling wall', *The Weekend Australian Magazine*, 28–29 July, p. 21.

Broom, D.M. (1991a) 'Animal welfare: concepts and measurement', *Journal of Animal Science*, 69(10): 4167–75.

—— (1991b) 'Assessing welfare and suffering', *Behavioral Processes*, 25(2–3): 117–23.

—— (1998) 'Welfare, stress, and the evolution of feelings', in A.P. Moller, M. Milinski, and P.J.B. Slater (eds) *Stress and Behavior: Advances in the Study of Behavior*, San Diego, CA: Academic Press, pp. 371–404.

Brophy, B. (1965) 'The rights of animals', *Sunday Times*, 10 October.

Brower, M. (2005) 'Trophy shots: early North American photographs of nonhuman animals and the display of masculine prowess', *Society & Animals*, 13(1): 13–31.

Brown, K., Turner, P.K., Hameed, H. and Bateman, I. (1997) 'Environmental carrying capacity and tourism development in the Maldives and Nepal', *Environmental Conservation*, 24(4): 316–25.

Brown, J.L., Wielebnowski, N. and Cheeran, J.V. (2008) 'Pain, stress, and suffering in elephants', in C. Wemmer and C.A. Christian (eds) *Elephants and Ethics: Toward a Morality of Coexistence*, Baltimore, MD: Johns Hopkins University Press, pp. 121–45.

Brownstein, O. (1969) 'The popularity of baiting in England before 1600: a study in social and theatrical history', *Educational Theatre Journal*, 21(3): 237–50.

Bryan, H. (1977) 'Leisure value systems and recreational specialization: the case of trout fishermen', *Journal of Leisure Research*, 9(3): 174–87.

Bryant, B. (1990) 'The richness of the child–pet relationship: a consideration of both benefits and costs of pets to children', *Anthrozoos*, 3: 253–61.

Bryant, T.L. (2005) 'Similarity or difference as a basis for justice: must animals be like humans to be legally protected from humans?', UCLA School of Law Research Paper No. 05–21. Online. Available at: <http://papers.ssrn.com/sol3/papers.cfm?abstract_id=796205> (accessed 2 September 2010).

Bulbeck, C. (1999) 'The "nature dispositions" of visitors to animal encounter sites in Australia and New Zealand', *Journal of Sociology*, 35(2): 129–48.

—— (2005) *Facing the Wild: Ecotourism, Conservation & Animal Encounters*, London: Earthscan.

Bull, W. (2005) 'Rights and duties under the law of nature: contractarianism and the moral status of animals', *ethic@, Florianópolis*, 4(1): 39–53.

Burford, A. (1960) 'Heavy transport in classical antiquity', *The Economic History Review*, 13(1): 1–18.

Burge, B.L. (1983) 'Impact of Frontier 500 off-road vehicle race on desert tortoise habitat', Proceedings of the 1983 Annual Symposium of the Desert Tortoise Council, pp. 27–38.

Burgess-Jackson, K. (1998) 'Doing right by our animal companions', *Journal of Ethics*, 2(2): 159–85.

Burghardt, G.M. (2009) 'Cognitive ethology', in J. Baird Callicott and R. Frodeman (eds) *Encyclopedia of Environmental Ethics and Philosophy*, vol. 1, Detroit, MI: Gale, pp. 156–9.

Burns, G.L. and Howard, P. (2003) 'When wildlife tourism goes wrong: a case study of stakeholder and management issues regarding dingoes on Fraser Island, Australia', *Tourism Management*, 24(6): 699–712.

Burr, J.R., Reinhart, G.A., Swenson, R.A., Swaim, S.E. Vaughn, D.M. and Bradley, D.M. (1997) 'Biochemical values in sled dogs before and after competing in long-distance races', *Journal of the American Veterinary Association*, 211(2): 175–9.

Butler, R.W. (1980) 'The concept of tourist area cycle of evolution: implications for management of resources', *The Canadian Geographer*, 24(1): 5–12.

Butynski, T.M. and Kalina, J. (1998) 'Gorilla tourism: a critical look', in E.J. Milner-Gulland and R. Mace (eds) *Conservation of Biological Resources*, Oxford: Blackwell Science, pp. 280–300.

Cahoone, L. (2009) 'Hunting as a moral good', *Environmental Values*, 18: 67–89.

Cain, L. and Meritt, D. (2007) 'The demand for zoos and aquariums', *Tourism Review International*, 11(3): 295–306.

Caius, J. (1576/1969) *Of Englishe Dogges*, trans. A. Fleming, Amsterdam: Da Capo.

Calgary Herald (2010) 'Vancouver generated $2.5 billion', 18 December. Online. Available at: <http://www.calgaryherald.com/sports/Vancouver+Olympics+generated+bill ion/3997570/story.html> (accessed 30 January 2011).

Callicott, J. Baird (1980) 'Animal liberation: a triangular affair', *Environmental Ethics*, 2(4): 311–38.

—— (1985) 'Intrinsic value, quantum theory, and environmental ethics', *Environmental Ethics*, 7: 257–75.

—— (1986) 'The search for an environmental ethic', in T. Regan (ed.) *Matters of Life and Death: New Essays in Moral Philosophy*, 2nd edn, New York: Random House, pp. 381–424.

—— (1989) 'Biosocial moral theory', in J. Baird Callicott (ed.) *In Defense of the Land Ethic: Essays in Environmental Philosophy*, Albany, NY: SUNY Press.

Calvert, B. and Williams, P. (1999) 'Low consumptive angler behaviour and preferred management strategies: the case of sport fishing in British Columbia's tidal waters', in *Evaluating the Benefits of Recreational Fisheries. Fisheries Centre Research Report*, 7(2), 58–62.

Cameron, A. (1976) *Circus Factions: Blues and Greens at Rome and Byzantium*, Oxford: Clarendon Press.

Campbell, B. (2005) 'On "Loving Your Water Buffalo More Than Your Own Mother": relationships of animals and human care in Nepal', in J. Knight (ed.) *Animals in Person: Cultural Perspectives on Human–Animal Intimacy*, New York: Berg, pp. 79–100.

Canada Revenue Agency (2011) 'Consultation on proposed guidance for The Promotion of Animal Welfare and Charitable Registration'. Online. Available at: <http://www.cra-arc. gc.ca/chrts-gvng/chrts/plcy/cnslttns/pwcr-eng.html> (accessed 3 May 2011).

Caras, R. (1970) *Death as a Way of Life*, Boston, MA: Little, Brown.

Carruthers, J. (2005) 'Changing perspectives on wildlife in southern Africa, c.1840 to c.1914', *Society & Animals*, 13(3): 183–99.

Carruthers, P. (1989) 'Brute experience', *Journal of Philosophy*, 86(5): 258–69.

—— (1992) *The Animals Issue: Moral Theory in Practice*, Cambridge: Cambridge University Press.

—— (2000) *Phenomenal Consciousness*, Cambridge: Cambridge University Press.

Cartmill, M. (1993) *View to a Death in the Morning*, Cambridge, MA: Harvard University Press.

Carvalhedo Reis, A. (2009) 'More than the kill: hunters' relationships with landscape and prey', *Current Issues in Tourism*, 12(5–6): 573–87.

Cashell, K. (2009) *Aftershock: The Ethics of Contemporary Transgressive Art*, London: I.B. Tauris.

Casimir, M.J. (2009) 'On the origin and evolution of affective capacities in lower vertebrates', in B. Röttger-Rössler and H.J. Markowitsch (eds) *Emotions as Bio-cultural Processes*, New York: Springer, pp. 55–93

Cater, C. and Cater, E. (2007) *Marine Ecotourism: Between the Devil and the Deep Blue Sea*, Wallingford, Oxon: CABI.

Catibog-Sinha, C. (2008) 'Zoo tourism: biodiversity conservation through tourism', *Journal of Ecotourism*, 7(2&3): 160–78.

Catlin, J., Jones, T., Norman, B. and Wood, D. (2010a) 'Consolidation in a wildlife tourism industry: the changing impact of whale shark tourist expenditure in the Ningaloo Coast region', *International Journal of Tourism Research*, 12(2): 134–48.

Catlin, J., Jones, R., Jones, T., Norman, B. and Wood, D. (2010b) 'Discovering wildlife tourism: a whale shark tourism case study', *Current Issues in Tourism*, 13(4): 351–61.

Causey, A.S. (1989) 'On the morality of hunting,' *Environmental Ethics*, 11: 327–43.

Cavalieri, P. (2001) *The Animal Question: Why Nonhuman Animals Deserve Human Rights*, Oxford: Oxford University Press.

Cavalieri, P. and Singer, P. (1993) 'Preface', in P. Cavalieri and P. Singer (eds) *The Great Ape Project: Equality Beyond Humanity*, New York: St Martin's Press, pp. 1–3.

Cavazzoni, E., Lister, B., Sargent, P. and Schibler, A. (2008) 'Blue-ringed octopus (*Hapalochlaena sp.*) envenomation of a 4-year-old boy: a case report', *Clinical Toxicology*, 46(8): 760–1.

Cavell, S. (1995) *Philosophical Passages: Wittgenstein, Emerson, Austin, Derrida*, Oxford: Blackwell.

Chandroo, K.P., Duncan, I.J.H. and Moccia, R.D. (2004) 'Can fish suffer? Perspectives on sentience, pain, fear, and stress', *Applied Animal Behaviour Science*, 86(3): 225–50.

Chappuis, F., Justafré, J.C., Duchunstang, L. and Taylor, W.R. (2004) 'Dengue fever and long thoracic nerve palsy in a traveller returning from Thailand', *Journal of Travel Medicine*, 11(2): 112–4.

Chang, K.C. (1977) 'Introduction', in K.C. Chang (ed.) *Food in Chinese Culture*, New Haven, CT: Yale University Press, pp. 1–22.

Chen, L.H. *et al.* (2009) 'Illness in long-term travellers visiting GeoSentinel clinics', *Emerging Infectious Diseases*, 15(11): 1773–82.

Chinadaily (2005) 'HK Disneyland draws fire over soup'. Online. Available at: <http://www.chinadaily.com.cn/english/doc/2005–05/24/content_445139.htm> (accessed 11 May 2011).

Christ Unlimited Ministries (n.d.) *Bible on the Web*. Online. Available at: <http://www.bibleontheweb.com/Bible.asp> (accessed 1 March 2010).

Christie-Miller, A. (2011) 'Turkey: tradition of camel wrestling making a comeback', *Eurasianet.org*. Online. Available at: <http://www.eurasianet.org/node/62784> (accessed 9 May 2011).

Clark, S.R.L. (1997) *Animals and their Moral Standing*, London: Routledge.

Clarke, C.H.D. (1958) 'Autumn thoughts of a hunter', *Journal of Wildlife Management*, 22(4): 420–7.

Clayton, S., Fraser, J. and Saunders, C.D. (2009) 'Zoo experiences: conversation, connections, and concerns for animals', *Zoo Biology*, 28(5): 377–97.

Clubb, R. and Mason, G. (2003) 'Animal welfare: captivity effects on wide-ranging carnivores', *Nature*, 425: 473–574.

Clubb, R., Rowlkiffe, M., Lee, P.C., Mor, K.U., Moss, C. and Mason, G.J. (2008) 'Compromised survivorship in zoo elephants', *Science*, 322: 1649.

Clubb, R., Rowlkiffe, M., Lee, P.C., Mor, K.U., Moss, C.J. and Mason G.J. (2009) 'Fecundity and population viability in female zoo elephants: problems and possible solutions', *Animal Welfare*, 18(3): 237–47.

Clutton-Brock, J. (2007) 'How domestic animals have shaped the development of human societies', in L. Kalof (ed.) *A Cultural History of Animals in Antiquity*, New York: Berg, pp. 71–96.

Cohen, C. (1997) 'Do animals have rights?', *Ethics & Behavior*, 7(2): 91–102.

Cohen, Erik (2009) 'The wild and the humanized: animals in Thai tourism', *Anatolia* 20(1): 100–18.

—— (1972) 'Toward a sociology of international tourism', *Social Research*, 39(1): 164–82.

Cohen, Erik and Avieli, N. (2004) 'Food in tourism: attraction and impediment', *Annals of Tourism Research*, 31(4): 755–78.

Cohen, Esther (1994) 'Animals in medieval perception: the image of the ubiquitous other', in A. Manning and J. Serpell (eds) *Animals and Human Society: Changing Perspectives*, London: Routledge, pp. 59–90.

Cohen, K. and Sanyal, N. (2008) 'Catch and release tourism: community, culture and consumptive wildlife tourism strategies in rural Idaho', in B. Lovelock (ed.) *Tourism and the Consumption of Wildlife: Hunting, Shooting and Sport Fishing*, London: Routledge, pp. 227–38.

Cole, D.N. and Spildie, D.R. (1998) 'Hiker, horse and llama trampling effects on native vegetation in Montana, USA', *Journal of Environmental Management*, 53(1): 61–71.

Cole, D.N., Van Wagtendonk, J.W., McClaran, M.P., Moore, P.E. and McDougold, N.K. (2004) 'Response of mountain meadows to grazing by recreational pack stock', *Journal of Range Management*, 57(2): 153–60.

Collins, J., Hanlon, A., More, S.J. and Duggan, V. (2008) 'The structure and regulation of the Irish equine industries: links to consideration of equine welfare', *Irish Veterinary Journal*, 61(11): 746–56.

Comninou, M. (1995) 'Speech, pornography, and hunting', in C.J. Adams and J. Donovan (eds) *Animals and Women: Feminist Theoretical Explorations*, Durham, NC: Duke University Press, pp.126–48.

Companion Air Corporation (2011) 'Companion Air'. Online. Available at: <http://www.companionair.com> (accessed 31 March 2011).

Compassion in World Farming (2011) *Compassion in World Farming: Resources*. Online. Available at: <http://www.ciwf.org.uk/resources/publications/default.aspx> (accessed 18 January 2010).

Connelly, N. and Brown, T. (2010) 'Assessing the economic importance of recreational fishing for communities along Lake Ontario', *Tourism in Marine Environments*, 6(2/3): 63–71.

Cooke, S.J. and Cowx, I.G. (2006) 'Contrasting recreational and commercial fishing: searching for common issues to promote unified conservation of fisheries resources and aquatic environments', *Biological Conservation*, 128(1), 93–108.

Cooke, S.J. and Philipp, D.P. (2004) 'Behaviour and mortality of caught-and-released bonefish (*Albula spp.*) in Bahamian waters with implications for a sustainable recreational fishery', *Biological Conservation*, 118, 599–607.

Cooke, S.J. and Sneddon, L.U. (2007) 'Animal welfare perspectives on recreational angling', *Applied Animal Behaviour Science*, 104(3/4): 176–198.

Cooke, S.J. and Suski, C.D. (2005) 'Do we need species-specific guidelines for catch-and-release recreational angling to effectively conserve diverse fishery resources?', *Biodiversity and Conservation*, 14, 1195–209.

Corkeron, P.J. (2004) 'Whale watching, iconography, and marine conservation', *Conservation Biology*, 18(3), 847–9.

Corson, S.A. and Corson, E.O. (1981) 'Companion animals as bonding catalysts in geriatric institutions', in B. Fogle (ed.) *Interrelation Between People and Pets*, Springfield, IL: Charles C. Thomas, pp. 146–74.

Costelloe, T.M. (2003) 'The invisibility of evil: moral progress and the "Animal Holocaust"', *Philosophical Papers*, 32(2): 109–31.

Coulton, G.G. (1967) *Life in the Middle Ages*, III, 2nd edn, Cambridge: Cambridge University Press.

Craig-Smith, S.J. and Dryden, G.M. (2008) 'Australia as a safari hunting destination for exotic animals', in B. Lovelock (ed.) *Tourism and the Consumption of Wildlife: Hunting, Shooting and Sport Fishing*, London: Routledge, pp. 268–80.

Cronen, W. (1991) *Nature's Metropolis: Chicago and the Great West*, New York: W.W. Norton & Co.

Cross, G. (1990) *A Social History of Leisure Since 1600*, State College, PA: Venture.

Crouch, D. (2000) 'Places around us: embodied lay geographies in leisure and tourism', *Leisure Studies*, 19(2): 63–76.

Curry, C.H., McCarthy, J.S., Darragh, H.M., Wake, R.A., Todhunter, R. and Terris, J. (2002) 'Could tourist boots act as vectors for disease transmission in Antarctica?' *Journal of Travel Medicine*, 9(4): 190–3.

Curtin, D. (1991) 'Toward an ecological ethic of care', *Hypatia*, 6(1): 60–74.

Curtin, S. (2005) 'Nature, wild animals and tourism: an experiential view', *Journal of Ecotourism*, 4(1): 1–15.

Curtin, S. and Wilkes, K. (2005) 'British wildlife tourism operators: current issues and typologies', *Current Issues in Tourism*, 8(6): 455–76.

—— (2007) 'Swimming with captive dolphins: current debates and post-experience dissonance', *International Journal of Tourism Research*, 9(2): 131–46.

Cuthbertson, R. (2010) 'Review shines light on lack of direction at zoo', *Calgary Herald*. Online. Available at: <http://www.calgaryherald.com/health/Review+shines+light+lack +direction/3177513/story.html> (accessed 21 June 2010).

Darwin, C. (1872) *The Expression of the Emotions in Man and Animals*, London: John Murray.

Davallon, F. and Davallon, J. (1987) 'Du musée au parc: exposer le vivant', *Society and Leisure*, 10(1): 23–43.

Davenport, J. and Switalski, T.A. (2006) 'Environmental impacts of transport related to tourism and leisure activities', in J. and J. Davenport (eds) *The Ecology of Transportation: Managing Mobility for the Environment*, Dordrecht: Kluwer, pp. 333–60.

Davey, G.C.L. (1993) 'Factors influencing self-rated fear to a novel animal', *Cognition and Emotion*, 7(5): 461–71.

—— (1994) 'Self-reported fears to common indigenous animals in an adult UK population: the role of disgust sensitivity', *British Journal of Psychology*, 85(4): 541–54.

—— (2007a) 'Public perceptions in urban China toward zoos and their animal welfare', *Human Dimensions of Wildlife*, 12(5): 367–74.

—— (2007b) 'Visitors' effects on the welfare of animals in the zoo: a review', *Journal of Applied Animal Welfare Science*, 10(2): 169–83.

Davie, P.S. and Kopf, R.K. (2006) 'Physiology, behaviour and welfare of fish during recreational fishing and after release', *New Zealand Veterinary Journal*, 54(4), 161–72.

Davis, D., Banks, S., Birtles, A., Valentine, P. and Cuthill, M. (1997) 'Whale sharks in Ningaloo Marine Park: managing tourism in an Australian marine protected area', *Tourism Management*, 18(5): 259–71.

Davis, M.S., McKiernan, B., McCullough, S., Nalson, S. Jr. Mondsagar, R.E., Willard, M. and Dorsey, K. (2002) 'Racing Alaskan sled dogs as a model of "Ski asthma"', *American Journal of Respiratory and Critical Care Medicine*, 166: 878–82.

Davis, R.E., Kassel, J. and Schwagmeyer, P. (1976) 'Telencephalic lesions and behaviour in teleosts, *macropodus opercularis*: Reproduction, startle reaction, and operant behaviour in the male', *Behavioral Biology*, 18(2), 165–77.

Davis, S.G. (1997) *Spectacular Nature: Corporate Culture and the Sea World Experience*, Berkeley, CA: University of California Press.

Dawkins, M.S. (1990) 'From an animal's point of view: motivation, fitness, and animal welfare', *Behavioral and Brain Sciences*, 13(1): 1–61.

—— (1998) 'Evolution and animal welfare', *Quarterly Review of Biology*, 73(3): 305–28.

—— (2000) 'Animal minds and animal emotions', *American Zoologist*, 40(6): 883–8.

—— (2006) 'The scientific basis for assessing suffering in animals', in P. Singer (ed.) *In Defense of Animals: The Second Wave*, Malden, MA: Blackwell Publishing, pp. 26–39.

Dawn, K. (2006) 'Moving the media: from foes, or indifferent strangers, to friends', in P. Singer (ed.) *In Defense of Animals: The Second Wave*, Malden, MA: Blackwell Publishing, pp. 196–205.

Dawson, J. and Lovelock, B. (2008) 'Environmental values of consumptive and non-consumptive marine tourists', in B. Lovelock (ed.) *Tourism and the Consumption of Wildlife: Hunting, Shooting and Sport Fishing*, London: Routledge, pp. 129–40.

De Fatima Filla, G. and De Araujo Monteiro-Filho, E.L. (2009) 'Monitoring tourism schooners observing estuarine dolphins (*Soltalia guianensis*) in the estuarine complex of Cananéia, south-east Brazil', *Aquatic Conservation: Marine and Freshwater Ecosystems*, 19(7): 772–8.

DeGrazia, D. (1996) *Taking Animals Seriously: Mental Life and Moral Status*, Cambridge: Cambridge University Press.

—— (1999) 'Animal ethics around the turn of the twenty-first century', *Journal of Agricultural and Environmental Ethics*, 11(2): 111–29.

de Leeuw, A.D. (1996) 'Contemplating the interest of fish: the angler's challenge', *Environmental Ethics*, 18(4): 373–90.

Deleuze, G. and Guattari, F. (1987) *A Thousand Plateaus: Capitalism and Schizophrenia*, Minneapolis, MN: University of Minnesota Press.

Del Sesto, S.L. (1975) 'Roles, rules, and organization: a descriptive account of cockfighting in Louisiana', *Southern Folklore Quarterly*, 38(1): 1–14.

Denver, M., Perez, J. and Aguirre, B.E. (2007) 'Local search and rescue teams in the United States', *Disaster Prevention and Management*, 16(4): 503–12.

de Pender, A.M.G., Winkel, K.D. and Ligthelm, R.J. (2006) 'A probable case of Irukandji syndrome in Thailand', *Journal of Travel Medicine*, 13(4): 240–3.

Derlet, R.W. (2008) 'Backpacking in Yosemite and Kings Canyon National Parks and neighboring wilderness areas: how safe is the water to drink?', *Journal of Travel Medicine*, 15(4): 209–15.

Derrida, J. (2002) 'The animal that therefore I am (more to follow)', *Critical Inquiry*, 28(2): 369–418.

de Veer, M.W., Gallup, G.G. Jr., Theall, L.A., van den Bos, R. and Povinelli, D.J. (2002) 'An eight-year longitudinal study of mirror self-recognition in chimpanzees (*Pan troglodytes*)', *Neuropsychologia*, 41(2): 229–34.

Devendra, C. and Chantalakhana, C. (2002) 'Animals, poor people and food insecurity: opportunities for improved livelihoods through efficient natural resource management', *Outlook on Agriculture*, 31(3): 161–75.

de Villiers, M., Bause, M., Giese, M. and Fourie, A. (2006) 'Hardly hard-hearted: heart rate responses of incubating Northern Giant Petrels (*Macronectes halli*) to human disturbance on sub-Antarctic Marion Island', *Polar Biology*, 29(8): 717–20.

De Waal, F.B.M. (2005) *Our Inner Ape: A Leading Primatologist Explains Why We Are Who We Are*, New York: Riverhead.

Diamond, J. (2005) *Guns, Germs and Steel: A Short History of Everybody for the Last 13,000 Years*, London: Vintage.

Diaz, G. (2000) 'Iditarod dog deaths unjustifiable', *Orlando Sentinal*, 5 March. Online. Available at: <http://articles.orlandosentinel.com/2000-03-05/sports/0003050070_1_dog-iditarod-race> (accessed 24 February 2011).

Diaz, J.H. (2008a) 'Recognizing and reducing the risks of Chagas disease (American Trypanosomiasis) in travelers', *Journal of Travel Medicine*, 15(3): 184–95.

—— (2008b) 'The evaluation, management, and prevention of stingray injuries in travelers', *Journal of Travel Medicine*, 15(2): 102–9.

Dijkstra, M.E. (2004) 'The animal prop: animals as play objects in Dutch folklorist games', *Western Folklore*, 63(1&2): 169–88.

Dinnerstein, D. (1987) *The Rocking of the Cradle and the Ruling of the World*. London: Women's Press.

Dionys de Leeuw, A. (1996) 'Contemplating the interests of fish: the angler's challenge', *Environmental Ethics*, 18(4): 373–90.

Dixon, B.A. (1996) 'The feminist connection between women and animals', *Environmental Ethics*, 18(2): 181–94.

Dobson, J. (2009) 'Towards a utilitarian ethic for marine wildlife tourism', Proceedings of the Coastal and Marine Tourism Conference, Nelson Mandela Bay, South Africa, 23–26 June.

Dod, J. and Cleaver, R. (1608) *A Plaine and Familiar Exposition of the Eleventh and Twelfth Chapters of the Proverbes of Salomon*, London: R. Bradocke for T. Man.

Dolphin Project (n.d.) 'Ric O'Barry's Dolphin Project'. Online. Available at <http://www.dolphinproject.org) (accessed 8 August 2011).

Domalain, J.-Y. (1978) *The Animal Connection*, London: Heinemann.

Domeier, M.L., Dewar, H., and Nasby-Lucas, N. (2003) 'Mortality rate of striped marlin (*Tetrapturus audax*) caught with recreational tackle', *Marine and Freshwater Research*, 54, 435–45.

Donahue, J. and Trump, E. (2006) *The Politics of Zoos: Exotic Animals and their Protectors*, Dekalb, IL: Northern Illinois University Press.

Donald, D. (2006) 'Pangs watched in perpetuity: Sir Edwin Landseer's pictures of dying deer and the ethos of Victorian sportsmanship', in The Animal Studies Group (eds) *Killing Animals*, Urbana, IL: University of Illinois Press, pp. 50–68.

Donlon, J.G., Donlon, J.H. and Agrusa, J. (2010) 'Cultural tourism, camel wrestling, and the tourism "bubble" in Turkey', *Anatolia*, 21(1): 29–39.

Donovan, J. (1990) 'Animal rights and feminist theory', *Journal of Women and Culture in Society*, 15(2): 350–68.

—— (2009) 'Tolstoy's animals', *Society and Animals*, 17(1): 38–52.

Druce, C. and Lymbery, P. (2002) *Outlawed in Europe: How America is Falling Behind Europe in Farm Animal Welfare*, New York: Archimedian Press.

Duffus, D.A. and Dearden, P. (1990) 'Non-consumptive wildlife-oriented recreation: A conceptual framework', *Biological Conservation* 53(3): 213–31.

Duffy, R. and Moore, L. (2010) 'Neoliberalising nature? Elephant-back tourism in Thailand and Botswana', *Antipode*, 42(3): 742–66.

Dunaway, F. (2000) 'Hunting with the camera: nature photography, manliness, and modern memory', *Journal of American Studies*, 34(2): 207–30.

Dunayer, J. (2004) *Speciesism*, Derwood, MD: Ryce Publishing.

Dundes, A. (1993) 'Gallus as Phallus: a psychoanalytic cross-cultural consideration of the cockfight as fowl play', in L.B. Boyer, R.M. Boyer and S.M. Sonnenberg (eds) *The Psychoanalytic Study of Society*, vol. 18, Hillsdale, NJ: The Analytic Press, pp. 23–66.

—— (1994) 'Gallus as Phallus: a psychoanalytic cross-cultural consideration of the cockfight as fowl play', in A. Dundes (ed.) *The Cockfight: A Casebook*, Madison, WI: University of Wisconsin Press, pp. 241–82.

Dunlap, J. and Kellert, S.R. (1989) *Informal Learning at the Zoo: A Study of Attitude and Knowledge Impacts*, Philadelphia, PA: Zoological Society of Philadelphia.

Dunlop, R., Millsopp, S. and Laming, P. (2006) 'Avoidance learning in goldfish (*Carassius auratus*) and trout (*Oncorhynchus mykiss*) and implications for pain perception', *Application of Animal Behaviour Science*, 97(2): 255–71.

Duran, J. (1994) 'Commentary', *Between the Species*, 10: 8–9.

Durant, W. (1935/1963) *Our Oriental Heritage*, New York: Simon and Schuster.

—— (1939/1966) *The Life of Greece*, New York: Simon and Schuster.

Durrheim, D.N. and Leggat, P.A. (1999) 'Risk to tourists posed by wild mammals in South Africa', *Journal of Travel Medicine*, 6(3): 172–9.

Echeverria, P., Piyaphong, S., Bodhidatta, L., Hoge, C.W. and Tungsen, C. (1994) 'Bacterial enteric pathogens in uncooked foods in Thai markets', *Journal of Travel Medicine*, 1(2): 63–7.

Edington, J.M. and Edington, M.A. (1986) *Ecology, Recreation and Tourism*, Cambridge: Cambridge University Press.

Ehrlich, P. (2000) *Human Natures: Genes, Cultures, and the Human Prospect*, New York: Penguin.

Ehrlich, P. and Ehrlich, A. (1981) *Extinction: The Causes and Consequences of the Disappearance of Species*, New York: Random House.

Eliason, S.L. (2008) 'A statewide examination of hunting and trophy nonhuman animals: perspectives of Montana hunters', *Society and Animals*, 16(3): 256–78.

Emel, J. (1995) 'Are you man enough, big and bad enough? Ecofeminism and wolf eradication in the USA', *Environment and Planning D: Society and Space*, 13(6): 707–34.

Engber, D. (2006) 'How deadly are stingrays? The numbers behind the Crocodile Hunter's death', *Slate*. Online. Available at: <http://www.slate.com/id/2148992> (accessed 11 May 2011).

Ericsson, C.D., Malgarejo, N.A., Jelinek, T. and McCarthy, A. (2009) 'Travelers' preferences for the treatment and prevention of acute diarrhea', *Journal of Travel Medicine*, 16(3): 172–8.

Ericsson, G., Heberlein, T.A., Karlsson, J., Bjärvall, A. and Lundvall, A. (2004) 'Support for hunting as a means of wolf (*Canis lupis*) population control in Sweden', *Wildlife Biology*, 10(4): 269–76.

Etter, H.-J., Meister, R. and Atkins, D. (2005) 'ICAR and its importance in avalanche rescue', in K. Elder (ed.) *Proceedings ISSW 2004. International Snow Science Workshop*, 19–24 September, Jackson Hole, WY, pp. 360–9.

European Cetacean Bycatch Campaign (2011) 'Animal welfare and the treaty of Amsterdam'. Online. Available at: <http://www.eurocbc.org/page673.html> (accessed 11 April 2011).

Evans, E.P. (1906/1987) *The Criminal Prosecution and Capital Punishment of Animals*, London: Faber and Faber.

Evans, S. (2009) 'Pugmarks, tyre-tracks and footprints: the actual and potential roles of ecotourism in protecting wild tigers in India', in J. Hill and T. Gale (eds) *Ecotourism and*

Environmental Sustainability: Principles and Practice, Farnham, UK: Ashgate Publishing, pp. 125–37.

Everett, S. (2009) 'Beyond the visual gaze? The pursuit of an embodied experience through food tourism', *Tourist Studies*, 8(3): 337–58.

Fa, J.E. (1992) 'Visitor-directed aggression among the Gibraltar macaques', *Zoo Biology*, 11(1): 43–52.

Farm Animal Rights Movement (2010) 'Number of farmed animals killed in USA drops!'. Online. Available at: <www.blog.farmusa.org> (accessed 2 June 2010).

Farm Animal Welfare Council (2009) 'Five Freedoms'. Online. Available at: <http://www.fawc.org.uk/freedoms.htm> (accessed 3 May 2011).

Farnham, A. (1992) 'A bang that's worth ten billion bucks', *Fortune*, 9 March. Online. Available at: <http://money.cnn.com/magazines/fortune/fortune_archive/1992/03/09/76155/index.htm> (accessed 15 February 2011).

Fennell, D.A. (2000) 'Ecotourism on trial: the case of billfishing as ecotourism', *Journal of Sustainable Tourism*, 8(4): 341–5.

—— (2006) *Tourism Ethics*, Clevedon, UK: Channel View Publications.

—— (2008a) *Ecotourism*, 3rd edn, London: Routledge.

—— (2008b) 'Responsible tourism: A Kierkegaardian perspective', *Tourism Recreation Research*, 33(1): 3–12.

—— (2009) 'The nature of pleasure in pleasure travel', *Tourism Recreation Research*, 34(2): 123–34.

Fennell, D.A. and Ebert, K. (2004) 'Tourism and the precautionary principle', *Journal of Sustainable Tourism*, 12(6): 461–79.

Fennell, D.A. and Malloy, D.C. (2007) *Codes of Ethics in Tourism: Practice, Theory, Synthesis*, Toronto, ON: Channel View.

Fennell, D.A. and Nowaczek, A. (2010) 'Moral and empirical dimensions of human–animal interactions in ecotourism: deepening an otherwise shallow pool of debate', *Journal of Ecotourism*, 9(3): 239–55.

Fenner, P.J. (1998a) 'Dangers in the ocean: the traveller and marine envenomation. I. Jellyfish', *Journal of Travel Medicine*, 5(3): 135–41.

—— (1998b) 'Dangers in the ocean: the traveller and marine envenomation. II. Marine invertebrates', *Journal of Travel Medicine*, 5(4): 213–6.

Finch, A. and Nash, S. (2001) *Greyhound*, London: Trafalgar Square Press.

Fine, A.H. (2002) *Handbook of Animal Assisted Therapy: Theoretical Foundations and Guidelines for Practice*, San Diego, CA: Academic Press.

Finkelstein, Jacob J. (1981) 'The ox that gored', *Transactions of the American Philosophical Society*, 71(2): 1–89.

Finkelstein, Joanne (1989) *Dining Out: A Sociology of Modern Manners*, Cambridge: Polity.

Fjellström, R. (2002) 'Specifying speciesism', *Environmental Values*, 11(1): 63–74.

Flesness, N.R., Lukens Jr., D.R., Porter, S.B., Wilson, C.R. and Grahn, L.V. (1995) 'ISIS and studbooks: very high consensus correlation for the North American zoo population – a reply to Earnhardt, Thompson, and Willis', *Zoo Biology*, 14(6): 509–17.

Florida Museum of Natural History (2011) 'Whale shark research on the Belize barrier reef'. Online. Available at: <http://www.flmnh.ufl.edu/fish/sharks/whaleshark/whalebelize/tourism.htm> (accessed 6 May 2011).

Floyd, T. (1999) 'Bear-inflicted human injury and fatality', *Wilderness and Environmental Medicine*, 10(2): 75–87.

Fogle, B. (1988) 'Search-and-rescue dogs', *Canadian Veterinary Journal*, 29: 536–7.

Food and Agriculture Organization of the United Nations (FAO) (2006) 'Livestock impacts on the environment', *Magazine of the Agriculture and Consumer Protection Department*. Online. Available at: <http://www.fao.org/ag/magazine/0612sp1.htm> (accessed 11 May 2011).

—— (2009) *Capacity Building to Implement Good Animal Welfare Practices*. Report of the FAO Expert Meeting, FAO Headquarters (Rome), 30 September–3 October.

Forsyth, C.J. and Evans, R.D. (1998) 'Dogmen: the rationalization of deviance', *Society and Animals*, 6(3): 203–18.

Foucault, M. (1979) *Discipline and Punish*, trans. A. Sheridan, New York: Random House.

Fowler, G.S. (1999) 'Behavioural and hormonal responses of Magellanic penguins (*Spheniscus magellanicus*) to tourism and nest site visitation', *Biological Conservation*, 90(2): 143–9.

Fox, M.A. (1999) *Deep Vegetarianism*, Philadelphia, PA: Temple University Press.

Fox Mayshark, J. (2010) 'Deadly fungus threatens total extinction of state bat population', *MetroPulse*. Online. Available at: <http://www.metropulse.com/news/2010/may/19/deadly-fungus-threatens-total-extinction-state-bat> (accessed 11 May 2011).

Francione, G.L. (1996) *Rain Without Thunder: The Ideology of the Animal Rights Movement*, Philadelphia, PA: Temple University Press.

Francis, L.P. and Norman, R. (1978) 'Some animals are more equal', *Philosophy*, 53(206): 507–27.

Frank, J. (2002) 'A constrained-utility alternative to animal rights', *Environmental Values*, 11(1): 49–62.

Franklin, A. (1996) 'Australian hunting and angling sports and the changing nature of human–animal relations in Australia', *Australian and New Zealand Journal of Sociology*, 32 (3): 39–56.

—— (1999) *Animals and Modern Cultures, a Sociology of Human–Animal Relations in Modernity*, London: Sage Publications.

—— (2001) 'New-Darwinism leisures, the body and nature: hunting and angling in modernity', *Body and Society*, 7(4): 57–76.

—— (2008) 'The "animal question" and the "consumption" of wildlife', in B. Lovelock (ed.) *Tourism and the Consumption of Wildlife*, London: Routledge, pp. 31–44.

Franklin, A. and White, R. (2001) 'Animals and modernity: changing human–animal relations, 1949–98', *Journal of Sociology*, 37(3): 219–38.

Franklin, A., Emmison, M., Haraway, D. and Travers, M. (2007) 'Investigating the therapeutic benefits of companion animals: problems and challenges', *Qualitative Sociology Review*, 3(1): 42–58.

Franklin, J.H. (2005) *Animal Rights and Moral Philosophy*, New York: Columbia University Press.

Fraser, J., Gruber, S. and Condon, K. (2007) 'Exposing the tourist value proposition of zoos and aquaria', *Tourism Review International*, 11(3): 279–93.

Fraser, J., Reiss, D., Boyle, P., Lemcke, K., Sickler, J., Elliott, E., Newman, B. and Gruber, S. (2006) 'Dolphins as popular literature and media', *Society and Animals*, 14(4): 321–49.

Frazer, J.G. (1890/1959) *The New Golden Bough: A Study in Magic and Religion*, abridged edn, ed. T.H. Gaster, New York: Macmillan.

Free From Harm (2011) '59 Billion Land and Sea Animals Killed for Food in the US in 2009'. Online. Available at: <http://freefromharm.org/farm-animal-welfare/59-billion-land-and-sea-animals-killed-for-food-in-the-us-in-2009> (accessed 12 May 2011).

Frey, R.G. (1980) *Interests and Rights: The Case Against Animals*, Oxford: Oxford University Press.

—— (1983) *Rights, Killing, and Suffering*, Oxford: Basil Blackwell.

Frohoff, T.G. (2004) 'Stress in dolphins', *Encyclopedia of Animal Behaviour*, Westport, CT: Greenwood Press.

Frohoff, T.G. and Packard, J.M. (1995) 'Human interactions with free-ranging and captive bottlenose dolphins', *Anthrozoos*, 8(1): 44–53.

Frost, W. (2011) 'Rethinking zoos and tourism', in W. Frost (ed.) *Zoos and Tourism: Conservation, Education, Entertainment?*, Toronto, ON: Channel View Publications, pp. 1–8.

Fudge, E. (2005) 'Two ethics: killing animals in the past and the present', in The Animal Studies Group (eds) *Killing Animals*, Urbana, IL: University of Illinois Press, pp. 99–119.

Gallup, G.G., Jr. (1970) 'Chimpanzees: self-recognition' *Science*, 167: 86–7.

Gallup, G.G., Anderson, J.R. and Shillito, D.J. (2002) 'The mirror test', in M. Bekoff, C. Alen, and G. Burghardt (eds) *The Cognitive Animal*, Cambridge, MA: MIT Press, pp. 325–34.

Garner, R. (2004) *Animals, Politics and Morality*, New York: Manchester University Press.

—— (2005) *The Political Theory of Animal Rights*, New York: Manchester University Press.

Garrod, B. (2007) 'Marine wildlife tourism and ethics', in J. Higham and M. Luck (eds) *Marine Wildlife and Tourism Management: Insights from the Natural and Social Sciences*, Wallingford, Oxon: CABI, pp. 257–71.

Gautret, P., Schwartz, E., Shaw, M., Soula, G., Gazin, P., Delmont, J., Parola, P., Soavi, M.J., Matchett, E., Brown, G. and Torresi, J. (2007) 'Animal-associated injuries and related diseases among returned travellers: a review of the GeoSentinel Surveillance Network', *Vaccine*, 25(14): 2656–63.

Geertz, C. (2005) 'Deep play: notes on the Balinese cockfight', *Daedalus*, 134(4): 56–86.

Geiser, K. (1999) 'Establishing a general duty of precaution in environmental protection policies in the United States: a proposal', in C. Raffensperger and J.A. Tickner (eds) *Protecting Public Health and the Environment: Implementing the Precautionary Principle*, Washington, DC: Island Press, pp. xxi–xxvi.

Geneletti, D. and Dawa, D. (2009) 'Environmental impact assessment of mountain tourism in developing regions: a study in Ladakh, Indian Himalaya', *Environmental Impact Assessment Review*, 29(4): 229–42.

George, K. (1992) 'The use and abuse of scientific studies', *Journal of Agricultural and Environmental Studies*, 5(2): 217–33.

Gershwin, L.-A. (2007) '*Malo kingi*: a new species of Irukandji jellyfish (Cnidaria: Cubozoa: Carybdeida), possibly lethal to humans, from Queensland, Australia', *Zootaxa*, 1659: 55–68.

Gill, J.E. (1969) 'Theriophily in antiquity: a supplementary account', *Journal of the History of Ideas*, 30(3): 401–12.

Gilligan, C. (1982) *In a Different Voice: Psychological Theory and Women's Development*, Cambridge, MA: Harvard University Press.

Girgen, J. (2003) 'The historical and contemporary prosecution and punishment of animals', *Animal Law*, 9: 97–133.

Goedeke, T.L. (2004) 'In the eye of the beholder: changing social perceptions of the Florida manatee', *Society & Animals*, 12(2): 99–116.

Goodwin, H. (1996) 'In pursuit of ecotourism', *Biodiversity and Conservation*, 5: 277–91.

Goodpaster, K. (1978) 'On being morally considerable', *Journal of Philosophy*, 75(6): 308–25.

Grabowski, P. and Behrens, R.H. (1996) 'Provision of health information by British travel agents', *Tropical Medicine and International Health*, 1(5): 730–2.

Grady, J.D. and Burnett, J.W. (2003) 'Irukandji-like syndrome in South Florida divers', *Annals of Emergency Medicine*, 42(6): 763–6.

Graft, D. (1997) 'Against strong speciesism', *Journal of Applied Philosophy*, 14(2): 107–18.

Gray, G.G. (1993) *Wildlife and People: The Human Dimensions of Wildlife Ecology*, Chicago, IL: University of Illinois Press.

Gray, J. (1991) 'On the morality of speciesism', *Psychologist*, 4(5): 196–8.

Gray, S. (1979) *Southern African Literature: An Introduction*, Cape Town: David Philip.

Green, R. and Higginbottom, K. (2001) 'The negative effects of wildlife tourism on wildlife', Wildlife Tourism Research Report Series No. 5, Sustainable Tourism Cooperative Research Centre, Gold Coast, Australia.

Greenblat, S. (2004) *Will in the World: How Shakespeare Became Shakespeare*, New York: W.W. Norton.

Greensboring (2011) 'Tijuana donkey show'. Online. Available at: <http://greensboring.com/viewtopic.php?f=21&t=328> (accessed 10 January 2011).

Greenwood, Z., Black, J., Weld, L., O'Brien, D., Leder, K., Von Sonnenberg, F., Pandey, P., Schwartz, E., Connor, B.A., Brown, G., Freedman, D.O. and Torresi, J. (2008) 'Gastrointestinal infection among international travelers globally', *Journal of Travel Medicine*, 15(4): 221–8.

Gregoire, L. (2008) 'Cold warriors', *Canadian Geographic*, 128(5): 34–50.

Griffin, D.R. (2001) *Animal Minds: Beyond Cognition to Consciousness*, Chicago, IL: University of Chicago Press.

Griffin, E. (2005) *England's Revelry: A History of Popular Sports and Pastimes 1660–1830*, Oxford: Oxford University Press.

Grimaldi, W., Jabour, J. and Woehler, E.J. (2011) 'Considerations for minimising the spread of infectious disease in Antarctic seabirds and seals', *Polar Record*, 47(240): 56–66.

Griner, L. (1983) *Pathology of Zoo Animals: A Review of Necropsies Conducted Over a Fourteen-Year Period at the San Diego Zoo and San Diego Wild Animal Park*, San Diego, CA: Zoological Society of San Diego.

Grinnell, G.B. (1892) 'Shooting without a gun', *Forest and Stream*, 287.

Gross, R.M. (1997) 'Toward a Buddhist environmental ethic', *Journal of the American Academy of Religion*, 65(2): 333–53.

Gruen, L. (2010) 'The moral status of animals', *Stanford Encyclopedia of Philosophy*. Online. Available at: <http://plato.stanford.edu/entries/moral-animal> (accessed 19 October 2010).

Grundlingh, A. (2003) '"Gone to the dogs": the cultural politics of gambling – the rise and fall of British greyhound racing on the Witwatersrand, 1932–1949', *South African Historical Journal*, 48(1): 174–89.

Guillermo, K. (2004) 'Response to Nathan Snaza's "(Im)possible witness: viewing PETA's 'Holocaust on Your Plate'"', *Animal Liberation Philosophy and Policy Journal*, 2(2): 1–2.

Gunn, A.S. (1983) 'Traditional ethics and the moral status of animals,' *Environmental Ethics*, 5(2): 133–53.

Gurung, D.B. and Seeland, K. (2009) 'Ecotourism benefits and livelihood improvement for sustainable development in the nature conservation areas of Bhutan', *Sustainable Development*. Online (subscription required). Available at: <http://onlinelibrary.wiley.com/doi/10.1002/sd.443/pdf> (accessed 19 February 2011).

Hadley, J. (2004) 'Using and abusing others: a reply to Machan', *Journal of Value Inquiry*, 38(3): 411–4.

Hall, C.M. and Sharples, L. (2003) 'The consumption of experience or the experience of consumption? An introduction to the tourism of taste', in C.M. Hall, Sharples, L.,

Mitchell, R., Macionis, N. and Cambourne, B. (eds) *Food Tourism Around the World: Development, Management, Markets*, New York: Butterworth-Heinemann, pp. 1–24.

Hall, D. and Brown, F. (2006) *Tourism and Welfare: Ethics, Responsibility and Sustained Well-being*, Wallingford, Oxon: CABI.

Hall, D., Roberts, L., Wemelsfelder, F. and Farish, M. (2004) 'Animal attractions, welfare and the rural experience economy', in D. Hall , L. Roberts, and M. Mitchell (eds), *New Directions in Rural Tourism*, London: Ashgate, pp. 90–101.

Hall, M.J., Anthony, N.G., Ursono, R.J., Holloway, H. Fullerton, C. and Casper, J. (2004) 'Psychological impact of the animal–human bond in disaster preparedness and response', *Journal of Psychiatric Practice*, 10(6): 368–74.

Hallie, P.P. (1977) 'The Ethics of Montaigne's "De la cruauté"', in R.C. La Charité (ed.) *O un Amy! Essays on Montaigne in Honor of Donald M. Frame*, Lexington, KY: French Forum.

Hamill, T.A. (2009) 'Cockfighting as cultural allegory in early modern England', *Journal of Medieval and Early Modern Studies*, 39(2): 375–406.

Hancocks, D. (2001) *A Different Nature: The Paradoxical World of Zoos and their Uncertain Future*, Berkeley, CA: University of California Press.

Haraway, D.J. (1989) *Primate Visions: Gender, Race, and Nature in the World of Modern Science*, London: Routledge.

—— (1991) *Simians, Cyborgs, and Women: The Reinvention of Nature*, New York: Routledge.

Hare, B., Brown, M., Williamson, C. and Tomasello, C. (2002) 'The domestication of social cognition in dogs', *Science*, 298(5598): 1634–6.

Harker, D. and Bates, D.C. (2007) 'The black bear hunt in New Jersey: a constructionist analysis of an intractable conflict', *Society and Animals*, 15(4): 329–52.

Harris, I. (2009) 'Buddhism', in J. Baird Callicott and R. Frodeman (eds) *Encyclopedia of Environmental Ethics and Philosophy*, Detroit, MI: Gale, pp. 120–5.

Harris, J. (1993) 'Horse riding impacts in Victoria's Alpine National Park', *Australian Ranger*, 27: 14–6.

Harrison, P. (1989) 'Theodicy and animal pain', *Philosophy*, 64: 79–92.

—— (1991) Do animals feel pain? *Philosophy*, 66: 25–40.

—— (1992) 'Descartes on animals', *Philosophical Quarterly*, 42(167): 219–27.

—— (1997) 'Do animals feel pain?' in E. Soifer (ed.) *Ethical Issues: Perspectives for Canadians*, Peterborough, Ontario: Broadview Press.

Harrison, R. (1964) *Animal Machines: The New Factory Farming*, London: Vincent Stuart.

Harrison, S.L., Leggat, P.A., Fenner, P.J., Durrheim, D.N. and Swinbourne, A.L. (2004) 'Reported knowledge, perceptions, and behavior of tourists and North Queensland residents at risk of contact with jellyfish that cause the "Irukandji syndrome"', *Wilderness and Environmental Medicine*, 15(1): 4–10.

Harvey, S. (2007) 'Close encounters with wild animals: evaluating a new form of wildlife tourism', MA thesis, Nicholas School of the Environment and Earth Sciences, Duke University. Online. Available at: <http://hdl.handle.net/10161/424> (accessed 10 January 2011).

Håstein, T., Scarfe, A.D. and Lund, V.L. (2005) 'Science-based assessment of welfare: aquatic animals', *Revue scientifique et technique (International Office of Epizootics)*, 24(2): 529–47.

Hearne, V. (1987) *Adam's Task: Calling Animals by Name*, New York: Random House.

—— (1994) *Animal Happiness: A Moving Exploration of Animals and Their Emotions*, New York: Skyhorse Publishing.

Hediger, H. (1964) *Wild Animals in Captivity*, New York: Dover.

Heerwagen, J. (2009) 'Biophilia', in J. Baird Callicott and R. Frodeman (eds) *Encyclopedia of Environmental Ethics and Philosophy*, vol. 1, Detroit, MI: Gale, pp. 109–13.

Helgadottir, G. (2006) 'The culture of horsemanship and horse-based tourism in Iceland', *Current Issues in Tourism*, 9(6): 535–48.

Hemsworth, H. (2008) 'Ethical stockmanship', *Australian Veterinary Journal*, 85(5): 194–200.

Henderson, B. and Potter, T. (2001) 'Outdoor adventure education in Canada: seeking the country way back in', *Canadian Journal of Environmental Education*, 6(1): 225–42.

Henheffer, T. (2010) 'When the sea goes silent', *Maclean's*, 27 December issue. Online. Available at: <http://www2.macleans.ca/2010/12/16/when-the-sea-goes-silent> (accessed 10 February 2011).

Henry, P. (2000) 'Getting the message in Montaigne's *Essays*', *Philosophy and Literature*, 24(1): 165–84.

Herda-Rapp, A. and Goedeke, T.L. (2005) *Mad About Wildlife: Looking at Social Conflict over Wildlife*, Boston, MA: Brill.

Herrero, S. (1989) 'The role of learning in some fatal grizzly bear attacks on people', in M. Bromley (ed.) *Bear–People Conflicts: Proceedings of a Symposium on Management Strategies*, Northwest Territories Department of Renewable Resources, 6–10 April, Yellowknife, Canada, pp. 9–14.

Herrero, S. and Fleck, S. (1990) 'Injury to people inflicted by black, grizzly or polar bears: recent trends and new insights', *International Association of Bear Research and Management*, 8: 25–32.

Herrero, S. and Higgins, A. (1999) 'Human injuries inflicted by bears in British Columbia: 1960–97', *Ursus*, 11: 209–18.

Herrero, S., Smith, T., DeBruyn, T.D., Gunther, K. and Matt, C.A. (2005) 'From the field: brown bear habituation to people – safety, risks, and benefits', *Wildlife Society Bulletin*, 33(1): 362–73.

Herzog, H. (2002) 'Darwinism and the study of human–animal interactions', *Society & Animals*, 10(4): 361–7.

Herzog, H.A. and McGee, S. (1983) 'Psychological aspects of slaughter reactions of college students to killing and butchering cattle and hogs,' *International Journal for the Study of Animal Problems*, 4(2): 124–32.

Hester, J.J. (1967) 'The agency of man in animal extinctions', in P.S. Martin and H.E. Wright (eds) *Pleistocene Extinctions: The Search for a Cause*, New Haven, CT: Yale University Press, pp. 169–92.

Heuvelink, A.E., van Heerwaarden, C., Zwortkruis-Nohuis, J.T., van Oosterom, R., Edink, K., van Duynhoven, Y.T. and de Boer, E. (2002) '*Escherichia coli* O157 infection associated with a petting zoo', *Epidemiology and Infection*, 129(2): 295–302.

Higginbottom, K. (2004) 'Wildlife tourism: an introduction', in K. Higginbottom (ed.) *Wildlife Tourism: Impacts, Management and Planning*, Altona, Victoria: Common Ground Publishing, pp. 1–14.

Higginbottom, K., Tribe, A. and Booth, R. (2003) 'Contributions of non-consumptive wildlife tourism to conservation', in R. Buckley and D.B. Weaver (eds) *Nature-based Tourism, Environment and Land Management*, Wallingford, Oxon: CABI, pp. 181–92.

Hill, C.M. (2002) 'Primate conservation and local communities: ethical issues and debates', *American Anthropologist*, 104(4): 1184–94.

Hinchcliff, K.W. (1996) 'Performance failure in Alaskan sled dogs: biochemical correlate', *Research in Veterinary Science*, 61(3): 271–2.

Hoage, R.J., Roskell, A. and Mansour, J. (1996) 'Menageries and zoos to 1900', in R.J. Hoage and W.A. Deiss (eds) *New Worlds, New Animals: From Menagerie to Zoological Park in the Nineteenth Century*, Baltimore, MD: Johns Hopkins University Press, p. 10.

Hobson-West, P. (2007) 'Beasts and boundaries: an introduction to animals in sociology, science and society', *Qualitative Sociology Review*, 3(1): 23–41.

Hockings, K.J. (2009) 'Living at the interface: human–chimpanzee competition, coexistence and conflict in Africa', *Interaction Studies*, 10(2): 183–205.

Hoff, C. (1983) 'Kant's invidious humanism,' *Environmental Ethics*, 5(1): 63–70.

Holland, A.J. (1984) 'On behalf of moderate speciesism', *Journal of Applied Philosophy*, 1(2): 281–91.

Holland, S.M., Ditton, R.B. and Graefe, A. (1998) 'An ecotourism perspective on billfish industries', *Journal of Sustainable Tourism*, 6(2): 97–116.

Holland, S.M., Ditton, R.B. and Graefe, A. (2000). 'A response to "Ecotourism on Trial: The Case of Billfish Angling as Ecotourism"', *Journal of Sustainable Tourism*, 8(4): 346–51.

Honderich, T. (ed.) (1995) *The Oxford Companion to Philosophy*, New York: Oxford University Press.

Hopkins, Keith (1983) *Death and Renewal*, Cambridge: Cambridge University Press.

Hopkins, Kyle (2010) 'Iditarod ends with no dog deaths', *Anchorage Daily News*, 21 March. Online. Available at: <http://www.adn.com/2010/03/20/1192545/iditarod-ends-with-no-dog-deaths.html> (accessed 25 February 2010).

Horowitz, S. (2008) 'The human–animal bond: health implications across the lifespan', *Mary Ann Liebert, Inc.*, 14(5): 251–6.

Houlihan, P.F. (1996) *The Animal World of the Pharaohs*, London: Thames and Hudson.

Hughes, P. (2001) 'Animals, values and tourism: structural shifts in UK dolphin tourism provision', *Tourism Management*, 22(4): 321–9.

Humane Slaughter Association (2011) 'Fish Slaughter'. Online. Available at: <http://www.hsa.org.uk/Information/Slaughter/Fish%20slaughter.htm> (accessed 11 May 2011).

Humane Society International (HSI) (n.d.) 'Caribbean News'. Online. Available at: <http://www.hsi.org/world/caribbean> (accessed 10 August 2011).

Humphrey, N. (2002) *The Mind Made Flesh: Essays from the Frontiers of Psychology and Evolution*, Oxford: Oxford University Press.

Huntingford, F.A., Adams, C., Braithwaite, V.A., Kadri, S., Pottenger, T.G., Sandøe, P. and Turnbull, J. F. (2006). 'Current issues in fish welfare', *Journal of Fish Biology*, 68(2): 332–72.

—— (2007) 'The implications of feelings-based approach to fish welfare: a reply to Arlinghaus *et al.*', *Fish and Fisheries*, 8(3): 277–80.

Hursthouse, R. (2000) *Ethics, Humans and Other Animals*, New York: Routledge.

Hutchins, M. (2004) 'Zoo vs. sanctuary', *Communique*, August: 54–6.

Hutchins, M. and Keele, M. (2006) 'Elephant importation from range countries: ethical and practical considerations for accredited zoos', *Zoo Biology*, 25(3): 219–33.

Hyde, W.W. (1916) 'The prosecution and punishment of animals and lifeless things in the Middle Ages and modern times', *University of Pennsylvania Law Review*, 64(7): 696–730.

IATA (2011) 'Live Animals Regulations'. Online. Available at: <http://www.iata.org/ps/publications/Pages/live-animals.aspx?NRMODE=Unpublished> (accessed 3 May 2011).

Iossa, G., Soulsbury, C.C. and Harris, S. (2009) 'Are wild animals suited to a travelling circus life?', *Animal Welfare*, 18: 129–40.

Irvine, L. (2007) 'The question of animal selves: implications for sociological knowledge and practice', *Qualitative Sociology Review*, 3(1): 5–22.

—— (2009) *Filling the Ark: Animal Welfare in Disasters*, Philadelphia, PA: Temple University Press.

Irwin, P.J. (2002) 'Companion animal parasitology: a clinical perspective', *International Journal of Parasitology*, 32(5): 581–93.

Isbell, L.A. (2006) 'Snakes as agents of evolutionary change in primate brains', *Journal of Human Evolution*, 51(1): 1–35.

Isbister, G.K. (2001) 'Venomous fish stings in tropical northern Australia', *The American Journal of Emergency Medicine*, 19(7): 561–5.

Isidore, St. (2007) 'Etymologiae XII, 1, 1', in *The Etymologies of Isidore of Spain*, trans. S. Barney, Cambridge: Cambridge University Press.

Ito, M. (2008) 'Seeing animals, speaking of nature: visual culture and the question of animal', *Theory, Culture & Society*, 25(4): 119–37.

Ito, T. (2006) 'Between ideals, realities, and popular perceptions: an analysis of the multifaceted nature of London Zoo, 1828–1848', *Society & Animals*, 14(2): 159–78.

Iwama, G.K. (2007) 'The welfare of fish', *Diseases of Aquatic Organisms*, 75: 155–8.

Jacobs, M.H. (2009) 'Why do we like or dislike animals?', *Human Dimensions of Wildlife*, 14(1): 1–11.

Jamal, T., Borges, M, and Stronza, A. (2006) 'The institutionalization of ecotourism: certification, cultural equity and praxis', *Journal of Ecotourism*, 5(3): 145–75.

Jamieson, D. (2006) 'Against zoos', in P. Singer (ed.) *In Defense of Animals: The Second Wave*, Malden, MA: Blackwell Publishing, pp. 132–43.

Jamison, W.V. and Lunch, W.M. (1992) 'Rights of animals, perceptions of science, and political activism: profile of American animal rights activists', *Science, Technology, & Human Values*, 17(4): 438–58.

Jerolmack, C. (2008) 'How pigeons became rats: the cultural-spatial logic of problem animals', *Social Problems*, 55(1): 72–94.

Johns, B.G. (1996) 'Responses of chimpanzees to habituation and tourism in the Kibale Forest, Uganda', *Biological Conservation*, 78(3): 257–62.

Johnson, B. and Pierce, J. (2008) 'Morality in animals? Yes, no, maybe', *Environmental Philosophy*: 1–17.

Jones, E.L. (2009) 'The environmental effects of blood sports in lowland England since 1750', *Rural History*, 20(1): 51–66.

Jones, S.G. (1986) *Workers at Play: Social and Economic History of Leisure 1918–1939*, London: Routledge.

Jorgenson, J. (1997) 'Therapeutic use of companion animals in health care', *Journal of Nursing Scholarship*, 29(3): 249–56.

Jülg, B., Elias, J., Zohn, A., Köppen, S. Becker-Gaab, C. and Bogner, J.R. (2008) 'Bat-associated histoplasmosis can be transmitted at entrances of bat caves and not only inside caves', *Journal of Travel Medicine* 15(2): 133–6.

Junior, V.H., de Paulo Neto, J.B. and Cobo, V.J. (2006) 'Venomous mollusks: the risks of human accidents by Conus snails (Gastropoda: Conidae) in Brazil', *Revista da Sociedade Brasileira de Medicina Tropical*, 39(5): 498–500.

Kalof, L. (2007a) *A Cultural History of Animals in Antiquity*, New York: Berg.

——— (2007b) *Looking at Animals in Human History*, London: Reaktion Books.

Kalof, L. and Fitzgerald, A. (2003) 'Reading the trophy: exploring the display of dead animals in hunting magazines', *Visual Studies*, 18(2): 112–22.

Kalof, L. and Fitzgerald. A. (eds) (2007) *The Animals Reader: The Essential Classic and Contemporary Writings*, Oxford: Berg.

Kaltenborn, B.P., Bjerke, T. and Nyahongo, J. (2006) 'Living with problem animals – self-reported fear of potentially dangerous species in the Serengeti region, Tanzania', *Human Dimensions of Wildlife*, 11(6): 397–409.

Karatzanis, A.D., Bourolias, C.A., Prokopakis, E.P., Shiniotaki, I. Panagiotaki, I.E. and Velegrakis, G.A. (2009) 'Anaphylactic reactions on the beach: a cause for concern?', *Journal of Travel Medicine*, 16(2): 84–7.

Karpf, A. (2001) 'Comment: Farmers' grief leaves us all bereft', *The Guardian*, 12 April. Online. Available at: <http://www.guardian.co.uk/uk/2001/apr/12/footandmouth. comment?INTCMP=SRCH> (accessed 23 February 2011).

Katcher, A.H. and Friedmann, E. (1980) 'Potential health value of pet ownership', *Compendium of Continuing Education Practice Vet*, 2(2): 117–21.

Kaushik, S.J. (1999) 'Animals for work, recreation and sports', *Livestock Production Science*, 59(2–3): 145–54.

Kellert, S.R. (1979) 'Zoological Parks in American Society. Address to the American Association of Zoological Parks and Aquaria', *AAZPA Annual Conference Proceedings*, pp. 88–126.

—— (1980) 'Contemporary values of wildlife in American society', in W. Shaw and E. Zube (eds) *Wildlife Values*, US Forest Service, Rocky Mountain Forest and Range Experimental Station, Ser. Rep. 1, pp. 31–60.

—— (1993) 'Attitudes, knowledge, and behavior toward wildlife among the industrial superpowers: United States, Japan, and Germany', *Journal of Social Issues*, 49(1), 53–69.

Kellert, S.R. and Berry, J.K. (1987) 'Attitudes, knowledge, and behaviors toward wildlife as affected by gender', *Wildlife Society Bulletin*, 15(3): 363–71.

Kellert, S.R., Black, M., Rush, C.R. and Bath, A.J. (1996) 'Human culture and large carnivore conservation in North America', *Conservation Biology*, 10: 977–90.

Kemp, S.F. (1999) 'Sled dog racing: the celebration of co-operation in a competitive sport', *Ethnology*, 38(1): 81–95.

Kete, K. (2002) 'Animals and ideology: the politics of animal protection in Europe', in N. Rothfels (ed.) *Representing Animals*, Indianapolis, IN: Indiana University Press, pp. 19–34.

—— (2007) *A Cultural History of Animals: In the Age of Empire*, New York: Berg.

Kharel, M., Neopane, S.P. and Shrestha, R. (2008) 'Performance characteristics of the yak in Nepal and its crosses with mountain cattle'. Online. Available at: <http://agtr.ilri.cgiar. org/Casestudy/yak/pdf/Yak.pdf> (accessed 21 February 2011).

Kheel, M. (1985) 'The liberation of nature: a circular affair', *Environmental Ethics*, 7(2): 135–49.

—— (1995) 'License to kill: an ecofeminist critique of hunters' discourse', in C.J. Adams and J. Donovan (eds) *Animals and Women: Feminist Theoretical Explorations*, Durham, NC: Duke University Press, pp. 85–125.

—— (1996) 'The killing game: an ecofeminist critique of hunting', *Journal of the Philosophy of Sport*, 23(1): 30–44.

Kierkegaard, S. (1859/1939) *The Point of View for my Work as an Author*, trans. W. Lowrie, London: Oxford University Press.

Kim, C.J. (2007) 'Multiculturalism goes imperial: immigrants, animals, and the suppression of moral dialogue', *Du Bois Review*, 4(1): 233–49.

Kinjerski, G. (2010) 'Killer bat disease closes Cadomin cave', *Edmonton Sun*. Online. Available at: <http://www.edmontonsun.com/news/alberta/2010/05/14/13957581.html> (accessed 11 May 2011).

Kluger, J. (2002) 'Hunting made easy', *Time*, 11 March, p. 62.

Knight, J. (2005) 'Introduction', in J. Knight (ed.) *Animals in Person: Cultural Perspectives on Human–Animal Intimacy*, New York: Berg, pp. 1–14.

—— (2009) 'Making wildlife viewable: habituation and attraction', *Society and Animals*, 17(2): 167–84.

Knight, S. Nunkoosing, K., Vrij, A. and Cherryman, J. (2003) 'Using grounded theory to examine people's attitudes toward how animals are used', *Society & Animals* 11(4): 307–27.

Knight, S., Vrij, A., Bard, K. and Brandon, D. (2009) 'Science versus human welfare? Understanding attitudes toward animal use', *Journal of Social Issues*, 65(3): 463–83.

Kontogeorgopoulos, N. (2009) 'Wildlife tourism in semi-captive settings: a case study of elephant camps in northern Thailand', *Current Issues in Tourism*, 12(5–6): 429–49.

Koontz, F. (1995) 'Wild animal acquisition ethics for zoo biologists', in B. Norton, M. Hutchins, T.L. Maple and E. Stevens (eds) *Ethics on the Ark: Zoos, Animal Welfare and Wildlife Conservation*, Washington, DC: Smithsonian Institution Press, pp. 38–51.

Koopmans-de Bruijn, R. (2005) 'Fabled liaisons: serpentine spouses in Japanese folktales', in G.M. Pflugfelder and B.L. Walker (eds) *JAPANimals: History and Culture in Japan's Animal Life*, Ann Arbor, MI: Center for Japanese Studies, pp. 61–90.

Korsgaard, C. (1996) *The Sources of Normativity*, Cambridge: Cambridge University Press.

Korte, S.M., Olivier, B. and Koolhaas, J.M. (2007) 'A new animal welfare concept based on allostasis', *Physiology & Behavior*, 92(3): 422–8.

Kovacs, K.M. and Innes, S. (1990) 'The impact of tourism on harp seals (*Phoca groenlandica*) in the Gulf of St. Lawrence, Canada', *Applied Animal Behaviour Science*, 26(1–2): 15–26.

Kreger, M.D. (2008) 'Canvas to concrete: elephants and the circus–zoo relationship', in C. Wemmer and C.A. Christian (eds) *Elephants and Ethics: Toward a Morality of Coexistence*, Baltimore, MD: Johns Hopkins University Press, pp. 185–203.

Kruuk, H. (2002) *Hunter and Hunted: Relationships Between Carnivores and People*, Cambridge: Cambridge University Press.

Kümpel, N.F., Milner-Gulland, E.J., Cowlishaw, G. and Rowcliffe, J.M. (2010) 'Incentives for hunting: the role of bushmeat in the household economy in rural Equatorial Guinea', *Human Ecology*, 38(2): 251–64.

Kwint, M. (2002) 'The circus and nature in late Georgian England', in R. Koshar (ed.) *Histories of Leisure*, New York: Berg, pp. 45–60.

Lamb, D. (1982) 'Animal rights and liberation movements,' *Environmental Ethics*, 4: 215–33.

Langford, D.J., Crager, S.E., Shehzad, Z., Smith, S.B., Sotocinal, S.G., Levenstadt, J.S., Chanda, M.L., Levitin, D.J. and Mogil, J.S. (2006) 'Social modulation of pain as evidence for empathy in mice', *Science*, 312(5782): 1967–70.

Langley, R.L. (2008) 'Animal bites and stings reported by United States Poison Control Centres, 2001–2005', *Wilderness and Environmental Medicine*, 19(1): 7–14.

Lathrop, S.L. (2007) 'Animal-caused fatalities in New Mexico, 1993–2004', *Wilderness and Environmental Medicine*, 18(4): 288–92.

Leach, E. (1964) 'Anthropological aspects of language: animal categories and verbal abuse', in E.H. Lennenberg (ed.) *New Directions in the Study of Language*, Cambridge, MA: MIT Press.

Lee, A.D. (2002) 'Decoding late Roman law', *Journal of Roman Studies*, 92: 185–93.

Lee, S.A., Gibbons, J.A. and Short, S.D. (2010) 'Sympathetic reactions to the bait dog in a film of dog fighting: the influence of personality and gender', *Society and Animals*, 18: 107–25.

Leggat, P.A. and Speare, R. (2000) 'Traveling with pets', *Journal of Travel Medicine*, 7: 325–9.

Lemelin, R.H. (2006) 'The gawk, the glance and the gaze: ocular consumption and polar bear tourism in Churchill, Manitoba, Canada', *Current Issues in Tourism*, 9(6): 516–34.

Leonard, J.A., Wayne, R.K., Wheeler, J., Valadez, R., Guillén, S. and Vilà, C. (2002) 'Ancient DNA evidence for Old World origin of New World dogs', *Science*, 298(5598): 1613–6.

Leopold, A. (1966) *A Sand County Almanac: With Essays on Conservation from Round River*, Toronto, ON: Random House.

Lindsey, P.A., Alexander, R.R., du Toit, J.T. and Mills, M.G.L. (2005) 'The potential contribution of ecotourism to African wild dog *Lycaon pictus* conservation in South Africa', *Biological Conservation*, 123(3): 339–48.

Lindsey, P.A., Alexander, R., Frank, L.G., Mattñson, A. and Romahieach, S.S. (2006) 'Potential for trophy hunting to create incentives for wildlife conservation in Africa where alternative wildlife-based land uses may not be viable', *Animal Conservation*, 9(3): 283–91.

Lindstrom, T.C. (2010) 'The animals of the arena: how and why could their destruction and death be endured and enjoyed?', *World Archaeology*, 42(2): 310–23.

Linhart, P., Adams, D.B. and Voracek, T. (2008) 'The international transportation of zoo animals: conserving biological diversity and protecting animal welfare', *Veterinaria Italiana*, 44 (1): 49–57.

Linnard, A. (2007) 'People moving matters: theorizing tourism and migration on the Nepali "periphery"', School for International Training, Nepal. Online. Available at: <http://digitalcollections.sit.edu/cgi/viewcontent.cgi?article=1147&context=isp_collection> (accessed 22 February 2011).

Linzey, A. (1994) *Animal Theology*, London: SCM Press.

—— (2000) *Animal Gospel: Christian Faith as if Animals Mattered*, Louisville, KY: Westminster John Knox Press.

List, C.J. (1997) 'Is hunting a right thing?', *Environmental Ethics*, 19(4): 405–16.

Locke, J. (1690) 'Essay Concerning Human Understanding'. Online. Available at: <http://oregonstate.edu/instruct/phl302/texts/locke/locke1/Book4b.html#Chapter%20XI> (accessed 27 January 2010).

Loftin, R.W. (1984) 'The morality of hunting,' *Environmental Ethics*, 6(3): 241–50.

—— (1985) 'The medical treatment of wild animals,' *Environmental Ethics*, 7(3): 231–9.

LoGiudice, K. (2006) 'Toward a synthetic view of extinction: a history lesson from a North American rodent', *BioScience*, 56(8): 687–93.

Loisel, G. (1912) *Histoire des Ménageries de L'antiquité à Nos Jours*, vol. 2, Paris: Octave Dion et Fils and Henri Laurens.

Lopez, B. (1986) *Arctic Dreams: Imagination and Desire in a Northern Landscape*, New York: Scribner.

Lott, D.F. (1988) 'Feeding wild animals: the urge, the interaction, and the consequences', *Anthrozoos*, 1(4): 255–7.

Lovelock, B. (2008a) 'An introduction to consumptive wildlife tourism', in B. Lovelock (ed.) *Tourism and the Consumption of Wildlife: Hunting, Shooting and Sport Fishing*, London: Routledge, pp. 3–30.

—— (2008b) 'Conclusion: consumptive wildlife tourism – sustainable niche or endangered species', in B. Lovelock (ed.) *Tourism and the Consumption of Wildlife: Hunting, Shooting and Sport Fishing*, London: Routledge, pp. 281–7.

Ludwig, E.G. (1981) 'People at zoos: A sociological approach', *International Journal for the Study of Animal Problems*, 2(6): 310–16.

Luke, B. (1996) 'Justice, caring, and animal liberation', in J. Donovan and C.J. Adams (eds) *Beyond Animal Rights: A Feminist Caring Ethic for the Treatment of Animals*, New York: Continuum, pp. 77–102.

—— (1997) 'A critical analysis of hunters' ethics', *Environmental Ethics*, 19(1): 25–42.

Lund, V., Mejdell, C.M., Röcklingsberg, H., Anthony, R. and Håstein, T. (2007) 'Expanding the moral circle: farmed fish as objects of moral concern', *Diseases of Aquatic Organisms*, 75(2), 109–18.

Lusseau, D. and Higham, J.E.S. (2004) 'Managing the impacts of dolphin-based tourism through the definition of critical habitats: the case of bottlenose dolphins (*Tursiops* spp.) in Doubtful Sound, New Zealand', *Tourism Management*, 25(6): 657–67.

Lynch, J.L. (1994) 'Is animal pain conscious?', *Between the Species*, 10(1–2):1–7.

Lynn, W.S. (1998) 'Contested moralities: animals and moral value in the Dear/Symanski debate', *Ethics, Place and Environment*, 1(2): 223–42.

Maartens, F., Sharpe, B., Curtis, B., Mthembu, J. and Hatting, I. (2007) 'The impact of malaria control on perceptions of tourists and tourism operators concerning malaria prevalence in KwaZulu-Natal, 1999/2000 versus 2002/2003', *Journal of Travel Medicine*, 14(2): 96–104.

McCormick, J. (1997) 'The bullfight gentrified', *Culture and Society*, 34(4): 48–50.

McDermott, J.P. (1989) 'Animals and humans in early Buddhism', *Indo-Iranian Journal*, 32(4): 269–80.

MacDonnell, N. (2007) 'Live flesh', Dept. of Culture, *style.com*. Online. Available at: <http://www.style.com/stylefile/2007/11/live-flesh/> (accessed 27 May 2010).

McDougal, C. (1980) 'Some observations of tiger behaviour in the context of baiting', *Journal of the Bombay Natural History Society*, 77: 476–85.

McGregor, J. (2005) 'Crocodile crimes: people versus wildlife and the politics of postcolonial conservation on Lake Kariba, Zimbabwe', *Geoforum*, 36(3): 353–69.

Machura, L. (1954) 'Nature protection and tourism: with particular reference to Austria', *Oryx*, 2(5): 307–11.

Machan, T.R. (2002) 'Why human beings may use animals', *Journal of Value Inquiry*, 36(1): 9–14.

McIntosh, I.B., Reed, J.M. and Power, K.G. (1997) 'Travellers' diarrhoea and the effect of pre-travel health advice in general practice', *British Journal of General Practice*, 47(415): 71–5.

Macnaghten, P. and Urry, J. (1998) *Contested Natures*, London: Sage.

McNeill, M.R., Payne, T.A. and Bewsell, D.T. (2008) 'Tourists as vectors of potential invasive alien species and a strategy to reduce risk', Re-creating Tourism, New Zealand Tourism and Hospitality Conference, Hanmer Springs.

MacQueen, K. (2009) 'What Canadians really believe', *Maclean's*, 122(6): 46–50.

Macrokanis, C.J., Hall, N.L. and Mein, J.K. (2004) 'Irukandji syndrome in northern Western Australia: an emerging health problem', *Medical Journal of Australia*, 181(11/12): 699–702.

Madden, R. (2010) 'Imagining the greyhound: "racing" and "rescue" narratives in a human and dog relationship', *Continuum: Journal of Media and Cultural Studies*, 24(4): 503–15.

Malamud, R. (1998) *Reading Zoos: Representations of Animals and Captivity*, New York: New York University Press.

—— (2007) 'Introduction: famous animals in modern culture', in R. Malamud (ed.) *A Cultural History of Animals in the Modern Age*, New York: Berg, pp. 1–26.

—— (2008) 'Americans do weird things with animals, or, why did the chicken cross the road?', in T. Tyler and M. Rossini (eds) *Animal Encounters*, Boston, MA: Brill, pp. 73–96.

Malloy, D.C. and Fennell, D.A. (1998). 'Ecotourism and ethics: moral development and organisational cultures', *Journal of Travel Research*, 36 (Spring): 47–56.

Manson, I., Goodwin, R.A., Loyd, J.E. and des Prez, R.M. (1981) 'Histoplasmosis in normal hosts', *Medicine*, 60(4): 231–66.

Maple, T.L. (2007) 'Toward a science of welfare for animals in zoos', *Journal of Applied Animal Welfare Science*, 10(1): 63–70.

Marino, L., Bradshaw, G. and Malamud, R. (2009) 'The captivity industry: the reality of zoos and aquariums', *Best Friends Magazine*, March/April: 25–7.

Markwell, K. (2001) '"An intimate rendezvous with nature"? Mediating the tourist–nature experience at three tourist sites in Borneo', *Tourist Studies*, 1(1): 39–57.

Markwell, K. and Cushing, N. (2009) 'The serpent's stare meets the tourist's gaze: strategies of display at the Australian Reptile Park', *Current Issues in Tourism*, 12(5&6): 475–88.

—— (2010) *Snake-bitten: Eric Worrell and the Australian Reptile Park*, Sydney, NSW: UNSW Press.

Marvin, G. (1994) *Bullfight*, Illinois: University of Illinois Press.

—— (2002) 'Unspeakability, inedibility, and the structures of pursuit in the English foxhunt', in N. Rothfels (ed.) *Representing Animals*, Bloomington, IN: Indiana University Press, pp. 139–58.

—— (2007) 'Animal and human bodies in the landscapes of English foxhunting', in S. Coleman and T. Kohn (eds) *The Discipline of Leisure: Embodying Cultures of 'Recreation'*, New York: Berghahn Books, pp. 91–108.

Marx, M.B., Stallones, T.F., Garrity, J.R. and Johnson, T.P. (1988) 'Demographics of pet ownership among U.S. adults 21–64 years of age', *Anthrozoos*, 2(1): 33–7.

Mason, M.J. (1987) 'Wilderness family therapy: experiential dimensions', *Contemporary Family Therapy*, 9(1–2): 90–105.

Mason, J. (2005) *An Unnatural Order: The Roots of Our Destruction of Nature*, New York: Lantern Books.

Mason, P. (2000) 'Zoo tourism: the need for more research', *Journal of Sustainable Tourism*, 8(4): 333–9.

—— (2007) 'Roles of the modern zoo: conflicting or complementary?', *Tourism Review International*, 11(3): 251–63.

Massad, E. and Wilder-Smith, A. (2009) 'Risk estimates of Dengue in travellers to Dengue endemic areas using mathematical models', *Journal of Travel Medicine*, 16(3): 191–3.

Masson, J.M. and McCarthy, S. (1995) *When Elephants Weep: The Emotional Lives of Animals*, New York: Delta.

Maunula, M. (2007) 'Of chickens and men: cockfighting and equality in the South', *Southern Cultures*, 13(4): 76–85.

Mavroidi, N. (2008) 'Transmission of zoonoses through immigration and tourism', *Veterinaria Italiana*, 44(4): 651–6.

Mbaiwa, J.E. (2008) 'The success and sustainability of consumptive wildlife tourism in Africa', in B. Lovelock (ed.) *Tourism and the Consumption of Wildlife: Hunting, Shooting and Sport Fishing*, London: Routledge, pp. 141–54.

Mehmetoglu, M. (2005) 'A case study of nature-based tourists: specialists versus generalists', *Journal of Vacation Marketing*, 11(4): 357–69.

—— (2007) 'Typologising nature-based tourists by activity: Theoretical and practical implications', *Tourism Management*, 28(3): 651–60.

Meleshkevich, I. (2005) 'In the gloomy forest of modern photography', *Herald of Europe*. Online. Available at: <http://www.heraldofeurope.co.uk/Article.aspx?ArticleID=1042596108> (accessed 27 May 2010).

Menn, B., Lorentz, S. and Naucke, T.J. (2010) 'Imported and travelling dogs as carriers of canine vector-borne pathogens in Germany', *Parasites & Vectors*, 3: 34.

Midgley, M. (1983) *Animals and Why They Matter*, Harmondsworth: Penguin.

—— (1998) *Animals and Why They Matter*, Athens, GA: The University of Georgia Press.

—— (2002) *Beast and Man: The Roots of Human Nature*, London: Routledge.

Miller, B., Conway, W., Reading, R.P., Wemmer, C., Wildt, D., Kleiman, D., Monfort, S., Rabinowitz, A., Armstrong, B. and Hutchins, M. (2004) 'Evaluating the conservation mission of zoos, aquariums, botanical gardens, and natural history museums', *Conservation Biology*, 18(1): 86–93.

Miller, I. (2005) 'Didactic nature: exhibiting nation and empire at the Ueno Zoological Gardens', in G. Pflugfelder and B. Walker (eds) *JAPANimals: History and Culture in Japan's Animal Life*, Ann Arbor, MI: University of Michigan, pp. 273–313.

Millspaugh, J.J., Barke, T., van Dyk, G., Slotow, R., Washburn, B.E. and Woods, R.J. (2007) 'Stress response of working African elephants to transportation and safari adventures', *Journal of Wildlife Management*, 71(4): 1257–60.

Mimi (2011) 'Consumptive use', Environment. Online. Available at: <http://en.mimi.hu/environment/index_environment.html> (accessed 10 January 2011).

Mitchell, R. and Hall, C.M. (2003) 'Consuming tourists: food tourism consumer behaviour', in C.M. Hall, Sharples, L., Mitchell, R., Macionis, N. and Cambourne, B. (eds) *Food Tourism Around the World: Development, Management, Markets*, New York: Butterworth-Heinemann, pp. 1–24.

Montaigne (n.d.) 'Of Cruelty'. Online. Available at: <http://www.readbookonline.net/readOnLine/22099/> (accessed 7 July 2010).

Monz, C., Roggenbuck, J., Cole, D., Brame, R. and Yoder, A. (2000) 'Wilderness party size regulations: implications for management and a decisionmaking framework', USDA Forest Service Proceedings RMRS-P-15, vol. 4, pp. 265–73.

Mooney, J. (2009) 'Exposed: the evil world of badger baiting', *The Sunday Times*, 22 February. Online. Available at: <http://www.timesonline.co.uk/tol/news/world/ireland/article5781271.ece> (accessed 1 May 2011).

Mordue, T. (2009) 'Angling in modernity: a tour through society, nature and embodied passion', *Current Issues in Tourism*, 12(5–6): 529–52.

Morey, D.F. and Aaris-Sørensen, K. (2002) 'Paleoeskimo dogs of the eastern Arctic', *Arctic*, 55(1): 44–56.

Moriarty, P.V. (1998) 'Zoos and conservation programs', *Journal of Applied Animal Welfare Research*, 1(4): 377–80.

Moriarty, P.V. and Woods, M. (1997) 'Hunting ≠ predation', *Environmental Ethics*, 19(4): 391–404.

Morris, M.C. (2009) 'Middle Earth, Narnia, Hogwarts, and animals: a review of the treatment of nonhuman animals and other sentient beings in Christian-based fantasy fiction', *Society and Animals*, 17(4): 343–56.

Morris, R. and Morris, D. (1966) *Men and Apes*, London: Hutchinson.

Moscardo, G. (2007) 'Understanding visitor experiences in captive, controlled, and non-captive wildlife-based tourism settings', *Tourism Review International*, 11(3): 213–23.

Moscardo, G. and Saltzer, R. (2004) 'Understanding wildlife tourism markets', in K. Higginbottom (ed.) *Wildlife Tourism: Impacts, Management and Planning*, Altona, Victoria: Common Ground Publishing, pp. 167–85.

Moscardo, G., Taverner, M. and Woods, B. (2006) 'When wildlife encounters go wrong: tourist safety issues associated with threatening wildlife', in Y. Mansfeld and A. Pizam (eds) *Tourism, Security and Safety: From Theory to Practice*, Burlington, VT: Elsevier, pp. 209–27.

Moscardo, G., Woods, B. and Saltzer, R. (2004) 'The role of interpretation in wildlife tourism', in K. Higginbottom (ed.) *Wildlife Tourism: Impacts, Management and Planning*, Altona, Victoria: Common Ground Publishing, pp. 231–51.

Mosier, J.L. (1999) 'The big attraction: the circus elephant and American culture', *Journal of American Culture*, 22(2): 7–18.

Mullan, B. and Marvin, G. (1987) *Zoo Culture*, London: Weidenfeld and Nicolson.

Mullin, M. (1999) 'Mirrors and windows: sociocultural studies of human–animal relationships', *Annual Review of Anthropology*, 28: 201–24.

—— (2002) 'Animals and anthropology', *Society & Animals*, 10(4): 387–93.

Munsche, P.B. (1981) *Gentlemen and Poachers: The English Game Laws*, Cambridge: Cambridge University Press.

Munthe, A. (2011) 'Images of captivity'. Online. Available at: <http://www.imagesofcaptivity.com> (accessed 3 May 2011).

Nagasawa, M., Kikusui, T., Onaka, T. and Ohta, M. (2009) 'Dog's gaze at its owner increases owner's urinary oxytocin during social interaction', *Hormones and Behavior*, 55(3): 434–41.

Nagel, T. (1974) 'What is it like to be a bat?', *The Philosophical Review*, 83(4): 435–50.

Nájera-Ramírez, O. (1996) 'The racialization of a debate: the charreada as tradition or torture', *American Anthropologist*, 98(3): 505–11.

Namkoong, G. and Regan, T. (1988) 'The question is not, "Can they talk?"', *The Journal of Medicine and Philosophy*, 13(2): 213–21.

Narveson, J. (2001) *The Libertarian Idea*, Orchard Park, NY: Broadview Press.

Nash, R. (1979) 'The exporting and importing of nature: nature-appreciation as a commodity, 1850–1980', *Perspectives in American History*, 12: 519–60.

Nasta, P. *et al.* (1997) 'Acute histoplasmosis in spelunkers returning from Mato Grosso, Peru', *Journal of Travel Medicine*, 4(4): 176–8.

National Geographic (2010) 'Tourists killing chimps?'. Online. Available at: <http://video.nationalgeographic.com/video/player/animals/mammals-animals/apes/chimp_mahaleillness.html> (accessed 5 April 2011).

National Geographic (2011) 'Animal-to-Human Disease Watch'. Online. Available at: <http://video.nationalgeographic.com/video/player/news/animals-news/nathanwolfe-missions-wcvin.html> (accessed 11 May 2011).

Naylor, L.M., Wisdom, M.J. and Anthony, R.G. (2009) 'Behavioral responses of North American elk to recreational activity', *Journal of Wildlife Management*, 73(3): 328–38.

New, J., Cosmides, L. and Tooby, J. (2007) 'Category-specific attention for animals reflects ancestral priorities, not expertise', *Proceedings of the National Academy of Sciences*, 104(42), 16593–603.

Newman, A. (1990) *Tropical Rainforest*, New York: Facts on File.

Newmark, W.D. and Manyanza, D.N. (2002) 'The conflict between wildlife and local people living adjacent to protected areas in Tanzania: human density as a predictor', *Conservation Biology*, 8(1): 249–55.

Newmyer, S.T. (2005) 'Tool use in animals: ancient and modern insights and moral consequences', *Scholia*, 14: 3–17.

Newsome, D., Dowling, R.K. and Moore, S.A. (2005) *Wildlife Tourism*, Clevedon, UK: Channel View.

Newsome, D., Lewis, A. and Moncrieff, D. (2004) 'Impacts and risks associated with developing, but unsupervised, stingray tourism at Hamelin Bay, Western Australia', *International Journal of Tourism Research*, 6(5): 305–23.

Nibert, D. (2002) *Animal Rights and Human Rights: Entanglements of Oppression and Liberation*, New York: Rowman & Littlefield.

Nicholls, W. (2007) 'Venison seeks its spot in the US food chain', *Washington Post*, 17 October, p. F01.

Nordgreen, J., Garne, J.P., Janczak, A.M., Ranheim, B., Muir, W.M. and Horsberg, E. (2009) 'Thermonociception in fish: Effects of two different doses of morphine on thermal threshold and post-test behaviour in goldfish (*Carasius auratus*)', *Applied Animal Behaviour Science*, 119(1–2), 101–7.

Norton, B.G. (1982) 'Environmental ethics and nonhuman rights', *Environmental Ethics*, 4: 17–36.

Noske, B. (1997) *Beyond Boundaries: Humans and Animals*, Montreal: Black Rose Books.

—— (2008) 'Speciesism, anthropocentrism, and non-Western cultures', in C.P. Flynn (ed.) *Social Creatures: A Human and Animal Studies Reader*, New York: Lantern Books, pp. 77–87.

Nursey-Bray, M., Marsh, M. and Ross, H. (2010) 'Exploring discourses in environmental decision making: an indigenous hunting case study', *Society and Natural Resources*, 23(4): 366–82.

Nussbaum, M.C. (2006) *Frontiers of Justice: Disability, Nationality, Species Membership*, Cambridge, MA: The Belknap Press.

Odendaal, J.S.J. and Meintjes, R.A. (2002) 'Neurophysiological correlates of affiliative behaviour between humans and dogs', *The Veterinary Journal*, 165(3): 296–301.

Oh, M. and Jackson, J. (2011) 'Animal rights vs. cultural rights: exploring the dog meat debate in South Korea from a world polity perspective', *Journal of Intercultural Studies*, 32(1): 31–56.

Ohler, N. (2000) *The Medieval Traveller*, trans. C. Hillier, Woodbridge: The Boydell Press.

Öhman, A. (1986) 'Face the beast and fear the face: animal and social fears as prototypes for evolutionary analyses of emotion', *Psychophysiology*, 23(2): 123–44.

—— (2000) 'Fear and anxiety: evolutionary, cognitive, and clinical perspectives', in M. Lewis and J.M. Haviland-Jones (eds) *Handbook of Emotions*, 2nd edn, New York: The Guilford Press, pp. 573–93.

—— (2007) 'Has evolution primed humans to "beware the beast"?', *Proceedings of the National Academy of Sciences*, 104(42): 16396–97.

—— (2009) 'Of snakes and faces: an evolutionary perspective on the psychology of fear', *Scandinavian Journal of Psychology*, 50(6): 543–52.

Öhman, A., Carlsson, K., Lundqvist, D. and Ingvar, M. (2007) 'On the unconscious subcortical origin of human fear', *Physiology & Behavior*, 92(1–2): 180–5.

Okaeme, A.N. (1987) 'Arthropods as pest and disease vectors and tourism in Nigeria', *The Journal of the Royal Society for the Promotion of Health*, 107(5): 189–91.

Oklahoma Department of Wildlife Conservation (1997) 'Final Report: Evaluation of Procedures to Reduce Delayed Mortality of Black Bass Following Summer Tournaments', Federal Aid Grant No. F-50-R, Fish Research for Oklahoma Waters, Project No. 8, 1 March 1996 to 28 February 1997.

Olsen, L. (2003) 'Contemplating the intentions of anglers: the ethicist's challenge', *Environmental Ethics*, 25(3): 267–77.

Olson, P.N. (2002) 'The modern working dog – a call for interdisciplinary collaboration', *Journal of the American Veterinary Medical Association*, 221(3): 352–5.

O'Neill, R. (2000) 'Animal liberation versus environmentalism: the care solution,' *Environmental Ethics*, 22: 183–90.

Online Etymology Dictionary (2011) 'Animal'. Online. Available at: <http://www.etymonline.com/index.php?search=animal&searchmode=none> (accessed 4 May 2011).

Orams, M. (1995) 'Managing interaction between wild dolphins and tourists at a dolphin feeding program, Tangalooma, Australia. The development and application of an education program for tourists, and an assessment of "pushy" dolphin behaviour', PhD dissertation, The University of Queensland, Brisbane, Australia.

—— (2002) 'Feeding wildlife as a tourism attraction: a review of issues and impacts', *Tourism Management*, 23(3): 281–93.

Oundo, J.O., Kariuki, S.M. Boga, H.I., Muli, F.W. and Iijima, Y. (2008) 'High incidence of enteroaggregative *Escherichia coli* among food handlers in three areas of Kenya: a possible transmission route of travelers' diarrhea', *Journal of Travel Medicine*, 15(1): 31–8.

Oxford Centre for Animal Ethics (2011) 'Animal ethics'. Online. Available at: <http://www.oxfordanimalethics.com/about-the-centre/animal-ethics> (accessed 10 May 2011).

Oxford Dictionary (2011) 'Animal'. Online. Available at: <http://oxforddictionaries.com/view/entry/m_en_gb0028870#m_en_gb0028870> (accessed 4 May 2011).

Page, T. (1999) *Buddhism and Animals: A Buddhist Vision of Humanity's Rightful Relationship with the Animal Kingdom*, London: UKAVIS.

Pandey, P., Shlim, D.R., Cave, W. and Springer, M.F.B. (2002) 'Risk of possible exposure to rabies among tourists and foreign residents in Nepal', *Journal of Travel Medicine*, 9(3): 127–31.

Parsons, E.C.M. and Rawles, C.J.G. (2003) 'The resumption of whaling by Iceland and the potential negative impact in the Icelandic whale-watch market', *Current Issues in Tourism*, 6(5): 444–8.

Paul, E.S. (1995) 'Us and them: scientists' and animal rights campaigners' views of the animal experimentation debate', *Society and Animals*, 3(1): 1–21.

Paulrud, A. and Waldo, S. (2010) 'The Swedish recreational fishing industry', *Tourism in Marine Environments*, 6(4): 161–74.

Peace, A. (2002) 'The cull of the wild: dingoes, development and death in an Australian tourist location', *Anthropology Today*, 18(5): 14–19.

—— (2005) 'Loving Leviathan: the discourse of whalewatching in Australian ecotourism', in J. Knight (ed.) *Animals in Person: Cultural Perspectives on Human–Animal Intimacy*, New York: Berg, pp. 191–210.

Pearce, D.G. and Wilson, P.M. (1995) 'Wildlife-viewing tourists in New Zealand', *Journal of Travel Research*, 34(2): 19–26.

Pearson, R.A. and Dijkman, J.T. (1994) 'Nutritional implications of work in draught animals', *Proceedings of the Nutrition Society*, 53: 169–79.

Penman, D. (2008) 'Animals torn to pieces by lions in front of baying crowds: the spectator sport China DOESN'T want you to see', *MailOnline*. Online. Available at: <http://www.dailymail.co.uk/news/article-506153/Animals-torn-pieces-lions-baying-crowds-spectator-sport-China-DOESNT-want-see.html> (accessed 2 March 2011).

Pereira, P., Barry, J., Corkeron, M., Keir, P., Little, M. and Seymour, J. (2010) 'Intracerebral hemmorrhage and death after envenoming by the jellyfish *Carukia barnesi*', *Clinical Toxicology*, 48(4): 390–2.

Perrett, R.Y. (1997) 'The analogical argument for animal pain', *Journal of Applied Philosophy*, 14(1): 49–58.

PETA (2011a) 'Cockfighting'. Online. Available at: <http://www.peta.org/issues/animals-in-entertainment/cockfighting.aspx> (accessed 9 May 2011).

PETA (2011b) 'Bullfighting'. Online. Available at: <http://www.peta.org/issues/animals-in-entertainment/bullfighting.aspx> (accessed 2 April 2011).

PETA (2011c) 'Rodeos'. Online. Available at: <http://www.peta.org/issues/animals-in-entertainment/rodeos.aspx> (accessed 28 February 2011).

Pfeiffer, S. and Peter, H.-U. (2004) 'Ecological studies toward the management of an Antarctic tourist landing site (Penguin Island, South Shetland Islands)', *Polar Record*, 40(4): 345–53.

Phelps, N. (2004) *The Great Compassion: Buddhism and Animal Rights*, New York: Lantern Books.

Philo, C. (1995) 'Animals, geography, and the city: notes on inclusions and exclusions', *Environment and Planning D: Society and Space*, 13(6): 655–81.

Piyaphanee, W., Wattanagoon, Y., Silachamroon, U., Mansanguan, C., Wicheanprasat, P. and Walker, E. (2009) 'Knowledge, attitudes, and practices among foreign backpackers toward malaria risk in Southeast Asia', *Journal of Travel Medicine*, 16(2): 101–6.

Pluhar, E.B. (1993) 'On vegetarianism, morality, and science: a counter reply', *Journal of Agricultural and Environmental Ethics*, 6(2): 185–213.

—— (1995) *Beyond Prejudice: The Moral Significance of Human and Nonhuman Animals*, Durham, NC: Duke University Press.

Pocock, C. (2006) 'Turtle riding on the Great Barrier Reef', *Society and Animals*, 14 (2): 129–46.

Pollan, M. (2006) *The Omnivore's Dilemma: A Natural History of Four Meals*, New York: Penguin Books.

Polyface (2007) 'Polyface guiding principles'. Online. Available at: <http://www.polyfacefarms.com/principles/> (accessed 11 May 2011).

Poole J.H. and Moss C.J. (2008) 'Elephant sociality and complexity: the scientific evidence', in C. Wemmer and C.A. Christen (eds), *Elephants and Ethics: Toward a Morality of Coexistence*, Baltimore, MD: Johns Hopkins University Press, pp. 69–98.

Portavella, M., Vargas, J.P., Torres, B. and Salas, C. (2002) 'The effects of telencephalic pallial lesions on spatial, temporal, and emotional learning in goldfish', *Brain Research Bulletin*, 57(3–4), 397–9.

Povilitis, A.J. (1980) 'On assigning rights to animals and nature', *Environmental Ethics*, 2(1): 67–72.

Prakash, A., Bhattacharyya, D.R., Mohapatra, P.K., Gogoi, P., Sarma, D.K., Bhattacharjee, K. and Mahanta, J. (2009) 'Evaluation of Permanet 2.0 mosquito bednets against mosquitoes, including *Anopheles minimus s.l.*, in India', *The Southeast Asian Journal of Tropical Medicine and Public Health*, 40(3): 449–56.

Preece, R. (2002) *Awe for the Tiger, Love for the Lamb: A Chronicle of Sensibility to Animals*, Toronto, ON: UBC Press.

—— (2003) 'Darwinism, Christianity, and the great vivisection debate', *Journal of the History of Ideas*, 64(3): 399–419.

—— (2005) *Brute Souls, Happy Beasts and Evolution: The Historical Status of Animals*, Vancouver: UBC Press.

—— (2007) 'Thoughts out of season on the history of animal ethics', *Society and Animals*, 15(4): 365–78.

Preece, R. and Chamberlain, L. (1993) *Animal Welfare and Human Values*, Waterloo, ON: Wilfred Laurier University Press.

Princée, F.P.G. (2001) 'Research in zoological gardens', *Lutra*, 44(2): 75–80.

Prokop, P., Özel, M. and Usak, M. (2009) 'Cross-cultural comparison of student attitudes toward snakes', *Society and Animals*, 17(3): 224–40.

Provost, S. and Soto, J.C. (2002) 'Perception and knowledge about some infectious diseases among travelers from Quebec, Canada', *Journal of Travel Medicine*, 9(4): 184–9.

Quan, S. and Wang, N. (2004) 'Towards a structural model of the tourist experience: an illustration from food experiences in tourism', *Tourism Management*, 25(3): 297–305.

Quigley, H. and Herrero, S. (2005) 'Characterization and prevention of attacks on humans', in R. Woodroffe, S.J. Thirgood and A. Rabinowitz (eds) *People and Wildlife: Conflict or Co-existence*, New York: Cambridge University Press, pp. 27–48.

Quint, D. (1998) *Montaigne and the Quality of Mercy: Ethical and Political Themes in the Essays*, Princeton, NJ: Princeton University Press.

Rabb, G.B. (1994) 'The changing roles of zoological parks in conserving biological diversity', *American Zoologist*, 34(1): 159–64.

Rabb, J.D. (2002) 'The vegetarian fox and indigenous philosophy: speciesism, racism, and sexism', *Environmental Ethics*, 24(3): 275–94.

Rachels, J. (1990) *Created from Animals: The Moral Implications of Darwinism*, Oxford: Oxford University Press.

Raia, P. (2010) 'Sixth horse dies at Calgary Stampede', *The Horse.com*. Online. Available at: <http://www.thehorse.com/ViewArticle.aspx?ID=16679> (accessed 30 July 2010).

Reade, L.S. and Waran, N.K. (1996) 'The modern zoo: how do people perceive zoo animals?', *Applied Animal Behaviour Science*, 47(1): 109–18.

Regan, T. (1983) *The Case for Animal Rights*, Berkeley, CA: University of California Press.

—— (2004) *Empty Cages: Facing the Challenge of Animal Rights*, Toronto, ON: Rowman & Littlefield.

Reilly, S.C., Quinn, J.P., Cossins, A.R. and Sneddon, L.U. (2008) 'Behavioural analysis of a nociceptive event in fish: comparisons between three species demonstrate specific responses', *Applied Animal Behaviour Science*, 114(1), 248–59.

Reser, J.P. (1995) 'Whither environmental psychology? The transpersonal ecopsychology crossroads', *Journal of Environmental Psychology*, 15(3): 235–57.

Resl, B. (2007) 'Animals in culture, ca. 1000–ca. 1400', in B. Resl (ed.) *A Cultural History of Animals in the Medieval Age*, New York: Berg, pp. 1–26.

Reynolds, P.C., and Braithwaite, D. (2001) 'Towards a conceptual framework for wildlife tourism', *Tourism Management*, 22: 31–42.

Ritvo, H. (1987) *The Animal Estate: The English and Other Creatures in the Victorian Age*, Cambridge, MA: Harvard University Press.

—— (2008) 'The emergence of modern pet-keeping', in C.P. Flynn (ed.) *Social Creatures: A Human and Animal Studies Reader*, New York: Lantern Books, pp. 96–106.

Rodd, R. (1996) 'Evolutionary ethics and the status of non-human animals', *Journal of Applied Philosophy*, 13(1): 63–72.

Rodger, K., Moore, S.A. and Newsome, D. (2007) 'Wildlife tours in Australia: characteristics, the place of science and sustainable futures', *Journal of Sustainable Tourism*, 15(2): 160–79.

Rodrigue, C.M. (2005) 'James Blaut's Critique of Diffusionism through a Neolithic lens: early animal domestication in the Near East', *Antipode*, 37(5): 981–9.

Rollin, B.E. (1996) 'Rodeo and recollection – applied ethics and western philosophy', *Journal of the Philosophy of Sport*, 23: 1–9.

—— (2005) 'Reasonable partiality and animal ethics', *Ethical Theory and Moral Practice*, 8(1–2): 105–21.

Rolston III, H. (1988) *Environmental Ethics: Duties to and Values in the Natural World*, Philadelphia, PA: Temple University Press.

—— (1994) *Conserving Natural Value*, New York: Columbia University Press.

Romeo, V. (2010) 'Bullfighting ban a first for Spain', *Reuters*. Online. Available at: <http://uk.reuters.com/article/2010/07/28/uk-spain-catalonia-bullfighting-idUKTRE66R1PA20100728> (accessed 5 May 2011).

Romero, L.M. and Wikelski, M. (2002) 'Exposure to tourism reduces stress-induced corticosterone levels in Galápagos marine iguanas', *Biological Conservation*, 108(3): 371–4.

Rongstad O.J. (1980) 'Research needs on environmental impacts of snowmobiles', in R.N.L. Andrews and P. Nowak (eds) *Off-Road Vehicle Use: A Management Challenge*, US Department of Agriculture Office of Environmental Quality, Washington, DC.

Rose, J.D. (2002) 'The neurobehavioral nature of fishes and the question of awareness and pain', *Reviews in Fisheries Science*, 10(1), 1–38.

—— (2003) 'Do fish feel pain?', *Indepth*, 1: 4.

Roskaft, E., Bjerke, T., Kaltenborn, B., Linnell, J.D.C. and Anderson, R. (2003) 'Patterns of self-reported fear towards large carnivores among the Norwegian public', *Evolution and Human Behavior*, 24(3): 184–98.

Roszak, T. (1992) *The Voice of the Earth: An Exploration of Ecopsychology*, New York: Simon & Schuster.

Rothfels, N. (2002a) 'Introduction', in N. Rothfels (ed.) *Representing Animals*, Indianapolis, IN: University of Indiana Press, pp. vii–xv.

—— (2002b) *Savages and Beasts: The Birth of the Modern Zoo*, Baltimore, MD: Johns Hopkins University Press.

—— (2005) 'Immersed with animals', in N. Rothfels (ed.) *Representing Animals*, Bloomington, IN: University of Indiana Press, pp. 199–223.

Rowlands, M. (2009a) *Animal Rights: Moral Theory and Practice*, 2nd edn, London: Palgrave Macmillan.

—— (2009b) 'Consciousness', in J. Baird Callicott and R. Frodeman (eds) *Encyclopedia of Environmental Ethics and Philosophy*, Detroit, MI: Gale, pp. 166–9.

Rowlands, M. (2009) *Animal Rights: Moral Theory and Practice*, 2nd edn, London: Palgrave Macmillan.

Rozin, P. and Fallon, A.E. (1987) 'A perspective on disgust', *Psychological Review*, 94(1): 23–41.

Rozin, P., Haidt, J. and McCauley, C.R. (2000) 'Disgust', in M. Lewis and J.M. Haviland-Jones (eds) *Handbook of Emotions*, 2nd edn, New York: Guilford Press, pp. 637–53.

Ryan, C. (1998) 'Saltwater crocodiles as tourist attractions', *Journal of Sustainable Tourism*, 6(4): 314–27.

Ryan, C. and Saward, J. (2004) 'The zoo as ecotourism attraction – visitor reaction, perceptions and management implications: the case of Hamilton Zoo, New Zealand', *Journal of Sustainable Tourism*, 12(3): 245–66.

Ryder, R.D. (1970) 'Speciesism', privately printed leaflet, Oxford.

—— (1971) 'Experiments on animals', in S. Godlovitch, R. Godlovitch and J. Harris (eds) *Animals, Men and Morals: An Enquiry into the Maltreatment of Nonhumans*, New York: Taplinger.

—— (1993) 'Sentientism', in P. Cavalieri and P. Singer (eds) *The Great Ape Project: Equality Beyond Humanity*, New York: St Martin's Press, pp. 220–2.

Sable, P. (1995) 'Pets, attachment, and well-being across the life-cycle', *Social Work*, 40(3): 334–40.

Saloña Bordas, M.I. (2004) 'Animal rights? No, human responsibility', *Human Ecology*, 12: 149–60.

San Martín, J. *et al.* (2010) 'The epidemiology of Dengue in the Americas over the last three decades: a worrisome reality', *The American Society of Tropical Medicine and Hygiene*, 82(1): 128–35.

Sapontzis, S.F. (1987) *Morals, Reason and Animals*, Philadelphia, PA: Temple University Press.

Saraceno, J. (2004) 'As death toll of dogs rises, so does Iditarod's insanity', *USA Today*, 14 March. Online. Available at: < http://www.usatoday.com/sports/columnist/saraceno/2004-03-14-saraceno_x.htm> (accessed 25 February 2011).

Saul, J.R. (2001) *On Equilibrium*, Toronto, ON: Penguin.

Savolainen, P., Zhang, Y., Luo, J., Lundeberg, J. and Leitner, T. (2002) 'Genetic evidence for an East Asian origin of domestic dogs', *Science*, 298(5598): 1610–13.

Scarff, J.E. (1980) 'Ethical issues in whale and small cetacean management', *Environmental Ethics*, 2(3): 241–79.

Schalow, F. (2000) 'Who speaks for the animals? Heidegger and the question of animal welfare', *Environmental Ethics*, 22(3): 259–72.

Schänzel, H.A. and McIntosh, A.J. (2000) 'An insight into the personal and emotive context of wildlife viewing at the penguin place, Otago Peninsula, New Zealand', *Journal of Sustainable Tourism*, 8(1): 36–50.

Schlagenhauf, P., Chen, L.H., Wilson, M.E., Freedman, D.O., Tcheng, D., Schwartz, E., Pandey, P., Weber, R., Nadal, D., Berger, C., von Sonnenberg, F., Keystone, J. and Leder, K. (2010) 'Sex and gender differences in travel-associated disease', *Clinical Infectious Diseases*, 50(6): 826–32.

Schmid, J. (1995) 'Keeping circus elephants temporarily in paddocks – the effects on their behaviour', *Animal Welfare*, 4(2): 87–101.

Schmidtz, D. (1998) 'Are all species equal?', *Journal of Applied Philosophy*, 15(1): 57–66.

Schopenhauer, A. (1998) *On the Basis of Morality*, Indianapolis, IN: Hackett Publishing.

Schullery, P. (1980) *The Bears of Yellowstone*, Yellowstone National Park, WY: Yellowstone Library and Museum Association.

Schwab, A. (2003) *Hook, Line and Thinker: Angling and Ethics*, Ludlow, UK: Merlin Unwin Books.

Schwartz, E., Weld, L.H., Wilder-Smith, A., von Sonnenberg, F., Keystone, J. S., Kain, K. C., Torresi, J., and Freedman, D.O. (2008) 'Seasonality, annual trends, and characteristics of Dengue among returned travellers, 1997–2006', *Emerging Infectious Diseases*, 14(7): 1081–8.

Schweitzer, A. (1923) *The Decay and the Restoration of Civilization (Verfall und Wiederaufbau der Kultur)*, London: Black.

Scruton, R. (1996) *Animal Rights and Wrongs*, London: Demos.

—— (2002) 'Ethics and welfare: the case of hunting', *Philosophy*, 77(302): 543–64.

Scully, M. (2002) *Dominion: The Power of Man, the Suffering of Animals and the Call to Mercy*, New York: St Martin's Griffith.

Searle, J. (1998) 'Animal minds', *Etica & Animali*, 9: 37–50.

Sekhar, N.U. (2003) 'Local people's attitudes towards conservation and wildlife tourism around Sariska Tiger Reserve, India', *Journal of Environmental Management*, 69(4): 339–47.

Seligman, M.E.P. (1971) 'Phobias and preparedness', *Behavior Therapy*, 2: 307–20.

Semeniuk, C.A.D., Bourgeon, S., Smith, S.L. and Rothley, K.D. (2009a) 'Hematological differences between stingrays at tourist and non-visited sites suggest physiological costs of wildlife tourism', *Biological Conservation*, 142(8): 1818–29.

Semeniuk, C.A.D., Haider, W., Beardmore, B. and Rothley, K.D. (2009b) 'A multi-attribute trade-off approach for advancing the measurement of marine wildlife tourism: a quantitative assessment of heterogeneous visitor preferences', *Aquatic Conservation: Marine and Freshwater Ecosystems*, 19: 194–208.

Senior, M. (2007) 'Introduction: the animal witness', in M. Senior (ed.) *A Cultural History of Animals in the Age of Enlightenment*, Oxford: Berg, pp. 1–22.

Senn, N., D'Acremont, V., Landry, P. and Genton, B. (2007) 'Malaria chemoprophylaxis: what do the travellers choose, and how does pretravel consultation influence their final decision', *The American Society of Tropical Medicine and Hygiene*, 77(6): 1010–14.

Serpell, J. (1989) 'Pet-keeping and animal domestication: a reappraisal', in J. Clutton-Brock (ed.) *The Walking Larder: Patterns of Domestication, Pastoralism, and Predation*, London: Unwin Hyman, pp. 10–21.

—— (1996) *In the Company of Animals: A Study of Human–Animal Relationships*, Cambridge: Cambridge University Press.

Shackley, M.L. (1996) *Wildlife Tourism*, London: International Thomson Business Press.

Shaha, B.K.P. (2002) 'Economics of yak farming with relation to tourism in Nepal', in H. Jianlin *et al.* (eds) *Yak Production in Central Asian Highlands*, Proceedings of the Third International Congress on Yak held in Lhasa, P.R. China, 4–9 September, pp. 134–40.

Shanghai Star (2002) 'Dogs electrocuted en route to Korean dinner tables'. Online. Available at: <http://app1.chinadaily.com.cn/star/2002/0314/fe19–2.html> (accessed 11 May 2011).

Shani, A. and Pizam, A. (2008) 'Towards an ethical framework for animal-based attractions', *New Zealand Management* 20(6): 679–693.

Shanks, N. (2009) 'Speciesism', in J. Baird Callicott and R. Frodeman (eds) *Encyclopedia of Environmental Ethics and Philosophy*, vol. 2, Detroit, MI: Gale, pp. 278–9.

Shapiro, P. (2006) 'Moral agency in other animals', *Theoretical Medicine and Bioethics*, 27(4): 357–73.

Shaw, M.T.M. and Leggat, P.A. (2003) 'Life and death on the Amazon: illness and injury to travellers on a South American expedition', *Journal of Travel Medicine*, 10(5): 268–71.

Shelton, J-A, (2004) 'Dancing and dying: the display of elephants in ancient Roman arenas', in R.B. Egan and M. Joyal (eds) *Daimonopylai: Essays in Classics and the Classical Tradition*, Winnipeg, MB: University of Manitoba Press, pp. 363–82.

Sheets-Johnstone, M. (1992) 'Taking evolution seriously', *American Philosophical Quarterly*, 29(4): 343–52.

Sherpa, Y.D. and Kayastha, R.B. (2009) 'A study of livestock management patterns in Sagarmatha National Park, Khumbu region: trends as affected by socioeconomic factors and climate change', *Kathmandu University Journal of Science, Engineering and Technology*, 5(2): 110–20.

Shklar, J.N. (1982) 'Putting cruelty first', *Daedalus*, 111(3): 17–27.

Shubert, A. (1999) *Death and Money in the Afternoon: A History of the Spanish Bullfight*, New York: Oxford.

Sicard, S., Simon, F., Soula, G. and Gazin, P. (2009) 'Efficacy of antimalarial chemoprophylaxis for travelers', *Journal of Travel Medicine*, 16(1): 66–7.

Signorini, L., Colombini, B., Cristini, F., Motteelli, A., Codeo, B., Cosatini, C. and Viole, P. (2002) 'Inappropriate footware and rat-bite fever in an international traveler', *Journal of Travel Medicine*, 9(5): 275–6.

Silva, F.G., Figueiredo, A. and Varandas, L. (2009) 'Travelers' diarrhea in children visiting tropical countries', *Journal of Travel Medicine*, 16(1): 53–4.

Singer, P. (1972) 'Famine, affluence, and morality', *Philosophy and Public Affairs*, 1(3): 229–43.

—— (1975) *Animal Liberation*, New York: New York Review/Random House.

—— (1987) 'Animal Liberation or Animal Rights?', *The Monist*, 70(1): 3–14.

—— (1993) *Practical Ethics*, 2nd edn, Cambridge: Cambridge University Press.

—— (2003) 'Animal liberation at 30', *New York Review of Books*, 50(8), 15 May. Online. Available at: <http://www.nybooks.com/articles/16276> (accessed 15 July 2010).

—— (2011) *The Expanding Circle: Ethics, Evolution, and Moral Progress*, Princeton, NJ: Princeton University Press.

Skidmore, J. (2001) 'Duties to animals: the failure of Kant's moral theory', *Journal of Value Inquiry*, 35(4): 541–59.

Smith, E.A. and Wishnie, M. (2000) 'Conservation and subsistence in small-scale societies', *Annual Review of Anthropology*, 29: 493–524.

Smith, K.F., Acevedo-Whitehouse, K. and Pedersen, A.B. (2009) 'The role of infectious diseases in biological conservation', *Animal Conservation*, 12(1): 1–12.

Smith, L. and Broad, S. (2007) 'Do zoo visitors attend to conservation messages? A case study of an elephant exhibit', *Tourism Review International*, 11(3): 225–35.

Smith, L., Broad, S. and Weiler, B. (2008) 'A closer examination of the impact of zoo visits on visitor behaviour', *Journal of Sustainable Tourism*, 16(5): 544–62.

Smith, L., Weiler, B. and Ham, S. (2010) 'The rhetoric versus the reality: a critical examination of the zoo proposition', in W. Frost (ed.) *Zoos and Tourism: Conservation, Education, Entertainment?*, Toronto, ON: Channel View Publications, pp. 59–68.

Smith, T.S., Herrero, S. and DeBruyn, T.D. (2005) 'Alaskan brown bears, humans, and habituation', *Ursus*, 16(1): 1–10.

Sneddon, L.U., Braithwaite, V.A. and Gentle, M.J. (2003) 'Do fishes have nociceptors? Evidence for the evolution of a vertebrate sensory system', *Proceedings of the Royal Society B*, 270(1520): 1115–21.

Soo, P. and Todd, P.A. (2009) 'Fish in aquariums for aesthetically enhancing public spaces (AAEPS): an incipient welfare issue?', *Journal of Applied Animal Welfare Science*, 12(3): 263–72.

Sorenson, J. (2009) *Ape*, London: Reaktion Books.

Spira, H (1985) 'Fighting to win', in P. Singer (ed.) *In Defence of Animals*, New York: Blackwell, pp. 194–208.

Spradlin, T.R., Barre, L.M., Lewandowski, J.K. and Nitta, E.T. (2001) 'Too close for comfort: concern about the growing trend in public interactions with wild marine mammals', *Marine Mammal Society Newsletter*, 9(3): 3–5.

Stark, D., van Haal, S., Lee, R., Marriott, D. and Harkness, J. (2008) 'Leishmaniasis, an emerging imported infection: report of 20 cases from Australia', *Journal of Travel Medicine*, 15(5): 351–4.

Stedman, R.C. and Heberlein, T.A. (2001) 'Hunting and rural socialization: contingent effects of the rural setting on hunting participation', *Rural Sociology*, 66(4): 599–617.

Steffen, R., Tornieporth, N., Clemens, S.A., Chatterjee, S., Coloacariti, A.M., Collard, F., De Clercq, N., Dupont, H.L. and Sonnunberg, F. (2004) 'Epidemiology of travelers' diarrhea: details of a global survey', *Journal of Travel Medicine*, 11(4): 231–7.

Sterba, J.P. (1995) 'From biocentric individualism to biocentric pluralism', *Environmental Ethics*, 17(2): 191–207.

Stevens, P.M. and McAlister, E. (2003) 'Ethics in zoos', *International Zoo Yearbook*, 38: 94–101.

Stevenson, P. with Formosinho, J. (2008) 'Long distance animal transport in Europe: a cruel and unnecessary trade', Godalming: Compassion in World Farming. Online. Available at: <http://www.ciwf.org.uk/includes/documents/cm_docs/2008/t/transport_in_europe_report_2008.pdf> (accessed 11 May 2011).

Stokes, J. (2004) '"Lion griefs": the wild animal acts as theatre', *New Theatre Quarterly*, 20(2): 138–54.

Stokey, E. and Zeckhauser, R. (1978) *A Primer for Policy Analysis*, New York: W.W. Norton.

Sukumar, R. (2008) 'Elephants in time and space: evolution and ecology', in C. Wemmer and C.A. Christian (eds) *Elephants and Ethics: Toward a Morality of Coexistence*, Baltimore, MD: Johns Hopkins University Press, pp. 17–40.

Sullivan, D.M., Vietzke, H. and Coyne, M.L. (2008) 'A modest proposal for advancing animal rights', *Albany Law Review*, 71: 1129–36.

Sumner, L.W. (1981) *Abortion and Moral Theory*, Princeton, NJ: Princeton University Press.

Sung, V., O'Brien, D.P., Matchett, E., Brown, G.V. and Torresi, J. (2003) 'Dengue fever in travellers returning from Southeast Asia', *Journal of Travel Medicine*, 10(4): 208–13.

Sunquist, M. and Sunquist, F. (2002) *Wild Cats of the World*, Chicago, IL: University of Chicago Press.

Suntrarachun, S., Roselieb, M., Wilde, H. and Sitprija, V. (2001) 'A fatal jellyfish encounter in the Gulf of Siam', *Journal of Travel Medicine*, 8(3):150–1.

Süss, J., Klaus, C., Gerstengarbe, F.-W. and Werner, P.C. (2008) 'What makes ticks tick? Climate change, ticks, and tick-borne diseases', *Journal of Travel Medicine*, 15(1): 39–45.

Swan, J. (1995) *In Defense of Hunting*, New York: Harper.

Sykes, G.M. and Matza, D. (1957) 'Techniques of neutralization: A theory of delinquency', *American Sociological Review*, 22, (6), 664–70.

Sztybel, D. (2006) 'Can the treatment of animals be compared to the Holocaust?', *Ethics & the Environment*, 11(1): 127–31.

Tambe, S. and Rawat, G.S. (2009) 'Ecology, economics, and equity of the pastoral systems in the Khangchendzonga National Park, Sikkim Himalaya, India', *Ambio*, 38(2): 95–100.

TAMS (2006a) 'U.S. activity profile: wildlife viewing while on trips', prepared by Lang Research, Inc. and the Canadian Tourism Commission.

TAMS (2006b) 'Canadian activity profile: wildlife viewing while on trips', prepared by Lang Research, Inc. and the Canadian Tourism Commission.

Taylor, A. (1996a) 'Animal rights and human needs', *Environmental Ethics*, 18: 249–64.

—— (1996b) 'Nasty, brutish, and short: the illiberal intuition that animals don't count', *The Journal of Value Inquiry*, 30(1–2): 265–77.

—— (2003) *Animals and Ethics: An Overview of the Philosophical Debate*. Peterborough, ON: Broadview Press.

Taylor, A.R. and Knight, R.L. (2003) 'Wildlife responses to recreation and associated visitor perceptions', *Ecological Applications*, 13(4): 951–63.

Taylor, P. (1986) *Respect for Nature: A Theory of Environmental Ethics*, Princeton, NJ: Princeton University Press.

Taylor, S. (1998) 'The hierarchic structure of fears', *Behaviour Research and Therapy*, 36(2): 205–14.

Teodósio, R., Gonçalves, L., Atouguia, J. and Imperatori, E. (2006) 'Quality assessment in the travel clinic: a study of travelers' knowledge about malaria', *Journal of Travel Medicine*, 13(5): 288–93.

The Brooke (2011) 'Our work'. Online. Available at: <http://www.thebrooke.org/home> (accessed 5 May 2011).

Theodossopoulos, D. (2005) 'Care, order and usefulness: the context of the human–animal relationship in a Greek island community', in J. Knight (ed.) *Animals in Person: Cultural Perspectives on Human–Animal Intimacy*, New York: Berg, pp. 15–36.

Thomas, K. (1983) *Man and the Natural World: Changing Attitudes in England, 1500–1800*, London: Harmondsworth.

Thompson, D.M. (2010) 'Noninvasive Approaches to Reduce Human–Cougar Conflict in Protected Areas on the West Coast of Vancouver Island', unpublished Masters thesis, Department of Biology, University of Victoria, Canada.

Thompson, K. (2010) 'Narratives of tradition: the invention of mounted bullfighting as "the newest but also the oldest"', *Social Science History*, 34(4): 523–54.

Thorstad, E.B., Neasje, T.F. and Leinan, I. (2007) 'Long-term effects of catch-and-release angling on ascending Atlantic salmon during different stages of spawning migration', *Fisheries Research*, 85(3): 316–20.

Tisdell, C.A. (1989) 'Environmental conservation: economics, ecology, and ethics', *Environmental Conservation*, 16(2): 107–13.

—— (2003) 'Economic aspects of ecotourism: wildlife-based tourism and its contribution to nature', *Sri Lankan Journal of Agricultural Economics*, 5(1): 83–95.

Tobias, M. (2008) 'The anthropology of conscience', in C.P. Flynn (ed.) *Social Creatures: A Human and Animal Studies Reader*, New York: Lantern Books, pp. 88–95.

Tooby, J. and Cosmides, L. (1992) 'The psychological foundation of culture', in J. Barkow, L. Cosmides and J. Tooby, *The Adapted Mind: Evolutionary Psychology and the Generation of Culture*, New York and Oxford: Oxford University Press.

Toovey, S., Annandale, Z., Jamieson, A. and Schoeman, J. (2004) 'Zebra bite to a South African tourist', *Journal of Travel Medicine*, 11(2): 122–4.

Tremblay, P. (2001) 'Wildlife tourism consumption: consumptive or non-consumptive?', *International Journal of Tourism Research*, 3(1): 81–6.

—— (2002) 'Tourism wildlife icons: attractions or marketing symbols', *Journal of Hospitality and Tourism Management*, 9(2): 164–80.

—— (2008) 'Wildlife in the landscape: a top end perspective on destination-level wildlife and tourism management', *Journal of Ecotourism*, 7(2&3): 179–96.

Tribe, A. (2004) 'Zoo tourism', in K. Higginbottom (ed.) *Wildlife Tourism: Impacts, Management and Planning*, Altona, Victoria: Common Ground Publishing, pp. 35–56.

Tribe, J. (2002) 'Education for ethical tourism action', *Journal of Sustainable Tourism*, 10(4): 309–24.

Trone, M., Kuczaj, S. and Solangi, M. (2005) 'Does participation in dolphin–human interaction programs affect bottlenose dolphin behaviour?', *Applied Animal Behaviour Science*, 93(3–4): 363–74.

Tsukahara, T. (1993) 'Lions eat chimpanzees: The first evidence of predation by lions on wild chimpanzees', *American Journal of Primatology*, 29(1): 1–11.

Tuan, Y.-F. (1984) *Dominance and Affection: The Making of Pets*, New Haven, CT: Yale University Press.

Tucker, C. and MacDonald, C. (2004) 'Beastly contractarianism? A contractarian analysis of the possibility of animal rights', *Essays in Philosophy*, 5(2): Article 31.

Turley, S.K. (1999a) 'Conservation and tourism in the traditional UK zoo', *Journal of Tourism Studies*, 10(2): 2–13.

—— (1999b) 'Exploring the future of the traditional UK zoo', *Journal of Vacation Marketing*, 5(4): 340–55.

Turner, J. (1980) *Reckoning with the Beast: Animals, Pain, and Humanity in the Victorian Mind*, Baltimore, MD: Johns Hopkins University Press.

Turner, S.S. (2009) 'Negotiating nostalgia: the rhetoricity of thylacine representation in Tasmanian tourism', *Society and Animals*, 17(2): 97–114.

Tye, M. (2000) *Consciousness, Color, and Content*, Cambridge, MA: MIT Press.

UK Forestry Commission (2011) 'Wildlife'. Online. Available at: <http://www.forestry.gov.uk/fr/INFD-5V8EF3> (accessed 12 March 2011).

UNEP (2007) 'Pests and invasive species in Africa', in C.J. Cleveland (ed.) *Encyclopedia of Earth*, Environmental Information Coalition, Washington, DC. Online. Available at: <www.eoearth.org/article/Pests_and_invasive_species_in_Africa> (accessed 31 January 2011).

Valentine, P.S., Birtles, A., Curnock, M., Arnold, P. and Duristan, A. (2004) 'Getting closer to whale–passenger expectations and experiences, and the management of swim with dwarf minke whale interactions in the Great Barrier Reef', *Tourism Management*, 25: 647–55.

van Polanen Petel, T., Giese, M. and Hindell, M. (2008) 'A preliminary investigation of the effect of repeated pedestrian approaches to Weddell seals (*Leptonychotes weddellii*)', *Applied Animal Behaviour Science*, 112(1): 205–11.

Vardy, P. and Grosch, P. (1999) *The Puzzle of Ethics*, London: Harper Collins.

Varner, G. (1994) 'What's wrong with animal by-products?', *Journal of Agriculture and Environmental Ethics*, 7(1): 7–17.

—— (1998) *In Nature's Interests?: Interests, Animal Rights, and Environmental Ethics*, New York: Oxford University Press.

—— (2008) 'Personhood, memory, and elephant management', in C. Wemmer and C.A. Christian (eds) *Elephants and Ethics: Toward a Morality of Coexistence*, Baltimore, MD: Johns Hopkins University Press, pp. 41–68.

Veltre, T. (1996) 'Menageries, metaphor and meanings', in R.J. Hoage and W.A. Deiss (eds) *New Worlds, New Animals: From Menagerie to Zoological Park in the Nineteenth Century*, Baltimore, MD: The Johns Hopkins Press, pp. 19–32.

Verga, M. and Michelazzi, M. (2009) 'Companion animal welfare and possible implications on the human–pet relationship', *Italian Journal of Animal Science*, 8(1): 231–40.

Verlecar, X.N., Snigdha, Desai, S.R. and Dhargalkar, V.K. (2007) 'Shark hunting: an indiscriminate trade endangering elasmobranchs to extinction', *Current Science*, 92(8): 1078–82.

Viegas, J. (2009) 'At 2009 Iditarod, dog deaths stir controversy', *Discovery News*, 25 March. Online. Available at: <http://dsc.discovery.com/news/2009/03/25/iditarod-dog-deaths.html> (accessed 25 February 2011).

Vilà, C., Savotainen, P., Maldonado, J.E., Amarim, I.R., Rice, J.E., Honeycutt, R.L., Crandoll, K.R., Lundeberg, J. and Wayne, R.K. (1997) 'Multiple and ancient origins of the domestic dog', *Science*, 276(5319): 1687–9.

Vitali, T. (1990) 'Sport hunting: moral or immoral?', *Environmental Ethics*, 12: 69–82.

Voith, V. (1985) 'Attachment of people to companion animals', *Vet Clinics of North America: Small Animal Practice*, 15(2): 289–95.

von Sonnenburg, F., Tornieporth, N., Waiyaki, P., Lowe, B., Peruski Jr., L.F., DuPont, H.L., Mattewson, J.J. and Steffen, R. (2000) 'Risk and aetiology of diarrhea at various tourist destinations,' *Lancet*, 356:133–4.

Wade, M.L. (1990) 'Animal liberationism, ecocentrism, and the morality of sport hunting', *Journal of the Philosophy of Sport*, 17: 15–27.

Waldau, P. (2006) 'Religion and animals', in P. Singer (ed.) *In Defense of Animals: The Second Wave*, Malden, MA: Blackwell Publishing, pp. 69–83.

Walpole, M.J. (2001) 'Feeding dragons in Komodo National Park: a tourism tool with conservation complications', *Animal Conservation*, 4(1): 67–73.

Walpole, M.J. and Goodwin, H. (2000) 'Local economic impacts of dragon tourism in Indonesia', *Annals of Tourism Research*, 27(3): 559–76.

Walpole, M.J. and Leader-Williams, N. (2002) 'Tourism and flagship species in conservation', *Biodiversity and Conservation*, 11(3): 543–7.

Wang, M., Szucs, T.D. and Steffen, R. (2008) 'Economic aspects of travelers' diarrhea', *Journal of Travel Medicine*, 15(2): 110–18.

Warren, M.A. (1983) 'The rights of the nonhuman world', in R. Elliot and A. Gare (eds) *Environmental Philosophy*, St Lucia: University of Queensland Press, pp. 109–34.

—— (1992) 'The rights of the nonhuman world', in E.C. Hargrove (ed.) *The Animal Rights/ Environmental Ethics Debate: The Environmental Perspective*, Albany, NY: SUNY Press, pp. 185–210.

Wasser, S.K., Davenport, B., Ramage, E.R., Hunt, K.E., Parker, M., Clarke, C. and Stenhouse, G. (2004) 'Scat detection dogs in wildlife research and management: application to grizzly and black bears in the Yellowhead ecosystem, Alberta, Canada', *Canadian Journal of Zoology*, 82(3): 475–92.

Watson, R.A. (1979) 'Self-consciousness and the rights of non-human animals and nature', *Environmental Ethics*, 1: 99–129.

WAZA (2011) 'Zoos and Aquariums of the World'. Online. Available at: <http://www.waza.org/en/site/zoos-aquariums> (accessed 3 May 2011).

Wearing, S. and Jobberns, C. (2011) 'Ecotourism and the commodification of wildlife: animal welfare and the ethics of zoos', in W. Frost (ed.) *Zoos and Tourism: Conservation, Education, Entertainment?*, Toronto: Channel View Publications, pp. 47–58.

Weaver, D.B. (2001) *Ecotourism*, Milton, Queensland: John Wiley & Sons.

Weaver, D.B. and Fennell, D.A. (1997) 'The vacation farm sector in Saskatchewan: a profile of operations', *Tourism Management*, 18(6): 357–65.

Weese, B. (2009) 'Feds back Toronto Zoo's campaign to land pandas', *The Standard*, 11 December, section B9.

Weiler, B. and Smith, L. (2009) 'Does more interpretation lead to greater outcomes? An assessment of the impacts of multiple layers of interpretation in a zoo context', *Journal of Sustainable Tourism*, 17(1): 91–105.

Weinrich, M. and Corbelli, C. (2009) 'Does whale watching in southern New England impact humpback whale (*Megaptera novaeangliae*) calf production or calf survival?', *Biological Conservation*, 142(12): 2931–40.

Wells, K. (2009) 'Welfare implications of the use of working equine animals (horses, donkeys and mules) in the tourism industry', position paper for *The Brooke*, London. Online. Available at: <http://www.thetravelfoundation.org.uk/assets/files/our_work_with_industry/tools_for_action/animal_guidelines/Guidance%20on%20Working%20Equines.pdf> (accessed 18 February 2011).

Wemmer, C. and Christen, C.A. (2008) 'Introduction: never forgetting the importance of ethical treatment of elephants', in C. Wemmer and C.A. Christian (eds) *Elephants and Ethics: Toward a Morality of Coexistence*, Baltimore, MD: Johns Hopkins University Press, pp. 1–16.

Wenz, P.S. (1993) 'Contracts, animals, and ecosystems', *Social Theory and Practice*, 19(3): 315–44.

Wescoat J.L., Jr. (1995) 'The "right of thirst" for animals in Islamic law: a comparative approach', *Environment and Planning D: Society and Space*, 13(6): 637–54.

Westra, L. (1989) 'Ecology and animals: is there a joint ethic of respect?', *Environmental Ethics*, 11: 215–30.

Whaley, A.R., Wright, A.J., De Calventi, B. and Parsons, E.C.M. (2007) 'Humpback whale sightings in southern waters of the Dominican Republic lead to proactive conservation measures', *Marine Biodiversity Records*, 1: 1–3.

Whatmore, S. and Thorne, L. (1998) 'Wild(er)ness: reconfiguring the geographies of wildlife', *Transactions of the Institute of British Geographers*, 23(4): 435–54.

Whinam, J., Chilcott, N. and Bergstrom, D.M. (2005) 'Subantarctic hitchhikers: expeditioners as vectors for the introduction of alien organisms', *Biological Conservation*, 121(2): 207–19.

White, L., Jr. (1967) 'The historical roots of our ecologic crisis', *Science*, 155 (3767): 1203–7.

Wickins-Drazilová, D. (2006) 'Zoo animal welfare', *Journal of Agricultural and Environmental Ethics*, 19(1): 27–36.

Wilkins, K.T. (1982) 'Highways as barriers to rodent dispersal', *Southwest Naturalist*, 27(4): 459–60.

Wilkinson, G. (1986) 'Social grooming in the common vampire bat, *Desmodus rotundus*', *Animal Behaviour*, 34 (6): 1880–9.

Willard, L.D. (1982) 'About animals "having" rights', *Journal of Value Inquiry*, 16: 177–87.

Williams, R. (1983) *Key Words*, London: Fontana.

Wilson, C., and Tisdell, C. (2001) 'Sea turtles as a non-consumptive tourism resource especially in Australia', *Tourism Management*, 22, 279–88.

Wilson, D.A.H. (2009) 'Racial prejudice and the performing animals controversy in early twentieth-century Britain', *Society and Animals*, 17(2): 149–65.

Wilson, E.O. (1993) 'Biophilia and the conservation ethics', in S.R. Kellert and E.O. Wilson (eds) *The Biophilia Hypothesis*, Washington, DC: Island Press, pp. 31–41.

—— (1998) *Consilience: The Unity of Knowledge*, New York: Vintage.

Wilson, G. (1607) *The Commendation of Cockes, and Cockfighting. Wherein is shewed, that Cocke-fighting was before the coming of Christ*, London: Henrie Tomes.

Wilson, R.T. (2003) 'The environmental ecology of oxen used for draught power', *Agriculture, Ecosystems and Environment*, 97(1–3): 21–37.

Wilson, S. (2001) 'Carruthers and the argument from marginal cases', *Journal of Applied Philosophy*, 18(2): 135–46.

—— (2002) 'Indirect duties to animals', *Journal of Value Inquiry*, 36: 15–25.

Wise, S.M. (2000) *Rattling the Cage: Toward Legal Rights for Animals*. New York: Perseus Books.

—— (2002) *Drawing the Line: Science and the Case for Animal Rights*, Cambridge, MA: Perseus Books.

Wolch, J. (2002) 'Anima urbis', *Progress in Human Geography*, 26(6): 721–42.

—— (2003) 'Zoöpolis', in A.R. Cuthbert (ed.) *Designing Cities: Critical Readings in Urban Design*, Oxford: Blackwell Publishing, pp. 254–72.

Wolch, J. and Emel, J. (1995) 'Bringing the animals back in', *Environment and Planning D: Society and Space*, 13(6): 632–6.

Wolf, I.D. and Croft, D.B. (2010) 'Minimizing disturbance to wildlife by tourists approaching on foot or in car: a study of kangaroos in the Australian rangelands', *Applied Animal Behaviour Science*, 126(1): 75–84.

Wolfe, C. (2003) *Animal Rites: American Culture, the Discourse of Species, and Posthumanist Theory*, Chicago, IL: The University of Chicago Press.

Wolfe, M.L. (2008) 'Avoiding the blame game in managing problem black bears', *Human-Wildlife Conflicts*, 2(1): 12–4.

Wonders, K. (2005) 'Hunting narratives of the Age of Empire: a gender reading of their iconography', *Environment and History*, 11(3): 269–91.

Woodford, M.H., Butynski, T.M. and Karesh, W.B. (2002) 'Habituating the great apes: the disease risks', *Oryx*, 36(2): 153–60.

Woods, B. (2000) 'Beauty and the best: preferences for animals in Australia', *Journal of Tourism Studies*, 11(2): 25–35.

Working Traveller (2010) '12 cheap ways to volunteer with animals'. Online. Available at: <http://www.the-working-traveller.com/12-cheap-ways-to-volunteer-with-animals> (accessed 5 May 2011).

World Health Organization (2007a) 'Dengue/DHF Press Release'. Online. Available at: <http://www.searo.who.int/EN/Section10/Section332/Section2386_13110.htm> (accessed 11 May 2011).

World Health Organization (2007b) 'Fact sheet no. 237: Food safety and foodborne illness'. Online. Available at: <http://www.who.int/mediacentre/factsheets/fs237/en/index.html> (accessed 8 June 2010).

World Health Organization (2010) 'Fact sheet no. 94: Malaria'. Online. Available at: <http://www.who.int/mediacentre/factsheets/fs094/en> (accessed 8 June 2010).

World Health Organization (2011) 'Facts and figures: Water, sanitation and hygiene links to health'. Online. Available at: <http://www.who.int/water_sanitation_health/publications/factsfigures04/en> (accessed 7 April 2011).

World Society for the Protection of Animals (1994) *The Zoo Inquiry*, World Society for the Protection of Animals, Oxford.

World Society for the Protection of Animals (2011) 'Animal friendly tourism'. Online. Available at: <http://www.wspa-international.org/helping/animalfriendlyliving/travel.aspx> (accessed 30 January 2011).

World Tourism Organization (2002) *The Canadian Ecotourism Market*, Special Report no. 15, Madrid.

WWF (1993) *WWF Position Paper on Whaling*. Online. Available at: <http://www.highnorth.no/Library/Movements/WWF/ww-po-p.htm> (accessed 3 August 2011).

Wright, S., Suchet-Pearson, S., Lloyd, K., Burarrwanga, L.L. and Burarrwanga, D. (2009) '"That means the fish are fat": sharing experiences of animals though indigenous-owned tourism', *Current Issues in Tourism*, 12(5–6): 505–27.

Yates, R. (2004) 'The social construction of human beings and other animals in human–nonhuman relations. Welfarism and rights: A contemporary sociological analysis'. Online. Available at: <http://roger.rbgi.net/Understanding%20Boundaries.html> (accessed 13 January 2011).

Yue, S., Moccia, R.D. and Dunca, I.J.H. (2004) 'Investigating fear in domestic rainbow trout, *Oncorhynchus mykiss*, using an avoidance learning task', *Applied Animal Behaviour Scien*ce, 87.

Yung, C. and Ng, T. (2005) 'Disney ditches shark's fin', *The Standard*, 25 June. Online. Available at: <www.thestandard.com.hk/stdn/std/Metro/GF25Ak01.html> (accessed 20 April 2011).

Zamir, T. (2007) 'The welfare-based defense of zoos', *Society and Animals*, 15(2): 191–201.

Zell, S.C. (1997) 'Environmental and recreational hazards associated with adventure travel', *Journal of Travel Medicine*, 4(2): 94–9.

Zeppel, H. and Muloin, S. (2008) 'Conservation benefits of interpretation on marine wildlife tours', *Human Dimensions of Wildlife*, 13(4): 280–94.

Zoocheck Canada (n.d) 'Jurisdictions that have prohibited or severely restricted performing wild animal acts,' Online. Available at <http://www.zoocheck.com/campaigns_circuses_lawslist.html> (accessed 3 August 2011).

Zoocheck Canada (2006) *Performing Prisoners: A Case Against the Use of Wild Animals in Circuses, Traveling Shows & Novelty Acts*, Toronto, ON: Zoocheck Canada.

Index

A Thousand Plateaus 30
A Woman of No Importance 139
access consciousness 44
Adams, C. 65
Aedes aegypti 234
Aedes albopictus 234
African Big Five 162
airborne illnesses 239–40
Aldo Leopold camp 155
Aldo Leopold's land ethic 57
all-terrain vehicles (ATVs) 214–15
American Veterinary Medical Association 121
An Apology for Raymond Sebond 25
angling 176
Angus Reid Strategies 30
'animal advocates' 57
Animal Assisted Activity (AAA) 124
Animal Assisted Education (AAE) 124
Animal Assisted Therapy (AAT) 123, 124
animal baiting 133
animal bite 218
animal combat 131–54; badger baiting **136**; baiting 133–4; betting: greyhound racing 149–52; blood: bullfighting 142–6; bravado: rodeo 146, 148–9; bullfighting ban a first for Spain 147; cock throwing 139–40; crackdown appeal after swoops on badger-baiting ring 135; diversity of uses 132–3; dogs before a race **152**; ethics in action 152–3; fighting 134, 136–9; fox tossing **142**; historical reference points 131; hunting and fishing 139; mounted bullfighting **143**; other blood sports 140–2; protest against bullfighting **146**; Roman games 131–2; Turkey: tradition of camel wrestling making a comeback 141; types of blood sports **133**

animal competition 131–54
animal ethics: anthropocentric 'othering' **65**; completely lacking moral status 53–5; moral heterodoxy 59–68; moral orthodoxy 55–8; Swiss say no to animal lawyers 61; theories 52–68; tourism 248–56
animal fighting 134
'animal liberation' 62
animal mind 44–9; did animals sense tsunami was coming? 49; mentality 47–9; phenomenal consciousness 45–6; self-consciousness 46–7
animal sex tourism 128
animal threat 217–47; balance 243–6; humans as vectors 241–3; marine environment threat 226–30; terrestrial threat 219–26; zoonoses 230–41
animal welfare 55–7
animals 12; animal mind 44–9; at work in the service of tourism industry 103–30; British Columbia sled dog cull 2; camel riding at Naples Zoo **108**; categorization of animal visitor attractions 5; chink in the chain 50–2; Cohen's conceptual framework of human-animal engagement **4**; companion animals and tourism 120–9; companion animals owned in US population (2007) **121**; conceptual framework **10**; contemporary culture 29–35; criteria to assign moral values to animals with associated theory 37–69; cull of the wild 1–3; did animals sense tsunami was coming? 49; domestication 103–6; ethics in action 129–30; extension of liberty rights under the common law **51**; first rescue dogs 118; fish pain science and philosophy 176–83; German airports use honeybees

to sniff out air quality 119; great chain of being 37–40; hunting 155–76; IditArod Rules 115–16; improving equine welfare now and for the long term **111**; misothery 13–22; misothery and theriophily in religious, philosophical and cultural contexts 13–36; moral value 40–4; objectives 9–12; present relationship between tourism, animals and ethics in tourism studies **7**; pursued for sport and subsistence 155–86; sex tourism 128; Shanghai monkey working the streets for money **116**; species mentioned in participants' deliberations concerning where to 'draw the line' **52**; theories of animal ethics 52–68; theriophily 22–9; tourism ethics 1–12; use of draught animals worldwide **107**; used for their senses 117–19; used for their strength 106–16; Your Time Travels 127

anthropocentrism 39
anthropomorphism 39
anthropomorphophobia 40
anthroponosis 230
anthrozoology 8
anti-discrimination approach 251–2
anticipatory accommodation 251
Ape 157
aquaria 96–9; Lolita: slave to entertainment 98
'armigerous gentry's traditional *raison d'être*' 156
Arthropod-borne disease 232–7; female *Anopheles* mosquito **236**
ass 107
Association of Zoos and Aquariums (AZA) 79, 162
Astley, P. 91
atomism 185
'Attenborough effect' 201
autonoetic 47
Autonoetic Consciousness Paradigm (ACP) 47

Babe 35
Bailey Knows Travel 125–6
Banff National Park 251
Barnum, P.T. 93
bear attacks 220–2
'behavioral enrichment' programs 78
behavioral flexibility 46
behaviorism 43, 50
Bentham, J. 45

bequest value 194
bestiality 128
'Big Five' 157
biocentrism 67, 215
'biodetectives' 119
biophilia 13, 28–9
Boas, G. 22
Born Free Foundation (BFF) 82
bovine spongiform encephalopathy (BSE) 240
British Animals Act (1986) 28
British Cruelty to Animals Act (1835) 27
Broome, A. 28
Buddhism 24–5
Buechler, J. 61
Bugs Bunny 35
bullfighting 142–6

Caius, J. 117
Calgary Stampede 148
Calgary Zoo 86–7
Caliskan, V. 141
camel 107–8
camel wrestling 140
Campaign for the Abolition of Terrier Work (CATW) 134
captives 70–102; animals torn to pieces by lions in front of baying crowds 100; aquaria 96–9; Bear pit at Bern, Switzerland **77**; circus 91–6; education message regarding conservation **81**; elephant attacks 94; ethics in action 99–101; evolution of circus **92**; Lolita: slave to entertainment 98; menagerie 70–5; tourist attractions **71**; transporting the black Rhinoceros 74; zoo breeding programs **80**; zoos 75–91
'carceral archipelago' 91
Carruthers, P. 53
Carson and Barnes Circus (USA) 94
Carukia barnesi 228
Carybdeids 227
Catalonian nationalist party (CiU) 147
'cave disease' *see* histoplasmosis
Chagas disease 235
charreada 149
Chicken Run 35
Chirodropids 227
Chironex fleckeri 227
Christian People's Party 61
Ciguatera 240–1
circus 91–6; elephant attacks 94; evolution of **92**; vs zoos 93
Cirque de Soleil 96

Citak, M. 141
cock throwing 139
cockfighting 137
Coe, S. 34
coevolution 14
cognitive ethology 44
Communal Areas Management
    Programme for Indigenous Resources
    (CAMPFIRE) 58
Companion Air 126
companion animals: owned in US
    population (2007) **121**; tourism
    120–9; travel 124–6; travel veterinary
    kit **125**; Your Time Travels 127;
    zoophilia 126–9
consciousness 44–5
conservation 79–80
constructivist approach 164
consumptive use 188–9
contemporary culture 29–35; animal
    representation 30–3; animal themes that
    sell **31**; art, books and the screen 33–5;
    dog sledding as representative of the
    character of the 'north' **31**
Contested Natures 167
contractarianism 63–4
contractarianist approach 100–1
Convention for the Regulation of
    Whaling 58
Convention on International Trade in
    Endangered Species of Wild Fauna
    and Flora (CITES) 74
core disgust 16
Corea, R. 49
cougars 222
Cousteau, J-M. 97
Creutzfeldt–Jakob disease 240
crop-robbing 105
Cruelty in Perfection 19
Cubozoans 227

de Warenne, W. 133
'Declaration on Great Apes' 50
dengue fever 234, 235
Descartes, R. 53
Diaz, G. 114
dingo 223
direct values 194–5
'Disneyfication' 196
Disneyization 82
'Dog Adventures' product 125
dog sledding 113–14
Dolphin Interaction Programmes (DIP) 97–9
dolphins 209–10

domain specificity 29
Domalain, J-V. 73
domestication 103–6, 130
dopamine 123
draught animals 106–9; camel riding at
    Naples Zoo **108**; use of draught animals
    worldwide **107**
du Chaillu, P.B. 157

ecclesiastical trials 21
ecocentrism 57–8
ecopsychology 29
ecotourism 25, 191
ecotourist 193
Egilmez, I. 141
elephant 48, 108, 109–10
Ellis, J. 119
encephalitis 234
English Protectorate ordinance (1654) 27
enteroaggregative *E. coli* 237–8
Enumclaw case 128
Escherichia coli 240
ethics 215–16; animal combat and
    competition 152–3; animals at work in
    the service of tourism 129–30; animals
    pursued for sport and subsistence 183–5;
    captives 99–101; finding balance 243–6;
    Manatee tours **246**; process of species
    reinvention over time **245**; theories of
    animal ethics 52–68
ethology 29
European wall lizard, 212–13
existence value 195
exotic pets 122
extended self theory 122

faecal glucocorticoid metabolite (FGM)
    212
Fair Chase Statement 157
fear 129
Feldstein, S. 126
feminist theory 64–6
Ferrater-Mora, J. 32
'fetishistic voyeurism' 35
Finding Nemo 35
Finocchio, E.J. 148
First Stage of Cruelty 19
fish pain: ethics in action 183–5; human
    priorities and actions in recreational
    interactions with fish **182**; New South
    Wales Council of Anglers Code of
    Conduct 184; philosophy 180–3, 184;
    science 177–80; science and philosophy
    176–83

fishing 176
'Five Freedoms' of animal welfare 56
Flavivirus 234
Flipper 35, 96
foodborne illnesses 237–9
fox hunting 139
fox tossing 140
Fraser Island 223
Fricker, P. 2
Frisco, T. 94
funktionslust 86

Game Act (1671) 156
Game Reform Act 156
'Garden of Intelligence' 71
gastrointestinal (GI) infection 238
GeoSentinel Network 218, 234
German shepherds 117–18
Gibraltar macaques 219
Global Viral Forecasting Initiative 241
Goetschel, A.F. 61
Goodall, J. 43
Grammont Law 27–8
Great Ape Project (GAP) 59, 251
*Great Ape Project (GAP): Equality beyond
    Humanity* 50
great chain of being 37–40;
    anthropocentrism **39**; chink in the chain
    50–2; circus procession **40**; extension of
    liberty rights under the common law **51**;
    species mentioned in participants'
    deliberations concerning where to
    'draw the line' **52**; speciesism,
    anthropocentrism and anthropomorphism
    38–40; where to draw the line 50–2
greyhound racing 149–52
Griffin, D. 44
group fishing 183

habituation 205; and provisioning 204–15;
    bear-to-bear habituation 206; bear-to-
    human habituation 206; human-to-bear
    habituation 207; potential benefits
    and risks (costs) of bear-to-human
    habituation **207**
haemolytic-uraemic syndrome 240
Hagenbeck, C. 83
happy hunter 161
haq-i shurb 25
harness animals 113–17; IditArod Rules
    115–16; Shanghai monkey working the
    streets for money **116**
Harry Potter 34
higher-order thought processes (HOT) 53

hired hunter 161
Hirst, D. 34
Histoplasma capsulatum 241
histoplasmosis 241
Hogarth, W. 19
holism 185
holist hunter 161
holy hunter 161
homo catalan 145
homo europeus 145
homo hispanense 145
Homo sapiens 18, 41
honeybees 119
Hope Vale Aboriginal community 170
Hornaday, W. 73
horse 107, 110
hostile hunter 161
hot water immersion 230
human-animal interaction 4
'human chauvinism' 8
'humane movement' 57
Humane Society International (HSI) 248
humans 65; chink in the chain 50–2;
    contemporary culture 29–35; criteria to
    assign moral values to animals with
    associated theory 37–69; extension of
    liberty rights under the common law **51**;
    great chain of being 37–40; misothery
    13–22; misothery and theriophily in
    religious, philosophical and cultural
    contexts 13–36; theriophily 22–9
humpback whales 210
hunger 130
hungry hunter 161
hunting 57, 155–76, 189, 190, 194; ethics
    in action 183–5; history 155–60; hunting
    dogs with a day off **159**; in defense of
    167–73; in opposition to 173–6; legal
    hunting and its benefits **171**; market
    hunting in ivory **160**; percentage of
    Swedish groups in support of hunting
    option **164**; the hunter 160–7; total
    wildlife-related recreation **158**
hunting-as-masculine theme 165
Hutchins, M. 89
Hydrozoa 227

IditArod Rules 115–16
In Defense of Animals (IDA) 85
indirect values 195
International Air Transport Association
    (IATA) 75, 125
International Commission for Alpine
    Rescue (ICAR) 118

International Zoo Yearbook 76
Inward Government Theory (IGT) 26
Irish law (1635) 27
Irukandji syndrome 228
Irwin, S. 30
Islamic law 25
Ixodes 236

Jagdliches Brauchtum 166
Jaschinski, B. 30, 34
jellyfish 227–8

Katzenmusik 19
Kellert, S. 17
Komodo dragon *see Varanus komodoensis*

Lassie 35
Leishmania 235
Leishmania braziliensis 236
Leishmania infantum 125
leishmaniasis 235–6
Loch Ness Monster 196–7
Lyme borreliosis 236–7

Machiavellian Intelligence tests 48
Machiavellianism 26
mad cow disease *see* bovine spongiform
    encephalopathy (BSE)
mahouts 109
malaria 232–4
malaria chemoprophylaxis 233–4
Malo kingi 228
manatees 244, **246**
'marginal humans' 42
marine environment threat 226–30; human
    fatalities and marine animal
    envenomation **229**
marine iguanas 205–6
market hunting 160
Martin, R. 27
Martin's Act (1822) 27, 140
menagerie 70–5; capture 73–5
mentality 45, 47
meta-responsibility 122–3
Mgahinga National Park 196
Mickey Mouse 35
Middle Earth 35
Midgley, M. 67
mirror test 46, 47
misothery 13–22; attitudes of fear and
    disgust 13–22; Hogarth: *The First Stage
    of Cruelty* **20**; types of human attitudes
    toward animals **17**
moral agents 42

moral heterodoxy 59–68; animals have
    rights 59–62; contractarianism 63–4;
    postmodern, including feminist ethics
    64–6; respect 67–8; utilitarianism 62–3;
    virtue ethics 66–7
moral orthodoxy 55–8; animal welfare
    55–7; ecocentrism 57–8
moral patient 42
moral value: animals 40–4; circus
    procession **40**; great chain of being
    37–40; use of criteria to assign to
    animals and associated theories 37–69
Moriarty, M. 2
mule 107

Nagel, T. 50
'Narnia' 34–5
nature-based tourism 187–8, 191–4
Nature Ecotourism Accreditation Program
    (NEAP) 192
neoliberalism 109
New York Times 16
Nile crocodile 222
non-consumptive use 188–9
normative theory 69

Of Englishe Dogges **117**
Olympic Games 1
On Cruelty 26
option value 194
orang-utans 202–3
Orlando Sentinel 114
Overseas Job Centre 126
oxen 108
oxytocin 123

pack animals 111–13
pain 130
pet keeping 29, 120–1
'pet passport' 125
pet therapy 124
phenomenal consciousness 45–6
plasma β-endorphin 123
'poaching' 163
Post-Traumatic Stress Disorder (PTSD) 86
'practical autonomy' 51
preparedness theory 15
primary responsibility 123
primatocentrism 50
prion 240
provisioning 208
proximity 200–15; best practice for
    reducing disease transmission to great
    apes 214; habituation and provisioning

204–8; impacts 208–15; swimming with
    bottlenose dolphin **209**

rat-bite fever 240
reciprocal altruism 42–3
Recreational Anglers Code of Conduct 183
Regan, T. 41
religious theriophily 22–5; Buddhism
    24–5; Islamic law 25
respect 67–8
Rhodes, R.L. 152
riding animals 109–11
'right of thirst' 25
Rin-Tin-Tin 35
rodeo 146, 148–9
Rull, J. 147
Rutledge, A. 168
Ryder, R. 37

Safe Sea 228
San Diego Zoo 87
SARS epidemic 239–40
Save the Manatee Club 244
scala naturae 37
Scharf, G. 77
Scyphozoans 227
Sea World 96
seal hunting 191
seals 211
search and rescue (SAR) teams 118–19
Second Stage of Cruelty 19
secular theriophily 25–8
secular trials 21
self-consciousness 45, 46–7
self-recognition 46
Sendur, R. 141
sensitivity 44
sentiency 59–60, 62
shari'a 25
Sherman, C. 33
'shock art' 34
Singer, P. 41, 62
'sixth sense' 48, 49
Sled Dog Action Coalition 114
slip 150
'slipper' 150
snakebite 224–5
snakes 15
social psychological theory of mindfulness
    204; model of wildlife-based tourist
    experiences **205**
Society for the Prevention of Cruelty to
    Animals (SPCA) 28

*Some Comfort Gained from the Acceptance
    of the Inherent Lies in Everything* 34
speciesism 38–9
Spink, D. 128
Spirillum minus 240
sport hunting 160, 163, 173
St. Bernards 118
'Still Life' 33
stingray 228, 230; viewing 193, 211
Streptobacillus moniliformis 240
subsistence hunting 160
supererogation 253
Swiss Alpine Club 117
symbiosis 105

T. cruzi 235
Tait, J. 128
taniwha 197; rock craving **198**
'Tasmanian tiger' 196
Taylor, P. 67–8
Tedford, T. 2
'terrestrial bioindicators' 119
terrestrial threat 219–26; bear–human
    interactions **221**; local and systemic
    symptoms and signs of venomous
    snakebite **226**; relationship between
    various bear–human interactions **221**
The Boke of Saint Albans 156
The Brooke 130
*The Commendation of Cockes, and
    Cockfighting. Wherein is shewed, that
    Cocke-fighting was before the coming
    of Christ* 137
The Compleat Angler 167
*The Criminal Prosecution and Capital
    Punishment of Animals* 20
'the Darwin and the "Killer Ape" Legacy'
    167
*The Expression of the Emotions in Man
    and Animals* 43
The Four Stages of Cruelty 19
'The Grizzly Man' 30
The Lion King 35
The New York Review 62
'The numbers behind Crocodile Hunter's
    death' 231
The Physical Impossibility of Death in the
    Mind of Someone Living 34
The Postmodern Animal 34
The Reward of Cruelty 19
The Sexual Politics of Meat 65
The Theodosian Code 108
The Working Traveller 126

The Zoo Inquiry 82
theriophily 22–9; biophilia 28–9; religious theriophily 22–5; secular theriophily 25–8
Tibetan macaques 211–12
tick-borne encephalitis 236–7
Tijuana Donkey Show 127–8, 129
totem 23
tourism: animal ethics 1–12, 248–56; animals at work in the service of 103–30; companion animals 120–9; conceptual framework **10**; objectives 9–12; present relationship between tourism, animals and ethics in tourism studies **7**
Tourism Review International (2007) 76
traditional hunting 170
Travel Trade Gazette 108
travellers' diarrhoea 237–9
Treadwell, T. 30
trophy hunting 163
turtle riding 188–9

Ukrainian Nathalia Edenmont 33
Ulster Society for the Prevention of Cruelty to Animals (USPCA) 135
United States Poison Control Centres 217
US National Survey of Fishing, Hunting and Wildlife-Associated Recreation 158
utilitarianism 62–3

Varanus komodoensis 195
vasodentin 230
venationes 131
Versailles menagerie 72
Vick, M. 122, 134, 136, 154
violence 161
virtue ethics 66–7, 152
'visitor effect' 84
vivisection 35

waking state 44
Wallace, A.R. 157
Walton, I. 167
waterborne illnesses 237–9

Waterloo Cup 150
West Nile virus 234
whale shark 201–2; tourism 202
whale watching 189, 199, 210
whaling 189
white-nose syndrome 241–2
Whitehorse Star 129
Wilde, O. 139
wildlife photography 200
Wildlife Society 192
wildlife tourism 191–3
wildlife viewing 187–216; classification complexities 187–94; classification of wildlife appeal **199**; comparison to humans 198–200; ethics in action 215–16; making animal icons 196–8; monetarily 194–6; proximity 200–15; valuing animals 194–200
Wilson, G. 137
wolf 18
World Association of Zoos and Aquariums (WAZA) 74, 76
World Society for the Protection of Animals (WSPA) 82, 253, 254
World Wildlife Fund 189

yellow fever 234–5
Yolacan, P. 33
Your Time Travels 126, 127

'zoo as menagerie' 76
Zoocheck Canada 94, 95–6
zoological gaze 78
zoonoses 230–41; airborne or droplet-borne 239–40; animal host 240–1; Arthropod vector-borne 232–7; food- or waterborne 237–9
zoophilia 126–9
zoos 75–91, 190; advantages and disadvantages 90–1; Bear pit at Bern, Switzerland **77**; breeding programs **80**; continued evolution 79–84; education message regarding conservation **81**; vs circus 93; welfare evaluations 84–90; zoo education **83**